National Security, Journalism, and
Law in an Age of Information Warfare

THE OXFORD SERIES IN ETHICS, NATIONAL SECURITY, AND THE RULE OF LAW

Series Editors Claire O. Finkelstein and Jens David Ohlin
Oxford University Press

About the Series

The Oxford Series in Ethics, National Security, and the Rule of Law is an interdisciplinary book series designed to address abiding questions at the intersection of national security, moral and political philosophy, and the law. It seeks to illuminate both ethical and legal dilemmas that arise in democratic nations as they grapple with contemporary national security challenges. The series also seeks to create a synergy between academic researchers and practitioners as they focus on common problems in national security theory and practice. The aim of the series is ultimately to advance thinking about how to protect and augment the rule of law in the context of contemporary armed conflict and national security.

The book series grew out of the work of the Center for Ethics and the Rule of Law (CERL) at the University of Pennsylvania. CERL is a nonpartisan interdisciplinary institute dedicated to the preservation and promotion of the rule of law in twenty-first century warfare and national security. The only center of its kind housed within a major research university, CERL draws from the study of law, philosophy, and ethics to answer the difficult questions that arise in times of war and contemporary transnational conflicts.

National Security, Journalism, and Law in an Age of Information Warfare

Edited by

MARC AMBINDER, JENNIFER R. HENRICHSEN, AND CONNIE ROSATI

OXFORD
UNIVERSITY PRESS

Oxford University Press is a department of the University of Oxford. It furthers the University's objective of excellence in research, scholarship, and education by publishing worldwide. Oxford is a registered trade mark of Oxford University Press in the UK and certain other countries.

Published in the United States of America by Oxford University Press
198 Madison Avenue, New York, NY 10016, United States of America.

© Oxford University Press 2024

Chapter 2 © Matthew L. Schafer 2024

Chapter 11 © Reporters Committee for Freedom of the Press 2024

All rights reserved. No part of this publication may be reproduced, stored in a retrieval system, or transmitted, in any form or by any means, without the prior permission in writing of Oxford University Press, or as expressly permitted by law, by license, or under terms agreed with the appropriate reproduction rights organization. Inquiries concerning reproduction outside the scope of the above should be sent to the Rights Department, Oxford University Press, at the address above.

You must not circulate this work in any other form
and you must impose this same condition on any acquirer.

Library of Congress Cataloging-in-Publication Data
Names: Ambinder, Marc, editor. | Henrichsen, Jennifer R, editor. | Rosati, Connie, editor.
Title: National security, journalism, and law in an age of information
warfare / [edited by] Marc Ambinder, Jennifer R. Henrichsen, Connie Rosati.
Description: New York : Oxford University Press, 2024. | Series: Ethics national security
rule law series | Includes bibliographical references and index.
Identifiers: LCCN 2024017151 (print) | LCCN 2024017152 (ebook) |
ISBN 9780197756621 (hardback) | ISBN 9780197756638 (epub) |
ISBN 9780197756645 (updf) | ISBN 9780197756652 (online)
Subjects: LCSH: National security—Law and legislation. |
Digital media—Law and legislation. | Electronic surveillance—Law and legislation. |
Journalism—Law and legislation. | Information warfare.
Classification: LCC K3278 .A94 2024 (print) | LCC K3278 (ebook) |
DDC 343/.015033—dc23/eng/20240416
LC record available at https://lccn.loc.gov/2024017151
LC ebook record available at https://lccn.loc.gov/2024017152

DOI: 10.1093/oso/9780197756621.001.0001

Printed by Marquis Book Printing, Canada

Note to Readers
This publication is designed to provide accurate and authoritative information in regard to the subject matter covered. It is based upon sources believed to be accurate and reliable and is intended to be current as of the time it was written. It is sold with the understanding that the publisher is not engaged in rendering legal, accounting, or other professional services. If legal advice or other expert assistance is required, the services of a competent professional person should be sought. Also, to confirm that the information has not been affected or changed by recent developments, traditional legal research techniques should be used, including checking primary sources where appropriate.

(Based on the Declaration of Principles jointly adopted by a Committee of the American Bar Association and a Committee of Publishers and Associations.)

You may order this or any other Oxford University Press publication
by visiting the Oxford University Press website at www.oup.com.

Contents

Foreword — vii
   Gordon Stables
List of Contributors — ix
Editors' Introduction — xv
   Marc Ambinder, Jennifer R. Henrichsen, and Connie Rosati

PART I RIGHTS AND DUTIES OF JOURNALISTS AND NEWS ORGANIZATIONS

1. On Obtaining National Security Information — 3
   Frederick Schauer

2. National Security and Access, a Structural Perspective — 21
   Matthew L. Schafer

3. A Fourth Amendment Press Clause — 43
   Hannah Bloch-Wehba

4. Higher Restraint: National Security Reporting in an Age of Information Anarchy — 61
   Marc Ambinder

5. Open Source Imagery Intelligence: Security Implications in an Era of Unprecedented Access to Satellite Data — 85
   Allison Puccioni

PART II GOVERNMENT PUSHBACK AND GOVERNMENTAL DUTIES TO JOURNALISTS AND NEWS ORGANIZATIONS

6. The Government Pushes Back: Prosecuting Julian Assange in the War against Leaks—Trend or Aberration? — 99
   George W. Croner

7. Watchdogs in the Digital Age: Digital Surveillance, Information Security, and the Evolution of Journalist-Confidential Source Relationships — 125
   Deborah L. Dwyer

8. Charging Journalists under the Espionage Act: Have We
   Reached a Tipping Point? 155
   Barry J. Pollack and Brian J. Fleming

9. Using UK Law to Investigate Misuse of Data during the 2016
   US Election: Cambridge Analytica and the Internationalization
   of Voter Analytics 169
   David R. Carroll

10. Digital Shackles: The Political Economy of Surveillance
    Technologies and the Emergence of Transnational
    Surveillance Fascism 179
    Jennifer R. Henrichsen

11. Digital Surveillance and Its Impact on Media Freedom:
    Navigating the Legal Landscape 197
    *Jennifer R. Henrichsen, Hannah Bloch-Wehba, Gabe Rottman,
    Grayson Clary, and Emily Hockett*

PART III NATIONAL SECURITY, JOURNALISM, AND THE DIGITAL MEDIA ECOSYSTEM

12. Enemies Foreign *and Domestic*: America's Media Ecosystem
    and the Externalization of Domestic Threats 231
    Christopher J. Fuller

13. Securing the Digital Media Ecosystem 261
    Susan E. McGregor

14. On the Frontlines of the Information Wars: How Algorithmic
    Gatekeepers and National Security Impact Journalism 277
    Courtney C. Radsch

15. Weaponizing Images 301
    Susan D. Moeller

Index 321

Foreword

For thousands of years, access to basic information about how the world does (and does not) work was the domain of a privileged few.

Even in our recent history, after the convulsive wars and technological revolutions of the twentieth century, information was disseminated in one direction: an elite group of people would first bear witness to an event or discover something new; they would construct stories based on what they found to be true and important; they would then broadcast those stories to the public. This same group created social and political rules based on these same stories, and, on top of those rules, legal regimes and ethical schemas tied to the stories that billions of others were asked simply to accept.

Technological advances, however, have altered the information landscape, enabling multidirectional dissemination of information—and disinformation. The technological transformations of the past three decades have not simply democratized the tools of producing and disseminating information; they have also given people new ways to organize themselves around shared affinities, interests, and prejudices. They have thereby created tribal "information" echo chambers that they guard fiercely. Moreover, the sheer volume of information has increased exponentially, and information spreads liked wildfires in parched cheatgrass. The news business can no longer serve as a gatekeeper, keeping out disinformation and admitting only vetted information. How can you gate-keep a million new videos posted every single day to a site like TikTok?

As a consequence, the audiences—call them "publics"—have the power. And within these publics, those who are skilled in persuasion or in the art of deception can quickly reach new spaces and influence critical debates about power, privilege, and status.

With each spasm of public controversy, it becomes apparent that historical norms are under immense pressure. For the professionals working at the intersection of national security, journalism, and the rule of law, these norms have been inverted; where there was a need to know, there is now a presumption that what is not known is being kept secret for nefarious reasons; where invisible statecraft was seen as the key to efficient statecraft, it is now an indicator that the system is irreversibly perverted by private interests.

The national security official now must wrestle with the significant increases in visibility for actions of statecraft. The journalists for whom exposing powerful truths was always a mission, now must adjust their work to reconcile the complexities of a world where visibility can be lost amidst a sea of disinformation. Finally, those professionals charged with fostering a culture of respect for the rule of law must navigate moments where legal norms are regularly upended by technological developments. The pressure on one set of professionals reinforces the pressure on other professionals. Journalists reporting on national security have to manage new national security and legal risks, as a result of both new laws and evolving social norms. National security professionals more generally must attempt to manage an accelerated information cycle, which severely limits the time available to respond to any crisis.

This volume gathers work by some of the leading voices in national security, national security reporting, and First Amendment law, that seek to navigate these difficulties. Their contributions offer insights into how each of these professional communities is drawing upon their own rich histories and traditions, as well as their respective experiences, to address current and future challenges. The conveners of the conference at the Center for Ethics and the Rule of Law at the University of Pennsylvania Law School and the editors of this volume recognize the essential contributions each community must make to addressing the challenges they collectively face. Legal norms, journalistic practices, and national security principles cannot operate independently of one another. Even if these fields once developed policies that presumed some degree of autonomy, the urgency of democratic societies retaining their legitimacy requires sustainable and shared norms.

In that spirit of pursuing shared norms, readers will appreciate those contributions that reflect their authors' professional experience, as well as those chapters that expose and reflect upon tensions, both old and new. To thrive into the future, democratic societies need to develop and reinforce shared norms. This volume is an important interdisciplinary effort to building that future.

Gordon Stables
Director, School of Journalism
Clinical Professor of Communication & Journalism
Annenberg School for Communication & Journalism
University of Southern California

Contributors

Marc Ambinder is a misinformation policy lead at TikTok and an adjunct professor of journalism at the University of Southern California's Annenberg School of Communications and Journalism, where he teaches investigative, national security, and political reporting. He is the author of three books on national security and a former White House correspondent and has spent more than fifteen years in the trenches of print, digital, broadcasting, and magazine journalism. In 2017, he was a fellow at the Center for Ethics and the Rule of Law at the University of Pennsylvania Law School. He was recently awarded an N Square Fellowship from the Ploughshares Fund to work on innovative ways to communicate about the threat posed by nuclear weapons.

Hannah Bloch-Wehba is an Associate Professor of Law at Texas A&M University School of Law. She teaches and writes on law and technology. Her scholarship explores the intersection of tech and civil liberties, primarily focusing on free expression, privacy, and government accountability. Her interests include transparency and accountability for law enforcement, public access to information, and the use of new technologies in government decision-making. She is also an Affiliated Fellow at Yale Law School's Information Society Project, an Affiliated Scholar at NYU School of Law's Policing Project, and a Fellow at the Center for Democracy & Technology. Bloch-Wehba is a graduate of NYU School of Law, where she was an Institute for International Law & Justice/Law and Security Scholar, and of the University of Texas at Austin. Prior to joining the faculty at Texas A&M, Bloch-Wehba taught at Drexel University's Thomas R. Kline School of Law and at Yale Law School. Previously, she practiced law at the Reporters Committee for Freedom of the Press and at Baker Botts LLP.

David R. Carroll serves as an Associate Professor of media design at Parsons School of Design at The New School. He is known as an advocate for data privacy rights by legally challenging Cambridge Analytica in the United Kingdom in connection with the US presidential election of 2016, resulting in the only criminal conviction of the company by the Information Commissioner's Office. This work is featured in the BAFTA and Emmy nominated Netflix original documentary *The Great Hack* (2019), and his writings on the effort have been published in the *Elgar Research Handbook on Political Propaganda*, *WIRED*, *PAPER Magazine*, *Quartz*, *The Guardian*, *Motherboard*, and *The Boston Review*. He was awarded prizes from the Philosophical Society and the Law Society at Trinity College Dublin in 2019. He received an MFA from Parsons and a BA from Bowdoin College. A recovering entrepreneur, he co-founded a machine-learning startup seeded by Hearst with NYC Media Lab, an experience which acquainted him with what happens to our data privacy on the other side of the screen.

Grayson Clary is a staff attorney at the Reporters Committee for Freedom of the Press, where he works primarily with the organization's Technology & Press Freedom Project. His litigation, amicus, and advocacy portfolio focuses on press rights issues that arise in the context of national security, law enforcement accountability, and new technologies. Clary first joined the Reporters Committee as the Stanton Foundation National Security/Free Press Fellow in 2020, having previously clerked for then Judge Merrick Garland on the US Court of Appeals for the D.C. Circuit. Clary also serves as an Adjunct Assistant Professor at Georgetown University's Center for Security Studies, where he teaches a seminar on surveillance law and policy. He earned his law degree magna cum laude from Harvard Law School and his bachelor's degree summa cum laude from Yale College.

George W. Croner previously served in the Office of General Counsel at the National Security Agency (NSA) with legal oversight responsibility for NSA's signals intelligence (SIGINT) operations, including compliance with the Foreign Intelligence Surveillance Act (FISA). His responsibilities included service as NSA's principal litigation counsel in multiple espionage prosecutions and as the NSA representative to the White House interagency group assembled to review and, where possible, declassify intelligence information associated with the Iran-Contra investigation. In this capacity, he assisted the Tower Commission, congressional intelligence committees and the Independent Counsel regarding security matters related to NSA intelligence product. His performance in these roles led to his receiving two Defense Meritorious Service Medals and a letter of appreciation from President Ronald Reagan. Following his service with NSA (1984–1988), he spent twenty-eight years in private legal practice until retiring in 2016. Since retiring, he has written and lectured extensively on FISA and foreign intelligence collection issues with his publications appearing on multiple media platforms. He is a member of the Association of Former Intelligence Officers, serves as a Senior Fellow in the National Security Program at the Foreign Policy Research Institute, and is a member of the Advisory Council at the Center for Ethics and the Rule of Law (CERL) at the University of Pennsylvania.

Deborah L. Dwyer is a former communications professional with twenty-five years of experience in industries, including journalism, corporate, and nonprofit communications. She earned her doctorate in 2022 as a Roy H. Park Fellow in the Hussman School of Journalism and Media at the University of North Carolina at Chapel Hill. She conducts research that broadly examines the challenges that technological advances in news reporting and dissemination present for journalists who strive to uphold the profession's ethical standards of accuracy, fairness, and accountability. Her latest work focuses on the phenomenon of unpublishing, a growing issue facing newsrooms. Learn more at deborahldwyer.com.

Brian J. Fleming is a partner at Steptoe & Johnson in Washington, D.C., and focuses his practice on matters at the intersection of national security and international trade, with an emphasis on economic sanctions, export controls, and foreign direct investment. Fleming formerly worked in the Justice Department's National Security Division, where his responsibilities included investigating and prosecuting matters arising under the Espionage Act, such as media leaks.

CONTRIBUTORS xi

Christopher J. Fuller is an Associate Professor in modern US history at the University of Southampton. His research focuses on the origins and conduct of the War on Terror, the role of the internet in enhancing and undermining American national security, and the rise of the precision ethos in America's culture of war. *See It/Shoot It: The Secret History of the CIA's Lethal Drone Program* was published with Yale University Press in June 2017, and he has contributed further chapters on drone policy to *The Obama Doctrine* (Routledge, 2016), *The Civilianization of Warfare* (Cambridge, 2017), *Ethics of Drone Strikes* (Edinburgh, 2022), and *The Second Drone Age: The De Gruyter Handbook* (De Gruyter, 2024). He has written about the Reagan administration's foreign policy in *The Reagan Moment: America and the World in the 1980s* (Princeton, 2021), published "The Roots of U.S. Cyber (In) Security" in *Diplomatic History* (2018), and co-edited and contributed to *Between Crime and War: Hybrid Legal Frameworks for Asymmetric Conflict* (Oxford, 2023).

Jennifer R. Henrichsen is an Assistant Professor at the Edward R. Murrow College of Communication at Washington State University. She is also an Affiliated Fellow at the Information Society Project at Yale Law School and an Affiliated Fellow at the University of Pennsylvania and Rutgers University's joint Media, Inequality, and Change Center. Henrichsen received her PhD from the Annenberg School for Communication at the University of Pennsylvania. Henrichsen's research examines how adversaries exploit weaknesses in the spread of information across organizations and institutions to contaminate the information ecosystem and to erode trust in knowledge systems. Specifically, she assesses how these and other challenges—from state and corporate surveillance to physical and digital attacks against the media—are creating an epistemic crisis for journalism. Henrichsen's research has been published in top peer-reviewed journals, including *Digital Journalism*, the *International Journal of Communication*, *Journalism Practice*, *Journalism Studies*, *Communication, Culture & Critique*, *New Media & Society*, and *Media, War & Conflict*. She twice has been a consultant to UNESCO, where she produced global reports on the state of journalism, and she has served as a consultant to the Knight Foundation, the MacArthur Foundation, and the Ford Foundation. She has served on the Advisory Council for the Open Technology Fund and the Steering Committee for the Center for Media at Risk at Annenberg. Henrichsen has written articles about journalism and information security for *Columbia Journalism Review* and Poynter, and she was previously a freelance journalist and a political correspondent. Henrichsen has received fellowships from Yale University, Columbia University, the University of Pennsylvania, and the University of Fribourg in Switzerland, among others. A Fulbright Research Scholar, Henrichsen holds MA degrees from the University of Geneva and the University of Pennsylvania. In 2011, she co-wrote the book, *War on Words: Who Should Protect Journalists?* (Praeger), and in 2017, she assisted with the book, *Journalism After Snowden: The Future of the Free Press in a Surveillance State* (Columbia University Press).

Emily Hockett is the Reporters Committee's Technology and Press Freedom Project fellow. Emily attended the University of Virginia School of Law, where she was a member of the First Amendment Clinic, working on public records matters and amicus briefs under the supervision of Reporters Committee attorneys. Emily graduated from New York University in 2018.

Susan E. McGregor is a Research Scholar at Columbia University's Data Science Institute, where she also co-chairs its Center for Data, Media & Society. She is the author of two books: *Information Security Essentials: A Guide for Reporters, Editors and Newsroom Leaders* (Columbia University Press, 2021) and *Practical Python: Data Wrangling and Data Quality* (O'Reilly, 2021). Her research on privacy and security issues in the media industry has appeared in leading peer-reviewed security and privacy venues and has received support from the National Science Foundation, the Knight Foundation, Google, and multiple schools and offices of Columbia University. Before joining Columbia, McGregor was the Senior Programmer on the News Graphics team at the *Wall Street Journal* and a reporter for the *New York Amsterdam News*. McGregor was named a 2010 Gerald Loeb Award winner for her work on the *Wall Street Journal*'s "What They Know" series and a 2007 finalist for the Scripps Howard Foundation National Journalism Awards for Web Reporting. McGregor holds a master's degree in Educational Communication and Technology from New York University and a bachelor's degree in Interactive Information Design from Harvard University.

Susan D. Moeller is the Director of the International Center for Media and the Public Agenda (ICMPA), an academic center that forms a bridge between the College of Journalism and the School of Public Policy at the University of Maryland, College Park. She is Professor of Media and International Affairs in the Philip Merrill College of Journalism at the University of Maryland and an affiliated faculty member at the School of Public Policy. In 2008, Moeller was the recipient of a Carnegie Scholar Award from the Carnegie Corporation of New York, a $100,000 grant for research and writing on how media report on the intersection of Islam and terrorism. She also received the 2008 State of Maryland Board of Regents Teaching Award, which recognized her both for her work in the university classroom and for her work in helping to found a new global education program, the Salzburg Academy on Media and Global Change, where she serves as codirector and lead faculty member

Barry J. Pollack is a partner with the law firm of Harris St. Laurent & Wechsler in Washington, D.C. Pollack served as counsel to Jeffrey Sterling in the case detailed in the authors' contribution to this volume and has defended other clients being investigated or charged under the Espionage Act.

Allison Puccioni has been an imagery analyst for over twenty-five years, working within the military, tech, defense, media, and academic communities. After honorably serving in the US Army as an Imagery Analyst from 1991–1997, Puccioni continued the tradecraft within the Defense Industry, augmenting US and NATO operations in the Kosovo airstrike campaign, and as a Senior Analyst and Mission Planner for Naval Special Warfare Group One. After earning her master's degree in international policy, Puccioni established the commercial satellite imagery analysis capability for the British publication *Jane's Intelligence Review*, publishing Open Source imagery analysis for six years. In 2015, she joined Google to establish applications for its commercial small-satellites. Today, Puccioni is the Principal and Founder of Armillary Services, providing insight on commercial imaging satellites and associated analytics. Concurrently, she manages the multisensor imagery analysis team at Stanford University's Center for International Security and Cooperation.

Courtney C. Radsch is the Director of the Center for Journalism and Liberty at the Open Markets Institute. She holds a PhD from American University and is the author of *Cyberactivism and Citizen Journalism in Egypt: Digital Dissidence and Political Change* (Palgrave-Macmillan, 2016). Her research focuses on media sustainability and the platformization of journalism; AI governance and information ecosystems; and the evolving socioeconomic and technopolitical effects of media and technology. As a journalist, scholar, and advocate focused on the intersection of technology, media, and rights, her work has been published in peer-reviewed journals and by leading media outlets including the *New York Times*, *The Guardian*, and *Newsweek*, featured on the likes of PBS Frontline, CNN, and the BBC, and cited by policymakers in the United States, Europe, Africa, and the United Nations. She has testified before Congress, parliaments, and international organizations on these topics, serves on several boards and advisory councils, and is a fellow at UCLA's Institute for Technology, Law & Policy, the Brookings Institute, the Center for Democracy and Technology, and the Center for International Governance Innovation. Previously, she worked for the Committee to Protect Journalists, UNESCO, and the *New York Times*.

Connie Rosati is Roy Allison Vaughan Centennial Professor in Philosophy and Professor of Law at the University of Texas at Austin. She received a PhD in Philosophy in 1989 from the University of Michigan and a JD in 1998 from Harvard Law School. She has previously held positions at Rutgers University, Northwestern University, the University of California, Davis, and the University of Arizona, as well as visiting positions at the University of San Diego Law School, Arizona State University Law School, and the University of Pennsylvania Law School. Her research interests lie principally in moral philosophy and the foundations of ethics and in the nature and interpretation of constitutions. Recent publications include "Welfare and Rational Fit," "The Makropulos Case Revisited: Reflections on Immortality and Agency," "Constitutional Realism," and "The Moral Reading of Constitutions."

Gabe Rottman is the director of the Reporters Committee's Technology and Press Freedom Project, which integrates legal, policy, and public education efforts to protect newsgathering and First Amendment freedoms as they intersect with emerging technological challenges and opportunities. Previously, he has worked at PEN America, the Center for Democracy and Technology, and the American Civil Liberties Union and in private practice with a focus on antitrust and national security foreign investment review law.

Matthew L. Schafer is Vice President, Assistant General Counsel, Litigation for Paramount Global. He handles content litigation across Paramount subsidiaries like CBS News, Showtime, and Paramount Pictures, with a focus on defamation, invasion of privacy, and copyright claims, as well as claims relating to access to government information. He also teaches media law at Fordham University School of Law and regularly writes on the history of press freedom in law reviews and the popular press. Previously, he was newsroom counsel at BuzzFeed News, where he advised reporters and editors on day-to-day liability stemming from gathering and reporting the news around the world, including advising the teams that broke the news that R. Kelly was holding women in an abusive "cult," that released thousands of secret records of misconduct at the NYPD, and that cataloged Russian-linked assassinations on UK soil, for which BuzzFeed News was a Pulitzer finalist. He began his career at the First Amendment firm Levine Sullivan Koch & Schulz, where a substantial amount of his practice was dedicated to government transparency issues at the federal and state level and in the military commissions at Guantanamo Bay. He holds degrees from Georgetown University, the University of Illinois, and Louisiana State University. Affiliations are provided for identification purposes only.

Frederick Schauer is David and Mary Harrison Distinguished Professor of Law at the University of Virginia and previously was Frank Stanton Professor of the First Amendment at Harvard University. A Fellow of the American Academy of Arts and Sciences and the British Academy and recipient of a Guggenheim Fellowship, Schauer is the author of *The Law of Obscenity* (BNA, 1976), *Free Speech: A Philosophical Enquiry* (Cambridge, 1982), *Playing by the Rules: A Philosophical Examination of Rule-Based Decision-Making in Law and in Life* (Oxford, 1991), *Profiles, Probabilities, and Stereotypes* (Harvard, 2003), *Thinking Like a Lawyer: A New Introduction to Legal Reasoning* (Harvard, 2009), *The Force of Law* (Harvard, 2015), and *The Proof: Questions of Evidence in Law, Politics, and Everything Else* (Harvard, 2022). He also is the editor of Karl Llewellyn, *The Theory of Rules* (Chicago, 2011), is a founding editor of *Legal Theory*, and has chaired the Section on Constitutional Law of the Association of American Law Schools and the Committee on Philosophy and Law of the American Philosophical Association. In 2005, he wrote the foreword to the *Harvard Law Review*'s Supreme Court issue, and he has written widely on freedom of speech and press, constitutional interpretation, evidence, legal reasoning, and the philosophy of law.

Editors' Introduction

The journalist's obligation to inform the public and hold powerful interests to account has often been in tension with the government's obligation to protect national security. In the United States, this tension has been historically long-standing, and it is undoubtedly permanent. Where conflicts have arisen, the parties have managed to resolve them, often on an ad hoc basis and often by means that allow reporters and federal authorities first, through public performance mediated by the press, to demonstrate that their claims of rightness have serious import and then, in private, to arrive at informal accommodations.[1] For more than a century, the government has occasionally threatened to enforce laws designed to punish anyone who publishes classified information.[2] Yet prosecutors are rightly reluctant to punish journalists for the "sin" of committing journalism. Norms of behavior have thus been powerful guardrails against censorship. In the even rarer instances when the federal government has gone to court to obtain prepublication injunctions, the judicial branch has responded by imposing constraints on the government that were not previously written into law.[3] For more than half a century, through wars, convulsive technological changes, a large expansion of the federal bureaucracy, and an explosion in the number of secrets declared and kept, this implicit bargaining, with sporadic appeals to the courts, has been sufficient to allow both journalism and government to meet their minimum obligations, thereby fulfilling their respective roles in a democracy.

---

[1] *See, e.g.*, David E. Pozen, "The Leaky Leviathan: Why the Government Condemns and Condones Unlawful Disclosures of Information," *Harvard Law Review*, 127, no. 2 (2013), 512–635. https://papers.ssrn.com/sol3/papers.cfm?abstract_id=2223703

[2] *See* Title 18, Criminal Code and Criminal Procedure, Chapter 37, "Espionage and Censorship," and specifically § 793e, which reads:

> Whoever having unauthorized possession of, access to, or control over any document, writing, code book, signal book, sketch, photograph, photographic negative, blueprint, plan, map, model, instrument, appliance, or note relating to the national defense, or information relating to the national defense which information the possessor has reason to believe could be used to the injury of the United States or to the advantage of any foreign nation, willfully communicates, delivers, transmits or causes to be communicated, delivered, or transmitted, or attempts to communicate, deliver, transmit or cause to be communicated, delivered, or transmitted the same to any person not entitled to receive it, or willfully retains the same and fails to deliver it to the officer or employee of the United States entitled to receive it . . . [shall be fined not more than $10,000 or imprisoned not more than ten years, or both].

[3] *New York Times Co. v. United States*, 403 U.S. 713 (1971).

During the Barack Obama administration, however, government officials became more aggressive in efforts to stop press leaks. And during the Donald Trump administration, hostility toward the press on the part of the president and other government officials made even the thought of using reason and bargaining to resolve tensions seem quaint. Attacks on the press were relentless, as the press struggled to keep the public informed in the face of a blizzard of lies, misinformation, and "alternative facts." In this environment, how could the government and the press *share* a responsibility to tend to the public square?

Beyond the United States, a contemporary wave of global illiberalism has emboldened governments to attack and curtail freedom of speech and press, and journalists everywhere find themselves under serious—even deadly—threat. Consider the brutal murder of journalist Jamal Khashoggi, allegedly at the hands of the Saudi Arabian government. Khashoggi was just one of at least 554 reporters to be killed because of their work over the past decade.[4] During the early June 2020 police reform protests in America, more than 100 credentialed journalists were detained by the police.[5] The threat to the press comes not only from governments but from a variety of sources. Hostile actors representing foreign nation-states, terrorist groups and amorphous cyber anarchists, corporations, and even private citizens now actively work to assault the foundations of a free press and, in so doing, undermine democratic processes.

Before Brexit, before the 2016 election of Donald Trump, and before the 2020 coronavirus pandemic, the business of news was in deep trouble; there were half as many reporters working in 2019 as there were in 2008.[6] The declining number of reporters is at odds with the fact there is *so much more* information to process, but it is readily explained by nearly frictionless access to social media platforms. There are fewer reporters, but there are many more people with the ability to function as de facto reporters. These new "reporters," however, generally do not feel obliged to follow traditional journalistic norms. Indeed, many of them flout these norms because they are convinced that legacy journalism served or was co-opted by special interests. At the same time, a number of powerful actors in the information ecosystem actively work to undermine whatever residue of legitimacy journalism retains. During the coronavirus pandemic, the lack of a shared sensibility about reporting led to the spread of deadly misinformation

---

[4] The Committee to Protect Journalists keeps a tally of journalists killed in the line of duty. *See* https://cpj.org/data/killed/?status=Killed&motiveConfirmed%5B%5D=Confirmed&motiveUnconfirmed%5B%5D=Unconfirmed&type%5B%5D=Journalist&type%5B%5D=Media%20Worker&start_year=1992&end_year=2024&group_by=year (accessed January 28, 2024).

[5] *See* https://pressfreedomtracker.us/, a project managed by the Freedom of the Press Foundation (accessed January 28, 2024).

[6] Mason Walker, "U.S. Newsroom Employment Has Fallen 26% Since 2008," Pew Research Center, July 13, 2021, https://www.pewresearch.org/short-reads/2021/07/13/u-s-newsroom-employment-has-fallen-26-since-2008/#:~:text=Since%202008%2C%20newsroom%20employment%20has,71%2C000%20jobs%20to%20about%2031%2C000 (accessed January 28, 2024).

and allowed agitators to turn misinformation into money-making and politically motivated disinformation campaigns with the goal and effect of civic paralysis and confusion. We urgently need to achieve a new consensus around norms that enable both government and journalism to carry out their vital roles, even as various actors and new technologies work to impede them.

The national security state has not been spared from the weaponization of information and misinformation. Politicians have long used the specters of secrecy and unaccountable powers to demonize or criticize opponents. In recent years, many have claimed themselves victims of a "deep state," actively attacking these supposed nefarious actors and spreading conspiracy theories. National security policies will always be controversial and in need of significant external policing from journalism, as well as strong internal policing, largely from inspectors general and congressional oversight committees. But the committees are increasingly polarized and dysfunctional; and it has become easy to fire inspectors general based on political whims. The US government suffers chronically from significant and damaging disclosures of classified information and struggles to adapt to a world in which control over national security information must be broadly distributed among different parts of the national security apparatus. Whistle-blowers find themselves in a precarious state, with no guidebook and few means of conveying their concerns responsibly, without facing a backlash that impugns their motives and undermines their efforts. They can be outed by presidents or their factotums.

Journalists engaged in national security reporting face both ethical and logistical challenges. The most fundamental challenge is deeply moral: *What constitutes responsible reporting in the national security context?* Although national security crises are inherently newsworthy, journalists must grapple with how to report the news, given that reporting can inflame a crisis. It can, for example, lead to more terrorist attacks by stoking public fear and providing terrorists with the kind of visibility they seek for their cause. Independent media coverage can expand the reach of terrorists' violent narratives, while inadvertently glorifying their image among vulnerable consumers of news. Beyond the coverage of terrorist acts, journalists' textual and photographic coverage of armed conflict and violent atrocities both at home and abroad can influence public opinion and negatively impact counterterrorism efforts. How should news outlets operate, given that what they choose to cover and how they choose to cover it may have such adverse effects?

Another ethical challenge concerns how to handle newsworthy information that comes from unauthorized disclosures of classified information by third parties or by quasi-journalistic outlets or independent platforms with cultures of disclosure that differ from the established media's formal processes and well-considered habits. In such cases, the disclosed information usually remains classified, and intelligence agencies are unlikely to acknowledge whether the leaks are based on bona fide classified documents, regardless of independent coverage. As classified information leaks become more frequent, whether by government officials or contractors such as Edward Snowden, or through third-party platforms like WikiLeaks, journalists must grapple with how to operate ethically. When dealing with these disclosures, when and how should news organizations that operate according to traditional journalistic ethics disseminate such information? Are journalists at all responsible for mitigating the potential damage to national security that might result from them?

Yet another ethical challenge has arisen; the use of the news form to create confusion and undermine a shared factual base among members of a democracy.[7] Although related to lying and to "bullshitting," as astutely analyzed by the philosopher Harry Frankfurt,[8] disinformation is a distinctive phenomenon. In contrast to misinformation, which involves mistakes about the facts, disinformation involves the intentional or knowing publication of nonsatirical false statements or stories, purported to be facts, with the aim of hiding the truth or making others believe what is false. Unfortunately, the term "fake news" has become increasingly used to discredit any reporting that reveals what the spreaders of false claims do not want revealed. The increasing dissemination of disinformation, often about life-or-death issues, has made it increasingly difficult to combat efforts to game the information ecosystem. Whether propagated by presidents, domestic agitators, or foreign sources, disinformation that aims to sow dissension, create distrust in democratic institutions, and subvert the electoral process well illustrates the threat such disinformation poses to national security and democracy.

Protecting democracy from political subversion through the dissemination of misleading news and content will require the efforts of multiple actors, including government and technology companies like Twitter/X, Google, TikTok, and Facebook/Meta. But what are the peculiar responsibilities of journalists? Irresponsible, secondary reporting of a noncorroborated story by major American news outlets can obscure the origins of the story and lend it credibility. Should American news outlets adopt a stronger editorial stance and stricter vetting procedures when it comes to republishing information first released by less credible sources? Government and journalistic outlets are each obligated, in their different ways, to ensure that the public is both safe and well informed. The difficulty for journalists comes with determining how to act on this obligation,

---

[7] Jennifer Kavanagh & Michael D. Rich, *Truth Decay: An Initial Exploration of the Diminishing Role of Facts and Analysis in American Public Life* (RAND Corporation, 2018), https://www.rand.org/pubs/research_reports/RR2314.html (accessed January 28, 2024).

[8] Harry Frankfurt, *On Bullshit* (Princeton University Press, 2005).

given the demonstrated susceptibility of the American public to internal and external disinformation campaigns and "weaponized news."

As they struggle with the moral issues raised by national security reporting, journalists must confront a host of logistical challenges that endanger them and impede their work. How are journalists to operate effectively and responsibly in the face of budgetary constraints and both legal and technological challenges? Because newsroom budgets have been paired down, journalists are often sent into disaster zones and "denied areas" without adequate support. Reporters are exposed to the dangers of warfare when they are deployed to war zones and especially when they are embedded in military units. How are journalists to operate under these conditions?

And what obligations does government have to protect them? The return of journalists to the battlefields of Syria and Iraq, as the Islamic State (ISIS) was being pushed back by coalition and local forces, reaffirmed the need to determine what protections they require and deserve. ISIS and, indeed, a variety of other substate actors in a region, may perceive these individuals as prime targets for ransom opportunities. The US government must communicate its stance on protecting journalists within combat zones, to ensure that journalists understand the risks when going to a combat zone, and to warn nonstate actors of the ramifications of harming or imprisoning a journalist, whatever those risks might be. Furthermore, the United States needs to work with the corporate sponsors of individual journalists at risk of physical harm or capture in these conflict areas to set clear legal and normative guidelines that govern their presence in the area, their involvement with combat units, and the contingencies in place should they become endangered or captured.

Advances in technology have degraded journalists' capacity to protect confidential sources. Previously, journalists may have refused to name their sources, even when subpoenaed to do so in a grand jury investigation. Yet, technological advances have made it increasingly difficult for journalists to protect their sources because communications metadata may reveal conversations between journalists and sources.

President Obama and President Trump after him took hard lines about breaches of their administrations' prerogatives to control information. This proclivity seems baked into the executive branch. The worry is that criminal investigations of journalists will become the norm, with more and more journalists facing subpoenas to reveal the identities of their sources or be held in contempt of court. The pursuit of journalists through the criminal law, especially if it became widespread, could result in institutionalized intimidation of individual journalists and media outlets for political gain. This worry may be mitigated by the President Joseph Biden administration's efforts to limit legal targeting of journalists, which in late 2022 culminated in the Justice Department, under Attorney General Merrick Garland, adopting a policy that bans, in most cases, the use of compulsory measures, such as subpoenas and search warrants, to gain confidential information from journalists.

Finally, journalists can face malevolent online harassment campaigns, mob censorship, hate-based attacks, or related physical threats or intimidation, due to their race, gender, religion, or nationality, and such conduct can affect the coverage of national security matters by overburdening journalists with safety concerns that impede efforts to fulfill the journalist's role as government watchdog.

The chapters collected in this volume are the work product of a conference on national security, journalism, and law organized by the Center for Ethics and the Rule of Law, while it was housed at the University of Pennsylvania's Law School, before moving to its current home in the Annenberg Public Policy Center. The authors of the chapters have worked in academia, government, and journalism. Drawing on their different experiences and expertise, each addresses some of the critical challenges that arise in national security reporting and reporting in a new information environment. Although their work primarily focuses on the United States and the United Kingdom, it draws on international perspectives and offers examples from countries with limited journalistic freedom. Together, these chapters both shed light on the problems of national security reporting and suggest how we might work toward a transformed set of legal, journalistic, and national security norms.

The volume is organized into three parts. The chapters in Part I, "Rights and Duties of Journalists and News Organizations," explore the obligations of journalists and news organizations engaged in national security reporting and the cultural, social, legal, and institutional constraints they face. Many times each day, editors and journalists confront the fundamental ethical question of what constitutes responsible reporting in a national security context.

In "On Obtaining National Security Information," Frederick Schauer observes that as far back as the events surrounding the *Pentagon Papers* litigation in 1971, it has been widely understood that the right to publish national security information, even illegally obtained national security information, is different from and greater than the right to obtain that information in the first place. Although the Richard Nixon administration's clumsy attempt to influence the trial of Daniel Ellsberg derailed Ellsberg's prosecution, the understanding at the time was that Ellsberg could justifiably and constitutionally be punished for unlawfully obtaining the documents, even if the *New York Times* could not constitutionally be prohibited from (or punished for) publishing the information originally unlawfully obtained. More recently, however, events surrounding WikiLeaks and other individuals and entities that disclose confidential national security information have raised again the questions of the circumstances, if any, under which those who leak national security information can be punished and the circumstances, if any, under which those who publish such information might be punished as aiders or abettors of, or accessories to, the initial unlawful acts. This chapter explores these issues from the perspective of the First Amendment, the substantive criminal law, and the larger and deeper questions about journalists' responsibilities.

Since 1980, the US Supreme Court has recognized that the press and the public have a First Amendment right to attend criminal trials. But in "National Security and Access, a Structural Perspective," Matthew L. Schafer argues that the Court has failed to anchor that right in any particular theory. Sometimes it has adjudicated requests for access without invoking any theory whatsoever; at other times, it has maintained that access to information plays a "structural role" in a democracy, by ensuring that public debate is informed. Lack of clear guidance has allowed the government to erode public access across the board but especially in cases involving national security. Schafer situates the right of access within the broader structure of the US Constitution and argues that our current approach to access—especially in the national security context—improperly subordinates the right of access to other constitutional concerns.

He maintains that access crucially advances the Constitution's separation of powers by empowering the judiciary to serve as a check on the executive's ability to keep national security information from the public. Access also supports democratic self-governance by providing the public with the information it needs to engage in "uninhibited, robust, and wide-open" public debate. Finally, Schafer explains how failure to account for these structural principles creates confusion, which courts can eliminate by emphasizing that although there is no right to access in cases involving national security, access is nevertheless an essential ingredient of the US constitutional system.

Fourth Amendment "reasonableness" requires courts to balance the intrusiveness of a search, the kind of information sought, and the First Amendment rights implicated by investigative activity. Although existing regulatory protections are motivated by this kind of balancing, they are wholly inadequate to vindicate First Amendment rights. Hannah Bloch-Wehba, in "A Fourth Amendment Press Clause," argues that the Fourth Amendment's overarching requirement that searches be "reasonable" can serve as a much-needed "Press Clause" for criminal procedure, enabling courts to incorporate First Amendment analysis where it is urgently needed. It thus provides a pathway toward First Amendment protections that are enforceable, strong, and predictable.

In "Higher Restraint: National Security Reporting in an Age of Information Anarchy," Marc Ambinder explains that journalism has changed, in response to various pressures (e.g., economic, competitive, political), in ways that have allowed its constituents (e.g., readers, viewers, ordinary citizens) to call its authority into question. Even in the best of times, national security reporting—journalism that holds those who wield executive (and often lethal) power accountable—is challenging. Journalists have responded to near-unprecedented dysfunction within the executive branch, and to President Trump's personal attacks on the press while in office, by changing the tools they use. To some, the situation has turned into a civic emergency that requires new rules. Too often, though, the press has taken shortcuts that further undermine its authority. These include an unprecedented eagerness to publish classified national security information when doing so might amplify its side of the conflict, a diminution in vetting standards for certain types of investigative reportage, the quick publication of falsehoods without prominent corrections, and other errors of commission and omission. This chapter traces the evolution of national security reporting norms before the Trump presidency and examines the changes to these conventions that came after he took office. It offers a critical appraisal of the profession and suggests new norms that will serve to reinforce its core accountability function.

Allison Puccioni's chapter, "Open Source Imagery Intelligence: Security Implications in an Era of Unprecedented Access to Satellite Data," seeks to identify the ethical and national security issues surrounding the emergence of satellite imagery analysis in modern media. Multispectral high-resolution satellite imagery was long the province solely of the intelligence and military communities of the Cold War superpowers. But over the past fifteen years, it has become an unclassified, attainable data set in the open source community. Decades ago, satellite images of severe global events would have been disseminated strictly through diplomatic or military channels. Now, open source satellite imagery analysts working from home have sometimes been the first to view such images and to face ethical issues about whether to publish them.

The use of satellite imagery beyond their use by military and intelligence communities raises a host of problems. These include a lack of appropriate technical and peer review in the analysis of this medium by the media, a trend toward analyzing only images of a nation's military systems, which risks playing into an artificially hawkish or despotic media narrative of a nation, a lack of journalistic or tradecraft standards applied to the analysis of imagery data, and a lack of understanding of the implications of publishing such data in the wider media. Puccioni explains these problems by considering the March 2011 earthquake-triggered tsunami that led to a nuclear meltdown at the Fukushima Daiichi Nuclear Power Plant near Sendai City in Japan's Fukushima Prefecture. Between March 12 and March 15, 2011, reactors No. 1, No. 2, and No. 3 incurred severe damage and released radioactive material. At that time, the Japanese government minimized the extent of the damage, reporting that only two reactors were damaged and fixing the immediate evacuation zone in keeping with that report.

Concurrently, a commercial satellite company imaged the reactor in mid-March 2011 and forwarded the image to Puccioni while she was working at the magazine *Jane's Intelligence Review*. As Puccioni explains, upon inspecting it, she immediately concluded that, contrary to the Japanese government's report, all of the reactors were damaged. With a looming press deadline, she had to consider the possible consequences of making the image public and decide whether to publish the image in the global-facing media.

Part II, "Government Pushback and Governmental Duties to Journalists and News Organizations," addresses the duties of government to journalists and news organizations, as well as governmental efforts to control information. The US government often must contend with significant and damaging disclosures of classified information, and it struggles to adapt to a world in which control over national security information must be broadly distributed among different parts of the national security apparatus.

In May 2019, a grand jury in the Eastern District of Virginia returned a superseding indictment in *U.S. v. Julian Paul Assange*. In June 2022, the government of the United Kingdom accepted a request to extradite Julian Assange to the United States, but in May 2024, a London court ruled that Assange can appeal an extradition order to the US. These developments vastly expanded the criminal exposure faced by Assange. He is to stand trial for multiple violations of US espionage law in connection with his successful solicitation of Chelsea Manning's illegal disclosure of classified national security information, which Assange published on the WikiLeaks platform. George W. Croner's chapter, "The Government Pushes Back: Prosecuting Julian Assange in the War against Leaks—Trend or Aberration?" observes that given Assange's actions and his avowed purpose of exposing US national security information, charging him with espionage may not seem all that remarkable. But the new indictment's description of Assange's inculpatory conduct has reverberated throughout the world of media and social network platforms because, in many respects, his actions closely resemble what US news publications and media sites do to solicit, receive, and publish US classified information. The amended Assange indictment appears to presage a new chapter in the US government's approach to confronting leaks of classified national security information by the media. The problem of unauthorized disclosures has grown exponentially since the Vietnam War and the post-Watergate investigations of the US intelligence community in the 1970s, and it poses a classic conundrum in a democracy where the press has a constitutionally protected role of observing and reporting on government activities. Croner argues that while media proponents bemoan the expanded *Assange* indictment as impermissibly encroaching upon First Amendment activities, it is the press, not the government, that needs to recalibrate regarding the publication of classified national security information.

Although government has national security interests in retaining control of critical information, the government also has obligations, in ethics and in law, to news organizations and reporters who may publicize leaked information. The obligations of government extend to news organizations and journalists engaged in all national security related reporting. The US government provides protection for journalists who embed, and its policy of not directly paying ransom for kidnapped US persons applies to journalists. But the return of journalists to the battlefields of Syria and Iraq, as the Islamic State was being pushed back by coalition and local forces, made clear yet again the need to determine whether journalists required and deserved additional protection. How can the US government more effectively communicate its stance on protecting journalists within combat zones to ensure that journalists understand the risks and that nonstate actors understand the ramifications of harming or imprisoning journalists? How can the United States work with corporate sponsors of individual journalists at risk of physical harm or capture to set more effective legal and normative guidelines to govern their presence in conflict areas, their involvement with combat units, and the contingencies in place should they become endangered or captured?

The budgetary constraints that have afflicted news organizations create additional problems and raise additional questions about the obligations of government. Reporters are exposed to the dangers of warfare when they are deployed, without adequate support, to war zones and when they are embedded in military units. Journalists are even put at physical risk when reporting about drug cartels and transnational crime or covering protests and political rallies. The contemporary global wave of illiberalism and populism has emboldened some governments to attack and curtail freedom of speech and press, and journalists everywhere can find themselves under serious—even deadly—threat. How are journalists to operate under these conditions? And what obligations does government have to protect journalists?

The work of journalists often depends on the use of confidential sources. Although increased availability of encrypted communication channels has in some ways improved journalists' ability to protect confidential sources digitally, the overall reliance on digital technologies among journalists and sources and the inability to encrypt communications metadata have degraded the ability of journalists to keep sources confidential. For years, First Amendment campaigners and the media have called for better protections for journalists who refuse to name sources in defiance of a subpoena in a grand jury investigation in which the sources are deemed vital to the prosecution's case. Without such protection, journalists must choose between possibly betraying a confidential source or withholding the source's name and risking imprisonment for contempt of court. Either way, their ability to do their job is impaired. Complicating matters is the fact that a journalist's best efforts to protect critical sources can now be bypassed by using communications metadata to identify sources who may be reluctant to reveal their communications with the media. What obligations does government have to provide better protection for journalists and what might this look like?

National security concerns, advances in surveillance technologies, rising public interest in data privacy, and increased legal risks for sources engaging with the press pose a unique threat to the American news media. This rising pressure comes at a time when government criticism of the media (especially by the former Trump Administration) is at historic highs and public trust in media remains low. Deborah L. Dwyer's chapter, "Watchdogs in the Digital Age: Digital Surveillance, Information Security, and the Evolution of Journalist-Confidential Source Relationships," focuses on the journalist-confidential source relationship and the hazards government surveillance poses to the watchdog function of the news media. As information brokers and gatekeepers, journalists must protect confidential information and those made vulnerable by providing it. This makes news workers and their sources a likely target of surveillance by the government and other powerful entities. After an introduction to the problem, this chapter summarizes several incidents of journalist surveillance and information security breaches in the face of rising tensions between the news media and the American government. It then examines the critical role confidentiality plays in the journalist-source relationship and the challenges information security practices create for the news media. Subsequently, findings from prior research inform an understanding of the security challenges cited by working journalists. Lastly, the chapter offers a list of considerations to bolster both future academic inquiry and industry practices as information security tensions, challenges, and capabilities continue to evolve and mature.

In an effort to determine whether we have reached a tipping point that could lead to the prosecution of a journalist under the Espionage Act, the co-authored chapter by Barry J. Pollack and Brian J. Fleming, "Charging Journalists under the Espionage Act: Have We Reached a Tipping Point?" examines two cases from the Obama administration—one that typifies the more aggressive approach of the Justice Department during President Obama's first term (*United States v. Stephen Kim*) and one that illustrates the somewhat more restrained approach taken during Obama's second term (*United States v. Jeffrey Sterling*). The authors next examine public statements by President Trump and senior administration officials to assess whether threats lobbed at the news media—both explicit and implicit—should be taken seriously or disregarded as mere rhetoric. Finally, they look holistically at the recent cases, the current political climate, the legal and structural impediments to charging journalists for conduct related to their news gathering and reporting activities, and certain external factors that could ultimately determine whether this hypothetical scenario ever becomes reality.

Programmatic national security surveillance and criminal leaks investigations have resulted in widespread chilling effects on reporters and sources. This has led journalists to adopt burdensome new means of secure communication while creating substantial uncertainty about the normative and legal protections for the press against governmental investigative activity. Statutory and regulatory guidelines, such as the Privacy Protection Act of 1980, the Department of Justice Media Subpoena Guidelines, and the FBI's Domestic Investigations and Operations Guide, suggest that there are clear rules in place to shield journalists from unfettered investigations and demands for documentary materials, communications records, and work product.

In 2015, during the primary season, an obscure voter analytics company called Cambridge Analytica caught the eye of industry observers and researchers long before it became a household name around the world, after a stunning whistleblower story broke in March 2018. Emerging from a shadowy global syndicate of election management and psychological operations active in nations around the world, Cambridge Analytica now sits at the center of investigations in the largest democracies on Earth, namely, the United States, the United Kingdom, and India. David R. Carroll's chapter, "Using UK Law to Investigate Misuse of Data during the 2016 US Election: Cambridge Analytica and the Internationalization of Voter Analytics," explains how, with his understanding from early news coverage that the company was based in London, he became the first US. citizen to perform a Subject Access Request under the UK Data Protection Act of 1998 to gain full disclosure of his Cambridge Analytica voter profile. He filed an official complaint with the Information Commissioner's Office in July 2017 after receiving a noncompliant data request in March 2017. The company refused to comply with an official enforcement order to cede Carroll's requests for additional information, but the Information Commissioner's issuance of the order set an important precedent regarding the application of data protection laws internationally. It did not matter that he was a US citizen. The UK DPA and the GDPR that follows it do not exclude by citizenship. Because he proved that his data was processed in the United Kingdom, the Information Commissioner's Office can exert its jurisdiction. This chapter explores the legal questions probed by this test case and the implications for democracy and transnational election integrity in the twenty-first century.

Jennifer R. Henrichsen's chapter, "Digital Shackles: The Political Economy of Surveillance Technologies and the Emergence of Transnational Surveillance Fascism," examines how the use of spyware against journalists is increasing in many countries around the world as states strive to control information and as technologies used to surveil civilians become more sophisticated and inexpensive. This confluence of factors is creating a new reality for activists and journalists in many countries as they seek to express their ideas online. The creation and selling of sophisticated surveillance systems by companies in Western democracies to authoritarian regimes further facilitates this asymmetrical power dynamic between states and their citizens. Yet there has been limited examination of the political economy of surveillance technologies, which are often created in democratic countries and then used to suppress dissent or critical journalism in non-democratic countries. Henrichsen's chapter examines the companies that create spyware technologies and sell them to the Bahraini government, which has used these technologies to target journalists and activists. The findings shed light on the shrouded political economy of surveillance technologies and the implications these technologies have for human rights and journalism. Ultimately, this chapter argues that the close cooperation between the state and corporations in the development and sale of surveillance technologies is emblematic of an emerging phenomenon of *transnational surveillance fascism*.

The practice of journalism has never been more global than it is today. Reporters use Zoom and other video chat services to communicate with sources halfway around the world. Newsrooms rely on cloud storage to share and edit documents among far-flung teams working on stories of global import. Individuals and organizations increasingly turn to cutting-edge technologies to break and share important news. At the same time, new applications and services can pose risks to the security and integrity of communications. Journalists and news media organizations have increasingly been the targets of hacking. Edward Snowden's revelations in 2013 brought to the fore the broad reach of US surveillance programs both domestically and abroad. And while the Department of Justice has strengthened its internal guidelines governing the use of legal process to obtain information from, or records of, the news media, some details about the implementation of those reforms remain unclear, despite the urging of press advocates.

In "Digital Surveillance and Its Impact on Media Freedom: Navigating the Legal Landscape," Jennifer R. Henrichsen, Hannah Bloch-Wehba, Gabe Rottman, Grayson Clary, and Emily Hockett address this changing technological, policy, and legal environment by first providing an overview of the main statutes underpinning the US government's authorization to conduct communications surveillance in the foreign intelligence, national security, and criminal justice settings. The authors then provide information about how common journalistic tools expose reporters and sources to various risks, in light of existing legal statutes and the US Department of Justice's revised news media guidelines. Ultimately, this chapter provides journalists and news organizations with a better understanding of the legal architecture that facilitates government access to communications records and helps journalists make informed decisions about the types of security tools they should use to keep their information and their sources safe.

Part III, "National Security, Journalism, and the Digital Media Ecosystem," addresses national security problems and the impact on the journalism of social media platforms and other third-party actors. New ethical and legal challenges arise from the varied and burgeoning sources of information and disinformation for journalism and government, but also for social media platforms and other actors who do not operate in the same way as traditional news organizations.

Some platforms, like TikTok, try to reduce their public exposure to some of these conundrums by claiming that they are an "entertainment company." A platform might wish to be used in a certain way, but how it is actually used is more relevant to assessing its obligations to the larger community. TikTok, for example, was caught off guard when Russia invaded Ukraine in 2022, and TikTok users turned the site's short-form video content production suite into a source of news and streamed parts of the invasion, including graphic and violent incidents, using its Livestream feature.

Journalism, the government, and society must confront problems stemming from the rapid growth of "information" sources that do not adhere to journalistic norms or share journalism's fundamental aims, even when there are many views about what those aims should be. In 2021, for example, a number of US states tried to regulate social platforms that did not conform to an ostensibly neutral standpoint on moderating "political content," without providing any solid definition of how a platform could possibly adjudicate political content neutrally.[9] (What if, for example, one "side" simply presented more false claims than another?) Even as these companies have moved from a "falsity" standard to a "harm" standard for moderation policy development, basic empirical questions remain: What about social media precipitates harm? What are the links between on-platform misleading content and off-platform harm?

At present, the US government is struggling to confront the dangers posed by politically motivated groups or individuals and by foreign governments and their agents. In particular, ongoing Russian and Chinese interference in democratic institutions in the United States and Europe signals that disinformation campaigns, most often propagated through social media, will continue to present a substantial threat to democratic governments and to freedom of

---

[9] Uriel J. Garcia, "U.S. Supreme Court Blocks Texas Law Limiting Content Moderation by Social Media Companies," *Texas Tribune*, May 31, 2022, https://www.texastribune.org/2022/05/31/texas-social-media-law-blocked/ (accessed January 28, 2024).

the press. Faced with this threat, policymakers must determine how to reduce the prevalence and influence of these toxic forms of communication, without impinging upon the legal and constitutional protections guaranteeing freedom of the press and freedom of speech.

The Kremlin has long employed kompromat ("compromising material") as a domestic propaganda tool to discredit its political opponents and influence public opinion. While effective within the USSR's borders, however, Soviet propaganda repeatedly failed to penetrate the media landscape, and public psyche, of the United States during the height of superpower competition. George Kennan, the influential American Russianist in the early days of the Cold War, thus dismissed it as "basically negative and destructive" and therefore "relatively easy to combat."[10] More recently, however, due to Russia's evolving methods and new American vulnerabilities, this insidious tool has proved more effective. Witness the Kremlin's significant success in its efforts to discredit Hillary Clinton as a candidate during the 2016 US election. But efforts to explain the recent impact of kompromat have exaggerated Russia's information warfare capabilities while overlooking how significant US domestic weaknesses have enabled it to become an effective tool. Christopher J. Fuller's chapter, "Enemies Foreign *and Domestic*: America's Media Ecosystem and the Externalization of Domestic Threats," seeks to address this imbalance. It first explores the historical origins of kompromat, evaluating the reasons for its failures during the Cold War, before examining how changes in America's media landscape led to its recent success. This chapter argues that once we recognize and focus on the United States' weaknesses, as opposed to its opponent's strengths, we can reduce the Kremlin's influence upon American society through domestic reform.

In "Securing the Digital Media Ecosystem," Susan E. McGregor observes that information warfare—in the forms of "fake news" and social media manipulation—has captured the imagination of both policymakers and the American public. Despite explanations to the contrary, many of these "attacks" are neither technically sophisticated nor especially covert. With increased public attention, however, manipulation efforts will likely move toward exploiting the more universal insecurities of digital dissemination, such as the use of unauthenticated content. Though nearly real-time content alteration, fabrication, and misattribution are already possible, it is *also* possible to design a digital publication infrastructure that is robust against both present and near-future information manipulation attacks. Implementing these approaches at scale would offer both publishers and the public a path toward greater resilience against disinformation-based security threats.

---

[10] George Kennan, "Long Telegram," U.S. Department of State, February 22, 1946, https://digitalarchive.wilsoncenter.org/document/george-kennans-long-telegram (accessed February 15, 2024).

As Courtney C. Radsch observes in "On the Frontlines of the Information Wars: How Algorithmic Gatekeepers and National Security Impact Journalism," social media and other tech platforms emerged as a battleground in geopolitical conflicts of the twenty-first century, significantly influencing journalism, public opinion, and policy. Dominated by a few American corporations, these platforms play a critical role in determining the reach and visibility of information, forcing journalism to navigate a landscape shaped by sociotechnical interpretations of national security concerns. Based on empirical analysis and firsthand observation, Radsch's chapter delves into the complex relationship between journalism, technology, and national security, highlighting the role of tech platforms as algorithmic gatekeepers and the ways that content moderation shapes journalism. The impact of this platformization of journalism is explored through case studies that reveal how these platforms' policies and algorithmic decisions, under the guise of combating extremism and disinformation, inadvertently affect journalistic practices and content visibility. The challenges of censorship as a by-product of countering terrorism and violent extremism, and the consequences of combating "fake news" on journalistic freedom reveal how national security priorities indirectly dictate tech platform policies, significantly shaping the dynamics of modern journalism.

As the United States struggles with a surge of accelerationism, revanchism, and extremism, compounding deep political divisions that spill over into policy debates, hostile actors representing foreign nation-states, terrorist groups and amorphous cyber anarchists, corporations, and even private citizens actively work to continue a frontal assault the foundations of a free press. These sources often dispense false or misleading information and conspiracy theories in an effort to stoke tribal politics, feed distrust of journalists and the "mainstream" media, and undermine faith in democratic government. The media, of course, is not blameless: the process opacity that surrounds a reporter's work will always arouse suspicion of conspiracies, and like every other institution known to humankind, the media is wont to rally around its own. Most mistakes in journalism are accidents or are the process of editorial errors; these tend to be amplified by the voices of those who want to discredit the media. Even worse, at those rare moments when personal agendas do affect news agendas, the result can be terribly damaging. When, in 2021, it was revealed that the president of CNN, a top public relations executive, and aides to then New York Governor Andrew Cuomo had interacted in a way that was, at the very least, unprofessional, and at worst, amount to the interview subject's having had a say in the way an interview was conducted,[11] the network had no defense to the

---

[11] Tatiana Siegel, "'Cuomo-W. Trump-L.': How CNN's Jeff Zucker and His Cronies Manipulated the News," *Rolling Stone*, March 11, 2022, https://www.rollingstone.com/culture/culture-features/jeff-zucker-cnn-resign-affair-cuomo-trump-1319698/ (accessed January 28, 2024).

public charge that it had manipulated the news to favor a Democratic politician during a pandemic.

In "Weaponizing Images," Susan D. Moeller examines the way in which visual content is coming to dominate social media platforms, especially on mobile devices. Users engage more meaningfully with photos, video, and graphics than with other forms of media, and only a minimal encounter with them is needed for their impact to be felt. The lesson in these observations—for terrorists, for technology companies, and for public policy experts alike—is self-evident: seeing matters.

What we see and how we see have become preoccupations over the last several decades—among neuroscientists interested in unraveling the secrets of the brain, philosophers interested in unpacking the inclinations of the mind, entrepreneurs interested in monetizing how we construct our visual identity, art historians interested in changing presentations of the self, and journalists interested in using visual technologies to bring scenes of the world, cross-platform, to their audiences. Yet the question of why seeing matters has been neglected, perhaps because the answer has seemed self-evident. The dramatic turn toward visual communication has had extraordinary personal, economic, and political implications. The "why" does matter—a lot. And now, more than ever, because of the confluence and implications of two facts: (1) seeing is becoming the way the world chooses to transfer information, via tools/apps/platforms that are increasingly visual, and (2) seeing still remains—even in our manipulated world—a linguistic synonym for knowledge and understanding.

Protecting democracy from deception, from institutional damage, and from outright subversion through the dissemination of manipulated and misleading reporting will require the efforts of multiple actors, including government, journalists, their editors and publishers, civil society groups, lawyers, academics, and the executives who try to mitigate risk at Twitter/X, Google, Facebook/Meta, and TikTok. If common goods like access to the vote, to public health infrastructure, and to equitable treatment by institutions are to be secure, every actor in society with a grip on any lever of information creation, production, dissemination, and amplification must work to ensure, at the very least, that thoughtful stewardship of the information they *can* control helps to mitigate the problems of information they cannot.

The editors of this volume wish to thank the contributors, Claire Finkelstein (Faculty Director of the Center for Ethics and the Rule of Law), the CERL executive board and staff, and Michael X. Delli Carpini (Oscar H. Gandy Emeritus Professor of Communication at the University of Pennsylvania), as well as the Annenberg School for Communication at the University of Pennsylvania, Miller & Chevalier, the Center for Advanced Research in Global Communication, and the Middle East Center at the University of Pennsylvania for supporting and hosting CERL's conference on national security and journalism.

Marc Ambinder
Senior Fellow
Center on Communication Leadership and Policy
University of Southern California

Dr. Jennifer R. Henrichsen
Assistant Professor
Edward R. Murrow College of Communication
Washington State University

Connie Rosati
Roy Allison Vaughan Centennial Professor in
Philosophy and Professor of Law
The University of Texas at Austin

PART I
RIGHTS AND DUTIES OF JOURNALISTS AND NEWS ORGANIZATIONS

1
On Obtaining National Security Information

Frederick Schauer

I. Framing the Problem: A Fragment of History

At least in the United States, and even to some extent in other countries, journalists who focus on issues of national security treat the 1971 Supreme Court decision in the case of the *Pentagon Papers* as iconic. For many journalists, and many others, the *Pentagon Papers* case stands as an affirmation of the right of the press to publish information and commentary relating to matters of war, the military, and national defense, even, and perhaps especially, in the face of a government claim that the publication will be injurious to the security of the nation.[1]

The common celebration of the *Pentagon Papers* decision is based in large part on the decision's seeming rejection of the view that on questions of national security it is essential that the country speak with one voice, and that challenging government decisions, especially during time of war, is at least unpatriotic and perhaps even treasonous. But governments often exaggerate the national security risks of publications critical of official policy, or so the common rejoinder goes. Moreover, the rejoinder continues, government are also all too prone both to conflate criticism of officials with criticism of official policy and to conflate criticism of official policy with security-endangering and unpatriotic behavior.[2] In resisting the government's efforts to prevent the publication of documents—the *Pentagon Papers*—that strongly suggested the folly of America's Vietnam policy under the John Kennedy, Lyndon B. Johnson, and (implicitly) Richard Nixon administrations, the Supreme Court, so the standard appreciation of the

---

[1] *New York Times Co. v. United States*, 403 U.S. 713 (per curiam).
[2] *See* Thomas I. Emerson, *The System of Freedom of Expression* (Vintage Books, 1971), 55–95; Geoffrey R. Stone, *Perilous Times: Free Speech in Wartime, From the Sedition Act of 1798 to the War on Terror* (W.W. Norton, 2004); Martin H. Redish, "Unlawful Advocacy and Free Speech Theory: Rethinking the Lessons of the McCarthy Era," *University of Cincinnati Law Review*, 73 (2004), 9.

decision insists, recognized that exposure of official mistakes was just the kind of behavior that the First Amendment was designed to foster.[3]

In reality, the Supreme Court's decision was not nearly as robust an affirmation of the press's First Amendment rights to publish material claimed to be injurious to national security as the conventional journalistic wisdom takes it to be. For one thing, the Court decided only that a so-called prior restraint was impermissible,[4] leaving undecided the question whether a publisher such as the *New York Times* could be punished, civilly or criminally, subsequent to publication, for publishing material such as that contained in the *Pentagon Papers*.[5] Indeed, two members of the Court's majority—Justices Potter Stewart and Byron White—expressly left open the question whether the *Times* could have been subject to just such subsequent punishment for publishing the very same content that even they acknowledged could not be prohibited in advance by way of judicial injunction.

Even as a decision about prior restraint and not about subsequent punishment, the Court's *Pentagon Papers* ruling was, perhaps again to the surprise of some journalists, still not absolute. Forty years earlier, the Supreme Court's seminal prior restraint ruling in *Near v. Minnesota*[6] explicitly left open the possibility

---

[3] See Vincent Blasi, "The Checking Value in First Amendment Theory," *American Bar Foundation Research Journal*, 1977 (1977), 521; Mary-Rose Papandrea, "Lapdogs, Watchdogs, and Scapegoats: The Press and National Security Information," *Indiana Law Journal*, 83 (2008), 233. See also Michael Schudson, "Why Democracies Need an Unlovable Press," *in* Timothy E. Cook (ed.), *Freeing the Presses: The First Amendment in Action* (Louisiana State University Press, 2005), 73–86.

[4] See Louis Henkin, "The Right to Know and the Right to Withhold: The Case of the Pentagon Papers," *University of Pennsylvania Law Review*, 120 (1971), 271; Harry Kalven Jr., "Foreword: Even When a Nation Is at War," *Harvard Law Review*, 85 (1971), 3. And on the specific doctrine of prior restraint and its complexities, see Stephen Barnett, "The Puzzle of Prior Restraint," *Stanford Law Review*, 29 (1977), 539; Vincent Blasi, "Toward a Theory of Prior Restraint: The Central Linkage," *Minnesota Law Review*, 66 (1981), 11; John C. Jeffries Jr., "Rethinking Prior Restraint," *Yale Law Journal*, 92 (1983), 409; William T. Mayton, "Toward a Theory of First Amendment Process: Injunctions of Speech, Subsequent Punishment, and the Costs of the Prior Restraint Doctrine," *Cornell Law Review*, 67 (1982), 245.

[5] The distinction between prior restraint and subsequent punishment dates at least as far back as William Blackstone, who observed in 1769 that "[t]he liberty of the press is indeed essential to the nature of a free state: but this consists in laying no *previous* restraints on publications, and not in freedom from censure for criminal matter when published. Every freeman has an undoubted right to lay what sentiments he pleases before the public: to forbid this, is to destroy the freedom of the press: but if he publishes what is improper, mischievous, or illegal, he must take the consequences of his own temerity." William Blackstone, *Commentaries on the Laws of England* (Clarendon Press, 1969), 151–52. Although there are suggestions that the First Amendment was originally intended only to track the Blackstonian view that the press is to be protected *only* against prior restraints, see *Patterson v. Colorado*, 205 U.S. 454 (1907) (Holmes, J.), that view does not come close to representing current law, which, although providing even greater protection against prior restraint than against subsequent punishment, still protects even the latter to a very considerable degree, and even in the context of issues of war and national security. See "Symposium, National Security and the First Amendment," *William and Mary Law Review*, 26 (1985), 715.

[6] 283 U.S. 697 (1931). The context and history of the case can be found in Fred W. Friendly, *Minnesota Rag: The Dramatic Story of the Landmark Supreme Court Case That Gave New Meaning to Freedom of the Press* (Random House, 1981).

even of permissible prior restraints against the publication of "the sailing dates of transports or the number and location of troops."[7] And eight years after the *Pentagon Papers* decision, a US District Court enjoined a magazine entitled *The Progressive* from publishing an article entitled "The H-Bomb Secret—How We Got It, Why We're Telling It," an article that the government claimed would make it easier for people or nations so disposed to design and manufacture a hydrogen bomb, thus possibly "pav[ing] the way for thermonuclear annihilation."[8] This is not the place to relitigate the case of *The Progressive*, or the case of the *Pentagon Papers* for that matter. But it is important to remind journalists and others that the ability of the press to publish that which those in authority think dangerous to national security is not absolute, as well as that the First Amendment's protection of even information and commentary allegedly injurious to national security is extraordinarily strong and, when measured by international standards, almost uniquely so.[9]

Lurking behind the surface strength of the *Pentagon Papers* case and all that preceded it and followed it is an issue of pervasive and increasing importance, an issue that is revealed by recounting the full scenario in which the *Pentagon Papers* case arose. The full scenario, it will be recalled, commenced with Daniel Ellsberg, earlier an employee of the Rand Corporation, and even earlier an employee of the US Department of Defense with substantial Vietnam-related experience. In both his Rand and Defense Department capacities, Ellsberg had worked on portions of a top-secret 7,000-page report entitled "History of U.S. Decision-Making Process on Vietnam Policy, 1945–1967," and in working on it for Rand and the Defense Department became bound by confidentiality provisions both in the law and in his employment contracts. In violation of

---

[7] This qualification seems quaint today, as there is a scarcely a national television broadcast these days that does not include pretty much exactly what the Court in 1931 assumed could be prohibited in advance.

[8] *United States v. Progressive, Inc.*, 467 F. Supp. 990 (W.D. Wis.) (preliminary injunction issued March 28, 1979), *request for mandamus denied sub nom. Morland v. Sprecher*, 443 U.S. 709 (1979), *case dismissed*, 610 F.2d 819 (7th Cir. 1979). After obtaining the preliminary injunction, the government abandoned the effort, largely because it had come to light that the information that *The Progressive* sought to publish had already been published elsewhere. It is not clear, however, why this should be determinative. Most of us lock our cars and houses even as we know that there are thousands of thieves who could easily bypass or disable our locks and alarms, and we do so because we believe that our efforts nevertheless reduce the probability of theft, even if not to zero. Similarly, the government might have taken the position that increasing the availability of information useful to a potential hydrogen bomb maker would increase the probability of the aforesaid thermonuclear annihilation, even if the probability of such an occurrence as a result of the unauthorized creation of such a bomb was, prior to *The Progressive*'s proposed publication, greater than zero. And on the (generally negative) reaction of the mainstream press to *The Progressive*'s actions, *see* Lee C. Bollinger, *Images of a Free Press* (University of Chicago Press, 1991), 50–51.

[9] And much the same can be said about the American approach to freedom of speech and freedom of the press in general, even apart from questions about national security. Frederick Schauer, "The Exceptional First Amendment," *in* Michael Ignatieff (ed.), *American Exceptionalism and Human Rights* (Princeton University Press, 2005), 29–56.

those provisions and agreements, however, Ellsberg, increasingly disillusioned by the war in Vietnam and the prospects of a successful resolution, removed the report, later nicknamed the *Pentagon Papers*, from Rand. Subsequently, and after his Rand employment ended, Ellsberg delivered the entire report to Neil Sheehan of the *New York Times*, which subsequently published the report, as did a number of other major American newspapers. But even though the *Times* was subsequently determined by the Supreme Court to be protected by the First Amendment for publishing what it had received from Ellsberg, and even though other similarly situated publications have been and remain immunized from sanctions even in contemporary times,[10] the question remains: What about Ellsberg?

Although often forgotten today, Daniel Ellsberg (along with his friend, collaborator, and former Rand colleague Anthony Russo) was in fact prosecuted for removing the relevant documents—the *Pentagon Papers*—from their secure and top-secret-protected location.[11] The prosecution was based on Ellsberg's alleged violation of several federal statutes relating to secrecy and national security, and also on his unauthorized taking of government property, but in some respects the matter was conceptually similar to a host of more mundane crimes. At least on the assumption that there were locational limits on Ellsberg's access to the documents, then the violation of those locational limits—taking them away from where they were supposed to be, taking control of them, and then delivering them to the *Times* and then to other publications—was theft. Or larceny, to be more precise. And thus Ellsberg was, both figuratively and literally, prosecuted for being a thief,[12] even though his aim in stealing the documents was plainly to deliver what he had stolen to the press and thus, in his view, to eventually enlighten the American public about what he by then had perceived to be a grave mistake of both morality and policy.

The federal prosecution of Daniel Ellsberg and Anthony Russo never even came close to producing a verdict. In one of its many political and moral misjudgments, the Nixon administration, after the proceedings had commenced, was revealed to have wiretapped a conversation between Ellsberg

---

[10] "Similarly situated" in the sense that the published materials had originally been obtained unlawfully. *See, e.g., Landmark Communications, Inc. v. Virginia*, 435 U.S. 829 (1978), involving the publication of confidential court documents under circumstances in which the court employee who had removed and disclosed the documents had violated the law but in which the newspaper that had received and published the documents, the Norfolk *Virginian Pilot*, had violated no laws by taking possession of the documents.

[11] *See* David Rudenstine, *The Day the Presses Stopped: A History of the Pentagon Papers Case* (University of California Press, 1996); Sanford J. Ungar, *The Papers and the Papers: An Account of the Legal and Political Battle over the Pentagon Papers* (Dutton, 1972).

[12] The indictment charged Ellsberg and Russo with both theft and espionage.

and his lawyers. Because of this and because of the delay these revelations produced, US District Judge Matthew Byrne declared a mistrial and ordered a new jury to be empaneled. After the second trial commenced, however, it also became known that the offices of Ellsberg's psychiatrist had been burglarized by White House employees (the same Gordon Liddy and Howard Hunt who were at the center of the Watergate burglary) in a search for incriminating material about Ellsberg. This further revelation led Judge Byrne to grant the defense motion to dismiss all charges on the grounds of government misconduct, and with that the criminal case against Ellsberg and Russo came to an end. The government did not renew (and almost certainly could not have renewed) the prosecution, and as a result there was no definitive ruling on Ellsberg's (or Russo's) own criminal culpability.

As a matter of existing American constitutional law, the (more or less complete) immunity of the downstream media publishers of material lawfully obtained, coupled with the non-immunized criminal liability of the agent who engaged in the original illegality, is entirely representative. Under existing First Amendment doctrine,[13] the original illegality does not infect the First Amendment rights of subsequent publishers, who remain free to publish that which had originally been obtained unlawfully. But although the *Pentagon Papers* scenario is accurately representative of American constitutional law and American prosecutorial practice, important normative issues remain. *Should* those in Ellsberg's position be protected as a matter of constitutional law? *Could* they be? And even if those in Ellsberg's position cannot and should not be protected by the First Amendment, should prosecutors, in the exercise of their prosecutorial discretion, refuse to prosecute them in the interests of public awareness of governmental conduct and misconduct? Finally, should journalists who participate in (or commit) the original illegality be immunized for many of the same reasons, even if and when their conduct would otherwise be unlawful as a matter of standard criminal law principles? That these issues are now so timely in the context of the pending indictments of Julian Assange, creator of WikiLeaks, makes them especially salient, but there is no reason to suppose that the issues do not arise in other contexts, nor that they will not so arise in the future. Moreover, these issues blend into even larger issues about press and citizen access to government documents, information, and premises. The goal of this chapter is not to offer definitive answers or even strong opinions about any of these issues. Rather, the goal is to provide a conceptual, legal, and constitutional map of the issues and the problems, in the hope that such a map will expose the nature of the problems and the routes to possible solutions.

---

[13] *See Landmark Communications, supra* note 10.

II. The Problem Explained and Explored

In the context of this volume, the exceptional nature of American constitutional law on freedom of the press will largely be taken as a given. It is worth noting, however, that in most countries of the world the problem would hardly even arise. Outside of the United States, even those liberal industrialized democracies with a robust recognition of the importance of freedom of the press, and with a considerable degree of legal and constitutional protection to support that recognition, would still typically take the original illegality as grounds for withholding the right to publish the material illegally obtained.[14] But things are different in the United States. Not only in the context of prior restraint as in the *Pentagon Papers* case but also in the context of subsequent punishment, the right of the press to publish information, documents, and the like that were illegally obtained has been reaffirmed on multiple occasions.[15] As long as the publisher obtained the material lawfully, and was not a participant in the original illegality, the right to publish, as with the *Pentagon Papers*, now holds a moderately firm place in American First Amendment doctrine and theory.

The First Amendment right to publish, however, has not, as with Daniel Ellsberg and the *Pentagon Papers* case, been understood to immunize the original perpetrator. And as a matter of traditional First Amendment doctrine, this conclusion is unexceptional. If a speaker's speech is restricted merely incidentally to a law or practice of general application not directed to the content (or, as it is put, the "communicative impact" of the speech), then the First Amendment has been understood as presumptively not being implicated.[16] Although, for example, it violates the First Amendment for the federal government or the states to prohibit desecration of the American flag,[17] it is no affront to the First Amendment for the government to prosecute even a politically expressive and ideologically protesting flag burner under a general ordinance prohibiting

---

[14] *See* Pnina Lahav (ed.), *Press Law in Modern Democracies: A Comparative Study* (Longman, 1985).

[15] *See, e.g., Bartnicki v. Vopper*, 532 U.S. 514 (2001), protecting the publication of truthful information obtained as a result of an illegal wiretap, and *Landmark Communications, Inc. v. Virginia*, 435 U.S. 829 (1978), protecting publication of information about a judicial proceeding had been unlawfully disclosed by a court employee but which was obtained lawfully from the employee by the broadcaster.

[16] The summary in the text represents the now-standard understanding (*see especially* John Hart Ely, "Flag Desecration: A Case Study in the Roles of Categorization and Balancing in First Amendment Analysis," *Harvard Law Review*, 88 (1975), 1482) of the Supreme Court's approach in *United States v. O'Brien*, 391 U.S. 367 (1968). *See also* Laurence H. Tribe, *American Constitutional Law* (Foundation Press, 2d ed., 1987), 791–92; Michael C. Dorf, "Incidental Burdens on Fundamental Rights," *Harvard Law Review*, 109 (1996), 1175; Elena Kagan, "Private Speech, Public Purpose: The Role of Government Motive in First Amendment Doctrine," *University of Chicago Law Review*, 63 (1996), 413; Melvile Nimmer, "The Meaning of Symbolic Speech Under the First Amendment," *UCLA Law Review*, 21 (1973), 29.

[17] *Texas v. Johnson*, 491 U.S. 397 (1989), followed by *United States v. Eichman*, 496 U.S. 310 (1990).

public burning, assuming that the prosecution was not a selective one aimed at protesting an expressive burner but not others. And under a regulation prohibiting overnight sleeping in a public park, the Supreme Court has held that ideologically motivated sleepers can be prosecuted in just the same way as those who are merely tired.[18] As a result, prosecuting someone under a general prohibition of larceny for stealing a document for the purpose of having it published would be presumptively permissible, and the same would apply, although perhaps not quite as obviously, to someone, like Ellsberg, who violated a general confidentiality requirement not aimed at someone who intended, like Ellsberg, to transmit to the press the information obtained as a result of the violation.

In the abstract, it would be hard to fault the contours of the existing constitutional doctrine. Consider, for example, a reporter who breaks into the residence of a public official in order to rifle through the official's desk in search of documents relating to a current policy issue, or consider an ordinary burglar who does much the same thing in search of cash or jewels, but when apprehended claims that he was merely in search of documents that he intended to transmit to a journalist. As long as such possibilities loom, it is difficult to imagine very much of a change in existing doctrine even were there to be a strongly press-sympathetic Supreme Court.

Although such possibilities make it inconceivable that legal or constitutional doctrine could immunize even ideological thieves (or, as with contemporary events, hackers) from the ordinary criminal law, that is by no means the end of the analysis. For one thing, the criminal law has long recognized culpability for those who in some way assist the primary perpetrators in committing a crime. This is not the place to describe in any detail the law's approach to aiders and abettors, accessories before and after the fact, accomplices, conspirators and co-conspirators, and various other forms of what we might think of as secondary or vicarious or derivative criminal liability.[19] But if Daniel Ellsberg could be prosecuted for stealing documents even as he intended to deliver the fruits of his theft to the *New York Times*, could, counterfactually, someone who paid Ellsberg be prosecuted along with Ellsberg in much the same way as those who hire contract killers (or thieves) are prosecuted along with those who pull the trigger (or physically remove the goods)? And if, again as a matter of ordinary criminal law, such hirers-as-accessories may permissibly be prosecuted under analogous circumstances, do things change if the hirer is a newspaper or other First-Amendment-protected disseminator? Do things change if the recipient-disseminator provides assistance of some sort or another to the original violator? In other words, although there is no indication that the *New York Times*

---

[18] *Clark v. Community for Creative Non-Violence*, 468 U.S. 288 (1984).
[19] *See* Model Penal Code §2.06 (2001).

or its reporter Neil Sheehan had even the slightest before-the-fact involvement in Ellsberg's initial illegality, there appears to be nothing in existing criminal law principles or in existing First Amendment doctrine that would have immunized them if they had.

Assuming that the basic conclusions in the previous paragraph are sound, and thus that the *New York Times* could have been held criminally liable if it had, in advance, paid Ellsberg to steal and deliver the documents, or if it had provided instructions or material assistance to Ellsberg to facilitate the original removal of the documents, it seems moderately clear that the same would apply if the *Times* had agreed, prior to the theft, to pay upon delivery of the documents. COD, as it were. Less obviously, and plainly more controversially, the same result would seem to follow if the *Times* had, again prior to the removal and delivery of the documents, promised Ellsberg that they would publish them after delivery, as may, indeed, have possibly been the case.[20] If the promise of publication can be understood as a form of compensation, then the *Times* may, under this possibly hypothetical and possibly real scenario, be understood as having promised Ellsberg compensation for doing what the *Times* was less willing to do itself. And if the *Times* might have been criminally liable for paying one of its regular employees to engage in the burglary of the documents, then what actually transpired may be less removed from this scenario than is commonly supposed.

Further variations on this scenario can easily be imagined. If, subsequent to the actual publication of the *Pentagon Papers*, Ellsberg had unlawfully removed another and different trove of documents and delivered it to the *Times*, now reasonably knowing that the *Times* would publish those documents, would the *Times* have been criminally culpable in the case of this second removal? Here the theory behind a claim of culpability would be that the first publication was in effect an assurance of publication of the fruits of the second removal, with this assurance making the *Times* criminally culpable as an aider and abettor, or

---

[20] The exact pre-delivery discussions among Ellsberg, Russo, and Sheehan leave this open as a possibility. There is at least some likelihood that Ellsberg did not deliver the documents to Sheehan until after Sheehan had agreed to urge the *Times* to publish them. If this is so, it might have exposed Sheehan to liability as a matter of traditional criminal law. And, depending on the discussions, if any, between Sheehan and the *Times* prior to delivery, the *Times* may also have exposed itself to liability. *See* Douglas O. Linder, "The Pentagon Papers (Daniel Ellsberg) Trial: An Account," available at https://famous-trial.com/legacyftrials/ellsberg/ellsbergaccount.html. As a practical matter, and according to James Goodale, then General Counsel for the *Times*, "in the three months prior to publication, no one at the Times thought there was any risk of prosecution under the Espionage Act." Owen Fiss & Douglas Rendleman (eds.), *Injunctions* (Foundation Press, 2d ed., 1984), 239–42. Whether the same degree of confidence would have been shared by publications less influential than the *Times* and publishers less prominent than Arthur Ochs Sulzberger is an important question going to just who does or does not benefit from the special aversion to prior restraint. It is possible that well-situated publishers and publications like Sulzberger and the *Times* have little to fear from the criminal law, and thus more to fear from targeted injunctions, but that for more socially vulnerable speakers and protesters, such as the typical flag burner or draft-card burner (*see United States v. O'Brien*, 391 U.S. 367 (1968)), the risks are exactly the opposite.

accessory, in the second removal. Or would the *Times*' actual publication of the actual *Pentagon Papers* have sent a message to other potential illegal removers of top-secret documents, perhaps, even more controversially, making the *Times* criminally liable for subsequent removals by non-Ellsberg subsequent removers, at least assuming subsequent publication? The analogy here would be to a serial receiver of stolen goods, a so-called fence. If the fence, known to be a fence, and knowing that the criminal community knows him to be a fence, receives goods stolen in a particular burglary, there are circumstances in which the fence would be criminally liable for receiving stolen goods, even as it would be otherwise if a burglar simply gives (or even sells) stolen goods to someone unaware that they were stolen.[21]

The lessons of the foregoing hypothetical explorations are straightforward: it would be difficult, in the abstract, to imagine a general immunity for those who violate existing laws of general application relating to the possession, use, and distribution of confidential government information; and it would be no easier to imagine such a general immunity even for only those who intended that their violations be precursors to otherwise constitutionally protected publication. Were it otherwise, as noted previously, the First Amendment would be understood to protect a wide range of what would otherwise be burglaries, larcenies, or even violations of other aspects of ordinary criminal and civil law. It is, for example, no defense to a charge of reckless driving that the driver is a journalist on the way to cover a breaking story. And a journalist who bribes an official to get favorable treatment of one sort or another receives no exemption from the bribery laws (nor does the official) even if the favorable treatment makes it easier for the journalist do her job, and even that in turn produces more genuinely valuable information for the public.[22] Indeed, although it is common for journalists to complain that this or that restriction prevents them from "doing their jobs," this question-begging observation presupposes both a contested view of what the job is and an equally contested view about the relationship between the law and "the job." Speed limits make it harder for UPS drivers to do their jobs, and air traffic control makes it harder for Federal Express pilots to do theirs, but we understand that "the job" is not under the exclusive definition and control of those who are doing it. And so too with the job of being a journalist. That does not

---

[21] A particularly comprehensive treatment of "fencing" under the criminal law is G. Robert Blakey & Michael Goldsmith, "Criminal Redistribution of Stolen Property: The Need for Law Reform," *Michigan Law Review*, 74 (1976), 1511.

[22] *See Cohen v. Cowles Media Corp.*, 501 U.S. 663 (1991), refusing to allow the press an exception for what would otherwise have been civil liability under contract law for breaking a promise to a source not to disclose his identity. "[G]enerally applicable laws do not offend the First Amendment simply because their enforcement against the press has incidental effects on its ability to gather and report the news." *See also Associated Press v. United States*, 326 U.S. 1 (1945), concluding that the First Amendment's protection of freedom of the press did not provide an exemption for what would otherwise be a violation of the Sherman Antitrust Act.

mean, of course, that some restrictions on journalists and their activities might not be unwise as a matter of policy or principle, but the mere pronouncement that a restriction on journalists' doing their jobs as journalists define the jobs gets us no closer to the difficult questions of policy and principle that lie behind the contested restrictions. And, to repeat, the fact that the job of being a journalist is in important ways protected by the First Amendment does not immunize journalists from laws of general application not targeted specifically, either in intent or effect, at the press *qua* press, or as journalists *qua* journalists.

Despite the virtual impossibility of the kinds of general immunities just discussed, there remains the possibility of somewhat more narrowly tailored immunities.[23] In particular, might the First Amendment be thought to justify (or demand, for that matter) a privilege, in the strict sense of a privilege as an exemption from a law of general application, for some violations of some general laws, where the claimant of the privilege could establish not only the requisite public-focused intent, but also that the violation of the general law caused, say, minimal damage to the public interest (or private interests) and a definite countervailing benefit to the public good? The law of evidence, for example, provides, to oversimplify egregiously, that all relevant evidence is to be admitted.[24] But even relevant evidence would not be admitted if it comes by way of confidential information revealed to a priest in the confessional,[25] to a lawyer in the process of consultation with a client,[26] or to a psychotherapist as part of treatment of a patient.[27] Similarly, and perhaps far more relevantly, the "free exercise" clause of the First Amendment[28] has occasionally been interpreted by the Supreme Court to require religiously based exemptions—privileges—from laws of general application, as with exempting the Old Order Amish from a Wisconsin law requiring school attendance until the age of sixteen.[29] Modern Supreme Court decisions have been decidedly more skeptical about such constitutionally required

---

[23] *See* Heidi Kitrosser, "Leak Prosecutions and the First Amendment: New Developments and a Closer Look at the Feasibility of Protecting Leakers," *William and Mary Law Review*, 56 (2015), 1221; Mary-Rose Papandrea, "National Security Information Disclosures and the Role of Intent," *William and Mary Law Review*, 56 (2015), 1381.

[24] *See Federal Rules of Evidence*, Rules 401, 402.

[25] Although the historical privilege extended only to those communications required by religious doctrine, of which communications to a priest in the confessional is the standard example, modern applications of the privilege routinely extend it to wide range of communications "made for spiritual guidance, comfort, or advice." Roger C. Park et al., *Evidence Law* (Thomson Reuters, 3d ed., 2011), § 12.20 at 481.

[26] For an overview of the lawyer-client privilege, including its history, rationale, and details of application, *see* Christopher Mueller, Laird Kirkpatrick, & Liesa Richter, *Evidence* (Wolters Kluwer, 6th ed., 2018), §§ 5.8–5.31.

[27] *See Jaffee v. Redmond*, 518 U.S. 1 (1996).

[28] "Congress shall make no law respecting an establishment of religion, or prohibiting the free exercise thereof;..." U.S. Const., amend. I.

[29] *Wisconsin v. Yoder*, 406 U.S. 205 (1972).

privileges for religious practices,[30] although in some instances statutes—the federal Religious Freedom Restoration Act being the most prominent—legislation has provided the exemptions that the Supreme Court has increasingly ruled are not provided by the Constitution itself.[31]

At various times over the last decades, the institutional press has argued that analogous privileges—exemptions from laws of general application—ought to apply to journalists (or their sources) as they seek to obtain and then publish otherwise unavailable information. Typically, those arguments arise in the context of claims by journalists to be exempt from the requirement—otherwise applicable to all citizens—to provide information necessary for law enforcement or criminal prosecution—with the widely publicized contempt sanctions against *New York Times* reporter Judith Miller being among the most prominent of relatively recent examples.[32] The Supreme Court has controversially refused to conclude that such privileges are required by the First Amendment, holding that the First Amendment does not exempt the press from what would otherwise be generally applicable and permissible requirements to comply with subpoenas and search warrants.[33] The Court's refusal to hold that the privilege is required as a matter of constitutional law, however, does not mean that a legislature could not do much the same thing as a matter of policy, or that state or federal courts could not do so in exercising their common law powers to recognize privileges, nor that particular agencies or individuals could not decide to do much the same thing.[34] So although the so-called journalist's privilege to refuse to disclose information received from sources with promises of confidentiality does not now have the status of constitutional requirement, much the same thing has been provided by legislative action or judicial decision in almost every state, and has often been embedded in the norms, practices, guidelines, and regulations of various state and federal agencies.[35] As a result, it would not be inconceivable for a legislature to decide that those in Ellsberg's position might be entitled to a defense from

---

[30] See *Employment Division v. Smith*, 494 U.S. 872 (1990).

[31] See *Burwell v. Hobby Lobby Stores, Inc.*, 134 S. Ct. 2751 (2014).

[32] See *In re: Grand Jury Subpoena, Judith Miller*, 397 F.3d 964 (D.C. Cir.), *cert. denied*, 545 U.S. 1150 (2005), *reissued*, 438 F.3d 1141 (2006). Among earlier examples, the most prominent is perhaps the (relatively brief) 1978 imprisonment of another *New York Times* reporter, Myron Farber, as discussed by Ronald Dworkin in "The Farber Case: Reporters and Informers," in Ronald Dworkin (ed.), *A Matter of Principle* (Harvard University Press, 1985), 373–80.

[33] See *Branzburg v. Hayes*, 408 U.S. 665 (1971) (subpoenas); *Zurcher v. Stanford Daily*, 4536 U.S. 547 (1978) (search warrants).

[34] Rule 501 of the Federal Rules of Evidence authorizes federal courts to create a "common law" of privileges in the federal system. As a matter or a prominent example of a federal court considering whether to recognize a reporter's privilege as a common law matter, see *In re Grand Jury Subpoena, Judith Miller*, 438 F.3d 1141 (D.C. Cir. 2005). Among the states, the Reporters Committee for Freedom of the Press documents that only Wyoming has neither a statutory shield law nor judicial doctrine recognizing the privilege.

[35] For the federal guidelines, see 28 C.F.R. 50.10, and Department of Justice Guidelines for Obtaining Evidence, § 9-13.400.

what would otherwise be a lawful prosecution (or other forms of discipline or punishment) if such a person could, say, prove that their intent from the outset was to provide information to the public, and to do so without personal financial gain.[36] Indeed, the now-common laws, regulations, and practices protecting so-called whistle-blowers are of the same genus.[37] There is nothing in the First Amendment that prohibits an employer, including a government employer, from imposing a requirement of confidentiality on its employees,[38] but various state and federal laws protecting whistle-blowers can be understood, in the same way as state shield laws, as legislative protections for what the First Amendment has not been deemed to do directly. And thus although blanket immunity for the original or upstream violator might be inconceivable or at least inadvisable for many of the reasons discussed previously, the possibility of more case-specific immunity, with some variety of ex post evaluation of intent as well as the balance of costs and benefits, might be a plausible solution to reconciling the advantages of disclosure, as in the *Pentagon Papers* themselves, with the necessities of government operating with at least some degree of secrecy for many of its operations, both in the context of national security and perhaps even more generally.[39]

III. The Question of Access

Much more could be said about the details and operation of a possible case-specific privilege just outlined, as well as about its advantages and disadvantages, but such details are best left to other occasions or other commentators. Instead, we can turn to an alternative method of achieving many of the same goals, the seemingly simpler policy of granting direct access to journalists, whether that be access to documents or to government facilities.

An obvious but often ignored aspect of the Ellsberg/*Pentagon Papers* scenario is the fact that the documents themselves were government documents,

---

[36] See Papandrea, *supra* note 23.

[37] For comprehensive treatments of statutes and policies regarding leaking, leakers, and whistle-blowers, see Rahul Sagar, *Secrets and Leaks: The Dilemma of State Secrecy* (Princeton University Press, 2013) David E. Pozen, "The Leaky Leviathan: Why the Government Condemns and Condones Unlawful Disclosures of Information," *Harvard Law Review*, 127 (2013), 512.

[38] *See*, controversially, *Snepp v. United States*, 444 U.S. 507 (1980).

[39] "Transparency" is the now-common term of praise, but what is transparency from one perspective is privacy from another. And on the frequent advantages but occasional disadvantages of transparency, see Frederick Schauer, "Transparency in Three Dimensions," *University of Illinois Law Review*, 2011 (2011), 1339. And for proposals along the lines suggested in the text, although somewhat broader than what I hint at here, see Heidi Kitrosser, "Leak Prosecutions and the First Amendment: New Developments and a Closer Look at the Feasibility of Protecting Leakers," *William and Mary Law Review*, 56 (2015), 1221; Mary-Rose Papandrea, "Leaker Traitor Whistleblower Spy: National Security Leaks and the First Amendment," *Boston University Law Review*, 94 (2014), 449.

prepared by government officials (or government contractors) for government use. And when the *Pentagon Papers* are described in this abstract way, we can see that Daniel Ellsberg was in an interesting way not strictly necessary to the fact of publication. Had the *Pentagon Papers* been part of the generally available repository of government documents and government information—had they been encompassed by the Freedom of Information Act, for example[40]—the *Times* and its reporters could simply have accessed (and then published) them directly, making Daniel Ellsberg in some important way unnecessary to the result.

In reality, of course, Ellsberg was necessary to publication for many reasons, but among them is the fact that the access just suggested was not in 1971 (or even now) available to the *Times*. Neil Sheehan, the journalist to whom Ellsberg delivered the documents, could in an alternative legal universe have simply gone to the Department of Defense and openly demanded access to the very same documents that he eventually received surreptitiously from Daniel Ellsberg.

When put this way, the question of press publication of information relating to national security raises the question of direct access by journalists to government documents and information. For more than a generation, some degree of access to government information, of course, is what is provided by the federal Freedom of Information Act, along with its state counterparts. As with the claims of the institutional press and its supporters about a constitutionally mandated right to a press exception for various regulatory laws of general application, parallel claims of the press for constitutionally mandated press access to government buildings, meetings, documents, and information have routinely been rebuffed by the Supreme Court. With the exception of the general public right of access to trials,[41] a right that includes but is not limited to the press, existing Supreme Court doctrine remains consistent with an often quoted 1975 observation of Justice Potter Stewart: "The Constitution itself is neither a Freedom of Information Act nor an Officials Secrets Act."[42]

As Justice Stewart well recognized, the most important word in this quote may well be "itself." Although the Constitution does not of its own require affirmative public or press access to government property or government documents and information,[43] nor does it prohibit it. There is nothing in the Constitution that forbids federal, state, or local governments or officials from allowing such access, or even from requiring such access as a matter of legislation or governmental

---

[40] *See generally* David E. Pozen & Michael Schudson (eds.), *Troubling Transparency: The History and Future of Freedom of Information* (Columbia University Press, 2018).
[41] *Richmond Newspapers, Inc. v. Virginia*, 448 U.S. 555 (1980).
[42] Potter Stewart, "Or of the Press," *Hastings Law Journal*, 26 (1975), 631, at 636.
[43] *See Houchins v. KQED*, 438 U.S. 1 (1978), in which Chief Justice Burger reaffirmed that "neither the First Amendment nor the Fourteenth Amendment mandates a right of access to government information or sources of information within the government's control." To the same effect, *see Saxbe v. Washington Post Co.*, 417 U.S. 843 (1974); *Pell v. Procunier*, 417 U.S. 817 (1974).

policy.[44] Just as the Constitution permits Congress to enact the Freedom of Information Act, the Constitution permits the Department of Defense to make documents available to the public or the press, and the Constitution permits the military to give reporters (or anyone else, for that matter) access to military operations, installations, and even plans, as is demonstrated by the existing practice of allowing embedded reporters to accompany military operations.

Unlike some number of industrialized democracies (Chile, Portugal, and, in some respects, France), the United States does not (and constitutionally could not) license journalists, although various forms of credentialing may often have similar effects. After all, it requires more than self-announcement as a journalist to be admitted to a White House press conference or to the reporters' gallery at Supreme Court arguments. And that it why reporters for student newspapers, for example, are rarely to be seen at such events or in such premises.[45] Still, the lack of an official license, credential, or certification for journalists makes it difficult to imagine very much of a distinction between journalists and curious members of the public, a distinction increasingly elusive in the era of the internet, social media, and the vast number of ways, some technological and some sociological, in which modern information dissemination differs from the ways in which it existed in an era when print newspapers and broadcast television dominated the public informational landscape.[46]

The increasing difficulty in delineating the category of journalists is among the reasons why, despite the efforts of the press community, Congress has remained unwilling to create a federal journalists' shield law.[47] But apart from the question whether Congress is right or wrong in not having done so, this one among the many reasons, some good and others not so much, for congressional inaction on the federal shield law is a signal toward the problems that would arise with attempting to institutionalize in any formal way a right of press access to national security information. Especially in an era in which existing judicial interpretations of the First Amendment, in particular the aversion to content regulation,[48] make it difficult or impossible, depending on the context, for the

[44] *See* Frederick Schauer, "Positive Rights, Negative Rights, and the Right to Know," *in* Pozen & Schudson, *supra* note 40, at 34–51.

[45] The press-controlled practice of press credentialing has not been without controversy or litigation. *See Schreibman v. Holmes*, 1999 U.S. App. LEXIS 25159 (D.C. Cir. 1999); *Consumers Union of United States, Inc. v. Periodical Correspondents' Association*, 515 F.2d 1341 (D.C. Cir. 1975). In *United Teachers of Dade v. Steiheim*, 213 F. Supp. 2d 1368 (S.D. Fla. 2002), a federal district court in Florida held unconstitutional the exclusion of a union newspaper from forms of access routinely granted to other newspapers.

[46] Although even now somewhat technologically obsolete, a good overview of the issues is Jeremy Harris Lipschultz, *Free Expression in the Age of the Internet* (Westview Press, 2000).

[47] *See* Rachel Harris, "Conceptualizing and Reconceptualizing the Reporter's Privilege in the Age of Wikipedia," *Fordham Laws Review*, 82 (2014), 1811.

[48] *See* Geoffrey Stone, "Content Regulation and the First Amendment," *William and Mary Law Review*, 25 (1983), 189; Susan H. Williams, "Content Discrimination and the First Amendment," *University of Pennsylvania Law Review*, 139 (1991), 615.

government to distinguish the *New York Times* from the *NS Bulletin* (the newsletter of the American Nazi Party) or from the website of the Communist Party USA, increasing formalization of access brings increasing legal and constitutional risks.

Lest the suggestion in the previous paragraph be taken as fantasy, consider the lawsuit brought by *The Nation* and other more or less left-wing magazines and press outlets[49] against the George H.W. Bush administration in 1991 in the context of press access to the press pools that had access to the front lines of battle during Operation Desert Shield—the first Gulf War.[50] When it turned out that admission to the press pools and thus to the battlefields in Kuwait was made available to mainstream wire services and print and broadcast outlets (the Associated Press, United Press International, Reuters, the *New York Times,* the *Washington Post, Time* magazine, the *Wall Street Journal,* ABC, CBS, NBC, etc.) but not others, and certainly not to left-wing critics of the war and the administration, these excluded publications brought suit. The suit, reflecting then- and now-existing First Amendment principles opposed to governmental viewpoint discrimination,[51] recognized that the government was not required to grant access to any publications but, having done so, was constitutionally obliged to grant that access on a viewpoint neutral basis.[52] As it turned out, the war in Kuwait was over before there could be a judicial resolution of *The Nation*'s claims, and the suit was dismissed as moot. But the issues, still never definitively resolved, are serious at both the constitutional and policy level. Constitutionally, the question is, as just noted, the enduring one of whether and when the government may draw distinctions based on point of view even as to privileges it need not have granted as a matter of right in the first place, as well as the related question whether a distinction based on size or impact or some other measure of "mainstream-ness" is a constitutionally impermissible proxy for viewpoint discrimination. But regardless of the outcome of a constitutional decision, the larger policy and principle question remains as to the extent to which access to government facilities and information should be based on a publication's or journalist's point of view. Or

---

[49] Among the plaintiff were *Mother Jones, The Guardian, The Progressive, The Village Voice,* and *Pacifica Radio News.*

[50] *Nation Magazine v. United States Department of Defense,* 762 F. Supp. 1558 (S.D.N.Y. 1991).

[51] *See, e.g., Reed v. Gilbert,* 135 S. Ct. 2218 (2015); *R.A.V. v. City of St. Paul,* 505 U.S. 377 (1992); *Texas v. Johnson,* 491 U.S. 397 (1989); *Boos v. Barry,* 485 U.S. 312 (1988); *Arkansas Writers' Project v. Ragland,* 481 U.S. 221 (1987); *News America Publishing, Inc. v. Federal Communications Commission,* 844 F.2d 800 (D.C. Cir. 1988). Although the government in its regulatory capacity is typically forbidden, as the foregoing cases demonstrate, from discriminating on the basis of point of view, that principle does not apply to the government's own communications. *Walker v. Texas Division, Sons of Confederate Veterans, Inc.,* 135 S. Ct. 2239 (2015); *Rust v. Sullivan,* 500 U.S. 173 (1991). In many access contexts, therefore, the question will be whether the government's grant or denial of access is a form of regulation or, instead, a form of government expression.

[52] *See Frank v. Herter,* 269 F.2d 245 (D.C. Cir. 1959) (Burger, J.).

whether, especially if we view a major function of the press as challenging mainstream positions, access should be granted on a privileged basis to those who in fact occupy and represent the mainstream. And if it should not, then there is still the question whether granting access only to allegedly mainstream or centrist publications and their reporters has the effect of entrenching mainstream points of view against challenges from outside the mainstream, whether those attacks come from the left or the right. It would be no surprise to discover that the mainstream media breathed a collective sigh of relief at the dismissal of *The Nation*'s lawsuit, for the granting of limited access increases the comparative advantage of the mainstream press over its non-mainstream competitors in a way that neither unlimited access nor no access can even approach. Indeed, the way in which selective access benefits the established or mainstream media may explain why, to the consternation of the plaintiffs in the suit brought by *The Nation*, the mainstream media refused to join that lawsuit,[53] and why the same mainstream media was willing to endure some restrictions, including censorship of their content, in order to secure and maintain their privileged access. And perhaps there is no better example of this phenomenon than the headline in the February 1991 edition of *Electronic Media*: "Cronkite calls for greater access, more censorship." For Walter Cronkite and other members of the mainstream media, enduring some degree of censorship was a price well worth paying for obtaining the access that they, unlike their less mainstream counterparts and competitors, were able to enjoy.

IV. Conclusion: The Dilemma of Access

The issues raised by *The Nation*'s complaint of denied access go to a much broader question. Even if we accept, as I do, that the national security apparatus of most nations, and certainly including the United States, is obsessively prone to secrecy beyond the needs of genuine national self-preservation, there remains the question of how information about national security should be made available to the larger public. Assuming, realistically, that direct public access will often be logistically difficult (or impossible), access to government information will require intermediaries. But if disempowering government requires empowering intermediaries, then we cannot avoid asking who the intermediaries are, and who they are not. Greater access entails greater power for selected intermediaries, which will increase the power differential between

---

[53] *See* Jonathan Mandell, "Panel Tackles Role of the Media During Gulf War," *Newsday*, May 9, 1991, at 70; Rich Brown, "War of Words on Coverage Continues," *Broadcasting*, March 25, 1991; Craig LeMay, "Media in Gulf War—Outwitted, Outflanked, Outmaneuvered," *The Record*, April 5, 1991, at B07; Tom Wicker, "Marketing the War," *New York Times*, May 8, 1991, at A23.

selected and unselected intermediaries at the same time that it reduces the power differential between the government and the selected intermediaries. And as long as there are selected and unselected intermediaries, then great power will reside in the selector, which, ironically, will often turn out to be the very government whose power the selected intermediaries seek to limit. That is the dilemma of access, and it is likely, even if unfortunate, that it can never be eliminated.

2
National Security and Access, a Structural Perspective

Matthew L. Schafer

I. Introduction

Movies like *All the President's Men* and *Snowden* romanticize the tradecraft of national security reporters.[1] It is the stuff of shadowy parking garages and confidential sources and, recently, anonymous digital rendezvous and encrypted communications. Another tool rarely seen in movies is far less dramatic but arguably more important: the right of access to government proceedings and records. This constitutional right of public access has pulled the veil back on spy swaps, revealed torture at CIA black sites, thrown a spotlight on a former president's purloining classified documents, disclosed sinister attempts to sow violence in the United States and abroad, and uncovered civil rights abuses by ever-burgeoning intelligence communities.

The United States has an "unbroken, uncontradicted history" of presumptively public access to court proceedings.[2] In 1907, the US Supreme Court explained that "the theory of our system is that the conclusions to be reached in a case will be induced only by evidence and argument in open court."[3] In the middle of the century, it emphasized that a "trial is a public event" and "[w]hat transpires in the court room is public property."[4] And, in *Richmond Newspapers, Inc. v. Virginia*, it held for the first time that the press and public have an enforceable constitutional right under the First Amendment to attend criminal trials.[5] "People in an open society do not demand infallibility from their institutions," a

---

[1] This chapter is adapted from an earlier article, Matthew L. Schafer, "National Security and Access, A Structural Perspective," *Journal of National Security Law & Policy*, 11 (2021), 689.
[2] *Richmond Newspapers, Inc. v. Virginia*, 448 U.S. 555, 573 (1980) (plurality op.).
[3] *Patterson v. Colorado*, 205 U.S. 454, 462 (1907).
[4] *Craig v. Harney*, 331 U.S. 367, 374 (1947); *see also, e.g., Estes v. Texas*, 381 U.S. 532, 541–42 (1965) (observing of courts that "reporters of all media, including television, are always present if they wish").
[5] For a comprehensive history of the Court's access jurisprudence, *see* Matthew L. Schafer, "Does *Houchins v. KQED, Inc.* Matter?," 70 *Buffalo Law Review* 1331 (2022).

plurality of justices wrote in 1980, "but it is difficult for them to accept what they are prohibited from observing."[6]

By the time the Court recognized a First Amendment right of access in *Richmond Newspapers, Inc.*, the theoretical underpinnings of its free speech jurisprudence were well established. Oliver Wendell Holmes' marketplace of ideas theory—the idea that over time, the truth will win out in the market when pitted against falsehood—was already sixty years old.[7] A theory for the access right, however, remains undeveloped. At worst, the Court's access jurisprudence can be read to eschew theory altogether in favor of a mechanical two-part test for determining when access to proceedings is presumed. At best, it suggests that the access right exists to "ensure that the individual citizen can effectively participate in and contribute to our republican system of self-government."[8] To make matters worse, since 1993, the Court has not clarified which reading is correct.[9] In fact, it has shown hostility to the doctrine, which makes the identification and elaboration of a theory for access all the more important.[10]

The Court's failure to develop a theory to guide application of the right of access has led to marked inconsistencies in how lower courts enforce that right. Nowhere is this more apparent than in disputes over access to court proceedings implicating national security. The executive branch has seized on this ambiguity to shut the public out of proceedings, arguing that only it can decide when classified or sensitive hearings and evidence may be disclosed to the public. According to the executive, courts are without power "to compel a breach in the security" that the executive branch "is charged to protect."[11] And courts, with little guidance from the Supreme Court, often defer to the executive branch, holding that the "judiciary is in an extremely poor position to second-guess the executive's judgment in this area of national security."[12]

As a result, more than twenty years after 9/11, the war on terror is not only covert on the battlefield but, many times, in the courtroom. As Carol Rosenberg, a reporter for the *New York Times* who has spent years at Guantanamo Bay, once reported, "Something Classified Was Scheduled at Guantánamo. A Judge Stopped It. What it was remains a mystery, and a federal court provided no information in halting it. Welcome to the military commission system."[13] This is

---

[6] *Richmond Newspapers, Inc.*, 448 U.S. at 572.
[7] *Abrams v. United States*, 250 U.S. 616, 630 (1919) (Holmes, J., dissenting).
[8] *Globe Newspaper Co. v. Super. Ct.*, 457 U.S. 596, 604 (1982).
[9] *El Vocero de Puerto Rico v. Puerto Rico*, 508 U.S. 147 (1993).
[10] *See generally McBurney v. Young*, 569 U.S. 221 (2013).
[11] Opening Br. for the United States at 19, In re: Certification of Questions of Law to the Foreign Intelligence Surveillance Court of Review (F.S.C.R. February 23, 2018).
[12] *Ctr. for Nat'l Sec. Studies v. Dep't of Justice*, 331 F.3d 918, 928 (2003).
[13] Carol Rosenberg, "Something Classified Was Scheduled at Guantánamo. A Judge Stopped It," *New York Times*, September 26, 2019, https://www.nytimes.com/2019/09/26/us/politics/guantanamo-classified.html (accessed July 15, 2023).

not new. The release of records in military commissions are often delayed for weeks or months, and, when finally released, records are replete with questionable redactions.[14] Even in traditional federal courts, it can take years to force disclosure of basic legal reasoning from opinions condoning, for example, mass surveillance.[15] And, of course, there are hearings—often held in terrorism prosecutions at Guantanamo Bay but in federal courts as well—that occur behind closed doors, making it doubtful the public will ever, truly, know what happened.[16]

Secret proceedings—even in the national security context—are anathema to the presumption of public access to judicial proceedings. As the Supreme Court observed decades ago, "[W]e have been unable to find, a single instance of a criminal trial conducted in camera in any federal, state, or municipal court during the history of this country."[17] With that tradition under threat, this chapter aims to reconceptualize the right of access in a way that accounts for its importance in our system of government and, in doing so, provides direction to lower courts confronting disputes over the right of access.

A right of access, I explain in section II, must be viewed as a structural requirement in a democratic republic. Although access plays a variety of structural functions, I highlight two prominent ones in sections III and IV. First, access plays a separation of powers role by ensuring the judiciary retains power to control its own proceedings and thereby act as an effective check on executive power. Second, access plays a democracy-enhancing role as it provides the electorate the information it needs to assess the conduct of its public officials and turn them out of office if necessary. Finally, in section V, I suggest how courts might recalibrate their approach to determining whether the access right attaches to a particular proceeding and, if so, whether it has been rebutted such that closure may nevertheless be proper.

II. A Structural Approach to Access

The words "access" and "transparency" are nowhere mentioned in the US Constitution. "Secrecy," however, is: Article I directs that "[e]ach House shall

---

[14] Carol Rosenberg, "Guantánamo Prosecutor Defends Retroactive Censorship of Public Hearing in 9/11 Case," *Miami Herald*, February 4, 2016, https://www.miamiherald.com/news/nation-world/world/americas/guantanamo/article58403068.html (accessed July 15, 2023).
[15] Sean Gallagher, "FBI Misused Surveillance Data, Spied on Its Own, FISA Ruling Finds," *Ars Technica*, October 9, 2019, https://arstechnica.com/tech-policy/2019/10/unsealed-fisa-ruling-slaps-fbi-for-misuse-of-surveillance-data.
[16] Mike Scarcella, "D.C. Circuit Abruptly Closes Courtroom in Guantanamo Case," *The Blog of LegalTimes*, April 5, 2010, https://legaltimes.typepad.com/blt/2010/04/dc-circuit-abruptly-closes-courtroom-in-guantanamo-case.html.
[17] *In re Oliver*, 333 U.S. 257, 266 (1948).

keep a Journal of its Proceedings, and from time to time publish the same, excepting such Parts as may in their Judgment require Secrecy."[18] From this, we can infer that the Founders intended access to congressional proceedings at least to be the default and secrecy to be the exception.[19] Some have suggested that the failure to explicitly mention transparency in the Constitution is probably owed to its being "taken so much for granted that it was deemed unnecessary to include it."[20] As US Senator Thomas Hennings Jr. said in 1959, "By 1787, the year the Constitution was written, there had developed in England the concept of a right in the people to know what their Government was doing."[21] And, he read the Constitution as evincing "an obvious intent to keep secrecy in government at a minimum."[22]

Today, things have changed. Secrecy in government is often the rule. This is especially the case in the national security context. Often, access in the judicial context, to the extent it is considered at all, is viewed as nothing more than a tool for encouraging procedural fairness (for example, the idea that witnesses are more likely to tell the truth if giving testimony publicly). Even when courts recognize that access may have a constitutional role to play, their analyses are often limited to First Amendment interests alone. But this devalues access, as it encourages courts to analyze the right of access only through a contemporary lens of individual rights rather than societal interests. While the "individual rights vision of the speech and press clauses powerfully illuminates a vital part of our constitutional tradition," it also obscures the structural role that the access plays in our government.[23]

A new approach is needed—one that accounts for this important role. Coming at the right of access from a structural perspective has support in text, history, and tradition.[24] The Founders "were concerned with broad principles, and wrote against a background of shared values and practices."[25] The Constitution is, after all, a structural document that, as John Hart Ely put it, ensures "a durable

---

[18] U.S. Const., art. I, § 5.

[19] *See also, e.g., Freeman's J.: or, the North-Am. Intelligencer* (Philadelphia), Mar. 14, 1784, at 2 (asserting that proposed changes to the Pennsylvania Constitution that would have prevented the reporting of the yeas and nays in the legislature was an attack on the liberty of the press).

[20] Thomas C. Hennings Jr., "Constitutional Law: The People's Right To Know," *American Bar Association Journal*, 45 (1959), 667, 668.

[21] *Id.*

[22] *Id.*

[23] Akhil Reed Amar, "The Bill of Rights as a Constitution," *Yale Law Journal*, 100 (1991), 1131, 1151–52.

[24] *New York State Rifle & Pistol Ass'n, Inc. v. Bruen*, 142 S. Ct. 2111, 2130 (2022) (noting focus on text, history, and tradition in constitutional interpretation).

[25] *See Globe Newspaper Co.*, 457 U.S. at 604; *see also* Thomas I. Emerson, *The System of Freedom of Expression* (1970), 5 ("Any study of the legal doctrines and institutions necessary to maintain an effective system of freedom of expression must be based upon the functions performed by the system in our society, the dynamics of its operation, and the general role of law and legal institutions supporting it.").

structure for the ongoing resolution of policy disputes."[26] "To understand the Constitution as a legal text," Laurence Tribe explained, "it is essential to recognize the sort of text it is: a *constitutive* text that purports, in the name of the People of the United States of America, to bring into being a number of distinct but interrelated institutions."[27] "Read in isolation," he added, "most of the Constitution's provisions make only a highly limited kind of sense."[28]

For these reasons, to understand the Constitution, emphasis must be placed on the "text and structure, both the structure within the text—the pattern and interplay in the language of the Constitution itself and its provisions" as well as "the structure (or architecture) outside the text—the pattern and interplay in the governmental edifice that the Constitution describes and creates, and in the institutions and practices it propels."[29] In short, "we must never forget that it is a constitution we are expounding."[30]

III. The Interbranch Function of Access

The tripartite government established by the Constitution cannot work without some degree of transparency. The Constitution is premised on the idea that separation of powers is "essential to the preservation of liberty" of the citizens who were creating the new government.[31] Separation of powers is the "foundation" for "separate and distinct" powers of each branch,[32] ensures that "the members of each department should be as little dependent as possible on those of the others," and gives "those who administer each department the necessary constitutional means and personal motives to resist encroachments of the others."[33] It prevents any branch from subsuming any of the others and infringing on the powers reserved by the People. For the Founders, Justice Frankfurter explained, "the doctrine of separation of powers was not mere theory; it was a felt necessity."[34]

Separation of powers cannot operate as intended, however, if each branch is able to close itself off from the others. It presupposes transparency of some degree. As James Wilson observed, "I believe, sir, that the observation which I am now going to make, will apply to mankind in every situation; they will act with

---

[26] John Hart Ely, *Democracy and Distrust: A Theory of Judicial Review* (1980), 80.
[27] Laurence H. Tribe, "Taking Text and Structure Seriously: Reflections on Free-Form Method in Constitutional Interpretation," *Harvard Law Review*, 108 (1995), 1221, 1235; *see also* David S. Ardia, "Court Transparency and First Amendment," *Cardozo Law Review*, 38 (2017), 835, 885–89.
[28] Tribe, *supra* note 27, at 1235.
[29] *Id.* at 1236.
[30] *McCulloch v. Maryland*, 17 U.S. 316, 407 (1819).
[31] THE FEDERALIST NO. 51 (James Madison).
[32] *Id.*
[33] *Id.*
[34] *Youngstown Sheet & Tube Co. v. Sawyer*, 343 U.S. 579, 593 (1952) (Frankfurter, J., concurring).

more caution, and perhaps more integrity, if their proceedings are to be under the inspection and control of another."[35] Secrecy, therefore, "may distort the system of checks and balances in the structure of the federal government" as it "will be very difficult, if not impossible," for example, "for the legislature to monitor the activities of the executive branch if information is concentrated there."[36] This holds true of the relationship between the executive and judicial branches as well.

Take one recent example: the executive's insistence that only it could decide whether to disclose to the public classified videos showing the force-feeding of a Guantanamo Bay detainee that were submitted as evidence in a habeas corpus case. The D.C. Circuit heard oral argument in that case, *Dhiab v. Obama*, after the lower court ordered the tapes released, relying on the right of access.[37] At argument, then Judge Merrick Garland pressed the government on its expansive understanding of its power to force proceedings to be held secrecy: "Your position is that no matter how central the document ... is to the resolution of a court case, the court under no circumstances can disclose it if the government has stamped it secret. Is that right?" "That is our position," the government responded.[38] That disturbed Judge Garland precisely because of the separation of powers issue, as it would mean that documents "fundamental to a decision in the courts cannot be disclosed" by the judiciary even if the government was "hiding something."[39] In such a case, the court may need to "exercise ... its discretion over its own proceedings" and unseal the documents to ensure the "public confidence" and the "integrity of the Judiciary."[40]

The executive generally advances three arguments to avoid the imposition of judicial power over disclosure of classified information, but ultimately none is persuasive.[41] First, it points to the "President's constitutional role as the head of the Executive Branch and as Commander-in-Chief" and to cases appearing to endorse that view.[42] In *Department of Navy v. Egan*, the government notes that the Supreme Court upheld the executive's denial of a security clearance to an individual because the "authority to classify and control access to information bearing on national security ... flows primarily from this constitutional

---

[35] Jonathan Elliot (ed.), *II Debates in the Several State Conventions on the Adoption of the Federal Constitution* (Taylor & Maury, 1854), 447.
[36] Cass R. Sunstein, "Government Control of Information," *California Law Review*, 74 (1986), 889, 897.
[37] *Dhiab v. Obama*, 787 F.3d 563, 565 (D.C. Cir. 2015).
[38] Recording of Oral Argument at 24:04, *Dhiab*, No. 14-5299; *see also Dhiab*, 787 F.3d at 565 (dismissing appeal).
[39] Recording of Oral Argument at 25:24, *Dhiab*, No. 14-5299.
[40] *Id.* at 27:18.
[41] Gov. Response to Standby Counsel's Memo. in Support of Defendant's Motion for Copy of Substitution at 2, United States v. Moussaoui, No. 01-455-A (E.D. Va. October 2003).
[42] Brief for the United States at 31, *Dhiab*, No. 16-5011 (D.C. Cir. March 3, 2016).

investment of power in the President."[43] Thus, the Court said, "courts traditionally have been reluctant to intrude upon the authority of the Executive in military and national security affairs."[44]

The government overreads *Egan* for at least two reasons. Initially, the Constitution does not vest sole authority over national security matters in the president, and *Egan* does not suggest otherwise. The legislative branch, for example, is charged with providing "for the common defense" and making "Rules for the Government and Regulation of the land and naval Forces," among other national security responsibilities.[45] Based on this authority, Congress regularly directs how classified information must be dealt with, including within the executive and judiciary.[46] And Congress has established rules governing disclosure of classified information by its own members. These rules have permitted release of classified information over the objection of the president—a provision that received much public attention during congressional investigations into Russian interference in the 2016 presidential election.[47]

Next, *Egan* does not stand for the proposition that the executive has power to dictate handling of judicial records containing classified information.[48] *Egan* dealt solely with the administration of classified information *within* the executive branch. It did not establish a roving rule of deference to the executive any time disclosure of classified information is at issue in any part of the government. Instead, it established a rule of judicial deference to the executive when it comes to the executive's intrabranch administration of classified information while remaining silent on the separate question of how the judiciary must handle its internal administration of access to classified information in judicial proceedings or records.[49]

---

[43] 484 U.S. 518, 527 (1988); *see also Bismullah v. Gates*, 501 F.3d 178 (D.C. Cir. 2007); *United States v. Smith*, 750 F.2d 1215 (4th Cir. 1984).

[44] *Egan*, 484 U.S. at 530.

[45] *See* U.S. Const., art. I, § 8 (giving Congress the power to "declare war," "raise and support armies," "provide and maintain a Navy," "organiz[e], arm[], and disciplin[e], the Militia"); *see also* Kenneth Mayer, *With the Stroke of a Pen: Executive Orders and Presidential Powers* (2001), 143 ("The legal and constitutional arguments concerning the balance of congressional-executive authority over classification suggest strongly that the pure presidency-centered view is overdrawn.").

[46] Pub. L. No. 93-502 (November 21, 1974) (granting courts power under FOIA to review classification decisions), 88 Stat. 1561; Pub. L. No. 111-258 (October 7, 2010) (ordering "Secretary of Homeland Security to develop a strategy to prevent the over-classification"), 124 Stat. 2649; *see also* 5 U.S.C. § 7211 (directing that government employees' right to furnish Congress information "may not be interfered with or denied"); 50 U.S.C. § 3091. For a general discussion of the current classification system, *see* Mayer, *supra* note 45.

[47] *See* Molly E. Reynolds, "The Little-Known Rule that Allowed Congress to Release Devin Nunes's Memo," *Lawfare*, January 30, 2018, https://www.lawfareblog.com/little-known-rule-allowed-congress-release-devin-nuness-memo (accessed July 15, 2023).

[48] *Marbury v. Madison*, 5 U.S. 137, 177 (1803).

[49] *Egan* can also be distinguished from other cases of forced access to the executive where some other constitutional principle is at issue, like individual rights. *See Egan*, 484 U.S. at 528 ("It should be obvious that no one has a 'right' to a security clearance."). Courts also show less deference when there are interbranch conflicts. *See id.* at 530 ("*unless Congress specifically has provided otherwise*, courts

Second, the government claims that Congress validated its authority over classified information by adopting two statutes. It contends that the Freedom of Information Act (FOIA), which requires disclosure of government records subject to an exemption for national security, demonstrates that courts "must accept... at face value" its classification decisions.[50] True, the Supreme Court held in *EPA v. Mink* that Congress never intended FOIA to subject classifications decisions "to judicial review."[51] But a year later, Congress overrode *Mink* (and a presidential veto) to make clear courts have such power.[52] Senator Edmund Muskie, the chief sponsor, explained, "I object to the idea that anything but full *de novo* review will give us the assurance that classification—like other aspects of claimed secrecy—has been brought under check."[53]

The executive also relies on the Classified Information Procedures Act (CIPA), which prevents the use of graymail in national security cases.[54] Under CIPA, the government can request an in camera pretrial hearing to determine the use of classified information at trial.[55] If the court determines that the information is relevant and admissible, it may authorize disclosure.[56] To avoid disclosure, the government can then concede the relevant facts for which the information is being offered or provide an unclassified summary of the information.[57] If it does neither, the court can order disclosure of the classified evidence anyway, or the government can move to dismiss the indictment.[58] As such, CIPA actually ensures a public trial and validates a court's authority over disclosure of classified information.[59]

Third, the executive asserts that the judiciary is not well placed to decide whether disclosure of classified information will cause harm.[60] Errors in

traditionally have been reluctant to intrude upon the authority of the Executive in military and national security affairs" (emphasis added) (citing, e.g., *Orloff v. Willoughby*, 345 U.S. 83 (1953)).

[50] Brief for Respondents-Appellants/Cross-Appellees at 33–34, *Dhiab*, No. 16-5011 (D.C. Cir. March 3, 2016) (citing *Morley v. CIA*, 508 F.3d 1108 (D.C. Cir. 2007); *Campbell v. Dep't of Justice*, 164 F.3d 20 (D.C. Cir. 1998)).
[51] 410 U.S. 73, 82 (1973).
[52] *Ray v. Turner*, 587 F.2d 1187, 1190 (D.C. Cir. 1978); *see also CIA v. Sims*, 471 U.S. 159, 181 (1985) (Marshall, J., concurring in judgment) (noting that at "one time, this Court believed that the Judiciary was not qualified to undertake this task," but "Congress, however, disagreed" (citation omitted)).
[53] As reprinted in Memorial Tributes Delivered in Congress, S. Doc. 104–17 at 95 (1996).
[54] *See United States v. Ressam*, 221 F. Supp. 2d 1252, 1256 (W.D. Wash. 2002).
[55] 18 U.S.C. App. 3 § 6(a).
[56] *Id.* § 6(c)(1).
[57] *Id.* § 6(c)(1)(A)–(B).
[58] *Id.* § 6(e)(2); *see also id.* § 8(a); Neil A. Lewis & David Johnston, "U.S. to Drop Spy Case Against Pro-Israel Lobbyists," *New York Times*, May 1, 2009, https://www.nytimes.com/2009/05/02/us/politics/02aipac.html (accessed July 15, 2023).
[59] *United States v. Rosen*, 487 F. Supp. 2d 703, 718 (E.D. Va. 2007); *see also id.* § 7(a) (permitting appeal from "a district court in a criminal case authorizing the disclosure of classified information").
[60] United States' Opp'n to Mot. of the Am. Civil Liberties Union for the Release of Ct. Records at 13, In re Opinions and Orders of this Court Containing Novel or Significant Interpretations of Law, No. 16-01 (F.I.S.C. June 8, 2017) (citation omitted).

predictive judgments of relative harms, it says, are "likely given that even judges with expertise in national security matters cannot 'equal [the expertise] of the Executive Branch.'"[61] Yet, in the context of domestic terrorism, the Supreme Court has rejected "the Government's argument that internal security matters are too subtle and complex for judicial evaluation."[62] The D.C. Circuit later extended that logic to the national security context.[63] According to the court, Congress's legislative override in *Mink* evidenced a "vote of confidence in the competence of the judiciary" and "affirms our own belief that judges do, in fact, have the capabilities needed to consider and weigh data pertaining to the foreign affairs and national defense of this nation."[64]

The executive's absolute claim of authority over disclosure of classified information also lacks support in case law emphasizing the role of separation of powers as between the executive and judiciary. In 1953, for example, the executive urged the Supreme Court to hold that only "executive department heads have power to withhold any documents in their custody from judicial view if they deem it to be in the public interest."[65] It argued that the Court was powerless to force it to disclose what it wished not to disclose.[66] The Court rejected that expansive argument. Instead, it held that the government could make *an assertion* of executive privilege to maintain secrecy. But, ultimately, the "court *itself* must determine whether the circumstances are appropriate for the claim of privilege."[67] "Judicial control over the evidence in a case," after all, "cannot be abdicated to the caprice of executive officers."[68] Were it so, that unbridled privilege "would lead to intolerable abuses."[69]

Then, in *New York Times v. United States*, the *Pentagon Papers* case, the government asked the Supreme Court to close portions of the oral arguments discussing classified information relating to whether the *New York Times* and the *Washington Post* could be restrained from publishing a secret and embarrassing government history of the Vietnam War. The Court denied that request and required that the argument be held in public (albeit while permitting a classified brief to be submitted by the government).[70] While no reason was given

---

[61] *Id.* (citing *Egan*, 484 U.S. at 529); *El-Masri v. United States*, 479 F.3d 296, 305 (4th Cir. 2007) ("the Executive ... occup[ies] a position superior to ... courts in evaluating the ... release of sensitive information").

[62] 407 U.S. 297, 320 (1972).

[63] *Zweibon v. Mitchell*, 516 F.2d 594, 642 (D.C. Cir. 1975) (en banc).

[64] *Id.*; *see also Halpern v. F.B.I.*, 181 F.3d 279, 291 (2d Cir. 1999) (noting that "Congress felt strongly" about de novo review of classification decisions in the FOIA context).

[65] *United States v. Reynolds*, 345 U.S. 1, 6 (1953).

[66] *Id.* at 6 n.9.

[67] *Id.* at 8.

[68] *Id.* at 9.

[69] *Id.*

[70] Recording of Oral Argument at 00:01, *N.Y. Times Co.*, No. 1873 (1971).

for denying the request, it takes little imagination to conclude that the Court knew the eyes of the nation were fixed on it. If the government was going to make a case for a court-enforced prior restraint to keep information about Vietnam from the public, it would have to do so in public.

Three years later, in *United States v. Nixon*, the issue was whether a subpoena should be quashed because it demanded "confidential conversations between a President and his close advisors."[71] The Nixon administration argued that "the separation of powers doctrine precludes judicial review of a President's claim of privilege."[72] In ordering the administration to turn over Watergate recordings, the Supreme Court explained that President Richard Nixon had the separation of powers argument backward, as granting the executive absolute immunity from disclosure would frustrate judicial administration: "The impediment that an absolute, unqualified privilege would place in the way of the primary constitutional duty of the Judicial Branch to do justice in criminal prosecutions would plainly conflict with the function of the courts under Art. III."[73] "Any other conclusion," the Court said, "would be contrary to the basic concept of separation of powers and the checks and balances that flow from the scheme of a tripartite government."[74]

The Fourth Circuit adopted a similar approach in a motion by the press for access to proceedings of a criminal prosecution of a Ghanaian spy.[75] The defendant was indicted on eight counts relating to espionage, and after negotiating a plea deal, the United States and Ghana made a motion to hold the plea colloquy behind closed doors.[76] The district court granted the motion.[77] Three days later, the *Washington Post* made a motion seeking the release of the transcript of the hearing and a right to participate in future hearings.[78] Thereafter, the reporter attempted to attend the sentencing hearing but was ejected from that hearing as well.[79] After the hearings were over, the court released the transcripts but continued to maintain several documents under seal. At the hearing on the *Post*'s motion, the district court complied "with the government's wishes" and agreed to keep several still-sealed documents under seal.[80]

On appeal, the government argued that traditional access "requirements should not apply where national security interests are at stake."[81] The Fourth Circuit disagreed and vacated and remanded. Although it recognized "the

---

[71] 418 U.S. 683, 703 (1974).
[72] *Id.*
[73] *Id.* at 707.
[74] *Id.* at 704.
[75] *In re Wash. Post Co.*, 807 F.2d 383 (4th Cir. 1986).
[76] *Id.* at 386.
[77] *Id.*
[78] *Id.* at 387.
[79] *Id.*
[80] *Id.*
[81] *Id.* at 391.

government's concern that dangerous consequences may result from the inappropriate disclosure of classified information," it held that a presumption of access attached to the proceeding.[82] The court framed its decision in terms of separation of powers: "A blind acceptance by the courts of the government's insistence on the need for secrecy, without notice to others, without argument, and without a statement of reasons, would impermissibly compromise the independence of the judiciary and open the door to possible abuse."[83] It is improper, the court said, for the judiciary to "abdicate its decisionmaking responsibility to the executive branch."[84]

Years later, when Lakhdar Boumediene, a detainee in the war on terror housed at the Guantanamo Bay, sought a writ of habeas corpus in *Boumediene v. Bush*, the government argued that civilian courts should not entertain such claims—in part because of the supposed risk that sensitive information would be publicly disclosed if those proceedings were permitted to go forward.[85] The Court rejected that argument too, finding that those concerns alone could not justify interference with the great writ.[86] Instead, the Court noted that while "the Government has a legitimate interest in protecting sources and methods of intelligence gathering," courts could "accommodate" that interest by deciding whether executive privilege was properly invoked—not reflexively closing proceedings.[87]

And in *In re Opinions & Orders*, two civil rights organizations sought access to classified "opinions evaluating the meaning, scope, and constitutionality of Section 215" of the USA PATRIOT Act.[88] An en banc Foreign Intelligence Surveillance Court recognized that the motion raised very real separation of powers concerns.[89] Breaking with the dissent and its concern over permitting nonparties to interfere in the government's protection of national security information,[90] the majority explained, citing *Egan*, that "courts rarely presume to review the Executive Branch's decisionmaking, at least without a statutory hook."[91] But, the court added, the classified information at issue was "not housed in the Executive Branch" but instead arose "within an Article III proceeding,

---

[82] *Id.*
[83] *Id.* at 392–93.
[84] *In re Wash. Post*, 807 F.2d at 391.
[85] *Boumediene v. Bush*, 553 U.S. 723, 796 (2008).
[86] *Id.* at 795.
[87] *Id.* at 795–97; *Ameziane v. Obama*, 620 F.3d 1, 6 (D.C. Cir. 2010) (construing *Boumediene* as a direction "to preserve to the extent feasible the traditional right of public access to judicial records grounded").
[88] In re Opinions & Orders of this Court Addressing Bulk Collection of Data under the Foreign Intelligence Surveillance Act, No. Misc. 13-08, 2017 WL 5983865 (F.I.S.C. November 9, 2017) ("*In re Opinions & Orders*").
[89] *Id.*
[90] *Id.* at *13–14.
[91] *Id.* at *8 (citing *Dep't of Navy v. Egan*, 484 U.S. 518, 538 (1988)).

and Plaintiffs seek access to portions of *judicial* opinions."[92] In other words, because the movants sought disclosure judicial records, the separation of powers argument broke in favor of the judiciary rather than executive.[93]

These cases all reflect the principle that separation of powers is "essential to the preservation of liberty."[94] Were a court to defer to the executive even as to disclosure of classified information in judicial proceedings, it would be abdicating its judicial responsibilities under the Constitution to another branch.[95] This would lead to intolerable abuses, where the executive could use secrecy for its owns aims. Judicially enforced access, however, prevents such a repugnant consolidation of power in the hands of the executive.

IV. The Equipping Function of Access

If the right of access's role plays a horizontal function in bolstering separation of powers, it also plays a vertical function by equipping the sovereign, that is, the People, with the information needed to engage in self-governance. This function, too, has grounding in text, history, and tradition. James Madison famously cautioned that a "people who mean to be their own governors must arm themselves with the power knowledge gives."[96] Thomas Jefferson explained that "[t]he way to prevent these [violent protests by the People] is to give them full information of their affairs through the channel of the public papers, and to contrive that those papers should penetrate the whole mass of the people."[97] He went on, "The basis of our governments being the opinion of the people, the very first object should be to keep that right."[98]

The People's right to know is implicit throughout the Constitution. The Preamble makes clear that the government being formed is a government of

---

[92] *Id.*

[93] Brief of Amicus Curiae at 29–30, *In re Certification of Questions of Law*, No. 18-01 ("Judicial opinions belong to the courts.... Should the Court find for the government, Art. II would trump Article III in an area of core Article III powers.").

[94] THE FEDERALIST NO. 51 (James Madison).

[95] *See, e.g., Stern v. Marshall*, 564 U.S. 462, 483 (2011) ("[T]he judicial Power of the United States' can no more be shared with another branch than the Chief Executive, for example, can share with the Judiciary the veto power, or the Congress share with the Judiciary the power to override a Presidential veto." (cleaned up) (citation omitted)); *Detroit Free Press v. Ashcroft*, 303 F.3d 681, 692–93 (6th Cir. 2002) (discussing separation of powers and access in national security matters); *Ex parte Drawbaugh*, 2 App. D.C. 404, 405 (D.C. Cir. 1894) ("this is a public court of record, governed by very different principles... from those that apply to an executive department.").

[96] 3 James Madison, *Letters and Other Writings of James Madison* (1884), 276; *see also* THE FEDERALIST NO. 3 (John Jay).

[97] 2 Thomas Jefferson, *Memoir, Correspondence, and Miscellanies, from the Papers of Thomas Jefferson* (1830), 85.

[98] *Id.*

the People: "We the People of the United States ... do ordain and establish this Constitution for the United States of America."[99] The "Constitution created a form of government under which 'The people, not the government, possess the absolute sovereignty.'"[100] Because the government established by the Constitution derives its authority from the People, "it logically and necessarily follows that the people have a right to know what the Government—which they themselves established—is doing."[101] The right to know, just as with the right to self-govern, is thus implicit in the Constitution.

It is also explicit. In Article I, Section 5, Clause 3, the House and the Senate are directed to "keep a Journal of its Proceedings, and from time to time publish the same."[102] That clause, the Supreme Court explained, "insure[d] publicity to the proceedings of the legislature."[103] By ensuring publicity, the "public mind is enlightened by an attentive examination of the public measures."[104] Under Article I, Section 9, Congress is required from "time to time" to publish a "Statement and Account of Receipts and Expenditures of all public Money."[105] And, under Article II, Section 3, the president "shall from time to time give to the Congress Information of the State of the Union."[106] This creates "a positive *duty* to provide information to the Congress," which, in turn, would provide it to the People.[107]

The Bill of Rights presupposes transparency too. The Sixth Amendment ensures that a criminal defendant is not tried in secret. In *Gannett Co., Inc. v. DePasquale*, the Court explained that "[t]here can be no blinking the fact that there is a strong societal interest in public trials."[108] This interest extends to all stages of a criminal prosecution.[109] And it exists in part because access ensures that "constitutionally protected 'discussion of governmental affairs' is an informed one."[110] In *Waller v. Georgia*, for example, the Court found that there was a clear public interest in being able to freely examine allegations that "police conducted general searches and wholesale seizures in over 150 homes, and eavesdropped on more than 800 hours of telephone conversations by means of effectively unsupervised wiretaps."[111]

---

[99] U.S. Const., pmbl.
[100] *N.Y. Times Co. v. Sullivan*, 376 U.S. 254, 274 (1964).
[101] Hennings Jr., *supra* note 20, at 669.
[102] U.S. Const., art. I, § 5.
[103] *Marshall Field & Co. v. Clark*, 143 U.S. 649, 670–71 (1892).
[104] *Id.*
[105] U.S. Const., art. I, § 9, cl. 7.
[106] *Id.*, art II, § 3.
[107] Hennings Jr., *supra* note 20, at 669.
[108] 443 U.S. 363, 383 (1979).
[109] *See, e.g., Waller v. Georgia*, 467 U.S. 39, 47 n.5 (1984) (citations omitted).
[110] *Id.*
[111] *Id.*

The First Amendment too is premised on transparency: "Implicit in [the First Amendment's] terms is a right to knowledge, including knowledge about what the government is doing."[112] The Supreme Court offered support for this view early on in *Grosjean v. American Press Co.*[113] There, it explained that the "predominant purpose of the grant of immunity here invoked was to preserve an untrammeled press as a vital source of public information ... since informed public opinion is the most potent of all restraints upon misgovernment."[114] In other words, "The evils to be prevented were not the censorship of the press merely, but any action of the government by means of which it might prevent such free and general discussion of public matters as seems absolutely essential to prepare the people for an intelligent exercise of their rights as citizens."[115]

Simply, to be able to effectively petition their government, the People need to be able to assemble to discuss public affairs; and to be able to effectively assemble and discuss their affairs, citizens must be able to share ideas about their government; and to be able to effectively share ideas, citizens must have access to information about the government, its officers, and their conduct.[116] Without access, the entire machine of self-government is breaks down. That is, First Amendment freedoms are not isolated from each other, they each are part of a shared ecosystem. Or, to mix metaphors, they are "a part of the working of the national government; ... a part of the flow of communication which is its lifeblood."[117]

In 1980, in *Richmond Newspapers, Inc. v. Virginia*, the Supreme Court began a journey toward recognizing as much when it found that the First Amendment guaranteed a right of access to criminal trials.[118] Notably, however, the plurality opinion said it was "not crucial" to link the right of access to any constitutional theory.[119] What the plurality did do was offer lower courts a two-part test to employ to decide whether a right of access applies. Under this "history and logic" test, a court first asks whether a proceeding historically has been open to the public and whether openness would promote the effective administration of justice.[120] If a court answers "yes" to both, then the proceeding is presumptively open to the public.[121] The test has its benefits. Through a mechanical application

---

[112] Hennings Jr., *supra* note 20, at 669.
[113] 297 U.S. 233 (1936).
[114] *Id.* at 250; *see also* Hennings Jr., *supra* note 20, at 669.
[115] *Grosjean*, 297 U.S. at 249–50 (citation omitted).
[116] *See, e.g.*, Charles Black, *Structure and Relationship in Constitutional Law* (1969), 41; *see also Branzburg v. Hayes*, 408 U.S. 665, 681 (1972) ("without some protection for seeking out the news, freedom of the press could be eviscerated.").
[117] Black, *supra* note 116, at 41.
[118] 448 U.S. at 558 (plurality op.); *id.* at 584 (1980) (Stevens, J., concurring); *id.* at 585 (Brennan, J., concurring in judgment); *id.* at 599 (Stewart, J., concurring in judgment).
[119] 448 U.S. at 576 (plurality op.).
[120] *Press-Enterprise Co. v. Super. Ct.*, 478 U.S. 1, 13–14 (1986).
[121] *Id.*

of it, courts have found a wide variety of government proceedings presumptively open.[122] But it has its disadvantages: it obscures the answer to the question of *why* there should be access to begin with.

Justice Brennan, in a concurrence, advanced a theory to answer just that question. Although traditionally the First Amendment was understood to make speech nearly inviolate, he admitted that the Court had not viewed it "as providing an equally categorical assurance of the correlative freedom of *access* to information."[123] But, he explained, the First Amendment was "more than a commitment to free expression" for its "own sake[]; it has a *structural* role to play in securing and fostering our republican system of self-government."[124] "The structural model," he said, "links the First Amendment to that process of communication necessary for a democracy to survive, and thus entails solicitude not only for communication itself, but also for the indispensable conditions of meaningful communication."[125] Thus, the First Amendment protected "the antecedent assumption that valuable public debate ... must be informed."[126] That is, the First Amendment protected both the ends and the means of informed debate.[127]

This theory, Brennan argued, was "not novel."[128] The Court often derived "specific rights from the structure of our constitutional government, or from other explicit rights."[129] The right to vote and the right of association—neither of which was mentioned in the Constitution but both of which were fundamental to democratic governance—were two such rights.[130] Pointing to Footnote 4 of *United States v. Carolene Products Co.*, he said that the recognition of such rights was especially important when government conduct purposefully undermined the Constitution's democratic processes that would normally "be expected to bring about" accountability.[131] In *Grosjean*, for example, the Court invalidated a tax aimed at crippling newspapers critical of the Louisiana governor not because the tax was facially invalid but because it was "a deliberate and calculated device ... to limit the circulation of information to which the public is entitled in virtue of the constitutional guaranties."[132] In such cases, courts had an obligation

---

[122] *See, e.g., N.Y. Civil Liberties Union v. N.Y.C. Transit Auth.*, 684 F.3d 286, 289 (2d Cir. 2012).
[123] *Richmond Newspapers, Inc.*, 448 U.S. at 585 (Brennan, J., concurring in judgment) (emphasis added).
[124] *Id.* at 587.
[125] *Id.* at 587–88.
[126] *Id.*
[127] Eugene Cerruti, "'Dancing in the Courthouse': The First Amendment Right of Access Opens a New Round," *University of Richmond Law Review*, 29 (1995), 237, 283 ("*Richmond Newspapers* does not vindicate a freedom of speech so much as it does a freedom of self-rule.").
[128] *Richmond Newspapers, Inc.*, 448 U.S. at 588 n.4 (Brennan, J., concurring in judgment).
[129] *Id.*
[130] *Id.* (citations omitted).
[131] *Id.* at 587 (citing 304 U.S. 144, 152 n.4 (1938)).
[132] *Id.* (citing 297 U.S. at 250).

to enforce "more exacting judicial scrutiny" to protect not just speech but self-governance itself.[133]

Although the plurality focused on its mechanical test, even it was forced begrudgingly to recognize that access played some structural role in our constitutional system. Because the explicit rights of free speech, press, and assembly "share a common core purpose of assuring freedom of communication on matters relating to the functioning of government," it admitted that the First Amendment should be understood as prohibiting the "government from limiting the stock of information from which members of the public may draw."[134] Justice Stevens, concurring in the judgment, observed similarly that without "some protection for the acquisition of information about the operation of public institutions . . . , the process of self-governance contemplated by the Framers would be stripped of its substance."[135]

And, although Justice Powell did not participate in *Richmond Newspapers, Inc.*, he previously laid the groundwork for the structural theory by observing that speech "must not only be unfettered; it must also be informed."[136] In that case, *Saxbe v. Washington Post Co.*, the press challenged a regulation limiting its ability to interview prisoners.[137] The majority concluded that the regulation did not implicate the First Amendment.[138] Powell, joined by Brennan and Marshall, disagreed. "Federal prisons," he wrote, were "public institutions" and "administration of these institutions, the effectiveness of their rehabilitative programs, [and] the conditions of confinement that they maintain . . . are all matters of legitimate societal interest and concern."[139] While the regulation did not directly infringe on the right to speak, it frustrated "the societal function of the First Amendment in preserving free public discussion of governmental affairs."[140]

Two years after *Richmond Newspapers, Inc.*, Brennan invoked the structural theory for the first time in an opinion for the Court in *Globe Newspaper Co. v. Superior Court*.[141] Invalidating a law requiring the mandatory exclusion of the public from certain portions of a trial, Brennan "eschewed any 'narrow, literal conception' of the [First] Amendment's terms."[142] Echoing his opinion in

---

[133] *Carolene Products Co.*, 304 U.S. at 152 n.4.
[134] *Richmond Newspapers, Inc.*, 448 U.S. at 575–76 (plurality op.).
[135] *Houchins v. KQED, Inc.*, 438 U.S. 1, 32 (1978) (Stevens, J., dissenting); *Richmond Newspapers, Inc.*, 448 U.S. at 584 (Stevens, J., concurring).
[136] *Saxbe v. Washington Post Co.*, 417 U.S. 843, 863 (1974) (Powell, J., dissenting); *see also id.* at 862–63 (First Amendment "embodies our Nation's commitment to popular self-determination").
[137] *Id.* at 843.
[138] *Id.* at 850.
[139] *Id.* at 861 (Powell, J., dissenting); *see also Waller*, 467 U.S. at 47 & n.5 (recognizing that the access right extended to suppression hearings in part because the public "has a strong interest in exposing substantial allegations of police misconduct to the salutary effects of public scrutiny.").
[140] *Saxbe*, 417 U.S. at 862 (Powell, J., dissenting).
[141] 457 U.S. at 606.
[142] *Id.*

Richmond Newspapers, Inc., he wrote that the amendment was "broad enough to encompass those rights that, while not unambiguously enumerated . . . are nonetheless necessary to the enjoyment of other First Amendment rights."[143] One such right was access to government proceedings that would ensure "the individual citizen can *effectively* participate in and contribute to our republican system of self-government."[144] The access right, he said, guaranteed that the "constitutionally protected 'discussion of governmental affairs' is an informed one."[145]

Brennan never again wrote a majority opinion in an access case. In two cases that followed, *Press-Enterprise I & II*, Chief Justice Burger, writing for the majority, dutifully applied the two-part history and logic test while downplaying the structural role access played.[146] At the same time, neither opinion expressly rejected Brennan's broader conception of the access right in *Globe Newspaper, Co.* A third case, resolved through a short per curiam opinion, also failed to address the theoretical tension in the Court's access jurisprudence.[147] And since that decision in 1993, the Court has been largely silent. As a result, although a majority of the Court signed on to Brennan's opinion in *Globe Newspaper Co.*, the structural theory was soon overshadowed by the work-a-day opinions in *Press-Enterprise I & II*, and the subsequent decisions in the lower courts apply its two-part test.

V. Toward a Structural Understanding

The failure of the Supreme Court to provide theoretical guidance for the right of access is evident in case law today—especially in the national security context. Currently, courts are directed to decide whether a particular proceeding is presumptively open to the public by applying the history and logic test and employees means-end scrutiny. Yet, as Judge Stephen F. Williams lamented in *Dhiab*, courts "have little guidance from the Supreme Court" as to when or why the right of access should be found to apply to any particular proceeding, including those containing or implicating classified information.[148] This indeterminacy is exacerbated by the absence of an underlying theory that might plot a course for this right otherwise adrift.

---

[143] *Id.*
[144] *Id.* (citing *Thornhill v. Alabama*, 310 U.S. 88, 95 (1940)).
[145] *Id.* at 604
[146] *Press-Enterprise II*, 478 U.S. 1; *Press-Enterprise Co. v. Super. Ct.*, 464 U.S. 501 (1984); *see also* Ardia, *supra* note 27, at 893 (Chief Justice Burger "did not adopt the expansive language" Brennan had).
[147] *El Vocero de Puerto Rico v. Puerto Rico*, 508 U.S. 147 (1993).
[148] *Dhiab*, 852 F.3d at 1103, 1107 (Williams, J.) (concurring in part and concurring in judgment).

Absent guidance from the Court, it is up to lower courts to chart a course. To do so, courts should move away from understanding access as strictly a matter of mechanical tests and procedural niceties and toward an understanding that is consistent with the structural role access plays in our democratic form of government. As discussed, when it comes to the executive trying to choke off access to national security proceedings, at least two structural principles are at stake. First, while the executive branch has an interest in protecting national security, courts must assert their interest exercising control over their own proceedings. Second, courts must view access as a protection against government-imposed information deficits that disenfranchise the citizenry by depriving it of information necessary for self-governance.

There is support for this approach in the case law, particularly in the national security context where some of the nation's and the public's weightiest interests are at stake. In *In re Washington Post*, the Ghanian spy case, the Fourth Circuit emphasized the separation of powers function of access—"we are equally troubled by the notion that the judiciary should abdicate its decisionmaking responsibility to the executive branch"—in finding that the right of access applied even to proceedings containing classified material.[149] Or, take the Sixth Circuit's decision in *Detroit Free Press v. Ashcroft*, where the question was whether in the wake of 9/11 the government could "secretly deport a class [of individuals] if it unilaterally calls them 'special interest' cases."[150] Emphasizing what it called the "selective[] control[of] information rightfully belonging to the people," the court held that those proceedings were subject to public access.[151]

But where courts fail to ground the right of access in these important roles, it is devalued. We know this to be true because, presented with the same question as the Sixth Circuit, the Third Circuit found no right of access to the same immigration proceedings. It did so in part by dialing down consideration of the benefits of access and dialing up the national security concerns: "Since the primary national policy must be self-preservation, it seems elementary that, to the extent open deportation hearings might impair national security, that security is implicated in the logic test."[152] This divergence is on display in other contexts

---

[149] *In re Wash. Post*, 807 F.2d at 391–92 ("A blind acceptance by the courts of the government's insistence on the need for secrecy . . . would impermissibly compromise the independence of the judiciary.").

[150] *Detroit Free Press*, 303 F.3d at 683.

[151] *Id.* Other courts uphold the access right based on the procedural protections that the right provides. *Rosen*, 487 F. Supp. 2d at 715; *see also United States v. Pelton*, 696 F. Supp. 156, 157–59 (D. Md. 1986). And still other courts make no mention at all why the access right should be honored. *See United States v. Almehmeti*, No. 16-cr-398, Dkt. 103 at 10–11 (January 23, 2018).

[152] *North Jersey Media Group, Inc. v. Ashcroft*, 308 F.3d 198, 202 (3d Cir. 2002); *see also Dhiab*, 852 F.3d at 1091–96 (Randolph, J.).

where courts sensitive to the roles access plays are more likely to uphold it than those who are blind to those interests.[153]

It does not have to be this way. First, courts can deploy a simple semantic fix. Describing access as a "right of access" may obscure the societal benefits access provides in a system where individual rights so often take precedence. So instead, courts should describe it as "*structural* access." This slight tweak is an ever-present reminder of the nature of the role access plays. Substantively, courts should also recalibrate the "experience and logic" test to place greater weight on the logic prong, which should be understood as embodying the structural roles access plays. This would temper the experience prong that may otherwise short circuit the access right without considering the societal benefits of providing access in a certain case.[154] As Justice Brennan explained in *Richmond Newspapers, Inc.*, a history of openness may have "special force," but what is "crucial" is "whether access to a particular government process is important in terms of that very process."[155]

Courts have done this before. In *Herald Company, Inc. v. Board of Parole*, for example, a court when confronted with a demand for access to parole board hearings employed a test calibrated just this way.[156] There, the court observed that "Justice Brennan set forth not only the historical analysis employed by Chief Justice Burger in the plurality opinion, but also a structural analysis in which he analyzed the function of the 1st Amendment in preserving free and open public discussion of governmental affairs."[157] Thus, although there was no history of access to parole board hearings, the court concluded that access should be found as a matter of overwhelming logic: "At a time when the merits of the parole process are being hotly debated, the 'structural value of public access' can scarcely be doubted."[158]

Moving from whether the presumption of access applies to whether that presumption has been overcome, courts conducting a means-end analysis should continue to be guided by the structural role that access plays rather than be beholden to a traditional strict scrutiny analysis. Indeed, although access may not

---

[153] *Compare also Cal. First Amend. Coal. v. Woodford*, 299 F.3d 868, 873 (9th Cir. 2002) (finding right of access to executions and emphasizing "public's right to be informed about how the State . . . implement[s] the most serious punishment"), *with Observer v. Patton*, 73 F. Supp. 3d 1318 (W.D. Okla. 2014) (no right of access to executions).

[154] *See, e.g., Phoenix Newspapers, Inc. v. U.S. Dist. Ct.*, 156 F.3d 940, 948 (9th Cir. 1998) (finding that the logic prong of the *Richmond Newspapers* test can be dispositive); *United States v. Simone*, 14 F.3d 833, 838 (3d Cir. 1994) (noting that the court "did not believe that historical analysis was relevant").

[155] *Richmond Newspapers, Inc.*, 448 U.S. at 589 (Brennan, J., concurring in judgment); *Press-Enterprise II*, 478 U.S. at 10 n.3 (noting that state courts had found that access right attached to pretrial proceedings because the "importance of the . . . proceeding" was obvious despite lacking a "historical counterpart").

[156] *Herald Co. v. Bd. of Parole*, 131 Misc. 2d 36 (Sup. Ct. Onondaga Cnty. 1985).

[157] *Id.* at 40.

[158] *Id.* at 46.

be overcome unless strict scrutiny is satisfied, strict scrutiny in the access context has become decidedly less strict than in other contexts.[159] No doubt this is due to the robust theoretical grounding that government intrusions on the right to speak enjoy as compared to the relative absence of a theory in the access context.[160] Simply, courts are more sensitive to intrusions on speech than on access.

The test for overcoming a presumption of access must therefore be recalibrated to account for the structural role access plays. Under the current approach, if a judge determines that there is a substantial likelihood of harm to compelling interest absent closure, then closure will be appropriate irrespective of any countervailing public interest.[161] This test is inappropriately weighted in favor of closure because the "interest inquiry seems to focus only on the importance of the government's ends: Is the interest compelling? If the answer is yes, the interest inquiry appears to stop."[162] The court never has a chance to consider the compelling interests in favor of access.

The means-end scrutiny must include consideration of these countervailing interests. This kind of public interest "gut check" has been proposed elsewhere. For example, where the question was whether national security journalists can be compelled to disclose their sources in a leak investigation, Judge David Tatel argued that "the court must weigh the public interest in compelling disclosure [of a journalist's source], measured by the harm the leak caused, against the public interest in newsgathering, measured by the leaked information's value."[163] A similar test can be adopted in the access context in light of the important role it plays, whereby courts consider whether the structural interests advanced by allowing access outweigh the harm disclosure might cause.

VI. Conclusion

Perhaps nowhere has secrecy been so derided as it has in the government's war on terror. Secrecy in national security proceedings is especially destructive of the constitutional system established by the Founders. It undercuts separation

---

[159] See Adam Winkler, "Fatal in Theory and Strict in Fact: An Empirical Analysis of Strict Scrutiny in the Federal Courts," *Vanderbilt Law Review*., 59 (2006), 793, 796, 849 ("Fifty percent of strict scrutiny applications in right-of-access cases uphold the challenged laws" compared with twenty-four percent in "most areas of the law").

[160] See Amar, *supra* note 23, at 1151–52.

[161] See *Ressam*, No. 99-cr-00666, slip. op. at 3 (W.D. Wash. November 29, 2001).

[162] Eugene Volokh, "Freedom of Speech, Permissible Tailoring and Transcending Strict Scrutiny," *University of Pennsylvania Law Review*, 144 (1996), 2417, 2439; see also id. at 2417 (reliance on rigid tests "risks leading courts ... to the wrong conclusions," "causes courts to apply the test disingenuously," and "distracts us from looking for a better approach").

[163] *In re Grand Jury Subpoena, Judith Miller*, 397 F.3d 964, 986 (D.C. Cir. 2005) (Tatel, J., concurring in judgment), superseded, 438 F.3d 1141 (D.C. Cir. 2006).

of powers and chokes off the flow of information central to democratic decision-making.[164] Too often, however, courts are simply blind to these harms that result from too much secrecy, and current jurisprudence offers little guidance as to how courts should deal with conflicts between secrecy and transparency.

The right of access is a constitutional right in search of a constitutional theory. I have attempted to identify the structural role that access plays with reference to the text, history, and structure of the Constitution and, in turn, argued that courts should recalibrate their approaches to deciding whether a right of access attaches to a particular proceeding and, if so, whether the presumption of access has been overcome. The Constitution demands this. As the Sixth Circuit observed, "When government begins closing doors, it selectively controls information rightfully belonging to the people. Selective information is misinformation. The Framers ... 'did not trust any government to separate the true from the false for us.'"[165]

In national security cases especially, it is too easy for courts to find that the access right, viewed by them as a mere procedural protection or right of the press alone, should be overcome in the face of national security interests. Courts should, therefore, jettison an overly mechanical, theoretically baseless approach to the right of access. Instead, they should recognize the fundamental role access plays and account for that role when deciding whether the executive can make secret national security information despite the interests of the judiciary, the press, and the public.

---

[164] *See, e.g.*, Eric Lictblaud, "In Secret, Court Vastly Broadens Powers of N.S.A.," *New York Times*, July 6, 2013, https://www.nytimes.com/2013/07/07/us/in-secret-court-vastly-broadens-powers-of-nsa.html (accessed July 15, 2023).

[165] *Detroit Free Press*, 303 F.3d at 683 (citation omitted).

3
A Fourth Amendment Press Clause

Hannah Bloch-Wehba[*]

I. Introduction

What effect will the anti-press politics of the Donald Trump era have on press freedom? Told to "shut up and listen" by alt-right guru and Trump political adviser Steven Bannon; called "scum" and "the enemy of the American People" by the president himself; accused of bias, falsity, and all-around incompetence by readers on the right and the left; the press has at once lost and found its footing, rattled by and arraying itself in force against this new hostile power.

Leak investigations—already the source of substantial tension between reporters and the executive branch before Trump took office—became a newly powerful weapon in the administration's war on the press. Take, for example, the unruly ascent and hasty downfall of Michael Flynn. What should have been a story about divided loyalties and violations of criminal law at the highest levels of government—Flynn's secret calls to Russian agents, his subsequent misleading statements to Vice President Mike Pence, and President Trump's decision to finally ask for Flynn's resignation after knowing of his misdeeds for weeks—instead quickly became a story about national security leaks and media malfeasance. Trump promised to go after the officials who had disclosed the information about Flynn and asked the FBI to investigate the "criminal leaks."[1] Leak investigations have reportedly tripled since Trump took office.[2] Reporters and news organizations wondered whether, in an atmosphere so hostile to press freedoms, Attorney General Jeff Sessions would continue to enforce and follow

---

[*] Associate Professor of Law, Texas A&M School of Law. I am grateful for helpful comments and insights from Colin Agur, Akhil Reed Amar, B.J. Ard, Jack Balkin, John Langford, and the participants at the 2015 Internet Law Scholars Works in Progress conference for their comments on an earlier version of this chapter.

[1] Charlie Savage & Eric Lichtblau, "Trump Directs Justice Department to Investigate 'Criminal Leaks,'" *New York Times*, February 16, 2017, https://www.nytimes.com/2017/02/16/us/politics/justice-department-leak-investigation-trump.html (accessed November 8, 2023).

[2] Charlie Savage & Eileen Sullivan, "Leak Investigations Triple under Trump, Sessions Says," *New York Times*, August 4, 2017, https://www.nytimes.com/2017/08/04/us/politics/jeff-sessions-trump-leaks-attorney-general.html (accessed November 8, 2023).

internal Department of Justice guidelines meant to protect journalists from searches, seizures, and subpoenas.[3]

Leak investigations, of course, are nothing new. The Obama White House pursued more prosecutions under the Espionage Act—the 1913 statute that prohibits unauthorized disclosure of classified information—than any other administration in history. But reporters and law enforcement had struck an uneasy bargain of mutual self-restraint: "[T]he government refraining from indiscriminately using its wide-ranging authority to stop or to punish leakers, and the press exhibiting concern for the consequences of disclosures and withholding information that might reasonably jeopardize lives or security."[4] Even as some argued that an upswing both in leak prosecutions and in accountability journalism based on massive leaks—Cablegate, the Snowden papers, the Panama papers—upset this delicate balance, the press itself continued to occupy a privileged position: its members remained free, while its sources went to prison.[5]

If this bargain was notable for the strength of its normative commitments, it was also striking for the absence of legal ones. The press enjoys social privilege, but no true *legal* privilege: federal law provides no escape hatch for reporters to avoid testifying against an indicted source. The rules of criminal law and procedure that govern leak investigations appear to offer virtually no enforceable protections to journalists who are not charged with a crime. The conventional wisdom is that no law prohibits the government from indicting a journalist for "aiding and abetting" a leak of classified information, or from searching or seizing journalists' records—in secret—to aid an Espionage Act investigation. And so-called bulk surveillance programs, which sweep up massive amounts of communications records, affect reporters and news organizations as much as—indeed, perhaps more than—they do everyone else.

Consequently, reporters and press groups have looked to legislation—the Privacy Protection Act, state shield laws, the oft-discussed but never passed federal shield law—regulatory protections, and norms to protect them from being dragged into criminal investigations, whether as suspects themselves or as sources of evidence. These subconstitutional rules offer general protections against unfettered investigations of journalists' documentary materials, communications records, and work product. In practice, however, existing protections have little power to prevent law enforcement from using secret, warrantless processes to investigate members of the press. In the context of the Trump

---

[3] Peter Sterne, "Sessions 'Not Sure' Whether He Would Prosecute Journalists," *Politico*, January 10, 2017, https://www.politico.com/blogs/on-media/2017/01/sessions-not-sure-whether-he-would-prosecute-journalists-233431 (accessed November 8, 2023).

[4] David McCraw & Stephen Gikow, "The End to an Unspoken Bargain? National Security and Leaks in a Post-Pentagon Papers World," *Harvard Civil Rights–Civil Liberties Law Review*, 48, no. 2 (Summer 2013), 473.

[5] 18 U.S.C. § 798(a)(3).

administration's hostility toward press institutions, it is all the more concerning that protections against unwarranted law enforcement investigations appear to be so ineffective.

But the US Constitution does offer one potential avenue to curb surveillance of reporters: the Fourth Amendment's reasonableness requirement. The Fourth Amendment's reasonableness requirement serves in part, I argue, as a "Fourth Amendment press clause" that imposes substantive constitutional requirements when the government seeks to search reporters' records for evidence of crime. Fourth Amendment reasonableness requires courts to balance factors including the intrusiveness of the search, the type of information sought, and the degree to which First Amendment rights are implicated by investigative activity. Though "reasonableness" is often denigrated as an ineffective safeguard against invasive law enforcement activity, I argue that the Fourth Amendment's "reasonableness" requirement provides an underappreciated path toward more substantive protections.

II. The Impact of National Security Surveillance and Leak Investigations on the Press

In February 2013, a few months before Edward Snowden's disclosures about the scope and extent of the National Security Agency's (NSA's) surveillance programs rocked America, the Supreme Court decided *Clapper v. Amnesty International USA*.[6] In *Clapper*, a number of public interest organizations, journalists, and lawyers challenged the constitutionality of Section 702 of the Foreign Intelligence Surveillance Act (FISA). Section 702 authorizes the government to target and collect the communications of non-US persons outside the United States for foreign intelligence purposes.[7] The plaintiffs argued that the surveillance impinged on their First and Fourth Amendment rights.[8] The likelihood that their communications with non-US persons would be intercepted was high, the plaintiffs alleged, and they had been "forced to take costly and burdensome measures to protect the confidentiality of their international communications."[9]

Like many national security cases, this one foundered on procedure.[10] In a 5–4 decision, the *Clapper* Court held that the plaintiffs lacked standing to

---

[6] 133 S. Ct. 1138 (2013).
[7] 50 U.S.C. § 1881a.
[8] *Amnesty Int'l. USA v. Clapper*, 638 F.3d 118, 121 (2d Cir. 2011).
[9] 133 S. Ct. at 1146.
[10] Stephen I. Vladeck, "The Demise of Merits-Based Adjudication in Post-9/11 National Security Litigation," *Drake Law Review*, 64, no. 4 (2016), 1035–36 ("[C]ourts faced with civil suits seeking remedies against allegedly unlawful government surveillance, detention, interrogation, rendition,

challenge the program. Characterizing the plaintiffs' fears as "highly speculative,"[11] the Court dismissed their "self-inflicted injuries" as not sufficient to give rise to standing.[12]

Only a few months later, Snowden's leaks about the scope of foreign intelligence surveillance became public. It was apparent that the government had embraced a sweeping interpretation of Section 215 of the USA PATRIOT Act, which authorized the government to make an application to the Foreign Intelligence Surveillance Court (FISC) for "an order requiring the production of any tangible things (including books, records, papers, documents, and other items) for an investigation ... to protect against international terrorism or clandestine intelligence activities."[13] Under Section 702 of the FISA Amendments Act, the government had conducted the PRISM program, under which certain electronic communications service providers—including Google, Microsoft, and Yahoo!—provide the contents of communications belonging to a target directly to the government.[14] Section 702 was also reported to be the statutory authority for Upstream surveillance, which refers to an NSA program to tap into "the telecommunications 'backbone' over which telephone and Internet communications transit."[15] The Snowden disclosures had a tremendous effect on public debate—there were immediate calls to end the surveillance, to reform the law, and to publicize information concerning the legal basis of these secret programs.[16]

---

and watchlisting, among myriad other initiatives, have refused to provide relief ... because of obstacles that, in the courts' views, barred them from even reaching the merits.").

[11] 133 S. Ct. at 1148.
[12] *Id.* at 1152.
[13] Glenn Greenwald, "NSA Collecting Phone Records of Millions of Verizon Customers Daily," *The Guardian*, June 6, 2013, https://www.theguardian.com/world/2013/jun/06/nsa-phone-records-verizon-court-order (accessed November 8, 2023).
[14] Barton Gellman & Laura Poitras, "U.S., British Intelligence Mining Data from Nine U.S. Internet Companies in Broad Secret Program," *Washington Post*, June 7, 2013, https://www.washingtonpost.com/investigations/us-intelligence-mining-data-from-nine-us-internet-companies-in-broad-secret-program/2013/06/06/3a0c0da8-cebf-11e2-8845-d970ccb04497_story.html (accessed November 8, 2023).
[15] Privacy & Civil Liberties Oversight Bd., "Report on the Surveillance Program Operated Pursuant to Section 702 of the Foreign Intelligence Surveillance Act," July 2, 2014, https://documents.pclob.gov/prod/Documents/OversightReport/ba65702c-3541-4125-a67d-92a7f974fc4c/702-Report-2%20-%20Complete%20-%20Nov%2014%202022%201548.pdf (accessed November 8, 2023).
[16] *See, e.g.*, *In re Orders of this Court Interpreting Section 215 of the PATRIOT Act* ("*In re Section 215 Orders*"), No. Misc. 13-02, 2013 WL 5460064, at *7 (FISC Sept. 13, 2013); *see also* Privacy & Civil Liberties Oversight Bd., "Report on the Telephone Records Program Conducted under Section 215," January 23, 2014, https://documents.pclob.gov/prod/Documents/OversightReport/ec542143-1079-424a-84b3-acc354698560/215-Report_on_the_Telephone_Records_Program.pdf (accessed November 8, 2023); President's Review Group on Intelligence & Communications Technologies, "Liberty and Security in a Changing World: Report and Recommendations," December 12, 2013, https://obamawhitehouse.archives.gov/sites/default/files/docs/2013-12-12_rg_final_report.pdf (accessed November 8, 2023).

A. Empirical Evidence of a Chilling Effect

A new project also arose from the disclosures: organizations and scholars dedicated to freedom of expression undertook studies to better understand how surveillance and leak investigations affected society. Those studies confirmed that surveillance has a palpable chilling effect on the public as a whole, as well as on reporters and their sources in particular.[17] It became apparent that reporters and the media were suffering a real impact as a result of bulk surveillance, in large part because journalists could not assure their sources that their relationship was truly confidential.

First, and most significantly, journalists reported that their relationships with sources have been made more difficult because of widespread surveillance. In 2014, PEN American Center reported that "writers are self-censoring their work and their online activity due to their fears that commenting on, researching, or writing about certain issues will cause them harm."[18] Fears of surveillance prompted writers to avoid social media and, at times, to avoid speaking about some topics using the phone or digital communications.[19] Respondents also reported increased difficulties in getting sources to speak "on the record."[20] A later study by the Pew Research Center confirmed that this tendency was affecting news gathering as well: 13 percent of respondents to the Pew survey said that "concerns about electronic surveillance and hacking led them to not reach out to a particular source."[21]

Surveillance also caused journalists to adopt new security precautions to protect sources. Respondents to surveys by the Pew Research Center, PEN, and Human Rights Watch reported using new techniques to avoid surveillance, including using email encryption, "burner" phones and anonymous email accounts, and meeting sources in person.[22] These kinds of additional precautions

---

[17] Leonard Downie & Sara Rafsky, "The Obama Administration and the Press: Leak Investigations and Surveillance in post-9/11 America," *Committee to Protect Journalists*, October 10, 2013, https://cpj.org/wp-content/uploads/2013/10/us2013-english.pdf ("CPJ Report") (accessed November 8, 2023); Human Rights Watch, "With Liberty to Monitor All: How Large-Scale Surveillance is Harming Journalism, Law and American Democracy," July 2014, https://www.hrw.org/report/2014/07/28/liberty-monitor-all/how-large-scale-us-surveillance-harming-journalism-law-and ("HRW Report") (accessed November 8, 2023); Pew Research Center and Tow Center for Digital Journalism at Columbia University, "Investigative Journalists and Digital Security," February 2015, http://www.journalism.org/2015/02/05/investigative-journalists-and-digital-security/ ("Pew Report") (accessed November 8, 2023); *and* PEN American Center, "Chilling Effects: NSA Surveillance Drives Writers to Self-Censor," November 2013, https://www.pen.org/chilling-effects ("PEN Report") (accessed November 8, 2023); Jonathon W. Penney, "Chilling Effects: Online Surveillance and Wikipedia Use," *Berkeley Technology Law Journal*, 31, no. 1 (2016), 117.
[18] PEN Report, *supra* note 17, at 6.
[19] *Id.*
[20] *Id.*
[21] Pew Report, *supra* note 17, at 3.
[22] *Id.* at 8; PEN Report, *supra* note 17, at 8; HRW Report, *supra* note 17, at 33.

take extra time and require technical know-how, not to mention "trade-offs with convenience."[23]

Leak investigations have also damaged relationships between sources and reporters. The PEN Report found that 81 percent of respondents were "very concerned about government efforts to compel journalists to reveal sources of classified information."[24] According to Human Rights Watch, some reporters "believed that surveillance may be a direct cause of the spike in leak investigations."[25] Widespread secrecy and legal uncertainty surrounding the minimization and use restrictions that apply to information gathered under foreign intelligence surveillance authorities prompted journalists to speculate that government agencies might share or use information in shadowy ways, including to bring criminal cases against sources.[26]

Obama administration officials defended the nine leak prosecutions as authorized and necessary. In 2013, the *New York Times* reported that from 2005 to 2009, 153 leak cases were referred to the Department of Justice for investigation and potential prosecution; the FBI investigated only 24, and no investigation had led to an indictment by the time Dennis Blair took office as director of national intelligence in 2009.[27] When asked about the chilling effect that leak prosecutions were having on the press, Bob Deitz, former general counsel of the NSA, said, "Leaking is against the law. Good. I want criminals to be deterred."[28] And in comments at the National Press Club, then Attorney General Eric Holder defended his record, saying that he disagreed that there was anything "inappropriate" about the leak prosecutions, and adding, "We have tried to be appropriately sensitive in bringing those cases that warranted prosecution. We've turned away substantially greater numbers of cases that were presented to us and where prosecution was sought."[29]

At the same time, there is no question that methods for investigating leaks implicate the media in several ways. First, several leak investigations have appeared to work backward from media reporting. For example, in a years-long battle that played out in federal court, the Justice Department attempted to compel *New York Times* journalist James Risen to testify against his purported source, Jeffrey Sterling, in a criminal trial based on Risen's

---

[23] HRW Report, *supra* note 17, at 42.
[24] PEN Report, *supra* note 17, at 8.
[25] HRW Report, *supra* note 17, at 29.
[26] *Id.* at 22.
[27] Sharon LaFraniere, "Math Behind Leak Crackdown: 153 Cases, 4 Years, 0 Indictments," *New York Times*, July 20, 2013, https://www.nytimes.com/2013/07/21/us/politics/math-behind-leak-crackdown-153-cases-4-years-0-indictments.html?pagewanted=all (accessed November 8, 2023).
[28] HRW Report, *supra* note 17, at 72.
[29] Speech of Eric Holder, National Press Club, February 17, 2015, http://www.press.org/news-multimedia/videos/npc-luncheon-eric-holder (accessed November 8, 2023).

reporting in his book *State of War*. On appeal, the Fourth Circuit held that Risen could claim no privilege to avoid testifying against Sterling.[30] Ultimately, however, the prosecution did not call Risen, averting a showdown that would have pitted the government against a journalist unwilling to reveal his source.[31] Instead, at trial, the government introduced evidence of the relationship between Risen and Sterling: Risen's credit card statement and records of telephone calls. Notwithstanding the government's long battle to compel Risen to testify, the Sterling conviction illustrates that it is possible to identify, prosecute, and convict a journalist's source without forcing the journalist to testify.

The Risen/Sterling case is not alone. In May 2013, the Department of Justice informed the Associated Press that it had subpoenaed two months' worth of toll billing records for twenty-one AP phone lines from a third-party phone provider in the course of its investigation of a 2012 AP article detailing a "CIA operation in Yemen that stopped an al-Qaida plot in the spring of 2012 to detonate a bomb on an airplane bound for the United States."[32] The Justice Department defended its actions as reasonable and necessary to the ongoing leak investigation.[33] But the media rebuked the Department for violating its own regulations by issuing such a broad subpoena and failing to notify the AP before doing so.[34]

Just one week later, the *Washington Post* reported that prosecutors had obtained a search warrant issued to Google for Fox News reporter James Rosen's personal email, naming him an unindicted co-conspirator in Espionage Act violations.[35] While the leaker in the Rosen case, Stephen Jin-Woo Kim, was ultimately indicted, pled guilty, and served time in federal prison,[36] Rosen himself was never charged, leading advocates for the press to suggest that his designation

---

[30] *United States v. Sterling*, 724 F.3d 482, 492 (4th Cir. 2013), *cert. denied sub nom. Risen v. United States*, 134 S. Ct. 2696, No. 13-1009 (June 2, 2014).

[31] Matt Apuzzo, "Times Reporter Will Not Be Called to Testify in Leak Case," *New York Times*, January 12, 2015, http://www.nytimes.com/2015/01/13/us/times-reporter-james-risen-will-not-be-called-to-testify-in-leak-case-lawyers-say.html (accessed November 8, 2023).

[32] Mark Sherman, "Government Obtains Wide AP Phone Records in Probe," *Associated Press*, May 13, 2013, https://www.ap.org/ap-in-the-news/2013/govt-obtains-wide-ap-phone-records-in-probe (accessed November 8, 2023).

[33] Letter from Deputy Attorney General James Cole to Gary Pruitt, May 14, 2013, https://archive.nytimes.com/www.nytimes.com/interactive/2013/05/15/us/politics/15leaks-letter.html?module=inline (accessed November 8, 2023).

[34] "AP President Pruitt Accuses of Rule Violations in Phone Records Case; Source Intimidation," *Associated Press*, June 19, 2013, https://www.ap.org/ap-in-the-news/2013/ap-president-pruitt-accuses-doj-of-rule-violations-in-phone-records-case-source-intimidation (accessed November 8, 2023).

[35] Ann E. Marimow, "A Rare Peek into a Justice Department Leak Probe," *Washington Post*, May 19, 2013, http://wapo.st/115Hzqg (accessed November 8, 2023).

[36] Peter Maass, "Destroyed by the Espionage Act," *The Intercept*, February 18, 2015, https://firstlook.org/theintercept/2015/02/18/destroyed-by-the-espionage-act/ (accessed November 8, 2023).

as a co-conspirator was "little more than pretext to seize his e-mails to build their case against the suspected leaker."[37]

B. Constitutional Protections

One might believe that using journalists' relationships with their sources to seek out evidence for criminal prosecution raises serious First Amendment concerns. But the courts have been reluctant to find that the First Amendment stands in the way of investigative activity. In 1972, the Supreme Court held in *Branzburg v. Hayes* that reporters have the same obligation "to respond to grand jury subpoenas as other citizens do. . . ."[38] Rejecting the argument for a broad reporter's privilege, the Court relied in part on the fact that "[e]stimates of the inhibiting effect of such subpoenas on the willingness of informants to make disclosures to newsmen are widely divergent and to a great extent speculative. It would be difficult to canvass the views of the informants themselves; surveys of reporters on this topic are chiefly opinions of predicted informant behavior and must be viewed in the light of the professional self-interest of the interviewees."[39] Dismissing concerns that refusing to shield reporters from grand jury subpoenas would result in a widespread chilling effect, the Court wrote, "Reliance by the press on confidential informants does not mean that all such sources will in fact dry up because of the later possible appearance of the newsman before a grand jury."[40]

Branzburg is contentious in part because advocates and courts have struggled to parse its seemingly contradictory imperatives. As the Court acknowledged, "without some protection for seeking out the news, freedom of the press could be eviscerated."[41] Yet in the next breath, the Court went on to cast doubt on the need for protection from law enforcement investigations, reasoning that the obligation to respond to the subpoena involved no effort to compel the press to publish, refrain from publishing, or other compulsion "related to the content of published material."[42]

Branzburg instructs that, at least when it comes to grand jury subpoenas, journalists stand in the same shoes as all other citizens. In a second case, the Court reasoned that the procedural safeguards of the Fourth Amendment were

---

[37] Ann E. Marimow, "Justice Department's Scrutiny of Fox News Reporter James Rosen in Leak Case Draws Fire," *Washington Post*, May 20, 2013, http://wapo.st/18ZTg9P (accessed November 8, 2023).
[38] 408 U.S. 665, 682 (1972).
[39] *Id.* at 693–94.
[40] *Id.* at 694.
[41] *Id.* at 681.
[42] *Id.*

sufficient to guard against the risk that investigations of the press might be abused. In *Stanford Daily*, a student newspaper sued for declaratory and injunctive relief after the police obtained a warrant to search the newsroom for evidence related to a "violent clash between demonstrators and police" at the Stanford University Hospital.[43] The district court granted relief, holding that "where the innocent object of the search is a newspaper, First Amendment interests are also involved and that such a search is constitutionally permissible" only under very limited circumstances.[44] The Ninth Circuit affirmed the decision.

The Supreme Court reversed, rejecting the newspaper's contention that the search was overly intrusive and that evidence should have been obtained using a subpoena.[45] Rather, the Court found that satisfaction of the warrant requirement was enough to insulate the *Daily* from "the harms that are assertedly threatened by warrants for searching newspaper offices."[46] Because "unrestricted power of search and seizure could also be an instrument for stifling liberty of expression,"[47] however, it was all the more essential that the Fourth Amendment protections in place possess real teeth. The Court highlighted that "the warrant requirement should be administered to leave as little as possible to the discretion or whim of the officer in the field."[48] Pointing to the relative rarity of warrants for searching newsrooms, the Court wrote, "This reality hardly suggests abuse; and if abuse occurs, there will be time enough to deal with it."[49]

C. Statutory Protections

Together, *Stanford Daily* and *Branzburg* stand for the proposition that journalists are subject to the same rules of criminal procedure as anybody else—and that the procedural safeguards for warrant and subpoena practice were sufficient to protect the press from overzealous intrusions. Lawmakers, however, disagreed. In response to the *Stanford Daily* holding, Congress enacted the Privacy Protection Act of 1980 (PPA), which generally forbids the government from searching journalists' work product and documentary materials.[50]

Notably, however, the PPA does not apply when there is probable cause to believe that a journalist has received or published information related to the

---

[43] *Zurcher v. Stanford Daily*, 436 U.S. 547, 550 (1978).
[44] *Id.* at 552.
[45] *Id.* at 563.
[46] *Id.* at 565.
[47] *Id.* at 564 (quoting *Marcus v. Search Warrant*, 367 U.S. 717, 729 (1961)).
[48] *Id.*
[49] *Id.* at 566.
[50] 42 U.S.C. § 2000aa.

national defense.[51] The PPA also provides no protection against intrusions that do not amount to Fourth Amendment "searches," such as pen registers, trap and trace orders, or demands for information under the Stored Communications Act. Nor does the PPA apply to National Security Letters or to programmatic national security surveillance that occurs under Executive Order 12,333 or under the FISA.[52] The result is that, when it comes to the use of many modern national security authorities to investigate leaks or other crimes, the PPA is silent.

D. Regulatory Protections

Internal Department of Justice and FBI guidelines and regulations also appear to impose additional requirements when the government seeks information from or relating to the news media. The Department of Justice Media Subpoena Guidelines and the United States Attorney's Manual generally require that the Department notify and attempt to negotiate with a journalist before obtaining a subpoena, warrant, or court order for that journalist's communications records. The Guidelines provide that—unlike almost anybody else—a journalist is supposed to get notice of a search warrant before the search is executed.[53]

Again, however, the utility of the Guidelines in the context of national security investigations is limited. The Guidelines' notice provisions do not apply if "the Attorney General determines that, for compelling reasons, such notice would pose a clear and substantial threat to the integrity of the investigation, risk grave harm to national security, or present an imminent risk of death or serious bodily harm."[54] In a leak investigation, it is easy to imagine how the government could demonstrate that notice to a reporter would threaten the investigation.

Moreover, the Guidelines simply appear not to hold much water in the context of offenses related to the possession or dissemination of classified or protected information. No provision of the Guidelines prevents a prosecutor from secretly naming a journalist as a co-conspirator, as the government did in the Rosen investigation, to trigger the PPA's "suspect exception." Most troubling

---

[51] 42 U.S.C. § 2000aa(a)(1) ("[A] search or seizure may be conducted under the provisions of this paragraph if the offense consists of the receipt, possession, or communication of information relating to the national defense, classified information, or restricted data.").

[52] Jennifer Henrichsen & Hannah Bloch-Wehba, "Electronic Communications Surveillance: What Journalists and Media Organizations Need to Know," *Reporters Comm. for Freedom of the Press*, 2017, https://www.rcfp.org/electronic-communications-surveillance (accessed November 8, 2023).

[53] 28 C.F.R. § 50.10(j)(1); *cf. Franks v. Delaware*, 438 U.S. 154, 169 (1978) ("The pre-search proceeding is necessarily ex parte, since the subject of the search cannot be tipped off to the application for a warrant lest he destroy or remove evidence.").

[54] 28 C.F.R. § 50.10(j)(2).

of all, the Guidelines create no enforceable rights.[55] Nor do any of the other internal guidelines that govern the Department of Justice and FBI's use of criminal investigative tools that may implicate First Amendment rights.[56]

For journalists and media organizations, national security surveillance and leak investigations have bred substantial mistrust and uncertainty about how investigatory methods might implicate press freedoms. The gaps and loopholes in the existing protections for journalists only exacerbate these concerns: ambiguity provokes uncertainty about whether or not to risk speaking at all.

III. The Inadequacy of Statutory and Regulatory Protections

As the Sterling case illustrates, even when the press itself is not the target of criminal prosecution or investigation, the rules of criminal procedure have deep implications for press freedom. Take, for example, a hypothetical leak investigation. Anonymous Leaker shares classified information concerning the conduct of the investigation into Paul Manafort's contacts with Russia—an investigation that involves extensive communications intelligence gathering—with Journalist, who publishes it. The government obviously knows the identity of Journalist, whose name appears on the byline, but seeks to identify Leaker.

First, the government seeks a court order compelling disclosure from Journalist's cell phone and email service providers of records concerning her communications on the basis that the records are relevant to an investigation.[57] The investigators seek, and obtain, a gag order preventing the providers from notifying Journalist of the request, on the basis that notification would have an "adverse result."[58] Designating Journalist a "subject" of an investigation arising out of her news-gathering activity, the Department of Justice opts not to provide notice under the Department of Justice Media Subpoena Guidelines.[59]

Searching Journalist's communications records, investigators find a significant number of text messages and emails between Journalist and a CIA employee. They find telephone records from the employee's desk at Langley

---

[55] 28 C.F.R. § 50.10(t) ("This policy is not intended to, and does not, create any right or benefit, substantive or procedural, enforceable at law or in equity by any party against the United States, its departments, agencies, or entities, its officers, employees, or agents, or any other person.").
[56] The Attorney General's Guidelines for Domestic FBI Operations (2008), https://www.justice.gov/archive/opa/docs/guidelines.pdf (accessed November 8, 2023); Emily Berman, "Regulating Domestic Intelligence Collection," *Washington & Lee Law Review*, 71, no. 1 (Winter 2014), 3, 32.
[57] 18 U.S.C. § 2703(d).
[58] 18 U.S.C. § 2705.
[59] 28 C.F.R. § 50.10.

(CIA's headquarters) reflecting several phone calls to Journalist's cell phone number and visitor records showing that Journalist went to Langley that very day. They subpoena Leaker's cell phone records and find additional records of text messages and phone calls between Leaker and Journalist. When the government indicts Leaker, it need not necessarily call Journalist to testify, nor tell Journalist that it rifled through her communications records; she may never find out.

In a situation like this one, existing protections do very little to guard against the possibility that journalists will become unwitting sources for law enforcement investigations. While the Department of Justice Media Subpoena Guidelines suggest that it is the exceptional circumstance in which a journalist will be a "subject or target" of an investigation arising out of news-gathering activities, there may be no way to verify this. The government's position that classified information is government property, and that stolen classified information is therefore contraband subject to seizure, would extend to many journalists and newspapers that cover national security.[60] But because electronic searches require no notice, we might never know.[61]

If the government ultimately indicts Journalist, perhaps as a co-conspirator, this background will all come to light in criminal discovery. But, of course, it's the rare case indeed in which a journalist might be prosecuted for doing her job. Indeed, in a perverse sense, the fact that the government typically does not go after reporters in leak cases actually undermines Journalist's privacy and news-gathering rights. By cloaking the investigation in secrecy, the government avoids admitting what it is, in fact, doing—using journalists as investigative sources without their knowledge or consent.

The absence of robust protections for the press is yet more problematic in light of the demonstrable impact that national security investigations have had on journalists and the media. Widespread chilling effects are exacerbated by the uncertainty that accompanies the rules, regulations, and procedures that govern investigations. Statutory and regulatory guidelines such as the Privacy Protection Act of 1980, the Department of Justice Media Subpoena Guidelines, and the FBI's Domestic Investigations and Operations Guide suggest that there are clear rules in place to prevent journalists from being used in this manner. But in the context of leak investigations and warrantless process, these rules are riddled with exceptions.

---

[60] As an example, see the search warrant for Huma Abedin's email, 1:16-mc-00464-PKC, ECF No. 13 (S.D.N.Y. December 20, 2016); *U.S. v. Morison*, 844 F.2d 1057 (4th Cir. 1988).

[61] Hannah Bloch-Wehba, "Exposing Secret Searches: A First Amendment Right of Access to Electronic Surveillance Orders," *Washington Law Review*, 93, no. 1 (March 2018), 145.

IV. First Amendment Substance in Fourth Amendment Reasonableness

How to get out of this mess? Returning to the principles that got us here in the first place is instructive. Taken together, *Branzburg* and *Stanford Daily* created a presumption that the rules of criminal procedure apply the same way to journalists as they do to everyone else. But those rules include substantially more protection for speech and press rights than has previously been recognized. The Fourth Amendment's overarching requirement that searches be "reasonable" means that courts must also consider the First Amendment harms that are likely to result from searches and surveillance.

Incorporating consideration of First Amendment values into Fourth Amendment analysis has a long history. The Fourth Amendment's protections from unfettered, unreasonable searches were partly a reaction to the use of general warrants and writs of assistance to single out political and religious dissenters. Two of the seminal pre-revolutionary cases of sweeping, abusive searches—*Entick v. Carrington* and *Wilkes v. Wood*—involved the printing of anonymous pamphlets that challenged and attacked royal authority.[62] The suspected authors were imprisoned, their houses ransacked, and their papers seized. As William Stuntz has noted, these cases were "classic First Amendment cases in a system with no First Amendment, no vehicle for direct substantive judicial review."[63] Instead, the mechanism for constraining government abuses came not from the principle of free expression or press freedom, but rather from the principle that the government could not simply rifle through one's papers without sufficient cause.

Later cases also recognized the close relationship between Fourth Amendment protections and freedom of expression. Consider *Mapp v. Ohio*, the first case to hold that the Fourth Amendment's exclusionary rule applied to the states rather than only federal law enforcement.[64] In *Mapp*, police entered Dollree Mapp's home without a warrant searching for a bombing suspect—only to find "lewd and lascivious" materials in her home. Mapp challenged her arrest on First Amendment grounds, arguing that the Ohio law that criminalized the mere possession of "obscene" material violated her "rights of free thought and expression."[65] Instead of taking up that issue, the Court held that the warrantless

---

[62] *Entick v. Carrington*, 19 Howell's State Trials 1029 (C.P. 1765); *Wilkes v. Wood*, 19 Howell's State Trials 1153 (C.P. 1763).
[63] William J. Stuntz, "The Substantive Origins of Criminal Procedure," *Yale Law Journal*, 105, no. 2 (November 1995), 393, 403.
[64] *Mapp v. Ohio*, 367 U.S. 643 (1961).
[65] *Id.* at 673 (Harlan, J., dissenting).

search of Mapp's home meant that the material could not be used as evidence against her in criminal proceedings.[66]

In theory, the Fourth Amendment's warrant requirement is sufficient to protect First Amendment rights. Generally speaking, searches and seizures without search warrants are "per se unreasonable under the Fourth Amendment."[67] But many warrantless surveillance programs do not constitute "searches" at all: a Fourth Amendment "search" takes place, implicating constitutional protections, only when government activities intrude on a person's "reasonable expectation of privacy."[68] Likewise, "what a person knowingly exposes to the public, even in his own home or office, is not a subject of Fourth Amendment protection."[69] As the Privacy and Civil Liberties Oversight Board pointed out in its report on the Section 215 telephony metadata program, "Although the Section 215 program encompasses much more information than the telephone numbers that a person dials, all of the information that the NSA collects under the program has been disclosed to telephone companies by their customers."[70] Because a "search" is defined narrowly, the Fourth Amendment's warrant clause is highly limited.

Even without the warrant requirement, all searches must be reasonable. Reasonableness is the ineffable "touchstone" of the Fourth Amendment.[71] However, courts rarely consider First Amendment rights in evaluating whether a search is "reasonable." One defendant, for example, challenged the constitutionality of communications surveillance under Section 702, asserting both First Amendment and Fourth Amendment interests.[72] In response, the government asserted that "First Amendment interests in a criminal investigation are protected by the Fourth Amendment," and therefore that only a Fourth Amendment analysis was required—or permitted.[73]

With respect to national security surveillance, the government typically argues that the Fourth Amendment's warrant requirement provides adequate protections for any First Amendment interests—even where the Fourth Amendment doesn't apply at all. In *Clapper*, for example, the government argued that because the Fourth Amendment does not apply to metadata collection pursuant to Section 215, there was no cognizable First Amendment violation: "Surveillance consistent with Fourth Amendment protections ... does

---

[66] *Id.* at 660.
[67] *Katz v. United States*, 389 U.S. 347, 357 (1967).
[68] *Id.* at 360.
[69] *Id.* at 351; *see also Smith v. Maryland*, 442 U.S. 735, 742 (1979).
[70] "Report on the Telephone Records Program Conducted under Section 215," *supra* note 16.
[71] *Florida v. Jimeno*, 500 U.S. 248, 250 (1991).
[72] *U.S. v. Mohamud*, No. 3:10-CR-00475-KI-1, 2014 WL 2866749, at *11 (D. Or. June 24, 2014), *aff'd*, 843 F.3d 420 (9th Cir. 2016).
[73] *Id.*

not violate First Amendment rights, even though it may be directed at communicative or associative activities."[74] Relying on the Supreme Court's holding in *Zurcher v. Stanford Daily* that where materials to be searched or seized "may be protected by the First Amendment, the requirements of the Fourth Amendment must be applied with 'scrupulous exactitude,'"[75] the government implied that if the Fourth Amendment does not apply to an investigative activity, there simply is no First Amendment inquiry. Rather, "when governmental investigative activities have an impact on the exercise of First Amendment freedoms, those interests are safeguarded by adherence to Fourth Amendment standards."[76]

These statements suggest that surveillance satisfies the First Amendment, so long as it is "reasonable" for purposes of the Fourth Amendment. Often, however, the cases attempting to "integrat[e] First Amendment concerns explicitly into the Fourth Amendment analysis"[77] ignore substantive inquiries under the reasonableness prong, instead focusing solely on procedural protections. Just so *Stanford Daily*, in which the Court concluded that "[p]roperly administered, the preconditions for a warrant—probable cause, specificity with respect to the place to be searched and the things to be seized, and overall reasonableness—should afford sufficient protection against the harms that are assertedly threatened by warrants for searching newspaper offices."[78]

In dissent, Justice Stevens was troubled by the Court's holding that search warrants targeting newsrooms could issue on a "reasonable belief that the files contain relevant evidence."[79] The fact that a newspaper possesses documentary evidence of crime, Justice Stevens pointed out, does not indicate that the newspaper is itself involved in or suspected in crime, nor does it suggest that the paper would not comply with a subpoena or other request to produce the evidence.[80] The intrusiveness of newsroom searches, however, raised "the question whether the offensive intrusion on the privacy of the ordinary citizen is justified by the law enforcement interest it is intended to vindicate."[81] In the case of searches for "mere evidence" rather than for "a criminal's weapons, spoils, or the like," Justice Stevens wrote, it was particularly necessary to ensure that searches were not conducted unreasonably.[82]

---

[74] *ACLU v. Clapper*, Defs. Mot. to Dismiss at 38, No. 1:13-cv-03994-WHP (filed August 26, 2013), ECF No. 33, *quoting Gordon v. Warren Consol. Bd. of Educ.*, 706 F.2d 778, 781 n.3 (6th Cir. 1983).
[75] 436 U.S. at 564 (1978).
[76] *ACLU v. Clapper*, Defs. Mot. to Dismiss at 38, No. 1:13-cv-03994-WHP (filed August 26, 2013), ECF No. 33.
[77] Akhil Reed Amar, "Fourth Amendment First Principles," *Harvard Law Review*, 107, no. 4 (February 1994), 757, 806.
[78] 436 U.S. at 565.
[79] *Id.* at 577 (Stevens, J., dissenting).
[80] *Id.* at 581.
[81] *Id.*
[82] *Id.* at 583.

Justice Stevens' dissent illustrates the limits of a strictly procedural approach to Fourth Amendment protections, which avoids examining the substance of surveillance programs to determine whether they are reasonable. But nothing about the Fourth Amendment prevents courts from taking account of a proposed search's impact on First Amendment rights when determining whether searches or surveillance are "reasonable." In fact, courts *must* determine whether searches are "reasonable" by looking at the "totality of the circumstances."[83] They must "balanc[e] the need to search against the invasion which the search entails."[84] This balancing must take into account intrusions on expressive, associational, and press freedoms, as well as other First Amendment liberties.

As a result, the "invasiveness" of a search is not limited to privacy intrusions, narrowly construed. In some surveillance cases, courts have asked whether "the protections that are in place for individual *privacy* interests are sufficient in light of the governmental interest at stake."[85] But that limitation on the individual interest in being free from unlawful surveillance is underinclusive, because, in fact, the Fourth Amendment was intended to safeguard free expression as well as privacy.[86]

It is more than appropriate for courts to consider the well-documented tendency of surveillance programs to chill expressive freedoms. A fuller conception of the Fourth Amendment's reasonableness guarantee could provide robust protection for the interests in dissent, free expression, and free association. This conception could begin with by asking whether the warrant requirement was met in a given case, but it should not stop there. Instead, a court could go on to examine whether investigative activity infringed on First Amendment rights and evaluate whether any infringement was reasonable when balanced against the government interest in the investigation. In cases in which reporters are the targets or subjects of investigation, it is all the more important for courts to take into account how investigative tools may impact press freedoms. That investigative methods might "unreasonably impair news gathering activities" is, indeed, the predicate for the Department of Justice's Media Subpoena Guidelines themselves;[87] courts need not stretch too far in an effort to account for this interest.

It is easy to imagine how First Amendment concerns might be folded into the substantive inquiry that determines whether an investigative method or surveillance program is "reasonable." In *Camara*, for example, the Court blessed a program of inspections intended to root out housing code violations, linking

---

[83] *Mohamud*, 2014 WL 2866749, at *19.
[84] *Camara v. Mun. Court of City & Cty. of San Francisco*, 387 U.S. 523, 537 (1967).
[85] *In re Directives Pursuant to Section 105B of Foreign Intelligence Surveillance Act*, 551 F.3d 1004, 1012 (Foreign Int. Surv. Ct. Rev. 2008).
[86] *Id.* at 8.
[87] 28 C.F.R. § 50.10.

the determination of "whether a particular inspection is reasonable" to the question of whether there is "probable cause."[88] The Court identified "persuasive factors" that, it held, "support[ed] the reasonableness of area code-enforcement inspections."[89] Those factors included a "history of judicial and public acceptance," the necessity of the search and absence of less intrusive alternatives, and the relative modesty of the intrusion at issue in that case.[90]

In the context of surveillance programs, for example, courts determining whether programmatic surveillance is "reasonable" under the Fourth Amendment already weigh multiple considerations to determine whether the government interest in surveillance outweighs an individual interest.[91] Reasonableness "balancing," for all its faults, also provides an avenue for courts to consider surveillance's substantive intrusions on First Amendment rights, without relying exclusively on the warrant clause's protections. Reasonableness might, for example, "take[] into account the gravity of the offense being investigated, the seriousness of the intrusion involved, and/or the availability of less restrictive alternatives in pursuing police objectives."[92] Applying the proposed approach, courts would consider not only the *extent* of the intrusion but also the different *kinds* of intrusion that are implicated—inquiring into the impact on individual speech, press, and associational freedoms, as well as likely chilling effects, in addition to the "privacy interest" that courts already consider. And in considering the "history of judicial and public acceptance" of a proposed search, courts would need to take into account the secret nature of many surveillance programs, the constitutionality of which is often adjudicated in secret, sealed opinions by the Foreign Intelligence Surveillance Court.

Critics have faulted the Supreme Court's embrace of a "broad reasonableness standard and an ill-defined balancing test" as insufficient to limit government searches.[93] And an even-handed "balancing" test is anathema to First Amendment advocates, who tend to prefer a thumb on the scale on the side of free expression.[94] But incorporating First Amendment interests into the substance of the Fourth Amendment does not endanger First Amendment rights any more than the current system of patchwork protections, which simply tend not to apply when the press needs them most.

---

[88] *Camara*, 387 U.S. at 535.
[89] *Id.* at 537.
[90] *Id.* ("it is doubtful that any other canvassing technique would achieve acceptable results.")
[91] *See, e.g., In re Directives, supra* note 85.
[92] Sherry F. Colb, "The Qualitative Dimension of Fourth Amendment Reasonableness," *Columbia Law Review*, 98, no. 7 (November 1998), 1642, 1673.
[93] Scott E. Sundby, "A Return to Fourth Amendment Basics: Undoing the Mischief of Camara and Terry," *Minnesota Law Review*, 72, no. 3 (February 1988), 383, 385.
[94] *Hart v. Elec. Arts, Inc.*, 717 F.3d 141, 150 (3d Cir. 2013) ("The interest in safeguarding the integrity of these protections therefore weighs heavily in any balancing inquiry.").

V. Conclusion

National security investigations and surveillance have had a dramatic chilling effect on the free press. Advocates have attempted to mitigate this harm through the use of statutory and regulatory protections, but these protections do not go far enough and contain gaps that prevent them from being effective. The Fourth Amendment's reasonableness requirement, however, requires courts to take into account the intrusiveness of a search or surveillance program—a question that incorporates the risk of chilling First Amendment freedoms. This more substantively oriented Fourth Amendment approach holds promise for those seeking more effective ways of protecting the press from law enforcement's demands.

4
Higher Restraint: National Security Reporting in an Age of Information Anarchy

Marc Ambinder

I. Powerful *and* Precarious

Though reporting on war in the West dates from Thucydides,[1] the genre of national security reporting germinated relatively recently, because the national security apparatus is a creation of modern democratic nation-states, tied to the architecting of a massive defense and intelligence establishment after World War II, the advance of telecommunication technologies, and a self-fashioned post-Vietnam and post-Watergate professional obligation to police the authorities for abuses of executive power. The degree to which national security journalism—broadly defined here as a narrative-based public disclosure of previously nonpublic information about national security institutions, their activities, and their secrets—enriches civic understanding of these opaque centers of power is often a function of contingent forces unrelated to the quality of the reporting.

The state of journalism, as a profession, is fractured. However one describes journalism's mission—holding powerful interests accountable, afflicting the comfortable, watchdogging in the public interest—the improvisational opera of the Trump administration deranged its course. The final year of Donald Trump's term saw a once-in-a-century pandemic collide with a rancorous presidential election where racial polarization and police violence were core issues, an attempt by one political party to suppress the franchise of largely minority voters from another party, the proliferation of misinformation with massive reach and scale. By the time the US Capitol was stormed by insurrectionists on January 6, 2021, journalists covering the pandemic, presidency, and policy were exhausted,[2] were hypervigilant regarding threats to themselves, their profession,

---

[1] Lawrence A. Tritle, *The Peloponnesian War* (Greenwood Press, 2004), 19.
[2] Al Tompkins, "COVID-19 Is Harming Journalists' Mental Health," *Poynter*, July 24, 2020, at https://www.poynter.org/reporting-editing/2020/covid-19-is-hurting-journalists-mental-health-a-new-study-found/ (accessed May 20, 2023).

and the country, collectively traumatized to the point of burnout.[3] It is hard to remember that the pre-pandemic news environment was hardly healthier. At that moment, the audience for news wanted less of the product: less news in general and less news reported about the news.[4] Journalists on the beat felt unusually exhausted in 2018.[5] Back then, the guardians of journalistic norms and ethics had been debating the same subject for at least two years, with acrimony befitting an existential crisis: how engrained habits of print, television, and digital journalism enable President Trump's worst instincts, ignored dramatic changes in culture and social expectations about communication, and amplified his cruel misinformation.[6] Not *whether*, but how. Many journalists felt an intuition that Trump had exploited, ruthlessly, the mental models of conventional reporting that kept democratic guardrails from rusting and corroding,[7] and somehow that the response of journalists to the threat posed by Trump in fact contributed to his capacity to damage them. Isolating Trump's first year in office helps us understand how this came to be.

During the president's first year in office, journalists uncovered a lie told to the vice president by the national security adviser;[8] they discovered cabinet members abusing the privilege of using chartered and military aircraft for personal travel, leading to a resignation; they revealed numerous ethical violations by members of the president's senior staff; they uncovered plagiarism by a key outside presidential adviser; they cast an unnerving spotlight on the thicket of financial entanglements the president and his family found themselves part of; they uncovered a major (classified) presidential policy directive on North Korea;[9] they revealed a major revision to the war plan for dealing with the Korean peninsula;[10] they became comfortable with directly reproaching presidential misstatements, exaggerations, and lies.

At the same time, the journalistic profession's preoccupation with the Brobdingnagian-like inner circle of President Trump, a space uniquely created

---

[3] In 2018, a level of true panic had set in. *See, e.g.*, Alexandria Neason, "The Burnout Year," *Columbia Journalism Review*, Winter 2018.

[4] Pew Research Survey of Attitudes Toward News, February 26, 2020.

[5] Sophie Maerowitz, "Surveys Show Pandemic Burnout Hitting TV Journalists and Advertising," *PR News*, April 12, 2021. https://www.prnewsonline.com/pandemic-burnout-hitting-tv-journalists-and-advertising-surveys-find/.

[6] *See, e.g.*, Jon Allsop & Pete Vernon, "How the Press Covered the Last Four Years of Trump," *Columbia Journalism Review*, October 23, 2020, https://www.cjr.org/special_report/coverage-trump-presidency-2020-election.php (accessed May 20, 2023).

[7] Author's interview with Chuck Todd, *NBC News*, January 2021.

[8] Maggie Haberman et al., "Michael Flynn Resigns As National Security Adviser," *New York Times*, February 13, 2017, https://www.nytimes.com/2017/02/13/us/politics/donald-trump-national-security-adviser-michael-flynn.html# (accessed May 20, 2023).

[9] Karen DeYoung, Ellen Nakashima, & Emily Rauhala, "Trump Signed Presidential Directive Ordering Actions to Pressure North Korea," *Washington Post*, September 30, 2017.

[10] "B1 Bombers Key to a US Plan to Strike North Korean Missile Sites," *NBC News*, August 9, 2017.

by Trump's highly provocative personality and his unusual daily online presence, focused public attention on the daily reality-show drama of the court and its courtiers.[11] But even here, the reporting was not lightweight. If the former secretary of state indeed called the president a "fucking moron" during a meeting at the Department of Defense;[12] if two generals on the National Security Council made a "private pact" where one kept tabs on the president at all times;[13] if three senior cabinet secretaries privately made a pact to resign en masse if the president decided to go after one of them; if US envoys regularly counseled their foreign charges that there were "cool heads" surrounding the president at the White House,[14] it meant that the president of the United States was treated by his cabinet members as a threat to the national security itself. Trump was an existential threat to the country, according to his own staff, not more than a year into his first term.

In biology, form follows function; in politics, personality, and policy cannot be untangled. To working journalists, academic efforts to create silos around "substance/policy" coverage and "personality" coverage betray a fundamental misunderstanding about how decisions get made. During Trump's presidency, they could make this case more easily, but it required practitioners to tread in uneasy waters. They had to admit that Trump differed from other presidents (in the modern media era) in such a profound and indelible way that it justified a different mental schema for coverage altogether. They did, by adopting the existential threat model. But that label, once affixed, carried significant consequences. In the short term, it increased public trust in journalism, as Democrats responded favorably to a pronounced oppositional edge that was more visible in coverage.[15] But a harder edge alone did not save the news, and it did not come without precedent and practice reversals that were harmful to the public's understanding of what the ground truth was.

For one thing, norms about publishing classified information were altered. Instead of publishing national security secrets as a last resort to hold the government accountable, it became broadly acceptable to publish them as a way to

---

[11] Amy Mitchell et al., "Covering President Trump in a Polarized Media Environment," *Pew Research Center*, October 2, 2017, https://www.pewresearch.org/journalism/2017/10/02/covering-president-trump-in-a-polarized-media-environment/ (accessed May 19, 2023).

[12] Carol E. Lee et al., "Tillerson's Fury at Trump Required an Intervention from Pence," *NBC News*, October 4, 2017, https://www.nbcnews.com/politics/white-house/tillerson-s-fury-trump-required-intervention-pence-n806451 (accessed May 19, 2023).

[13] James Kitfield, "Trump's Generals Are Trying to Save the World, Starting with the White House," *Politico*, August 4, 2017, https://www.politico.com/magazine/story/2017/08/04/donald-trump-generals-mattis-mcmaster-kelly-flynn-215455/ (accessed May 19, 2023).

[14] Daniel Hurst, "Rest Easy, Trump Surrounded by Cool Heads, Says US Envoy to Japan," *Asia Times*, September 29, 2017.

[15] Chris Kahn, "The Press, Branded as Enemy by Trump, Increasingly Trusted by Public: Reuters Ipsos Poll," *Reuters*, October 3, 2017.

underscore Trump's perfidy. For another, the inability (at best) or the negligence (at worst) to incorporate into the reporting editing and publishing processes what students of political science, psychology, and communication now know about how information is processed by individuals and audiences is exacerbated by the "weaponization of information,"[16] by actors who *do* understand these biases and heuristics, and who use the same tools, technology, language, and platforms that reporters rely on to influence political decisions, to make money or simply to stir up chaos for its own sake.

Finally, the turn toward threat coverage did not account for audience effects. When a tree falls, partisan audiences will determine for themselves whether a strong gust of wind blew it over, or whether a tiny man with a hacksaw chopped it down, believing their case to be strong even when the preponderance of evidence points to a third cause: perhaps the soil dried up. Coverage of President Trump's first year in office was overwhelmingly negative;[17] stories were perceived differently and reframed to highlight damning or exculpatory details. As political attitudes became certitudes, the press presented a reality that overlapped strongly with what many Democrats saw. Correspondingly, Trump exerted a nuclear force over the physics felt by Republican partisans.[18] If, in a largely binary political culture, one side has more of a purchase on truth, coverage asymmetry is inevitable. But did it become self-reinforcing?

II. Loss of Context as a Consequence

One uncomfortable truth is that while national security reporting has brought to the fore a significant amount of information about one of the most important stories of our time—the efforts by a foreign government to stir chaos inside the United States and elect a candidate more friendly to its interests—the public's understanding of this issue was partial, fractious, and conditioned by tribalism. The decision rules that informally govern national security reporting changed in a way that prioritized incremental and often contingent scoops over consensus and context.

Many stories turned out to be wrong. This is not remarkable; the body of Watergate reporting is replete with mistakes, too. But when public trust is low, when the political stakes are high, when the distance between professional and amateur journalists seems to be narrow, the mistakes can be highly consequential

---

[16] Mitchell et al., Pew Research Center, 2017.
[17] Mike Allen, "Astonishing Poll About Trump and Media," *Axios* July 4, 2017, https://www.axios.com/2017/12/15/exclusive-astonishing-poll-about-trump-and-media-1513303993 (accessed May 19, 2023).
[18] Casey Wexler, "What Do Americans Think about Trump and Russia," *CBS News*, June 8, 2017.

for the entire profession. Consider: Russia, it turns out, did not "attempt to hack" election databases in twenty-one states. (Russia scanned many of these databases as anyone with a fairly middling suite of software could, and did not try to hack more than a few. Wisconsin was initially told that its elections database was scanned; it turns out that Russian-connected cyber-probes looked at IP addresses belonging to an entirely different federal agency.)[19]

> Russia did not, it turns out, penetrate the country's electrical grid, as the *Washington Post* reported they had. (A tweet sent out by the *Post* on December 30, 2016, read thusly: Breaking: Russian hackers penetrated U.S. electricity grid through a utility in Vermont); other news outlets naturally ran with the story, often exaggerating the (incorrect) findings.[20]
>
> The truth: malware that bears a similarity to that used in the past by actors affiliated with Russia and other entities was found on the laptop of one employee who worked at a public utility.[21] The malware in question can be purchased online. The *Post* corrected its story by publishing a new one.[22]

How many intelligence agencies concluded in 2016 that Russia, in fact, engaged in a dedicated campaign to influence the election on behalf of Trump? Seventeen, according to the *New York Times* and the Associated Press,[23] a number that would be repeated endlessly on cable news in the weeks after the report.

There are (more than) seventeen US intelligence agencies, but only three provided raw information to the analysts who compiled the report in question, and it was written by the National Intelligence Council.[24] In 2024, we know more about the Russian efforts, including the link between then campaign manager Paul Manafort and a source for Russian intelligence, but the facts do not support the claim that Trump himself was a witting agent working on behalf of

---

[19] Scott Bauer, "Homeland Security Now Says Wisconsin Not Targeted," *AP*, September 27, 2017.

[20] ""Russian Malware Detected in US Electricity Grid—Report," *Reuters*, December 30, 2016.

[21] April McCullum, *Russian Hackers Strike Burlington Electric with Malware* (Burlington Free Press, December 30, 2016).

[22] Glenn Greenwald, "CNN Journalists Resign: Latest Example of Media and Recklessness on Russia Threat," *The Intercept*, June 6, 2017, https://theintercept.com/2017/06/27/cnn-journalists-resign-latest-example-of-media-recklessness-on-the-russia-threat/ (accessed May 19, 2023). Greenwald became the face of populist liberal media criticism about the Russia investigation and, as of 2021, has singled out numerous reporters, most of them women, for significant criticism. He has, to my mind, been more of a bully and may have unwittingly encouraged online mobs to subject individual journalists for abuse. Though there is significant evidence in the public domain about Russia's entanglements with the Trump campaign, Greenwald deserves credit for being sensitive to the compounding effects that these early mistakes have had on media trust, even as he toxically refuses to see the forest for the trees.

[23] Corrections: June 28, 2017, *New York Times*.

[24] Maggie Haberman, "Trump's Deflections and Denials on Russia Frustrate Even His Allies," *New York Times*, June 25, 2017.

Vladimir Putin,[25] nor does the magnitude of Russia's actual intervention justify overstatement.

What about this story? So concerned was President Barack Obama about Russian shenanigans that, months before the 2016 election,[26] he personally pulled aside Facebook's Mark Zuckerberg and warned him to intervene. Another blockbuster, but it turned out that Obama did not, in fact, refer once to Russian interference.

A consistent body of research shows that corrected stories do not have the same reach as the original erroneous one, and, indeed, that corrections themselves might serve to reinforce the original story because of human cognitive biases.[27] Further, hyperbolic reporting about Russia's influence campaign can lead to a bandwagon effect whereby protected political speech itself is delegitimized, although even the heaviest of skeptics ought to understand the difference between a dedicated campaign of persuasion by a foreign power to sew discord and spontaneous or organized pro-Kremlin points of view that deserve First Amendment protection.[28] I was not among the skeptics; years on, the body of evidence, public, private, and reported, suggests a rather significant and perhaps unprecedented effort to use misinformation and to game the affective biases of American voters to produce a more favorable (from Moscow's perspective) political climate. But the bad information produced by the campaign to cover this story has had a deleterious effect on the public's understanding of it.

III. President Donald Trump

The most significant nontechnology factor affecting the environment for national security journalists was the easiest to identify and the hardest to understand: the president himself.

There were, from the outset of his administration, two confounding complications. One was that the people working for the president evinced little

---

[25] Dan Mangan, "Trump Campaign Chief Manafort's Associate Kilimnik Gave Russia 2016 Election Strategy, U.S. Says," *CNBC.com*, April 15, 2021.

[26] Adam Entous, Elizabeth Dwoskin, & Craig Timberg, "Tried to Give Zuckerberg a Warning in Call over Fake News on Facebook," *Washington Post*, September 24, 2017, https://www.washingtonpost.com/business/economy/obama-tried-to-give-zuckerberg-a-wake-up-call-over-fake-news-on-facebook/2017/09/24/15d19b12-ddac-4ad5-ac6e-ef909e1c1284_story.html (accessed May 19, 2023).

[27] Brendan Nyhan & Jason Reifler, "When Corrections Fail: The Persistence of Political Misperceptions," *Political Behavior*, Advance Publication Copy (2017).

[28] Adrian Chen, "The Propaganda About Russian Propaganda," *New Yorker*, December 1, 2016, https://www.newyorker.com/news/news-desk/the-propaganda-about-russian-propaganda (accessed May 19, 2023).

trust in his capabilities to be commander in chief.[29] (It is not unprecedented for people working inside the executive branch to manifest distrust of the president. Richard Nixon had to deal with—and tried to cover up—the unsettling fact that his Joint Chiefs of Staff felt out of the loop and tasked a young navy yeomen to steal documents belonging to the National Security Council, copy them, and make sure that they were sent to the Pentagon.[30] At one point, on the instructions of an admiral, this yeoman went through Henry Kissinger's luggage.) So far as we know, President Trump's luggage (or that of Rex Tillerson's) remained unmolested.

The other was Trump's unprecedented vitriol toward the press itself, and toward other institutions that served him, particularly in the national security establishment. Within weeks of his election, Trump used the media's public agonizing over its disconnect with swaths of America as a weapon against the press, branding as "Fake News" reporting that questioned his dominance over the facts, over reality, and over his White House, even claiming that the *New York Times* had apologized for its coverage of him.[31] (It hadn't.) "Fake News" became his call to arms. I hesitate to say that journalists rededicated themselves to aggressive accountability reporting after the election because that presumes that they had lost it before the election, and it misstates causality: certainly, newsroom attitudes and habits influence coverage, but so does the news itself. Trump's pre-inauguration period produced a geyser, much of it touching on national security: Gen. Michael Flynn (ret.), lied about his pre-election contacts with the Russians. He misled the vice president about the nature of one of those contacts.[32] He was caught on a wiretap of the Soviet ambassador discussing the potential for sanctions relief.[33] The US intelligence community released an unclassified white paper concluding that Moscow had actively tried to undermine the liberal democratic order in the United States, which is common, but also that President Vladimir Putin "actively aspired" to help elect Trump, that these efforts represented a "significant escalation" compared to previous operations, and that the main vector of these efforts were cyber-based "covert influence operations."[34]

Trump may have sparked a revolt among the intelligence community that serves him; his transition team reminded reporters that these same organizations had concluded that Saddam Hussein was hiding a weapons of mass

---

[29] Daniel Drezner's continuing account is worth reading in full: "White House Aides Can't Stop Talking about the President Like He's a Toddler," *Washington Post*, August 21, 2017.

[30] James Rosen, "The Admiral and the Chiefs," *The Atlantic*, April 2001, https://www.theatlantic.com/magazine/archive/2002/04/nixon-and-the chiefs/302473/, (accessed May 19, 2023).

[31] Kelsey Sutton, "New York Times to Trump: We Did Not Apologize," *Politico*, March 29, 2017.

[32] Greg Miller & Adam Entous, "National Security Adviser Discussed Russian Sanctions with Ambassador Despite Denials," *Washington Post*, February 2, 2017.

[33] *Id.*

[34] The paper can be found at https://www.dni.gov/files/documents/ICA_2017_01.pdf (accessed May 19, 2023).

destruction program before the United States invaded in 2003;[35] the president-elect himself accused holdovers at these organizations of undertaking a massive campaign to undermine his presidency.[36] Trump's open defiance and disdain, quickly disseminated to the president's supporters via Tweets, was unprecedented. The result was open warfare about leaks themselves. Trump partisans began to assert that a hidden "Deep State" was treasonously working to denude the president of his power. Each new leak reinforced the conspiracy theory.

So prolific and headline-grabbing was the reporting by the *New York Times* and the *Washington Post* in particular that at times they acknowledged each other's work in a meta-narrative: a *Times* columnist wrote about becoming a *Post* subscriber; the *Times* followed up with a tongue-in-cheek tweet encouraging its followers to follow the *Post*'s Twitter account; the *Post* then used its account to post a GIF of two television characters, Fox Mulder and Dana Scully, the opposites-attract pairing from the *X Files* who pried (fictional) secrets out of a fictional Federal Bureau of Investigation.

So this, then, was the environment that national security reporters were operating in right after the election: a highly competitive arena, with news organizations bent on proving to their audiences and to themselves that they were relevant and legitimate, an operational assumption that the current president might not be fit for the job he occupied and a base of national security and intelligence sources who shared these assumptions and whose identities as patriots were being challenged almost daily by the man they pledged to serve. There may be no greater catalyst for leaks of classified information than an intelligence community that feels powerless. And then there was the story: one that the incoming administration had an active motive to fight back against, at best, and cover up, at worst.

Even still, the gusher of leaks aimed directly at undercutting Trump directly, and his policy, more generally, was astonishing. The president may never have intended to settle executive branch in public, or to provide a wide-open window into the inner most sanctums of the White House, but his own tweets, combined with the torrent of unauthorized disclosures, made his administration the most transparent in history. If the president cannot keep his own secrets, if he cannot keep secret the government's secrets, and if he cannot executive his powers efficiently, the executive branch can grind to a halt. There was a collusion of sorts between the president, who cannot help himself, and journalists, who have no reason to turn down the latest scoop. If Trump was indeed an existential threat to democracy, then adversarial journalism, even it sows confusion, disestablishes

---

[35] Stephen Collinson & Elise Labott, "Donald Trump Takes Aim at US Intelligence Community on Russia," *CNN*, December 11, 2016.

[36] Tom Porter, "Deep State: How a Conspiracy Theory Went from Political Fringe to Mainstream," *Newsweek*, August 2, 2017.

lines of authority, reduces efficiency, and prolongs decision-making, may seem justified no matter what the second-order consequences might be.

Indeed, one of those second-order consequences has been rapid and repeated disclosures of highly classified information. In just eight months, the public has been treated to a near-voyeuristic display of sensitive national security information:

- leaked the gist[37] of transcripts of petulant presidential phone calls with the president of Mexico and the prime minister of Australia (the substance of the conversations would most likely have been classified top secret at a minimum)[38]
- the later leak of those actual transcripts
- details of a secret CIA covert action program in Syria
- detailed reporting about NSA and FBI surveillance against Russian targets inside and outside of the United States
- a report that the United States had intelligence information describing how Russian leaders celebrated Trump's victory
- details about State Department plans for sanctions relief against Russia
- details about leak investigations, which are classified
- news that Trump decided to end a secret, four-year-old CIA covert action program arming anti-Assad rebels in Syria[39]

The president confirmed[40] this in a tweet, objecting to a part of the article.

Also:

- classified reporting that how U.S. reconnaissance satellites discovered that North Korea was arming its patrol boats with missiles capable of attacking other ships

President Trump simply retweeted this last item.

Did he realize that it was classified? Did he care? Does it matter? Does a tweet from a president constitute a decision from an original classification authority to declassify a fact?[41] The prompts to ask these questions are prima facie evidence that the information ecosystem changed journalistic decision rules quite quickly.

---

[37] "Gist" is a term of art; it refers to an abstract, usually in the form of a memorandum for the record.
[38] Michael S. Schmidt, Mark Mazzetti, & Matt Apuzzo, "Trump Aides Had Repeated Contacts with Russian Intelligence," *New York Times*, February 24, 2017.
[39] Greg Jaffe & Adam Entous, "Trump Ends Covert CIA Program to Arm Anti-Assad Rebels in Syria, a Move Sought by Moscow," *Washington Post*, July 19, 2017.
[40] Zachary Cohen, "Trump Retweets Fox News North Korea Story," *CNN*, August 8, 2017.
[41] The Justice Department insisted it did not.

One further example will serve to illustrate the point. On May 15, 2017, the *Washington Post* revealed that President Trump had revealed to Russian diplomats "highly classified information" that "jeopardized a critical source of information on the Islamic State."[42]

> The information the president relayed had been provided by a U.S. partner through an intelligence-sharing arrangement considered so sensitive that details have been withheld from allies and tightly restricted even within the U.S. government, officials said.[43]

So worried were national security officials about the ramifications of this disclosure that they contacted government agencies with liaison relationships with the ally and tried to contain the damage, the *Post* reported.

Quite naturally, the *Post* self-censored quite a bit; it did not report the name of the country; it did not report the type of intelligence that was shared; it did not report the content of the intelligence that was shared; it did not reveal anything about the method that was used to obtain it. The *Post*'s reporters and editors behaved as responsibly as could be expected, as did CNN, the *Wall Street Journal*, and the *New York Times*,[44] all of whom were able to confirm the story using their own sources within hours. Each news outlet told readers it had decided to withhold some details because of the perishability of the intelligence and because officials had convinced it that doing so was in the interest of national security. Here was an example of the media aggressively holding the president to account for a highly unusual violation of a norm, and doing so in a way that acknowledged the equities of the government at large.

The gravity of the story set in motion a frenzy among reporters to learn as much as possible about it, and the government could quite reasonably have expected certain other details to come out in the process, including the name of the partner. The next day, it did: the *New York Times* reported that Israel was the original source.[45] Even with the added detail, the public interest was served; with Israel being a close but fractious ally, it is hard to make a case that our understanding of the story was not enriched by knowing how easy it was for a president to seemingly undermine such a sensitive ally. The public (and the world) now knew that Israel had sources inside the Islamic State who knew

---

[42] Matthew Rosenberg & Eric Schmitt, "Trump Revealed Highly Classified Information to Russia, Officials Say," *New York Times*, May 15, 2017; Shane Harris, "White House Denies Trump Gave Classified Information to Russian Officials," *Wall Street Journal*, May 15, 2017.

[43] Rosenberg & Schmitt, *supra* note 42.

[44] Greg Miller & Greg Jaffe, "Trump Revealed Highly Classified Information to Foreign Minister and Ambassador," *Washington Post*, May 15, 2017.

[45] Adam Goldman, Eric Schmitt, & Peter Baker, "Israel Said to Be Source of Secret Intelligence Trump Gave to Russia," *New York Times*, May 16, 2017.

about bomb-making plots, and it was regularly passing along information to the United States. So long as the city in question was not named, the source would be protected. But a day later, that critical detail was added; it came by way of a tweet from a national security reporter for CBS News. Israel had not said what became of their source or method, but within forty-eight hours of the publication of the initial story, a story where reporters had originally and properly balanced equities, there were few secrets left to disclose. There is no journalistic hive mind, and different entities can come to different conclusions about how to best to protect national security information, but journalists tend to follow the collective in these matters. This is not a new pattern: news organizations feel competitive pressure to match and advance high-impact stories. But the mediums and platforms they use today are very different. Legitimizing Twitter as an outlet disclosing classified national security information all but guarantees that what some in government term as items of "secrecy porn" are revealed much more easily, and with much less forethought.[46]

Before the election, a dossier of President Trump's alleged connections to Russia circulated among journalists,[47] some of whom referenced its existence but did not publish it,[48] because they could not independently verify its claims. Eleven days before Trump was inaugurated, CNN reported that a synopsis of the dossier had been given to Trump in one of the post-election briefings he received about Russian interference in the election. The next day, BuzzFeed published the entire dossier.[49] ("A subhead noted: These Allegations are Unverified and The Report Contains Errors."). The reason: "[S]o that Americans can make up their own minds about allegations about the president-elect that have circulated at the highest levels of the US government." BuzzFeed editor-in-chief Ben Smith found himself on the receiving end of a barrage of complaints from journalists. False information was chum in the water; BuzzFeed was reveling in it. Smith would tell his interlocutors that the public's skepticism of the media, in general, demands more transparency from the profession; also, since the dossier had been briefed to the president, it was hardly not newsworthy. "I think we are now in a media

---

[46] The author has committed this error before; writing hours after the Joint Special Operations Command completed Operation Neptune's Spear and captured Osama bin Laden, I revealed, in a tweet, that a highly classified US surveillance drone had been hovering, undetected, over the site of the raid in Pakistan. The Director of National Intelligence sent me an email the next day taking me to task for revealing a highly perishable method. He was right. I was wrong. So much as I can reconstruct my thinking, I do not remember weighing national security concerns at all. That was the first, and last, time, I ever took to Twitter to reveal a classified fact.

[47] David Corn, "A Veteran Spy Has Given the FBI Information Alleging a Russian Operation to Cultivate Donald Trump," *Mother Jones*, October 16, 2016.

[48] Even Perez et al., "Intel Chiefs Presented Trump with Claims of Russian Efforts to Compromise Him," *CNN*, January 12, 2017.

[49] Ken Bensinger, Miriam Elder, & Mark Schoofs, "These Reports Allege Trump Has Deep Ties to Russia," *BuzzFeed*, January 10, 2017.

environment where you have to engage in false statements," he told NBC News's Chuck Todd. Todd wasn't having it. "You just published fake news. Why is that an unfair description?" Smith responded: "This was a real story about a real document that was really being passed around between the very top officials of this country."[50] President Trump memorably called the publication a "failing pile of garbage," after that. As of this writing, most of the material in the dossier has been disclaimed as either entirely false or unverifiable; a few items turned out to be true.

IV. Toward Transparency and the Presumption to Publish

The control of national security information, and the informal bargaining between journalists and the government, forms a sort of institutional equilibrium, governed by what David Pozen has called an "nuanced set of informal social controls."[51] Leaks (or formally directed but disclosures of classified information) occur in an interstitial space between the reach of laws and the habits of practice. In the main, journalists are not punished for leaking, even though they are not exempt from laws governing the publication of such information. The Joe Biden administration has made it harder for federal prosecutors to seek phone and email records from journalists. Still, the government insists upon the fact of a hurricane-like havoc that leaks leave in their wake, even though the national security bureaucracy seems resistant to statutory and regulatory efforts to build more effective firewalls. As Pozen has written, "There is a dramatic disconnect between the way our laws and our leaders purport to condemn leaking and the way they have condoned it—a rampant, pervasive culture of it—in practice."[52] That is because, as he and many others have noticed, leaks are extremely useful, often influential ways to effectuate policy change *over time*; they fill in the gaps between the public's misunderstandings of a complex issue and the government's need to prosecute a policy based on a firmer understanding; they allow for otherwise obscure personal and policy disputes to be litigated; they often serve the direct professional and culture equities of the leakers and the individuals they represent. So a tacit "permissive neglect" has settled over the nation's capital, and the result, over time, has been the maintenance of something approaching more trust in the executive branch and in its decision-making.[53]

---

[50] MSNBC Broadcast, Meet the Press Daily (accessed January 11, 2017); archives not online.
[51] David Pozen, "The Leaky Leviathon: Why the Government Condemns and Condones Leaks of Classified Information," *Harvard Law Review*, 127, https://harvardlawreview.org/print/vol-127/the-leaky-leviathan-why-the-government-condemns-and-condones-unlawful-disclosures-of-information/ (accessed May 19, 2023).
[52] *Id.* at 517.
[53] *Id.* at 575.

This dynamic has changed dramatically during the past decade, and it has been upended entirely since Trump's election. For one thing, though the number of actual or discrete leaks over time is hard to quantify, the volume of raw, unexpurgated secrets that have appeared in the public square has increased exponentially, because of WikiLeaks' serial revelations of classified information and then Edward Snowden's theft of classified information and its subsequent disclosure through traditional and new media outlets. Chelsea Manning, one of WikiLeaks' original sources, was a low-level analyst who developed an ideological aversion to the war she was fighting. Snowden's motives, if we take him at his word, were not institutional or dispositional. He opposed the growing reach of the surveillance state; one learned "the dangerous truth behind the U.S. policies that seek to develop secret, irresistible powers and concentrate them in the hands of an unaccountable few," getting the word out was not only inevitable, it was for him an imperative.[54] These were not the authorized "plants" of Pozen's taxonomy; they were simply huge dumps of highly sensitive information, often with only partial context, and at times related tangentially to questions about privacy. These disclosures significantly disrupted the functioning of the government.

Since its birth in 2006, WikiLeaks' stance toward curation and sifting has shifted from collaboration to confrontation. Its founder, Julian Assange, understands intuitively how large quantities of information can overwhelm dominant narratives in "unjust societies," splinter public opinion, and reduce the efficiency with which governments and corporations carry out their policies.[55]

In 2010, after obtaining more than 700,000 classified military and State Department cables from Manning, WikiLeaks collaborated with at least four news organizations to sift and filter them before publication.[56] There was no precedent for this type of information disclosure before. "Journalists getting handed a set of 250,000 primary source documents is unheard of."[57] The decision to outsource to several news outlets allowed WikiLeaks the feint of insisting that any collateral damage resulting from the leaks—sources and methods revealed, humans put in danger—were incidental to its own purpose and largely the fault of the journalists who had been given the chance to contextualize them.

The news organizations found plenty that was *new* within the document cache to justify their publication, but the sheer volume of secrets augured their

---

[54] Barton Gellman & Jerry Markon, "Edward Snowden Says Motive Behind Leaks Was to Expose 'Surveillance State,'" *Washington Post*, June 10, 2013.

[55] Essays by Assange can be found here: https://cryptome.org/0002/ja-conspiracies.pdf (accessed May 19, 2023).

[56] Richard Tofel, "Why Wikileaks' War Logs' Are No Pentagon Papers," *ProPublica*, July 26, 2010, https://www.propublica.org/article/why-wikileaks-war-logs-are-no-pentagon-papers (accessed May 19, 2023).

[57] Interview with C.W. Anderson, https://www.cfr.org/interview/how-wikileaks-affects-journalism (accessed May 19, 2023).

eventual publication anyway; given access to nonpublic information about an important subject, reporters will report it, because they are reporters. Daniel Ellsberg, one of the authors and subsequent leakers of the *Pentagon Papers* in 1969, compared the military leaks to his own, and lauded Manning.[58]

News organizations found their decisions thus blessed by the man whose leaks enshrined their right to publish (but not, to be sure, to publish without consequences), national security information without prior permission from the government. Fundamentally, the public interest justification was different. Certainly, both sets of Manning documents contained lots of *information*. But much of it may have been noise, albeit noise with a classification banner affixed to it. As even many journalists who lauded the leaks pointed out, the documents did not reveal discrepancies between what the US government was doing in public and what it was saying it private. They did not reveal lies or abuses by the executive branch. Indeed, the State Department cables painted a portrait of American diplomats that was largely positive; the foreign service upheld its ethical obligations in secret. It is hard to argue that they provided any significant context or an enhanced understanding of executive decision-making. The document dump did not change the direction of policy. President Obama had just added troops but promised to start withdrawing them by the next year when the War Logs were published;[59] public opinion did not appreciably move in any direction; the military did not give up its decades-long effort to convince civilian policymakers to let them "finish the job"; the aftermath of withdrawal still resonates.[60] What resulted was significant disruption to the US foreign policy establishment, a collection of people and interests that Assange finds to be, more than anything else, "evil."[61] Assange was quite satisfied.

The situation was novel. Journalists had to ask several foundational questions simultaneously: Was Assange a journalist like them? If they treated him differently, did that mean they might be treated differently by the government? Do his motives differ from those of journalists? Do different motivations matter? Did the enormous number of classified documents require an appreciably larger degree of vetting and/or deference to the government's own equities? The Justice Department decided to answer the question in 2019 by indicting Assange for conspiring with Manning to obtain the information.[62]

---

[58] "Pentagon Papers Leaker Praises Manning, Snowden," *NPR*, August 3, 2013.
[59] Sheryl Gay Stolberg & Helene Cooper, "Obama Adds Troops, But Maps Exit Plan," *New York Times*, December 2, 2009.
[60] Frank Rich, "Kiss This War Goodbye," *New York Times*, August 1, 2010.
[61] Raffi Khatchadourian, "Julian Assange, 'A Man Without a Country,'" *New Yorker*, August 28, 2017, https://www.newyorker.com/magazine/2017/08/21/julian-assange-a-man-without-a-country (accessed May 19, 2023).
[62] Read the indictment here: https://www.justice.gov/opa/pr/wikileaks-founder-charged-superseding-indictment (accessed May 19, 2023).

News organizations, however, answered these questions by publishing the information. In doing so, they signaled an adversarial change in their relationship with the government. The intellectual lineage of the presumption to publish model lies outside of formal, organized journalism. It is a guiding principle of a movement among the most enfranchised purveyors of the new information ecosystem: programmers, hackers, geeks, and techno libertarians—the citizen reporters who now compete with traditional news entities for attention, financial resources, and credibility. If they have a central credo, it is probably this: the more decentralized the *control* of information, the harder it is for governments and corporations to use information (and the internet) to oppress and malign.

In 2008, a prodigal programmer, engineer, and ideological entrepreneur named Aaron Schwartz wrote a crisp call to arms for his fellow activists called the "Guerilla Open Access Manifesto."[63] He had dedicated his professional career to the notion that information, once produced, ought to be free and widely circulated. He believed this in his marrow. Corporations and governments that kept public information from seeing the light of day, or who charged money for the right to simply share knowledge, were "blinded by greed." In the "grand tradition of "civil disobedience," it was time to "declare our opposition to this private theft of public culture." Schwartz first downloaded and then distributed about 20 percent of the Public Access to Court Electronic Records (PACER) database operated by the Justice Department on the grounds that it was immoral for the government to charge people access for information they, themselves, deemed to be public. Three years later, as a fellow at Harvard, he began to download reams of articles from the JSTOR database, intending to disseminate them widely. This time, he was arrested, was charged, and later settled with the government; he committed suicide in 2013. His friends and family blamed the stress associated with a highly aggressive, invasive prosecution by the government.[64]

Edward Snowden owes a lot to Aaron Schwartz.[65] While most reporters working on the Snowden cache consulted the government before publishing specific stories, the presumption to publish them at all was assumed; most of Snowden's journalistic interlocutors and their critics seemed to agree with his main premise. Journalists "are meant to stick up for the underdog and irritate the powerful," wrote John Cassidy in the *New Yorker*, in a piece about "taking sides." "Which side are you on?"[66] Snowden followed some of the traditional

---

[63] Read the manifesto here: https://openipub.com/?pub=GuerrillaOpenAccessManifesto.html (accessed May 19, 2023).
[64] Elizabeth Day, "Aaron Swartz, Hacker, Genius, Martyr?," *The Guardian*, June 2, 2013.
[65] Noam Scheiber, "Why'd He Do It," *New Republic*, June 10, 2013.
[66] John Cassidy, "Demonizing Edward Snowden: Which Side Are You On," *New Yorker*, June 24, 2013.

conventions that whistle-blowers take; he ignored others, giving journalists[67] the power to disclose (or not disclose) his secrets and insisted in certain redactions, usually related to direct non-intelligence defense capabilities of the United States and those that would protect US soldiers fighting in Afghanistan, Iraq, and elsewhere. To Snowden's credit, a number of important issues—the NSA's deliberate weakening of encryption standards, the ability of the NSA to retroactively query databases that contained un-minimized US persons information, and its reliance on aged legal authorities to collect communications metadata—were foist into the public square, hastening a public reckoning about the sheer volume of digital detritus we all possess, and how those bits and bytes are vacuumed up under the guise of intelligence collection.

But Snowden did not uncover any significant abuse of that power other than the breadth of permissible collection, which, in fairness to his point of view, he views as significant. He did not uncover any actual chilling of political speech; he did not uncover programs that had not been briefed to Congress; much of what he disclosed, and what the government later disclosed in response, revealed a years-long secret struggle to reconcile the voracious information demands of policymakers with technology that was insufficient to the task of sorting, analyzing, and sifting them properly. Snowden did not uncover a secret history to mislead the American people about government decision-making. To date, his revelations have resulted in minor changes to federal law; there is no significant public clamor for greater ones.[68] (Many highly consequential leaks, in fact, do not result in policy changes immediately; no affront to Snowden is intended.)

But his revelations did fundamentally change the relationship between the technology industry in the United States and the US government. Many of those companies cooperated in secret with the NSA under arguably coercive federal orders. Some—Apple, Google, Facebook, among others—found their inner libertarian instincts emboldened. Big Tech took a hard turn in favor of encryption-by-default, and toward a policy consensus about endpoint encryption (that it protects businesses, consumers, and even the government, and it ought to be standard). Companies with large overseas footprints and relationships with foreign governments were left trying to explain how they could simultaneously serve the interests of America's surveillance agency and some of its targets.[69]

Snowden's disclosures changed journalists' tradecraft, for the better. Virtually every major news organization prominently, and often obsequiously, solicits anonymous sources through their websites. Most use the service provided by

---

[67] Author's interview with several of the journalists who Snowden directly contacted and has interacted with.

[68] Julian Hattem, "Spying After Snowden: What's Changed and What Hasn't," *The Hill*, December 25, 2016.

[69] Jon Swartz, "NSA Surveillance Hurting Tech Firms' Business," *USA Today*, February 24, 2014.

SecureDrop, a project of the Freedom of the Press Foundation, a nonprofit set up to promote secure "adversarial" journalism.[70] They encourage their reporters to use Redbone and Signal, or other calling and chat apps with end-to-end encryption; that is, the keys to decrypt the messages exist only on the devices that the sender and receiver use and are not stored centrally. Journalists are routinely urged to use throw-away cell phones when calling sources directly, to study their personal/home ISP's data retention policies, to utilize virtual private networks (VPNs) to obscure their locations; others use Tor, the anonymized decentralized peer-to-peer file-sharing network, and Tails, a secure operating system that runs off a USB stick.[71] Many prominent journalists now advertise their secure communication keys on their Twitter or personal websites. But most do not.[72] "In an era when anything that can be hacked will be and when the president has declared outright war on the media, this should serve as a frightening wake-up call," two researchers who studied the issue have written.[73]

Correspondingly, the ability of governments and hostile actors to detect and discover those sources has increased. Surveillance of communications metadata can uncover patterns that allow investigators to piece together the provenance of information even when a widely used secure communications platform, like WhatsApp, employs solid end-to-end encryption. Indeed, Facebook Chief Operating Offer Sheryl Sandberg has acknowledged an obligation to share with governments communicants' metadata to protect against terrorism or to assist investigators, provided that proper warrants and procedures are followed in countries where the rule of law is respected.[74]

V. Gaming the System

In their influential work on mass media and communication, Doris Graber and Johanna Dunaway identify three main biases common to the practice of journalism:[75] affective, informational, and partisan/ideological. All three shade the tone, type, and content of stories and the decision to produce them. Since there is no objective starting point to measure these biases—a story without any obvious emotional markers is itself an obvious emotional marker—the relative influence of these biases depends on the social circumstances within which the journalism

---

[70] The author has worked with the Freedom of the Press foundation on a digital security project.
[71] *See* https://tails.boum.org/ (accessed May 19, 2023).
[72] Nikki Usher, "Why Haven't Reporters Mass-Adopted Secure Tools for Communicating with Sources?," *Slate*, July 2017.
[73] *Id.*
[74] Facebook's Sheryl Sandberg: "WhatsApp Metadata Informs Governments about Terrorist Activity in Spite of Encryption," *CNBC*, July 31, 2017.
[75] Doris Graber & Johanna Dunaway, *Mass Media and American Politics*, (CQ Press, 2016).

is produced. Like riding public transit, group therapy sessions, and professional wrestling, journalism is a social experience requiring some degree of cooperation among interested parties. It, too, has a bias, one that is difficult to grasp, but it is arguably the most vital to understand: the product of the interaction between journalistic decision rules and the rapidly evolving information ecosystem.

Journalists used to wait for printing presses or online editors to publish their own work, in full, after stories were thoroughly edited and finished; *now*, stories, particularly original breaking news and enterprise scoops, are rapidly thrown up on websites; journalists tweet out the headlines, often within moments of receiving information. Within hours, they're on cable news shows, discussing and analyzing articles that many have yet to finish writing. As of 2021, dozens of journalists left their edited platforms for new companies, like Substack, that gave them complete freedom, and often a healthy advance, to build their own brands and audiences.

Until the past decade, national security reportage benefited from journalistic decision rules and from an information ecosystem that allowed for pauses; *now*, because there is one continuous news cycle, there is only an information stream, to which national security reporting is added, often lacking the context that gives stories weight or subtlety. Journalists lack the time and space to think about how to best inform their readership about the background of a complicated issue; while reporters at top-flight news organizations still have more leeway and relatively more freedom to publish at their own pace, they cannot escape the demands imposed upon them by the means of production. It should not escape the notice of national security reporters that six in ten people who see a headline will share it on their Facebook feed without reading the story.[76] How can the public be expected to understand an issue as complex as "unmasking"—the practice by which a government official requests that the NSA provide the identity of a US person who has been incidentally or inadvertently caught in a surveillance net, when technical terms like "unmasking" are juxtaposed next to scare words like "scandal"?[77]

It has certainly not escaped the industry's notice that the advent of online publishing tools and the way that Facebook and Google have, until recently, visually conflated mainstream and partisan news sources makes it very easy for anyone to borrow the style of journalism and claim that journalism is being done.[78] It *did* escape the industry's notice that a foreign government—Russia—had done

---

[76] Caitlin Dewey, "6 in 10 of You Will Share This Link Without Reading It, a New, Depressing Study Says," *Washington Post*, June 16, 2016.

[77] David Harasanyi, "Reminder: Susan Rice Lied About Her Role in Unmasking Scandal," *The Federalist*, September 14, 2017.

[78] Charlotte Scott, "Spurning the Sidebar: Does Facebook Verify the Sponsored Articles That Appear in Its News Feeds?," *USC Annenberg Media*, March 20, 2017.

so during the 2016 election. How these weaponized efforts to rig the election in favor of one candidate actually influenced voters—or whether they did it all—is unknowable given how many factors determine whether individuals will actually vote. But the early indicators suggest that the information economy itself produces a sort of Gresham's law for news: bad news chases out good news; or, rather: poorly produced, skewed, or partisan news crowds out responsibly produced, responsibly sourced reporting. An Oxford study of information and news shared on Twitter during the final week of the 2016 election found that only 20 percent of all shares related to the election came from "professional news content," rivaling the percentage that came from the deliberately polarizing and conspiracy sources, including Russian bots and troll farms.[79]

Indeed, those bots-with-brains seem to respond more quickly to algorithm changes than humans do. And though Google and Facebook use human curators, along with machine learning, to try and identify points of information distribution that are fake, or false, the cycle of misinformation does not require that bots continually participate: all it takes is a sudden burst of linking, or retweeting (back when "X" was "Twitter"), or sharing, and real humans begin to see the results higher up in their newsfeeds and Facebook pages; as soon as they do, the bots can effectively silence themselves, because humans will do to the sharing. In the past several months, platform-based search results have been gamed right when major (legitimate) news stories have dropped. The day after President Trump purportedly disclosed classified information to Russian diplomats in the Oval Office, Google users searching for information about the story were treated to a false story about President Obama allegedly leaking classified information.[80]

After a sixty-four-year-old retired real estate speculator took a hammer to the windows of his Las Vegas hotel room and unleashed a gothic horror on concertgoers on October 1, 2017, Google and Facebook suffered major failures in their algorithmic efforts to distinguish true information from false information. On Facebook's safety check page, one of the most prominently displayed links sent readers to an alt-right blog that speculated about the shooter's political affiliation. The second, as BuzzFeed's Charlie Warzel noted, "is a random aggregation of site [with] gross chumbox ads everywhere." Twelve hours after the incident, one of the main links led to a bitcoin wallet.[81] Google, for its part, surfaced at the top of its feed a post by 4Chan that falsely identified the shooter. The

---

[79] Phillip N. Howard et al., "Social Media, News and Political Information during the US Election: Was Polarizing Content Concentrated in Swing States?," Comprop Data Memo 2017.8/September 28, 2017, available at http://comprop.oii.ox.ac.uk/wp-content/uploads/sites/89/2017/09/Polarizing-Content-and-Swing-States.pdf (accessed May 19, 2023).

[80] Noticed by @RVAwonk on Twitter and verified by the author.

[81] Charlie Warzel, "The Big Tech Platforms Are Still Botching Breaking News," BuzzFeed, October 2, 2017. See https://twitter.com/cwarzel/status/914882919440703488/photo/1 (accessed May 19, 2023). BuzzFeed set up a page devoted to all the hoax articles.

company, in a statement, said that the post was "replaced" algorithmically within "hours."[82] Outside sites that rely on Facebook and Twitter for their transmission, some of them partisan and others whose intentions can't be discerned, spread false rumors about shootings inside casinos.[83] Two and a half years before the coronavirus pandemic and the 2020 presidential election, the media and intermediary platforms were alerted to the dangers of news voids and their role in the harmful spread of misinformation.

VI. Conclusion

For four years, during the proliferation and powering up of news intermediaries, the press struggled to fill multiple new roles. Marty Baron, the then *Washington Post* editor and among the most admired voices in the industry, put it this way in a speech early in Trump's term:

> Many journalists wonder with considerable weariness what it is going to be like for us during the next four—perhaps eight—years. Will we be incessantly harassed and vilified? Will the new administration seize on opportunities to try intimidating us? Will we face obstruction at every turn?[84]

Yes, to all that. But then: all those leaks, too. Baron has elsewhere insisted that the *Post* never declared war on Trump.[85] Perhaps journalism has become war by another name. Trump's actions suggested that he perceived the press to be an existential threat to him, albeit a useful demon: he could frame the press as an enemy in the well-worn language of the culture wars.[86] He regularly encouraged the demonization of individual reporters, threatened to tighten libel laws, even set journalists up for physical violence at his rallies by pointing out the press pens and insulting the beat reporters en masse. It took his lies about the 2020 election for Twitter and Facebook to remove his calls to violence from their platforms.

In late December of 2017, Breitbart editor-in-chief Matthew Boyle said of his (and the President's) adversaries:

---

[82] Gerrit DeVynck, "Fake News Fills Information Vacuum in Wake of Las Vegas Shooting," *Bloomberg*, October 10, 2017.

[83] Noticed by @RBAWonk, https://twitter.com/RVAwonk/status/914743535211024384 (accessed May 19, 2023).

[84] Martin Baron, "Speech in Honor of the Hitchens Prize," *New York*, November 30, 2016.

[85] Nico Salvatori, "Editor Martin Baron: Post Not at War with Trump," *GoErie.com*, August 18, 2018.

[86] Matthew Yglesias, "Donald Trump Versus the NFL Explained," *Vox.com*, September 25, 2017.

The media is an industry in crisis that refuses to admit that it's an industry in crisis. It's almost like an alcoholic refusing to admit that they have a problem ... Journalistic integrity is dead. There is no such thing anymore. So, everything is about weaponization of information.[87]

The stakes are quite high. And Boyle's tribal threats represent only one of the sources of pressure.

Journalism holds powerful interests accountable and informs the public; the government protects national security and superintends national security information; the bearers of these prerogatives and responsibilities have been at daggers drawn since before the first Constitutional Convention. How they are debated and resolved—formally, informally, *or* ad hoc—have been critical forcing functions for our evolving democratic institutions.

Today, national security journalists find themselves under threat not just from their own governments but also from hostile actors representing foreign nation-states, from terrorist groups, from amorphous cyber anarchists, and even from ordinary internet trolls who can disrupt their nonprofessional lives with campaigns of harassment and bullying. The effect of their journalism is often *nullified* by ubiquity of misinformation, skewed information, the easily gamified information economy, and by a growing mistrust of their motives.[88]

The floor has been low for a decade or more. In 2007, a full 61 percent of those surveyed questioned the *accuracy* of "traditional journalists." That's about as many who questioned the accuracy of "citizen journalists." When the quality of information produced by self-styled professionals is subject to the same level of skepticism as that produced by people without formal training or an inculcation in that profession's culture, the authority and influence of the former cannot be assumed or willed into existence. Political tribalism has been transformed by the development of online sharing communities (Subreddits, Twitter retweets, TikTok posts, Telegram chat groups, Facebook self-sharing) into hardened certitudes that fill the void of trust with a constant stream of curated, precontextualized information. The financial dominance of these platforms—Facebook, YouTube, Snapchat, Google, Twitter—over news outlets (CBS, the *New York Times*, AP) means that when readers and viewers consume information from traditional media, they are bringing to their experience the values of their preferred platform as an initial reference point.[89] Prefiltered news consumption is a high bar for traditional journalists to vault.

---

[87] Charlie Warzel, InfoWarzel.com newsletter, https://tinyletter.com/Infowarzel/letters/journalistic-integrity-is-dead-is-the-mainstream-media next (accessed May 19, 2023).
[88] *See* Gallup's trendline in "Media Use and Evaluation," Gallup, as of September 9–10, 2017, http://news.gallup.com/poll/1663/media-use evaluation.aspx (accessed May 19, 2023).
[89] John Herrman, "The Land of Internet Subcultures," *New York Times*, August 13, 2017.

Effective national security journalism requires a bond of trust between the reader and the reporter; not every source can be described or revealed, and not every story can come quickly, nor should it. It must survive daily treks through the turbulent, ungovernable, easily gameable information landscape, a tense, tribal public that craves good, reliable news but has a habit of rejecting it when it poses a threat to their identity, technology that facilitates the easy creation and maintenance of cast-iron echo chamber, and the brain-rewiring imposition of intermediaries like Facebook, Google, and Twitter.

Publishing classified information today is not the same as publishing a report thirty years ago, or even ten years ago; it lands differently. Journalists need to remain humble: they did not know if the main effect of aggressive leaks, a focus on President Trump's norm-violating habits and on his disruptive communication practices would have, in the main, the consequence of grinding executive branch policymaking to a halt, or whether it would fortify his support, or whether it would bear fruit as a mechanism to hold him accountable. Journalists ought to be humble about the future: the imposition of machine learning, artificial intelligence, the close-to-zero cost to distribute information far and wide are permanent features of reality; they will persist even when the president does not view the press an enemy, or if political tribalism somehow suddenly declines. If good national security reporting loses its ability to persuade and inform, then what is its purpose? To survive, the profession should consider these issues thoroughly.

My principal recommendation is to treat journalism, and national security journalism in particular, as a craft that must be taught, repeated, and explored in order to be mastered. There are prodigies who need no instruction, but if journalism schools do not specifically encourage their students to learn the very particular set of skills necessary to report on these sensitive topics, there will be simply be more bad stuff out there, and less good stuff. Having established the first course in national security reporting at one of the nation's top journalism schools, I can attest to student interest. Journalism schools have successfully reconstituted their curricula to account for technological changes to the profession, and they're wrestling with questions about finance and sustainability. Good. But they must also engage, just as deeply, with questions of substance. What is going on in the world, right now, that journalism needs to apply itself to?

There are other recommendations that follow from a close analysis of President Trump's first year in office.

1. Fast publishing of national security information (through Twitter, or elsewhere) should NOT the norm be unless there is a vital interest that is extremely time-sensitive.
2. The informal collaboration model, where journalists and the government bargain over how much national security information ought to be

disclosed in each story, must be revived, but it must be acknowledged openly by both sides.
3. Journalists will engage more openly with their audiences, often crowdsourcing reporting and soliciting tips, but they must fashion themselves as conversation leaders and work to provide history and context.
4. Those who report on a subject that requires subject matter expertise must learn as much as possible about the subject; journalists should study Terrorism Management Theory; the effect of framing, priming, contrasts, motivated reasoning, and other cognitive biases on the reception of news coverage.
5. Journalists should practice technologically better tradecraft when dealing with sources, particularly anonymous ones, and they should reconsider the presumption to publish model whenever a source's motivations cannot be discerned.
6. Journalists must be open to the possibility that the information they receive anonymously or even through a trusted broker is, in fact, a weapon of a foreign government or serves the interests of another nefarious actor, using mechanisms of attribution that are impossible to discern.

While transparency, adversarial journalism, and the exposure of secretive national security practices are often inherent political goods and, more often than not, have redounded to the benefit of the country, they are not goods in and of themselves. Especially when the tools of journalists can now be subverted as effortlessly as a hapless Hungarian in a John LeCarré novel, journalists ought to respect the presumption to publish as a public trust, and they should not automatically assume that their untraditional practices will reproduce prior forms of credibility from skeptical audiences. Indeed, they should not assume that aggression and speed enhance persuasion, or that it equips citizens with the accurate context and facts to make more informed decisions.

5
Open Source Imagery Intelligence: Security Implications in an Era of Unprecedented Access to Satellite Data

Allison Puccioni

I. Introduction

Long relegated to the intelligence and military communities of the Cold War superpowers, high-resolution satellite imagery has emerged over the past fifteen years as an unclassified, attainable data set in the open source community. This relatively new medium carries the veracity associated with the tradecraft of intelligence as well as a heightened interest from a public that was long denied access to such information.

II. Emergence of High-Resolution Imaging Satellites in the Open Source Community

Militaries have attempted aerial reconnaissance since the invention of cameras and aerial platforms. While biplanes, balloons, and pigeons successfully collected photographic reconnaissance during World War I, aircraft-mounted photographic reconnaissance and the tradecraft of imagery analysis took form in World War II. During this war, British and American "photographic interpreters" analyzed pictures taken from reconnaissance aircraft, such as Britain's Supermarine Spitfire, and developed a method of identifying unique features of military equipment and military facilities that remains the keystone of imagery intelligence today.

But it was the Cold War and the potential for unprecedented war on a global scale with nuclear weapons and the rockets that could deliver such weapons at intercontinental range that prompted a race toward developing satellites that required as much treasure and scientific talent as the US and USSR respective race for nuclear weapons and space rocketry. After World War II and the ensuing pursuit of nuclear weapons, the United States employed long-range strategic aircraft, including the Lockheed-Martin U2 "Dragon Lady," which flew at a near-stratospheric altitude, to fly over Russian territory and photograph strategic and military activity. Simultaneously, the United States and Russia were developing satellite technology both as a means to demonstrate their technological prowess to the world and to propagate a means to collect imagery from space, beyond even the farthest reaches of sophisticated missile systems that could potentially even target the U2. The successful shoot-down of a U2 over Soviet territory in 1960, then the Cuban Missile Crisis in 1962 (during which another U2 was shot down in Cuba) forced both parties to redouble efforts to develop space-based sensors. By the early 1960s, the United States successfully launched a satellite platform that collected crude but useful photographs of Soviet territory beyond the reach of even the most sophisticated surface-to-air missile system.[1] Use of spy satellites was broadly legitimized as a part of an overall nuclear verification process throughout multiple nuclear arms summits in the 1950s and 1960s, and the legacy of freedom of image collection from space has extended to the realm of commercial satellites. Though information about the United States' early satellite program exists, the ensuing generations of satellites have been a closely held secret: that the United States only acknowledged its existence by accident in the 1970s when President Jimmy Carter inadvertently alluded to them in a speech at NASA's Kennedy Space Center.

Yet somehow, by the 1990s, the US government began supporting companies intent on building satellites commercially, raising the question: Why would a nation support the advancement of a capability that comprised a key intelligence apparatus into the open-source community? Several factors likely influenced the US decision. Firstly, overhead pictures provide answers to prominent intelligence questions while simultaneously *prompting* many more questions, creating a near-insatiable need for such an intelligence force-multiplier. No matter how prodigious the US national technical means of space-based surveillance was, the capability was always surpassed by the need for more. Moreover, many defense industry companies charged with building customized imagery intelligence systems may have addressed their remit, but in many cases these systems were so specialized that innovation, cost-effectiveness, or technological translation to wider applications stagnated. Concurrently, the American technological sector was at the time flourishing, promising at worst comparable capability and at best a windfall of next-generation imaging technology.

---

[1] "NGA in History—Defining Moments," Springfield, VA, National Geospatial-Intelligence Agency, CORONA Program, 2023, https://www.nga.mil/defining-moments/CORONA_Program.html (accessed March 15, 2023).

By the late aughts (the decade from 2000 to 2009), American commercial companies had successfully launched four high-resolution commercial satellites. One such satellite, the GeoEye-1, cost about a half-billion dollars to build and launch.[2] This was a reported fraction of a similar such system built by the US defense industry.[3] By 2011, two American companies and one French company were manufacturing high-resolution satellites; and by 2013, two Silicon Valley–accelerated companies by the name of SkyBox and Planet Labs successfully integrated components from common electronics like cell phones to drastically reduce the size and weight of high-resolution imaging satellites.[4] Imaging platforms once the size of a Mercedes minibus could now be scaled down to the size of a beer keg. Commercial rocketry became more commercialized as well, now dozens of "beer kegs" (much more commonly known as "small-sats" or their smaller "cube-sat" counterparts) could be launched simultaneously exponentially reducing launch costs.

In 2006, there was one one-meter resolution satellite called the Ikonos, and another higher resolution satellite (submeter) called the QuickBird. By comparison, today there are over fifty submeter/high-resolution satellites that have over the course of twenty years collected hundreds of millions of kilometers' worth of archival satellite imagery over the earth's surface.

Accordingly, satellite imagery analysis has increased transparency over territories that have long sought to deny access to and understanding of their strategic activities. However, there are significant ethical implications associated with satellite imagery including a lack of appropriate technical and peer review in the nascent stages of this medium, a trend toward analysis only of a nation's military systems, which can tend to play into an artificially hawkish or despotic media narrative of a nation, a lack of journalistic or tradecraft standards applied to the analysis of this data, and a lack of understanding of the implications of publishing this popular data in the wider media. These disadvantages, combined with the popularity of this data, contribute to a unique quandary attached to high-resolution satellite imagery during a decade that has seen an order-of-magnitude increase in space launches of these sensors.

In the United States and most of the world's intelligence communities, the tradecraft of imagery analysis is largely relegated to groups with clearances that work within intelligence agencies. As of 2023, there is no semester-length

---

[2] J. Bloom, "Way Up There—And Personal," *The Guardian*, January 28, 2009, https://www.theguardian.com/technology/2009/jan/28/satellite-photography-privacy (accessed March 17, 2023).

[3] P. Taubman, "The Demise of a Pricey U.S. Spy Satellite Program," *New York Times*, November 11, 2007, https://www.nytimes.com/2007/11/11/world/americas/11iht-spy.4.8286181.html (accessed March 15, 2023).

[4] R. Meyer, "Silicon Valley's New Spy Satellites," *The Atlantic*, January 7, 2014, https://www.theatlantic.com/technology/archive/2014/01/silicon-valleys-new-spy-satellites/282580/ (accessed March 20, 2023).

academic curriculum for analyzing imagery. But the medium of satellite imagery is becoming increasingly available, and the utility in the open source community is no different than it is within the classified confines of the intelligence communities that developed the data-collection and analytical capabilities.

Imagery analysis has been conducted—in fits and starts—in the media since the 1990s, when policy think tanks like the Federation of American Scientists used medium-resolution satellite imagery available from France's *Satellite pour L'Observation de la Terre* (SPOT) to study strategic events and activity, such as nuclear proliferation and military activity. Organizational open source imagery analysis was significantly hindered by lack of high-resolution imagery, which was not commercially available until January 2000, and by the continuing scarcity of such images throughout the 2000–2010 time frame, resulting from too few satellites to build a deep archive of imagery for historical context of change over time.

In the 2010s, however, many media outlets were covering imagery analysis conducted from a handful of organizations, like the British publication company Janes, which produced *Jane's Intelligence Review* and *Jane's Defence Weekly* and academically funded think tanks, including the Center for Nonproliferation Studies (at Middlebury Institute) and the Stimson Center. Many think-tank-produced articles received continual, widespread coverage in the media, including satellite imagery of a North Korean rocket just after launch, Russian maneuvers of mobile-launched nuclear missile TELs, the evolution of Iran's rocket and space launch capability, the deployment of China's first nuclear weapons–enabled submarine, or the production of weapons-grade plutonium in North Korea.

III. Inherent Ethical Implications of Satellite Journalism

With the expansion of the conventional high-resolution satellite constellation in the 2010s and the concurrent advent of small-satellites capable of imaging comparable but vastly cheaper imagery, the market experienced a deluge of quality satellite images. Several media outlets, like the *New York Times*, began to incorporate in-house satellite imagery analysis into their routine publication. Student and postgraduate imagery analysts proliferated at the Center for Nonproliferation Studies, and small open source imagery "experiments" got started at Stanford University's Center for International Security and Cooperation. Today, there are approximately sixty-six self-described open source imagery analysts with experience in assessing nuclear capabilities, but only a small handful—less than half a dozen—of these practitioners of open source imagery analysis have a conventional (i.e., military- or intelligence agency–trained) education in imagery intelligence.[5]

The dearth of competent imagery analysts in the open source community is a substantial ethical quandary of its own: without consistent literacy in this tradecraft, there are few people to collaborate, to conduct peer-review research, or to refute poor imagery analysis that gets published. Imagery analysis within the government or military intelligence sphere is, per tradecraft, sent through a standardized process for quality control requiring several trained imagery analysts by contrast. Moreover, satellite imagery amplifies the exposure of an article, conferring notoriety to the report and the originating analyst. With too few experienced analysts, a public hunger for a medium that is often conflated with "spycraft," and a widespread public illiteracy in the tradecraft, incomplete or incorrect journalism is published and misinterpreted as fact.

IV. Examples of Ethical Quandaries in Satellite Journalism

On balance, satellite imagery has added a layer of quantitative verification that can break news on its own or corroborate traditional reporting. It has the ability to hold leaders and militaries accountable. Constant satellite image collection over the 2022 war in Ukraine has enabled research institutions, media agencies, "enthusiasts," and hobbyists alike to better understand military activity and battle damage in Ukraine as it transpires. However, like every new informative medium, there are significant drawbacks to dissemination of material that was long the sole domain of military commanders, diplomats, or elected officials. The following examples depict several quandaries and drawbacks we find with the publication of this former keystone of intelligence communities in this "Wild West" era of emerging satellite imagery.

V. First-to-Witness

There are hundreds of millions of square kilometers' worth of archived images available for sale, with millions more taken each day. Much of this is purchased by governments or mapping companies for private or commercial use. Some of this is purchased by open source imagery analysts for research. An imagery analyst can only scroll over 100 square kilometers of imagery in an eight-hour shift,

---

[5] K. Leede, *Spies in the Public Eye: A Comparative Community Analysis of Nuclear Sleuths and Government Intelligence Agencies, 2021–2022* (2022), 50 (Stanford Center for International Security and Cooperation Honors Program Thesis, Stanford University).

and there are only several dozen commercial satellite imagery analysts, the vast majority of satellite images are never seen by the public. In most cases, therefore, open source imagery analysts are the only people in the public domain to actually see any of the satellite imagery they purchase. Occasionally, an imagery analyst observes an exigent event within the image that is either overlooked by the media, or deliberately unreported by a state actor. In this instance, the analyst alone must decide if or how to publish this information.

In March 2011, an earthquake-triggered tsunami led to a nuclear meltdown in the nuclear reactors at the Fukushima Daiichi Nuclear Power Plant near Sendai City in Japan's Fukushima Prefecture. Between March 12 and March 15, 2011, reactors No. 1, No. 2, and No. 3 incurred severe damage and released radioactive material into the environs. At that time, the Japanese government minimized the extent of the damage, reporting that only two reactors incurred damage, and set the immediate zone of evacuation to correspond with that report. Concurrently, a commercial satellite company imaged the reactor in mid-March 2011 and forwarded it to me while I was working for the magazine *Jane's Intelligence Review*. Upon first glance of the image, I immediately concluded there was unequivocal damage to *all* of the reactors, in contrast to what was being reported by the Japanese government. Within a time frame of several hours before a press deadline, I faced a quandary in which I had to decide whether I should have published the image in the global-facing media and what possible public reactions the publication of this image could incur. My editors and I approached this with the following questions in mind: Should we publish the image in the widespread media? What possible reaction might this image incur? What could be the result if we refrained from publishing?

I received the image in the evening (Pacific time), which was early morning at the UK publishing house, giving my editors and me several hours to make a decision. We wanted to achieve a balance of providing information to the public and preserving safety during a nuclear catastrophe. An ongoing mass evacuation was underway. Radiation sickness and long-term rates of cancer are indeed associated with nuclear power plant disasters, but it should be noted that no one died of immediate radiation exposure at Fukushima, no one died at the US Three Mile Island accident in 1979, and between thirty and fifty people died from Acute Radiation Sickness in the immediate aftermath of the Chernobyl disaster. Radiation is dangerous, but I suspected the Japanese government may have calculated a lower risk of injury or death than if panic spread through an active evacuation campaign.

Ultimately, my editors and I decided not to immediately publish this information, which we believed was only known to us at that time. The information was published several days afterward by other media outlets at a later stage in the evacuation campaign.

VI. Artificial Portrayal of an Entire Nation

High-resolution imaging satellites were originally developed in the United States for one specific purpose: to locate and monitor nuclear weapons–related facilities and the rocket and missile systems that could deliver said weapons to an intercontinental range. Though imagery is used within and beyond the intelligence community for far more than nuclear proliferation monitoring, the majority of open source satellite imagery reporting aligns with the original charter of such satellites. The corpus of articles and their popularity may create an artificial image of a nation. In the case of North Korea, this steady stream of satellite imagery articles can feed the popular media notion that this country is despotic, militaristic, and nothing beyond. A nation may undertake a massive campaign to promote stability and security within its society, but it will likely be wholly overlooked as a research topic by the imagery analyst or a topic for publication by a media outlet. Put another way, no one spends two years to find and track the increase of orphanages or hospitals in the provincial cities in North Korea, and if they do, the media is less than willing to publish such articles.

After fifteen years publishing satellite imagery research, I have yet to be asked to interpret satellite images that may show a nation's infrastructure and society in a positive light. Yet from personal accounts from organizations like the Swiss Development Agency and Chosun Exchange, there are indeed measures being taken by North Korea to improve daily life in the country. Open source satellite imagery analysis is often a culprit in enforcing an existing narrative of a nation's political climate, temperament, and intent.

VII. Tipping Off the Subject of Analysis

Over the past decade, several institutions have published "gotcha" imagery articles revealing new military or strategic systems. My first such article was on an unsuspected deployment of China's Type 094 SSBN submarine to the South China Sea despite widespread belief it was still in early stages of shipbuilding thousands of kilometers north. Though China often displays its land and sea ordinance in full view of overhead observation (I believe as a purposeful effort to project strategic prowess to a wider audience), China and other nations take great pains to conceal some of their most sensitive facilities. If a satellite imagery article is published over these facilities, illustrating the visual features of the facility that indicated its nature, the nation subject to the imagery report will often make significant efforts to obfuscate or move the system that was revealed and described in the article. But in an effort to publish, and keep publishing, many journalists are happy to get the "scoop" even if it means the nation will take measures to conceal it once the report is published.

In 2013, North Korea resumed operations at its only working nuclear reactor as a means to expend fuel from uranium rods, which yields weapons-grade plutonium.[6] When this particular nuclear reactor was *critical* and operating, it used upstream-incoming cold water from the nearby Yalu River to cool the reactor's core. This fresh water became hot from absorbing the reactor core's heat and was expressed into a downstream "basin" at the Yalu River, as part of a continual water-cooling process at this facility. Visually, this presented as a flow of water emanating from the cooling system pipe connecting the reactor to the river. Every time this gust of "effluent"—which looked like a tiny white, diaphanous shape—was visible, one could confidently estimate the reactor was operating and producing plutonium.

Many articles on this effluent, and a few other key visual signatures associated with that reactor, were published by dozens of journalists picked up by hundreds of media outlets, especially those in East Asia, the United States, and Europe. Within months of the first onslaught of satellite images of this reactor in operation, North Korea buried the cooling system pipe to obfuscate that effluent. When analysts found another visual signature that confirmed water was emanating into the river, North Korea mounted a campaign to re-engineer the cooling system, further precluding an analysts' ability to assess whether North Korea was producing weapons-grade plutonium.

Another example involves the use of a relatively new type of open source satellite imagery. *Multispectral* or *hyperspectral* imagery has long been collected from cameras and aircraft sensors to determine very granular features of the earth's surface associated with its color. Unique spectral "signatures" are embedded within each pixel of this special imagery that can reveal anything from crop type to mineral content of the soil. New satellites like those launched by the Spanish-Argentinian company *Satellogic* collect this high-quality, spectrally detailed imagery from space. Recent studies by the Center for Nonproliferation Studies and the Center for International Security and Cooperation have used multispectral imagery to identify the spectral signatures associated with possible locations of uranium mines in North Korea.[7] As both institutions have successfully published these articles, they have potentially *shown* North Korea the areas within its borders where uranium is likeliest to exist. North Korea has one known uranium

---

[6] D. Sanger, "North Korea Appears to Restart Plutonium Reactor," *New York Times*, September 11, 2013, https://www.nytimes.com/2013/09/12/world/asia/north-korea-appears-to-restart-plutonium-reactor.html (accessed March 25, 2023).

[7] S. Park & F. Derby, "New Study Seeks Evidence of Uranium Mining Activity in North Korea," *Jane's Intelligence Review*, September 4, 2019, https://www.janes.com/ (accessed March 30, 2023).

mine, but these articles may have provided the nation with several dozen more potential mines by using cutting-edge imaging technology and applied analytics.

VIII. Publishing Imagery over Active Military Operations

The United States dominated the high-resolution satellite image commercial market until 2012. All imagery analysts were subject to the rules of the satellite data provider, which were in part supervised by the US Department of Commerce. Both American satellite companies, GeoEye and DigitalGlobe, broadly required end users of their data may not publish imagery analysis of US or NATO-aligned military operations underway. When Airbus began to provide high-resolution satellite data, they largely followed this rule as well. In several instances, I've seen satellite imagery of NATO or NATO-affiliated forces that set up an operational forward-deployed facility in other nations during wartime or peacekeeping mission efforts. The imagery over these facilities revealed details of the security associated with these military bases, and the areas of vulnerabilities in the security perimeters of the sites. In each case, I have personally declined to report on or publish this imagery and analysis in accordance with the guidance of the satellite data providers. Today, however, small-sat imagery constellations in the United States and many other countries are vastly increasing the amount of imagery collected. As regulations are diminishing, many other nations are emerging and selling satellite imagery. There is still a significant lack of reporting over American or NATO military events and activity because most of the current commercial imagery analysts concentrate solely on the nations of North Korea, Iran, Syria, Russia, and China, with an emerging increase of concentration in Ukraine. But it is wholly possible to commercially procure imagery over military facilities from any point on earth, and increasing numbers of imagery journalists will likely yield an increasing focus on American and NATO military operations.

IX. Right to Privacy

Currently, commercial satellites collect high-resolution imagery equating to a clarity of 100 centimeters of ground space per pixel to a much clearer 30 centimeters of actual ground space contained within each pixel of the image. Commercial imaging companies are developing new methods to collect even higher-resolution imagery from space, with either space-based or "stratollite" (stratospheric balloons that can be posted in an unregulated region of airspace above the jurisdiction of the International Civil Aviation Organization) platform, that can collect an exquisite-level resolution at about 15 centimeters per pixel. With some context clues, this resolution would be clear enough to recognize and identify individual people. What was once used to determine if a nation has nuclear weapons can now be used to viably find and track an individual, whether that be a terrorist or an ex-wife.

Nations like Germany are already considering regulating the collection of ultra-high resolution satellite image collections as a breach of any national or international conventions on the right to privacy. But other entities, namely, the American tech industry, are inclined to develop this technology as a means of enhancing common applications to help an individual determine whether they left the light on at their house, or how busy their nearest outdoor café is. In the race toward space technology, ethical implications are often overlooked for the sake of both commerce and a determination to advance privatized space operations.

X. Israel's Curtailment of Commercial Satellite Imaging within Its Borders

In 1997, the US Congress passed the Kyl-Bingaman Amendment that prohibited US-based satellite companies from collecting and disseminating high-resolution imagery over Israel. This was passed *before* there was such a company with an operational high-resolution commercial satellite. This amendment was in effect until 2021, when it was dissolved. During that twenty-four years, American satellite companies that collected high-resolution imagery over Israel were unable to view or process their own imagery until it was "sanitized" to a much lower resolution. Legally, lower-resolution imagery significantly impeded open source analysis during this time over nuclear and military activity within the boundaries of this nation. As a result, there were fewer articles in the open source community pertaining to Israeli activity even during globally critical events including the 2008–2009 war in Gaza or the commencement of the construction of a second nuclear reactor at Negev.

Israel lobbied for the Kyl-Bingaman Amendment in the United States in part because the United States was on the precipice of allowing the commercial launch and operation of satellites that could view details of sensitive facilities from space, under the ostensible justification of enhancing Israel's own regional security. Historically, Israel has been reticent about disclosing the nature, details, and very existence of its own nuclear program, including its Negev nuclear reactor. But after the Kyl-Bingaman Amendment was dissolved in 2021, Israel became the final nation on earth to become "fair game" for commercial high-resolution satellite image targeting.

Excluding Israel, high-resolution commercial satellite imaging has remained almost wholly unobstructed since its existence. Most nations, explicitly the United States, prefer to practice obfuscation of sensitive strategic and military facilities through conventional means of concealment, which includes simply hiding activities in buildings, underground, or undercover. Israel's conspicuous insistence on preventing satellite image collection within its borders illustrates an overarching desire to prevent satellites from imaging their territory. This compels some important ethical questions about satellite imaging in general: Should a nation have the right to their national privacy, or the privacy of its companies and citizens? Can other countries successfully lobby the United States to bar satellite image collection over their territories? Is information about nuclear weapons capability—an issue that affects everyone—a public right, and therefore more important than a nation's right to privacy?

XI. Conclusion

Satellite imagery is quickly becoming an established, critical component of journalism. Those who ascribe to the notion that information is a public right must thereby support the judicious use of the decades-old tradecraft of satellite imagery interpretation, a lifeblood for intelligence agencies sophisticated enough to develop, launch, and operate imaging satellites. But these emerging data sets and the means to analyze them, juxtaposed directly against a veritable sea change in how news media is presented or consumed, make for a hazardous environment for open source researchers and journalists and the audience they serve.

PART II

GOVERNMENT PUSHBACK AND GOVERNMENTAL DUTIES TO JOURNALISTS AND NEWS ORGANIZATIONS

6
The Government Pushes Back: Prosecuting Julian Assange in the War against Leaks—Trend or Aberration?

George W. Croner

I. The Assange Indictment and the Media Reaction

On May 23, 2019, a grand jury in the Eastern District of Virginia handed down a superseding indictment in Criminal No. 1:18-cr-111 (CMH),[1] better known as *U.S. v. Julian Paul Assange*, that vastly expanded the charges against Julian Assange to include multiple violations of the US espionage statutes.[2] Given Assange's conduct and avowed purpose of exposing US national security information, the idea of charging him with espionage may not seem all that remarkable. But the amended indictment's description of Assange's inculpatory conduct reverberated throughout the Fourth Estate since, in many respects, the conduct alleged closely resembles what mainstream US news publications do to solicit, receive, and publish US classified information.

The similarities struck too close to home for many journalists. Twitter was afire with adverse commentary from journalists, politicians, and activists. The American Civil Liberties Union noted, "For the first time in the history of our country, the government has brought criminal charges against a publisher

---

[1] The May 2019 *Assange* superseding indictment can be found at https://www.justice.gov/opa/press-release/file/1165556/download (accessed June 14, 2023). The government superseded the *Assange* indictment again in June 2020 adding, inter alia, allegations that Assange and WikiLeaks sought to entice other leakers by advertising their efforts to assist Edward Snowden in evading arrest. The June 2020 superseding indictment can be found at https://www.justice.gov/opa/pr/wikileaks-founder-charged-superseding-indictment (accessed June 14, 2023). References in this article to the "superseding indictment," "the indictment," or "the Assange indictment" refer to the content of the June 2020 superseding indictment.

[2] The superseding indictment charges Assange with violating multiple parts of 18 U.S.C. § 793 by disclosing national defense information. Generally speaking, and without quoting the statute at full length here, § 793 criminalizes a broad range of activities associated with the gathering, possession, or communication of information relating to the "national defense" (including activities that may bear little resemblance to "classic espionage") with intent or reason to believe the information could "be used to the injury of the United States or to the advantage of any foreign nation." Section 793 is included in Chapter 37 of Title 18, titled "Espionage and Censorship."

George W. Croner, *The Government Pushes Back: Prosecuting Julian Assange in the War against Leaks—Trend or Aberration?* In: *National Security, Journalism, and Law in an Age of Information Warfare*. Edited by: Marc Ambinder, Jennifer R. Henrichsen, and Connie Rosati, Oxford University Press. © Oxford University Press 2024.
DOI: 10.1093/oso/9780197756621.003.0006

for the publication of truthful information."[3] Gabe Rottman at the Reporters Committee for Freedom of the Press declared that the Justice Department "now seeks to punish the pure act of publication of newsworthy government secrets under the nation's spying laws."[4] Former Alaska Senator Mike Gravel, a frequent apologist for Assange, called the indictment "a disgrace" and, on Twitter, insisted that Assange be pardoned. Not surprisingly, the notorious leaker Edward Snowden also weighed in. Snowden, whose journalistic bandwidth generally is limited to the character limits imposed by Twitter and who has never been confused with Joseph Pulitzer, breathlessly announced that the Justice Department "just declared war—not on Wikileaks, but on journalism itself. This case will decide the future of media."[5]

The June 2020 superseding indictment, and subsequent US efforts in 2021 and 2022 to have Assange extradited from the United Kingdom to stand trial in the United States, drew similar condemnation from media advocates who insist that perpetuating the Assange prosecution represents a continuation of the hostility of the Donald Trump administration to a free press.[6]

Affording such respect as may be due to these opinions and countless others expressing similar levels of consternation, the end of the Republic is not at hand. Although, for journalists who have increasingly solicited, received, and published classified information with veritable impunity for decades, the indictment may signal that the government no longer considers the media immune from the consequences that the espionage statutes, at least on their face, contemplate for such conduct.[7] Still, if the *Assange* indictment truly signals a new response by the government to the publication of classified national security

---

[3] Brian Barrett, "The Latest Julian Assange Indictment is an Assault on Press Freedom," *wired.com*, May 23, 2019, https://www.wired.com/story/julian-assange-espionage-act-threaten-press-freedom/ (accessed June 14, 2023).

[4] Gabe Rottman, "The Assange Indictment Seeks to Punish Pure Publication," *Lawfare*, May 24, 2019, http://www.lawfareblog.com/assange-indictment-seeks-punish-pure-publication (accessed June 14, 2023).

[5] Edward Snowden (@snowden (May 23, 2019), "The Department of Justice Just Declared War--Not on Wikileaks, But on Journalism Itself," *Twitter*, https://twitter.com/Snowden/status/1131657973745496066?s=17 (accessed May 23, 2019).

[6] *See*, e.g., Jameel Jaffer, "The Biden Administration Should Drop the Assange Case," *Just Security*, February 8, 2021, https://www.justsecurity.org/74614/the-biden-administration-should-drop-the-assange-case/ (accessed June 14, 2023).

[7] One example of the media's disclosure of classified national security information that seriously compromised critical intelligence gathering is the story of initial NSA efforts to monitor the communications of Osama Bin-Laden. Following the bombings of the US embassies in Kenya and Tanzania in 1998, Bin-Laden became NSA's priority intelligence target and the agency was successful in monitoring his satellite telephone communications until that information was gratuitously disclosed in an August 21, 1998, article by Martin Sieff published in the *Washington Times*. The 9/11 Commission identified the Sieff article as alerting Bin-Laden to the monitoring of his satellite telephone calls and Bin-Laden promptly ceased his use of the phone depriving NSA of its best source of information regarding Bin-Laden's intentions. *See* National Commission on Terrorist Attacks Upon the United States, *The 9/11 Commission Report: Final Report of the National Commission on Terrorist Attacks Upon the United States* (W.W. Norton, 2004), 127.

information, the change might represent the beginning of a seismic shift in its approach and, given the relatively parsimonious jurisprudence on the subject, predicting the reaction of the courts (and one court, in particular) to such an approach is, at best, educated guesswork.

The fact of the matter is that the US government leaks like a sieve. Administrations come and go, and every one of them bemoans the persistent flow of classified information to the media from unauthorized, anonymous sources. Intelligence professionals decry the consequences. And yet, the laws that arguably can be employed to stem the leaks are almost never enforced. The stark contrast between the persistent handwringing about unauthorized disclosures in the abstract and the condoning of those leaks in practice have been defining features of executive policy for the better part of the past fifty years. The principal question raised by the *Assange* indictment is whether this enforcement action represents an isolated response to an ignominious "leaker" whose conduct, while reflecting certain significant similarities to that of mainstream national security journalists, also differs in sufficiently material respects so that the government's treatment of Assange may not signal a broader initiative to pursue prosecutions of the conventional media for unauthorized disclosures.

I shall undertake here to examine the Assange superseding indictment from the standpoint of what it may portend with respect to the government's potential response to future unauthorized disclosures of classified national security information. This chapter will examine the scope of the leak problem, the history of the government's reaction (or lack thereof) to that problem, the actions, both in terms of governmental policy and journalistic approach, that have led to the current posture regarding the publication of classified information, and what, if anything, the superseding *Assange* indictment suggests by way of prospective government response to the unauthorized disclosure of classified national security information.

II. Impediments to Enforcement Efforts against Leaks

The scope of the leak problem is undeniable, and it has existed for years.[8] Legislators demand that laws be enforced because, they insist, "the unauthorized

---

[8] "Leaks are a 'routine daily occurrence' for the government," Report of the Interdepartmental Group on Unauthorized Disclosures of Classified Information (March 31, 1982), reprinted in Presidential Directive on the Use of Polygraphs and Prepublication Review: Hearings Before the Subcomm. on Civil and Constitutional Rights of the H. Comm. on the Judiciary, 98th Cong. 166, 169 (1985) (hereinafter the *Willard Report*). Nothing about the *Willard Report's* characterization of the problem has changed in the ensuing thirty-seven years. *See, e.g.,* Disclosures of National Security Information and Impact on Military Operations: Hearing Before the H. Comm. on Armed Services, 112th Cong. (2012); National Security Leaks and the Law: Hearing Before the Subcomm. on Crime,

release of classified information is a crime—it is a crime because it threatens our national security and puts the lives of those who are sworn to defend our Nation in jeopardy. Everyone agrees [this] is criminal conduct."[9] And, yet, the number of criminal prosecutions has been minuscule. Moreover, despite the introduction of numerous bills over the years, no single piece of congressional legislation unequivocally banning the unauthorized disclosure of classified information has ever been enacted into law.[10] By any accepted counting methodology, the federal government has brought no more than a dozen leak prosecutions in the century since the Espionage Act was enacted, and never once in the past half century has the government proceeded against a member of the media for publishing or possessing leaked information.[11]

But this paucity of enforcement effort cannot be attributed entirely, or even principally, to the shadow cast by the First Amendment. The reality is that the timidity in combating leaks historically exhibited by the executive branch, which

---

Terrorism, and Homeland Sec. of the H. Comm. on the Judiciary, 112th Cong. (2012) (addressing impact of unauthorized disclosures on defense and national security).

[9] Steven Aftergood, "Not All Leaks of Classified Information Violate the Law," Federation of American Scientists, June 13, 2012 (quoting a statement by Senator John Cornyn), https://fas.org/publication/not_all_leaks/ (accessed June 14, 2023). As Aftergood notes, despite the perception among at least some legislators that "the unauthorized release of classified information is a crime," no law categorically prohibits the release of classified information.

[10] As recently as 2017, a bill introduced in the House of Representatives sought to address this absence by providing for such prophylactic coverage. "Classified Information Protection Act of 2017," H.R. 3448, 115th Cong. (2017). The bill was in a congressional subcommittee when the 115th congressional session expired. Numerous other bills that would have criminalized leaks of classified information by government employees have similarly failed to become law, including H.R. 319, 104th Cong. § 2 (1995), H.R. 271, 103d Cong. § 2 (1993), H.R. 363, 102d Cong. § 2 (1991), H.R. 279, 101st Cong. § 2 (1989), and H.R. 3066, 100th Cong. (1987).

[11] See Jessica Lutkenhaus, "Note: Prosecuting Leakers the Easy Way: 18 U.S.C. § 641," 114 Columbia Law Review, 1167, 1168 n.6 (2014) ("The standard view is that President Obama's administration has prosecuted six cases (the addition of Edward Snowden makes seven), while all previous administrations combined have prosecuted three." Charlie Savage, "Nine Leak-Related Cases," New York Times, June 20, 2012, http://www.nytimes.com/2012/06/20/us/nine-leak-related-cases.html (accessed June 14, 2023) (on file with the Columbia Law Review). See also David Pozen, "The Leaky Leviathan: Why the Government Condemns and Condones Unlawful Disclosures of Information," 127 Harvard Law Review, 512, 534 & n.114 (2013) ("The common wisdom is that there have been eleven such cases, including Edward Snowden's and Donald Sachtleben's. Depending on how one counts and on some unknown facts, the correct figure may be double that . . . Only one Espionage Act case in recent memory has been brought against someone other than the initial source, and only a miniscule number of leak investigations appear to have yielded prosecutions for derivative offenses, such as perjury or destruction of evidence. Although it has contemplated doing so several times, the government has never once, over the past half century, proceeded against a member of the media for publishing or possessing leaked information."). More recently, the Washington Post reported that the Obama administration "brought eight prosecutions for media leaks—more than all previous administrations combined—and the Trump Administration has upped the ante, bringing seven prosecutions in the space of two years." Elizabeth Goitein, "The U.S. Says Julian Assange 'Is No Journalist.' Here's Why That Shouldn't Matter," Washington Post, May 25, 2019, https://www.washingtonpost.com/outlook/2019/05/25/us-says-julian-assange-is-no-journalist-heres-why-that-shouldnt-matter/ (accessed June 14, 2023).

is both the arbiter and repository of classified national security information, is attributable to a variety of factors that include institutional ambivalence, self-inflicted impediments, and genuine prosecutorial conundrums. The first of these is perhaps best encapsulated in the observation: "The ship of state is the only known vessel that leaks from the top."[12]

Leaks have become an accepted part of the political dynamic in Washington. From presidents to officials significantly lower on the government food chain, leakers seek to skew public debate in their favor by selectively disclosing intelligence that supports their favored policy positions.[13] Of course, from every leaker's perspective, such disclosures are salutary when made to advance the "correct" viewpoint and become unauthorized disclosures only when employed to promote contrary positions. As Lyn Nofziger famously commented, "I just want to leak my leaks, not your leaks."[14] No rational approach to the problem of unauthorized disclosures can lay this aspect of the problem at the feet of the media. Nor is it a problem of prosecutorial limitation; instead, it is a nuanced dynamic reflecting the confluence of executive action implemented through bureaucratic governance in the modern national security state. Absent more aggressive action to pursue and prosecute the sources of unauthorized disclosures, there is little genuine likelihood that this form of leaking will disappear, or abate, anytime soon. And although more aggressive pursuit of policy leakers would have a decided impact on those mainstream journalists who feast on such leaks, the unauthorized disclosure of classified national security information depicted in the *Assange* superseding indictment has nothing to do with this form of "semi-official" communication that seems to have become part of the permanent patois of Washington.

Policy-driven leaks aside, the magnitude of unauthorized disclosures is also a direct consequence of self-imposed government restrictions that handicap, and in many instances completely handcuff, any effort to combat the problem. Constraining its ability to investigate and prosecute leak cases, the Department of Justice (DOJ) has long-standing internal guidelines imposing special procedures on the issuance of subpoenas to journalists.[15] First announced in

---

[12] Attributed to an aide to President John F. Kennedy, the comment was made after Kennedy, in an attempt to pressure Robert McNamara into accepting the post of secretary of defense, leaked to the *Washington Post* that McNamara had been offered the job. *See* Robert Dallek, *An Unfinished Life: John F. Kennedy (1917–1963)* (Little, Brown & Co., 2003).

[13] These ostensibly policy-driven disclosures have been described as occurring in the gray area between authorized and unauthorized disclosures leading some to describe them as *pleaks* (combining an authorized "plant" of information with the unauthorized "leak"). Pozen, *supra* note 11, at 515.

[14] Tom Wicker, "In the Nation; Leak On, O Ship of State," *New York Times*, January 26, 1982.

[15] 28 C.F.R. § 50.10. In July 2021, Attorney General Merrick Garland issued a memorandum to all levels of the federal prosecutorial chain further clarifying DOJ policy on the "Use of Compulsory Process to Obtain Information From, or Records of, Members of the News Media." The restrictions in Garland's memorandum arguably impede the government's ability to pursue a prosecution under 18 U.S.C. § 798, which, unlike other statutes codified under the Espionage Laws, proscribes the act

August 1970, and then codified in 1973, the guidelines prohibit use of subpoenas, search warrants, and court orders except as a last resort and only with the express authorization of the attorney general because, according to the rules, when used with respect to "non-consenting members of the media," these customary enforcement tools represent "extraordinary measures, not standard investigative practices."[16]

Ostensibly justified as serving First Amendment values,[17] all evidence suggests that this policy substantially depresses the number of subpoenas issued, and the concomitant lack of access to journalists' records and testimony makes it substantially more difficult to identify and build cases against leakers.[18] This approach is especially incongruous with the DOJ's unflinching position in criminal cases that journalists have no constitutional or common law privilege to withhold confidential source information because the practical impact of the regulatory policy amounts to creation of a qualified reporter's privilege[19]—a privilege which the DOJ has adamantly and consistently opposed affording any federal statutory recognition. Whatever policy considerations might be offered to explain the institutional ambivalence reflected in these seemingly contradictory positions, the effect is to interpose a significant impediment to any genuine effort to combat unauthorized disclosures of classified information.

The DOJ's internal prosecutorial policies only serve to exacerbate these regulatory restrictions for intelligence community components (particularly the CIA and NSA) seeking to redress unauthorized disclosures of classified national security information. The structural framework for intelligence community reporting of those leaks to the DOJ is found in a 1995 memorandum of understanding (MOU),[20] and the reports generated pursuant to the procedures in that

---

of publishing classified information concerning the communication intelligence activities of the United States. *See* George Croner, "A Flaw in the Attorney General's Policy against Seizing Reporter's Records," *Just Security*, August 11, 2021, https://www.justsecurity.org/77726/a-flaw-in-the-attorney-generals-policy-against-seizing-reporters-records/ (accessed June 17, 2023).

[16] *Id.* at § 50.10(a)(3).
[17] The "Statement of Principles" to 28 C.F.R. § 50.10 opens with: "Because freedom of the press can be no broader than the freedom of members of the news media to investigate and report the news, the Department's policy is intended to provide protection to members of the news media from certain law enforcement tools, whether criminal or civil, that might unreasonably impair newsgathering activities." Having unilaterally tied one hand behind its back, the provision then states: "The policy is not intended to extend special protections to members of the news media who are subjects or targets of criminal investigations for conduct not based on, or within the scope of, newsgathering activities." *Id.*
[18] Pozen, *supra* note 11, at 538–39.
[19] *See* Adam Liptak, "The Hidden Federal Shield Law: On the Justice Department's Regulations Governing Subpoenas to the Press," *N.Y.U. Annual Survey of American Law*, 227 (1999), 236 (characterizing the guidelines as "a shadow federal shield law").
[20] *See* Memorandum of Understanding: Reporting of Information Concerning Federal Crimes, https://irp.fas.org/agency/doj/mou-crimes.pdf (accessed June 14, 2023).

MOU are known as "crimes reports."[21] No "crimes report" has ever resulted in a media prosecution,[22] not least because the initial step in any effort to pursue a media leak begins with the DOJ's infamous (at least in the intelligence community) "Media Leak Questionnaire,"[23] which lists eleven inquiries preliminary to consideration for prosecution including requiring of the reporting agency, inter alia, "will the information be made available for use in a prosecution, and if so, what is the name of the person competent to testify to its classification?" Thus, from the start, any prosecution of a media disclosure of classified national security information effectively requires that the reporting agency be prepared to fully compromise the source or method in question, and do so in a public proceeding. Little wonder that none of the 120 crimes reports filed with the DOJ in 2017, or the 88 filed in 2018, has led to the prosecution of any media entity for the unauthorized disclosure of classified national security information.[24]

III. The Role of the First Amendment

Contrary to the fervent arguments of those in the conventional media and their supporters, then, a variety of factors other than purely First Amendment considerations explains the anomaly between the government's expressed concerns about leaks and the absence of any enforcement action. Stated differently, the absence of enforcement actions against the press cannot be attributed entirely to perceived First Amendment protections. With the government having roused itself to address Assange's receipt and publication of classified national security information (however ephemeral this enforcement action may prove to be), the recognition that the First Amendment may not inoculate such conduct helps frame the true parameters of the *Assange* debate because, while the First Amendment assuredly provides a level of protection for what the press

---

[21] Steven Aftergood, "'Crimes Reports' and the Leak Referral Process," Federation of American Scientists, December 17, 2012.

[22] The term "crimes reports" may have received its greatest notoriety in an exchange occurring during the hearings on George Tenet's nomination to be Director of Central Intelligence. Commenting on the severity of the leaks problem, Tenet observed that the CIA "file[d] crimes reports every week." "Say again," said Senator Robert Kerry, apparently unfamiliar with the term, to which Tenet responded, "We file crimes reports with the Attorney General every week about leaks, and we're never successful in litigating one." Nomination of George Tenet to be Director of Central Intelligence, Hearing Before the Senate Select Committee on Intelligence, S. Hrg. 105–134 at 108 (May 6, 1997).

[23] Aftergood, *supra* note 21. A copy of the DOJ Media Leak Questionnaire is available at https://www.google.com/url?sa=t&rct=j&q=&esrc=s&source=web&cd=&ved=2ahUKEwibkbeZncT_AhU0EFkFHVkqAoQQFnoECBIQAQ&url=https%3A%2F%2Firp.fas.org%2Fagency%2Fdoj%2Fleak-questions.pdf&usg=AOvVaw3kOcQM7s3uqMpzcrQ2G1mP (accessed June 14, 2023).

[24] Letter dated March 29, 2019, from U.S. Department of Justice to Steven Aftergood, Federation of American Scientists, Re: FOIA/PA #19-106, reporting that the number of crimes reports in CY 2017 totaled 120, and the number of crimes reports in CY 2018 totaled in 88.

publishes, that First Amendment protection is not, and never has been, absolute. The recognition in every jurisdiction of, for example, defamation and invasion of privacy claims, and of time, place, and manner restrictions, where appropriate, confirms that there are circumstances where the First Amendment will not protect every form of publication.

This is especially so where national security matters are at issue. And although it is difficult to discern from some of the more heated commentary that followed the release of the amended *Assange* indictment, in truth, the debate the indictment raises is not about whether the First Amendment prevents the government from prosecuting "journalists" who violate the espionage laws (despite it having never done so). Rather, it is about how far the reach of the First Amendment may extend to protect those journalists who engage in conduct that is arguably criminal when performed by nonjournalists. Evaluating the impact of the *Assange* indictment in this context requires determining whether the government and, ultimately, the courts view Julian Assange as a journalist entitled to the full panoply of First Amendment protections afforded journalists and, if not, how his conduct materially differs from that of many national security journalists and mainstream publications such that the First Amendment tolerates the punishment of Assange but protects these more "conventional" journalists from government prosecution.

IV. Who Is a Journalist? And What Is Journalistic Conduct?

One senses that the government, having moved on Assange, is in no hurry to pick a broader fight. The Justice Department insists that "Julian Assange is no journalist,"[25] but those remonstrations have done little to ease the anxiety amongst many mainstream reporters. The problem, for them, is that nothing in the text of the First Amendment plausibly allows for drawing a constitutionally sustainable distinction between what Assange is charged with doing and the types of activities in which national security journalists routinely engage in their efforts to pry classified information from those with legitimate access. From the DOJ's perspective, for example, Assange may not be among those protected by the regulatory limitations found in the Code of Federal Regulations[26] that place limitations on the use of subpoenas and other investigative techniques against journalists engaged in "newsgathering" activities because, in the DOJ's view, Assange was not engaged in a "newsgathering" activity. But this is a relatively self-serving distinction that depends entirely on the definition of "newsgathering"—a term

---

[25] Goitein, *supra* note 11.
[26] *See* 28 C.F.R. § 50.10.

clearly absent from the First Amendment and susceptible to widely divergent definitions that, realistically, afford no objective protection sufficient to placate professional journalists.

Similarly, the DOJ also has expressed the view that Assange "is not charged simply because he is a publisher" or for "passively obtaining government information" but for publishing "a narrow set of classified documents in which Assange also published the names of innocent people who risked their safety" to help the United States.[27] These "assurances" may also be true, insofar as they describe the motivations behind the amending of the *Assange* indictment; but they, too, lack the constitutional substance necessary to create enduring protection for those journalists reporting for mainstream publications on national security matters. Consequently, it was no surprise that, while Assange is no acolyte of the Code of Ethics of the Society of Professional Journalists, that organization nonetheless quickly moved to condemn the government's expansion of the *Assange* indictment, observing that "[q]uestions about whether or not Assange was acting as a journalist became irrelevant once the Espionage Act was brought into play. WikiLeaks is clearly a publisher. If this dangerous precedent were applied more broadly, it could have a chilling effect on the publication of newsworthy classified information."[28]

Taken at face value, the organization's remarks suggest that the First Amendment forbids any form of punitive government action premised on the act of publishing classified national security information, regardless of how obtained—an absolutist view of the First Amendment that has never commanded a majority of the justices of the US Supreme Court.[29] According to the Society of Professional Journalists, the concern is with "the effects this [the *Assange* prosecution] could have on journalists seeking to publish lawfully obtained classified information in the public interest."[30] Yet, at least with respect to journalists, "lawfully obtained classified information" is a non sequitur; a transparently manufactured phrase with neither legal nor practical meaning other than as referring to one possessing both the requisite level of government security clearance and the "need to know" warranting access to a particular piece of classified information—a duality that no uncleared reporter can ever "lawfully" possess.

---

[27] Natasha Bertrand, "DoJ Accuses Assange of Violating Espionage Act," *Politico*, May 23, 2019.
[28] Society of Professional Journalists, News Release, May 24, 2019 (Contact: J. Alex Tarquinio, SPJ National President, 212-283-0843, atarquinio@spj.org, Jennifer Royer, SPJ Director of Communications and Marketing, 317-361-4134, jroyer@spj.org).
[29] While some Supreme Court justices (e.g., Hugo Black) over the years have embraced the idea of First Amendment absolutism, that position "has never commanded a majority of the Supreme Court." *U.S. v. Rosen*, 445 F. Supp. 2d 602, 638 (E.D. Va. 2006).
[30] Society of Professional Journalists, *supra* note 28.

All of this suggests that an analysis seeking to assess the *Assange* indictment in the context of the First Amendment is unlikely to be productive if predicated upon manufacturing strained distinctions between Assange's conduct and that engaged in by mainstream journalists. And it is precisely the difficulty of drawing principled, constitutionally based distinctions between Assange's actions and those often employed by mainstream reporters that helps explain why the concerns of those reporters are best encapsulated in the opening paragraph of the *Assange* indictment, which alleges: "To obtain information to release on the WikiLeaks website, ASSANGE encouraged sources to (i) circumvent legal safeguards on information; (ii) provide that protected information to WikiLeaks for public dissemination; and (iii) continue the pattern of illegally procuring and providing protected information to WikiLeaks for distribution to the public."

As many journalists in the mainstream media surely recognize, this is precisely what national security reporters and their publications often encourage government officials or contractors to do. Experienced journalists reporting on national security, intelligence, and defense-related matters will generally know, or strongly suspect, that the information they are pursuing or, put more accurately, that they are encouraging others with access to pursue, is classified. As Jack Goldsmith has described, the news organizations' encouragement of this almost clandestine pursuit of classified information "is underscored by the mechanisms they provide for sources to convey information securely and anonymously."[31] They also know that individuals who furnish them with such classified information are violating the law; hence, the extensive security precautions available for sources to transmit the information to the media. In much the same way as WikiLeaks did, these mainstream media outlets encourage sources to provide them with "protected information" (as the *Assange* indictment describes it) and to obtain that information in whatever manner it can be secured and transmitted, regardless of legality. In fact, given the laws and regulations that govern the handling of classified information in the US government, there is no approved means by which anyone handling such information who is not the classifying authority for that information is authorized to release such information to a third party, including the media.[32] Otherwise, there would have been no reason for Snowden, for example, to have relied on the deceit and subterfuge in

---

[31] Jack Goldsmith, "The U.S. Media is in the Crosshairs of the New Assange Indictment," *Lawfare*, May 24, 2019. As Goldsmith describes: "The New York Times's menu includes SecureDrop, an 'encrypted submission system set up by The Times [that] uses the Tor anonymity software to protect [the] identity, location and the information' of the person who sends it." The Washington Post has reported that journalists "wisely use encryption applications such as Signal to converse with, and receive information from, sources." Margaret Sullivan, "Traditional Journalists May Abandon WikiLeaks' Assange at Their Own Peril," *Washington Post*, April 11, 2019.

[32] Executive Order 13526, which establishes the current classification standards in the executive branch, provides that information is only classifiable if "its unauthorized disclosure could reasonably be expected to cause identifiable or describable damage to the national security."

which he engaged to steal, and then disclose, some of the nation's most sensitive secrets. As noted earlier, the notion that, for the press, there is "lawfully obtained classified information" is an oxymoron.

V. The Journalistic Challenge to Classification and Restricted Disclosure

Another facet of the *Assange* indictment that resonates uncomfortably with reporters is the government's emphasis on the WikiLeaks website's acknowledgment that "WikiLeaks accepts classified, censored, or otherwise restricted material of political, diplomatic, or ethical significance." These "standards" for acceptance are strikingly similar to those that publishers and editors of mainstream publications would apply in making their own decision regarding the publication of classified information. As former *Washington Post* editor Leonard Downie once acknowledged, "'Highly classified' doesn't mean anything to me ... The question is, is it important for the American public to know that its government is acting in its name in this particular way?"[33] Indeed, the view is almost talismanic to any American journalist that the responsibility of a reporter is to publish information of interest to the public—even where that includes publishing government secrets.[34]

This attitude has produced a dramatic change in journalistic norms over the past few decades, with mainstream media entities far more willing to publish national security secrets now that would not have been reported in the past. In an article addressing the May 2019 *Assange* superseding indictment, Goldsmith identifies eight reasons why those norms have changed, how those norms have changed, and why journalists are more willing to publish more, and more types of, classified national security information.

1. Journalists perceive a special duty to make public how the endless, unprecedentedly secretive, and sometimes morally ambiguous post-9/11 wars are being waged.
2. Journalists have grown increasingly cynical about the government's claimed need for secrecy.[35]

---

[33] Goldsmith, *supra* note 31.
[34] *Id.* Goldsmith ascribes this view to a former executive editor of the *New York Times*.
[35] This cynicism has produced an unprecedented level of animosity and distrust which, in turn, has spawned a media ethos that "reporting on the secret acts of government officials or powerful financial actors—including by publishing documents taken without authorization—is at the core of investigative journalism." Glenn Greenwald, "As the Obama Administration Concluded, Prosecution of Julian Assange for Publishing Documents Poses Grave Threats to Press Freedom," *The Intercept*, November 16, 2018 (inducing those with access to steal government secrets readily fits with this ethos).

3. The secrecy bureaucracy has grown enormously—there are many more secrets than before.
4. These secrets leak to journalists more readily than in the past because of the digitalization of classified information and because a vastly greater number of government officials with traditional incentives to leak have access to the information.[36]
5. The globalized growth of journalistic coverage of the US intelligence community (for example, *The Guardian, Der Spiegel, The Intercept*) means more extensive coverage and publication of the intelligence community's global activities.
6. Competition from these foreign or cosmopolitan outlets makes it harder for US journalists to sit on stories out of deference to US national security claims.
7. The government has, despite all of the hemming and hawing about leak crackdowns, largely accepted these changes in norms, or at least has done remarkably little about the changes.
8. Journalists saw huge public interest benefits from the massive leaks by Chelsea Manning and Edward Snowden, and from the enormous growth in more discrete leaks. They also saw that they suffered remarkably few legal consequences as a result.[37]

I find little with which to disagree in Goldsmith's analysis, but his last two points are, in my view, particularly relevant. Since Watergate, the end of the Vietnam War, and the 1970s congressional investigations of US intelligence activities, the media has grown increasingly aggressive in the face of decades of US government passivity regarding the protection of classified national security information. Couple this more aggressive reporting with increasing media suspicion about the legitimacy of government classification decisions and a skepticism that unauthorized disclosures genuinely produce discernible damage to

---

[36] It has been argued that the government's recourse is to pursue the original leaker of unauthorized disclosures; i.e., the government employee who provides the information to the journalist. But, of course, the press wants no part of any effort to unmask a reporter's source and routinely relies on the First Amendment to also justify a refusal to disclose the identity of sources—even in the face of the exceedingly rare issuance of a compulsory subpoena. As discussed earlier, the government has unilaterally handicapped itself in the effort to unmask those who actually leak by restricting the use of conventional investigative techniques (e.g., subpoenas and search warrants) where those techniques "might unreasonably impair news gathering activities." 28 C.F.R. § 50.10(a). Indeed, for years there have been calls from mainstream media entities for a federal "shield" law, similar to those found in many states, that would assure journalists that they will never have to reveal the identity of a source. While no such effort has ever made it out of Congress and those efforts are persistently resisted by the Justice Department, the DOJ's regulatory restrictions on the use of customary investigative tools in pursuing leaks essentially has produced a de facto shield law. *See, e.g.*, Liptak, *supra* note 19, at 227, 236 (characterizing the guidelines as "a shadow federal shield law").

[37] Goldsmith, *supra* note 31.

the national security (a skepticism fed, if not spawned, by the absence of any apparent military or foreign policy damage from the disclosure of the *Pentagon Papers*) and the combination has produced the seductive illusion that secrecy is largely employed by government solely to further activities that are inimical to democracy and that, if exposed, would be rejected by the polity that the government is intended to serve.

A few years ago, a former counsel of the *New York Times*, David McGraw, essentially acknowledged that the *Times*' hesitancy about publishing national security secrets had been lowered in the wake of the Snowden experience which convinced its legal counsel "that there is no legal consequence from publishing leaks" of classified information.[38] Combining Goldsmith's cogent synopsis of the factors encouraging the publication of classified national security information with the historically flaccid response of the government to these unauthorized disclosures and it is easy to understand the boldness with which the mainstream media now views the publication of classified information that may have been acquired in ways that do not significantly differ from the manner in which Assange secured the information that he then published to the world via WikiLeaks.

VI. Liability for Publishing Classified National Security Information

Whether or not media organizations have much concern for any adverse consequences that might attend the publication of the nation's secrets, my prior experience at the National Security Agency (NSA) tells me that, in the intelligence community, the concern about the deleterious effects of unauthorized disclosures on intelligence activities has never abated.[39] For many years, those concerns have failed to outweigh the political and/or public relations concerns that invariably entered into the cost/benefit analysis of bringing a leak prosecution—concerns which find expression in the DOJ's regulatory restrictions on the use of investigative tools "that unreasonably impair newsgathering activities" and in the DOJ "Media Leak Questionnaire." As recently as 2013, for example, the Barack Obama administration reportedly rejected the idea of

---

[38] *Id.* quoting David McGraw speaking at a forum on "National Security and Transparency in This Administration and the Next," *Just Security*, November 2, 2016.

[39] My past personal experience, and current research, have been in the area of foreign intelligence electronic surveillance. To the extent I offer personal views on the damage and impact of unauthorized disclosures of classified national security information, those views are drawn from that experience and research relating to the activities, operations, sources, and methods related to foreign intelligence activities. In expressing those personal viewpoints, I exclude comment on classified military information (e.g., war plans and weapons systems) and diplomatic secrets, not because those areas are any less important to the national security but because I can competently offer no personal observations in those areas.

prosecuting Assange because of what has been reported as "The New York Times problem"—a shorthand description for the purported recognition that it was "impossible to prosecute Assange for publishing classified documents without also prosecuting *The New York Times, The Washington Post, The Guardian* and others for doing exactly the same thing."[40] This sort of political and public relations calculus has been employed repeatedly to squelch intelligence community appeals for more aggressive steps to stanch the leaking. All the while, the losses from leaks accumulate: some of those losses are permanent and irreversible; others can be recovered, though sometimes only partially, and only with the expenditure of substantial resources that could well be utilized elsewhere.

The revelations do not go unnoticed by foreign adversaries. A former Russian military intelligence officer once wrote: "I was amazed—and Moscow was very appreciative—at how many times I found very sensitive information in American newspapers. In my view, Americans tend to care more about scooping their competition than about national security, which made my job easier."[41]

This government lethargy, coupled with more people than ever having access to more classified information than ever in a digitized age, has created fertile ground for reporters searching for secrets. Combine these features with an emboldened new breed of journalist wedded to the concept that "it is legal and constitutional to publish secret documents even if the sources of those documents obtained them through illicit or even illegal means"[42] and you have a leak problem that has reached deluge proportions.

The original *Assange* indictment contained a single count alleging that Assange conspired with Chelsea Manning to crack the computer password affording Manning access to the secrets that were then transmitted to WikiLeaks.

---

[40] Greenwald, *supra* note 35.

[41] Stanislav Lunev, *Through the Eyes of the Enemy* (Washington, D.C.: Regnery Publishing, Inc. (1988). Prior to his defection to the United States in 1992, Lunev, a former Russian GRU intelligence officer, worked in the United States under journalistic cover, ostensibly as a correspondent for the Russian news organization TASS. Unauthorized disclosures have been plaguing US intelligence operations for over a half century. A small, but representative, sampling includes: A *New York Times* article in 1958 that enraged President Dwight Eisenhower by disclosing details of the US ability to monitor Soviet nuclear testing operations; a 1971 column in the *Washington Post* that revealed the United States was successfully intercepting telephone conversations from the limousines of Soviet Politburo members—a collection coup that abruptly stopped after the public disclosure in the *Post*; and a 1975 piece in the *Los Angeles Times* that disclosed the CIA's effort to recover a sunken Soviet submarine using the *Glomar Explorer*. As former Director of Central Intelligence William Colby later observed: "There was not a chance that we could send the *Glomar [Explorer]* out again on an intelligence project without risking the lives of our crew and inciting a major international incident... The *Glomar* project stopped because it was exposed." James Bruce, "The Consequences of Permissive Neglect," *Studies in Intelligence*, 47, no. 1 (2003), https://www.google.com/url?sa=i&rct=j&q=&esrc=s&source=web&cd=&ved=0CDgQw7AJahcKEwjoguWaocT_AhUAAAA AHQAAAAAQAw&url=https%3A%2F%2Fwww.cia.gov%2Fstatic%2FConsequences-Permissive-Neglect.pdf&psig=AOvVaw05tugDIvox8fNU9_MeACv3&ust=1686883589404839 (accessed June 14, 2023).

[42] *Id.*

That charge presented no First Amendment difficulty and was not perceived as doing so.

But the June 2020 superseding indictment adds seventeen counts under the espionage statute, 18 U.S.C. Section 793. Most of these counts focus on Assange's urging Manning to illegally disclose classified information to WikiLeaks. Manning unquestionably committed a crime by leaking the information in violation of the duty that Manning had voluntarily assumed when going to work handling confidential government data. As interpreted by the courts,[43] 18 U.S.C. Sections 793(d) and (e), which forbid the unauthorized disclosure of national defense information to "one not entitled to receive it," are not limited to classic espionage involving transfers to a foreign agent but apply to any situation where one having possession of national defense information (whether that possession is authorized (§ 793(d)) or unauthorized (§ 793(e)) then transfers that information to anyone not authorized to receive it. The government's theory is that Assange himself committed a separate crime by aiding, abetting, procuring, and willfully causing Manning's unlawful activities.

This is an entirely plausible theory since soliciting a specific crime by another is itself criminal, and unprotected by the First Amendment. As the US Supreme Court has declared, "Offers to engage in illegal transactions are categorically excluded from First Amendment protection,"[44] and this applies to the solicitation of illegal transactions like those charged in the indictment. Each of these counts alleging Assange's urging of Manning's theft of confidential government data essentially employs an "aiding and abetting" theory that is a perfectly acceptable basis for imposing criminal liability.[45] That said, Assange's activities as described in these counts have been acknowledged by many journalists commenting on the *Assange* indictment as representing the same or similar forms of conduct in which many a national security reporter has engaged in urging a source to leak particular documents or types of information containing national defense secrets. It is this seeming similarity to the activities of mainstream national security journalism that seems to have sent such a chill down the collective spines of national security reporters—and media advocates more generally.[46]

---

[43] *See, e.g., U.S. v. Morison*, 844 F.2d 1057, 1064–1067 (4th Cir. 1988), *cert. denied*, 488 U.S. 908 (1988) (explaining the distinction between 18 U.S.C. § 793, "intended to apply to disclosure of the secret defense material to *anyone* 'not entitled to receive it,'" and 18 U.S.C. § 794 that was "to apply narrowly to classic spying") (emphasis in original).

[44] *U.S. v. Williams*, 553 U.S. 285 (2009).

[45] When one "aids, abets, counsels, commands, induces or procures [a crime]," the person engaging in that conduct is punishable as a principal. 18 U.S.C. § 2. Consequently, in the superseding *Assange* indictment, Assange is charged with thirteen counts of aiding and abetting liability based upon soliciting Chelsea Manning to obtain and disclose to WikiLeaks classified national security information in violation of 18 U.S.C. § 793(c), (d), and (e).

[46] As Professor Steve Vladeck has Tweeted: "The issue isn't whether Assange is a 'journalist'; this will be a major test case because the text of the _Espionage Act_ doesn't distinguish between what Assange allegedly did and what mainstream outlets sometimes do, even if the underlying facts/

There is legal support for the idea that reporters cannot be liable for publishing information that is illegally obtained if they have no role in the illegal acquisition (even if they know of the illegal gathering but were not involved).[47] The Supreme Court has said that "state action to punish the publication of truthful information seldom can satisfy constitutional standards," and that "if a newspaper lawfully obtains truthful information about a matter of public significance then state officials may not constitutionally punish publication of the information, absent a need ... of the highest order."[48] But it is those qualifying phrases, "lawfully obtains" and "absent a need ... of the highest order" on which the government seems to be relying to reject the otherwise general prohibition against punishing the act of publication where leaks of national defense information are involved. If so, the government appears to be pursuing what was left undecided in the *Pentagon Papers* case:[49] in addressing sanctions for a publication of truthful information, is there a meaningful distinction between prior restraint and a postpublication penal sanction? A plethora of Supreme Court precedent repeatedly holds that only a state interest "of the highest order" can be asserted to sustain penalizing the publication of truthful information. The *Assange* case may now provide the first meaningful opportunity to receive judicial review at the highest level regarding if, or when, national security concerns satisfy that "highest order" of state interest in punishing, after the fact, the publication of truthful national security information acquired unlawfully.

Espionage prosecutions are not immune from First Amendment scrutiny, but the First Amendment does not presumptively preclude employing the espionage laws where the press publishes unlawfully procured classified national security information. First Amendment scrutiny will surely be a principal feature of any such prosecution, but if the actions by which classified national security information is acquired and subsequently disclosed meet all of the elements

motives are radically different." Steve Vladeck @steve_vladeck, May 23, 2019, https://twitter.com/steve_vladeck/status/1131654501562224640?s=17 (accessed June 14, 2023).

[47] In *Bartnicki v. Vopper*, 532 U.S. 514 (2001), for example, a radio commentator played on the air and furnished to others the contents of an intercepted cell phone conversation, knowing that the call had been intercepted without the consent of the participants and that such activity violated both federal and Pennsylvania law. The Supreme Court concluded that the radio commentator could not be held liable for publication despite knowing that the contents of the call had been obtained illegally.

[48] *Smith v. Daily Mail Publishing Co.*, 443 U.S. 97 (1979); *Landmark Communications, Inc. v. Virginia*, 435 U. S. 829 (1978).

[49] *New York Times v. U.S.*, 403 U.S. 713 (1971). Never directly revisited by the Supreme Court, the per curiam opinion issued in the *Pentagon Papers* case rejected the government's request for an injunction restraining further publication of the classified study of the origins and history of the Vietnam War. However, the case also produced six concurring opinions and three dissents that, considered collectively, indicate that a majority of the Court at that time would have concluded that the First Amendment presented no obstacle to a postpublication prosecution of the newspapers (the *New York Times* and the *Washington Post*).

constituting the proscribed offense, the prevailing jurisprudence suggests that there is no constitutional impediment to Congress's right to protect the nation's security and penalize that conduct. While invoking national security does not free Congress from the restraints of the First Amendment, invoking the First Amendment does not provide journalists with "immunity for every possible use of language." *Frohwerk v. U.S.*, 249 U.S. 204, 206 (1919). "The societal value of speech must, on occasion, be subordinated to other values and considerations,"[50] or, as Justice Frankfurter aptly put it, "[t]he demands of free speech in a democratic society as well as the interest in national security are better served by a candid and informed weighing of the competing interests, within the confines of the judicial process, than by announcing dogmas too inflexible for the non-Euclidian problems to be solved."[51]

In other words, the collision of national security and First Amendment values are resolved by "an assessment of the competing societal interests"[52] at stake and proceeding to the "delicate and difficult task" of weighing those interests "to determine whether the resulting restriction on freedom can be tolerated."[53] In sum, Congress retains considerable latitude in reconciling the conflict between the basic values of free speech and security and, in the Solomonic pursuit of striking the "right" balance, judicial scrutiny of any government restriction on "the free flow of information and ideas essential to self-government" must recognize that the disclosure of certain information may be properly restricted in service of the nation's security because "no governmental interest is more compelling than the security of the Nation."[54] The right to free speech in pursuit of an informed citizenry must, on occasion, yield to the government's efforts to ensure "the environment of physical security which a functioning democracy requires."[55] Expressed directly, "Free speech is subject to prohibition of those abuses of expression which a civilized society may forbid."[56]

U.S. v. Rosen[57] is a relatively contemporaneous judicial decision affording some insight into the issues raised by the *Assange* indictment's application of 18 U.S.C. Section 793 to the unauthorized disclosure of classified information. In *Rosen*, the district court rejected a First Amendment challenge to the prosecution

---

[50] *Dennis v. U.S.*, 341 U.S. 494, 503 (1951).
[51] *Id.* at 524–25 (Frankfurter, J. concurring).
[52] *U.S. v. Morison*, 844 F.2d at 1082 (quoting *Saxbe v. Washington Post Co.*, 417 U.S. 843, 859–60 (1974) (Powell, J., dissenting)).
[53] *U.S. v. Robel*, 389 U.S. 258, 264 (1967).
[54] *Haig v. Agee*, 453 U.S. 280, 307 (1981).
[55] *U.S. v. Morison*, 844 F.2d at 1082 (Wilkinson concurring).
[56] *Dennis v. U.S.*, 341 U.S. at 523 (Frankfurter, J. concurring).
[57] *U.S. v. Rosen*, 445 F. Supp. 2d 602 (E.D. Va. 2006). The judge in Rosen (Thomas Ellis) shared the view that an interpolation of the opinions produced in the *Pentagon Papers* case supported the view that a majority of the justices did not view the First Amendment as precluding the postpublication prosecution of the newspapers. *Id.* at 638–39.

of two American Israel Public Affairs Committee (AIPAC) employees, who received illegally leaked information and then forwarded it to various journalists.

> [D]efendants here contend that the First Amendment bars Congress from punishing those persons, like defendants, without a special relationship to the government for the disclosure of [national defense information]. In essence, their position is that once a government secret has been leaked to the general public and the first line of defense thereby breached, the government has no recourse but to sit back and watch as the threat to the national security caused by the first disclosure multiplies with every subsequent disclosure. This position cannot be sustained. Although the question whether the government's interest in preserving its national defense secrets is sufficient to trump the First Amendment rights of those not in a position of trust with the government is a more difficult question, and although the authority addressing this issue is sparse, both common sense and the relevant precedent point persuasively to the conclusion that the government can punish those outside of the government for the unauthorized receipt and deliberate retransmission of information relating to the national defense.[58]

While the outcome in *Rosen* is informative, it is not necessarily a harbinger of judicial reaction to an effort to prosecute an acknowledged member of the press for the act of receiving, and then publishing, national security information unlawfully disclosed by another. The *Rosen* defendants were not journalists (although they provided information to journalists) and Section 793 does not specifically forbid, or mention, publishing.[59] Given that *Rosen* yielded no appellate decision on the substantive First Amendment questions, it is of limited precedential value. If Assange is ever extradited and the *Assange* case proceeds to trial, the outcome will almost certainly be pursued on appeal and produce a result far more likely to affect prosecutorial and media practices, especially if Assange is viewed by the courts as a legitimate avatar of the press entitled to the full protection of the First Amendment.

In truth, from the government's perspective, this uncertainty regarding the judicial response to an effort to wield Section 793 to punish the *publication* of national security information has undoubtedly contributed to the DOJ's historical reluctance to make any effort to do so. Given this institutional inertia, it requires

---

[58] *Id.* at 637.

[59] In his concurring opinion in the *Pentagon Papers* case, Justice Douglas noted that § 793 does not specifically forbid "publishing" while noting that, among the "eight sections in the chapter on espionage and censorship," three sections specifically mention "publish" as among the proscribed acts indicating that "it is apparent that Congress was capable of and did distinguish between 'publishing' and 'communication' in the various sections of the Espionage Act." *New York Times Co. v. U.S.*, 403 U.S. at 721 (Douglas, J. concurring).

no great speculative leap to conclude that the decision to finally pull the trigger and use Section 793 in a leak prosecution against someone other than the leaker rests in no small part on the DOJ's view that Assange's conduct can be readily distinguished from that employed by "traditional" journalists. The DOJ's insistence upon this distinction,[60] coupled with the sheer antipathy that Assange seems to inspire among both reporters and the public at large, suggests that prosecuting Assange may represent less of a long-term shift in government policy against unauthorized disclosures than the opportunity for the DOJ to take action against a bête noire of the intelligence community, while perhaps avoiding a direct First Amendment challenge to Section 793 carrying genuine gravitas.

Perhaps most ominously in the eyes of media advocates, counts 15 to 17 of the superseding *Assange* indictment appear to charge Assange with criminal conduct based simply on having published (in violation of 18 U.S.C. § 793(e)) material that he knew was improperly leaked and was related to the national defense within the meaning of the statute. To convict on these counts, a jury need not find that Assange was complicit in the initial leak and, according to critics, punishes the pure act of publication in violation of the First Amendment.[61] Regardless of how assiduously the DOJ seeks to differentiate Assange from mainstream national security reporters, it is difficult to plausibly distinguish what is described in counts 15 to 17 (i.e., that Assange "having unauthorized possession of documents relating to the national defense" [albeit without alleging that Assange engaged in any wrongdoing in connection with the initial misappropriation of those documents] communicated, delivered, or transmitted the contents of those documents "to persons not entitled to receive them") from the conduct that leads to the publication of classified national security information in the nation's leading newspapers on a recurring basis.

Whether and when the First Amendment permits the government to punish the sort of third-party, arm's-length publication of national defense information charged in counts 15 to 17 of *Assange*'s superseding indictment is a complicated question informed by relatively sparse judicial precedent. Over eighty years ago, in *Near v. Minnesota*,[62] the Supreme Court opined that "[n]o one would question but that a government might prevent actual obstruction to its recruiting service or the publication of the sailing dates of transports or the number and location of troops." Similarly, does anyone sincerely doubt that the First Amendment would

---

[60] At the press briefing announcing the superseding *Assange* indictment, Assistant Attorney General for National Security John Demers stressed: "Julian Assange is no journalist. This [*sic*] made plain by the totality of his conduct as alleged in the indictment—i.e., his conspiring with and assisting a security clearance holder to acquire classified information, and his publishing the names of human sources." Department of Justice Press Release, Remarks from the Briefing Announcing the Superseding Indictment of Julian Assange, May 23, 2019.

[61] *See, e.g.*, Rottman, *supra* note 4.

[62] *Near v. Minnesota*, 283 U.S. 697, 716 (1931).

have precluded a government effort to punish, and even restrain, publication of the secrets of the Manhattan Project, or the details of the D-Day invasion, during World War II? But, is that where the First Amendment draws the line on punishing publication of national security secrets—is it necessary that the nation be at war? These are the matters potentially at issue as the *Assange* case proceeds and, just as invoking national security does not foreclose a First Amendment analysis, neither does invoking the First Amendment provide limitless protection to speech or newsgathering activities—especially when those activities may amount to soliciting another to commit a crime.

Whether one agrees with the DOJ's characterization of him or not, Assange is certainly not the archetype of a conventional journalist and is rather poorly positioned to present some of the thornier constitutional arguments that will be raised to challenge the application of Section 793(e) to his conduct. Given some of what are arguably Assange's unique characteristics, the mainstream media is unlikely to accept any conviction as precedent that appropriately applies to their activities, regardless of the similarity between Assange's actions and their own. Similarly, from a legal standpoint, the conventional press will insist that Assange's conduct provides no basis for applying Section 793 to their own activities, because publishing is not included within the activity that is proscribed in the statute.

These considerations indicate that Section 793 may not be the best available provision of the espionage laws for prosecuting a newspaper or website for publishing classified national security information. In the absence of congressional action to directly address, through specific legislation, the problem of media publication of unauthorized disclosures, prosecution might better be pursued under another of the statutes included among the espionage laws where the challenged disclosure falls within its ambit.

Enacted virtually simultaneously with the last congressional amendment of Section 793, Section 798 of Title 18[63] makes it a crime to, inter alia, publish classified information concerning a variety of cryptographic activities, as well as any

---

[63] Subsection (a) of § 798 reads: "(a) Whoever knowingly and willfully communicates, furnishes, transmits, or otherwise makes available to an unauthorized person, **or publishes**, or uses in any manner prejudicial to the safety or interest of the United States or for the benefit of any foreign government to the detriment of the United States any classified information—
  (1) concerning the nature, preparation, or use of any code, cipher, or cryptographic system of the United States or any foreign government; or
  (2) concerning the design, construction, use, maintenance, or repair of any device, apparatus, or appliance used or prepared or planned for use by the United States or any foreign government for cryptographic or communication intelligence purposes; or
  (3) **concerning the communication intelligence activities of the United States or any foreign government; or**
  (4) **obtained by the processes of communication intelligence from the communications of any foreign government, knowing the same to have been obtained by such processes—**
Shall be fined under this title or imprisoned not more than ten years, or both." (emphasis added).

classified information "(3) concerning the communication intelligence[64] activities of the United States or any foreign government" and any classified information that is "(4) obtained by the processes of communication intelligence from the communications of any foreign government, knowing the same to have been obtained by such processes." As the congressional reports that accompanied its passage reflect, the specific narrow construction of Section 798 was designed to apply to "only a small category of classified matter, a category which is both vital and vulnerable to an almost unique degree."[65] Among the Espionage Laws, it is a scalpel, not a sledgehammer, and its careful circumscription has led commentators to remark that "compared to sections 793 and 794 it is a model of precise draftsmanship."[66] So well-crafted and limited were the proscriptive provisions of Section 798 that the bill not only passed the House without debate and the Senate with virtually none but was also supported by the American Society of Newspaper Editors.[67]

The limited reach of Section 798 is clear from its text: it applies solely to cryptographic and communication intelligence activities, which, as Congress acknowledged, represent two categories of classified matter vital and vulnerable to an almost unique degree. From a constitutional standpoint, Section 798's limited scope provides the more favorable basis for prosecuting media publication of classified information. Policy and public relations issues aside, the First Amendment should not present an impediment to a properly structured prosecution for publishing classified information concerning the communications intelligence activities of the United States.

Still, an unused scalpel affords no protection to even the most sensitive of government secrets, and no prosecution of a media entity has ever been pursued using Section 798. When the *New York Times* published the details of the Stellar Wind collection program in December 2005, the government did nothing and allowed the *Times*, in the words of executive editor Bill Keller, to "satisf[y] ourselves that we could write about this program . . . in a way that would not expose any intelligence-gathering methods or capabilities that [were] not already

---

[64] "Communication intelligence" is statutorily defined as "all procedures and methods used in the interception of communications and the obtaining of information from such communications by other than the intended recipients." Under Executive Order 12333, the NSA is responsible for all US communications intelligence activities.

[65] H.R. Rep. No. 81-1895 at 2 (1950); S. Rep. No. 81-111 at 2 (1949).

[66] Harold Edgar & Benno Schmidt Jr., "The Espionage Statutes and Publication of Defense Information," 73 *Columbia Law Review*, 929, 1065 (1973). As Edgar and Schmidt observe: "First, the statute and its history make evident that violation occurs on knowing engagement in the proscribed conduct, without any additional requirement that the violator be animated by anti-American or pro-foreign motives. Second, the use of the term 'publishes' makes clear that the prohibition is intended to bar public speech. Third, the inevitable vagueness in defining what cryptographic information is subject to restriction is substantially mitigated, although perhaps at the cost of overbreadth, by making classification an element of the offense." *Id.*

[67] *Id.* at 1069.

on the public record." Keller added that technical details of the program were withheld.[68]

Then, in the face of Snowden's theft of highly classified information and the subsequent publication of details of some of NSA's most sensitive collection programs in what former CIA deputy director Michael Morrell called the "most serious compromise of classified information in the history of the U.S. intelligence community,"[69] the government reacted by indicting Snowden, who remains in Russia under asylum, but took no action against any of the journalists or media entities responsible for publishing the fruits of Snowden's treachery. And make no mistake, without the assurance of media publication, Snowden and others like him have nowhere to go with their stolen secrets.

No provision in the US Constitution generally, and none in the First Amendment, appoints journalists as unelected ombudsmen for determining which national security secrets remain secret. In fact, only elected officials have the authority to designate information as secret and to dictate its handling. And one can have a healthy respect for the First Amendment and its protections consistently with supporting criminal sanctions against a journalist who violates the law regarding classified national security information. Given a journalistic ethos that "[h]ighly classified' doesn't mean anything to me," there are certain to be collisions between aggressive investigative reporting and the government's effort to protect classified national security information. Whatever weight one accords First Amendment interests in these collisions, the Constitution is no "suicide pact"[70] requiring perpetual government indolence as reporters, sometimes spurred by parochial and pecunious motivations, pursue exposure of the nation's most sensitive secrets.

Indeed, as I see it, the greater danger lies in effectively leaving the security of the nation's secrets in the hands of reporters who simply lack the experience, context, or depth of knowledge necessary to evaluate what their reporting exposes. Bill Keller of the *New York Times* may have felt comfortable that he could "write about [Stellar Wind] . . . in a way that would not expose any intelligence-gathering methods or capabilities"; but Keller was no more qualified to make that judgment than the Director of the NSA is to decide what content in the *Times* will maximize that newspaper's circulation and advertising

---

[68] Gabriel Schoenfeld, "Has The New York Times Violated the Espionage Act?," *Commentary Magazine*, March 2006, https://www.google.com/url?sa=t&rct=j&q=&esrc=s&source=web&cd=&ved=2ahUKEwitjLiPpMT_AhXFUjUKHb2-CccQFnoECA0QAQ&url=https%3A%2F%2Fwww.commentary.org%2Farticles%2Fgabriel-schoenfeld%2Fhas-the-new-york-times-violated-the-espionage-act%2F&usg=AOvVaw2kD6m0OBWIGn9N8tKOYkBb (accessed June 14, 2023).

[69] Janet Reitman, "Snowden and Greenwald: The Men Who Leaked the Secrets," *Rolling Stone*, December 4, 2013.

[70] *Aptheker v. Secretary of State*, 378 U.S. 500, 509 (1964).

revenue. Disclosures directly revealing sensitive intelligence operations create enough problems, but reporters often have little or no appreciation that what they print can contain sufficient detail to allow an American intelligence target, through use of its own proficient intelligence capabilities, to capitalize on the disclosure by either: (1) deducing the suspected source of the intelligence information published, (2) uncovering unique details of US intelligence tradecraft, or (3) ascertaining the level and capability of US exploitation sufficiently to neutralize that source. Even worse in many respects, capable adversaries may exploit the disclosure to facilitate the communication of future misleading disinformation. In the case of communications intelligence efforts by the NSA, for example, virtually every piece of classified information disclosed and then published without authorization may reveal both substantive intelligence product *and* critical data regarding the intelligence sources and methods by which the NSA acquired that substantive intelligence. The inclusion of such source-identifying detail is often either gratuitous or consciously employed to embellish the perceived journalistic credibility of the reporter or publication. To make matters worse, many stories containing leaked classified information are a tangle of accurate disclosure, partially accurate surmise, and completely inaccurate speculation. Yet, at least in terms of NSA and CIA foreign intelligence and FBI counterintelligence operations, the government can never address or ameliorate the effects of such misinformed or misguided reporting, since any correction, explanation, or rebuttal risks further compromising or degrading intelligence capabilities.

The media, often with no small level of sanctimony, justifies these disclosures as congruous with its self-appointed role as arbiter of the public's need to know and judge of what is or is not damaging to the national security, but the press exercises those claimed roles without any practical accountability—and power without accountability is a dangerously unbalanced combination.

VII. Conclusion

I frequently found myself at odds with the Trump administration's national security policies,[71] but my experience with the harms resulting from unauthorized disclosures of national security information convinces me that a more aggressive approach is needed to protect the country's secrets. If the seeds for

---

[71] *See*, e.g., George Croner, "Fact and Denial, Trump's Inexplicable Refutation of the U.S. Intelligence Community's Conclusion of Russian Election Interference," *FPRI E-Notes*, July 18, 2018, https://www.fpri.org/article/2018/07/fact-and-denial-trumps-inexplicable-refutation-of-the-u-s-intelligence-communitys-conclusion-of-russian-election-interference/ (accessed June 14, 2023).

such protection are sown in the decision to charge Assange under the espionage statutes, then perhaps, finally, the escalating cycle of debilitating, unauthorized disclosures can be slowed.

The *Assange* indictment certainly makes a point, but I suggest that the point made is that it is the media, not the government, that needs to recalibrate here. Pursuing Julian Assange may, or may not, be the best way to begin to stanch the hemorrhaging of classified national security information, but initiating the effort to do so is long overdue. For too long now, national security journalists have trolled the corridors of government agencies soliciting the indignantly underpaid, the ideologue, or the malcontent to pilfer secrets they are sworn to protect, publish those secrets, and then expect that the government will do another damage assessment, bear the costs of the unauthorized disclosure in both dollars and lost intelligence, and move on. The First Amendment does not afford carte blanche to engage in such conduct, and the overwrought reaction to the *Assange* indictment from mainstream media sources squirming from the uncomfortable proximity that their own conduct shares with Assange's reflects less that a constitutional line has been crossed and more that government torpidity has finally given way to action.

Whether indicting Julian Assange represents a first step in that necessary recalibration of the government/press relationship in the area of unauthorized disclosures of classified national security information remains to be seen; but, if not, the government has itself, not the First Amendment, to blame. An official reassessment of the self-imposed DOJ restrictions that hamper the investigation of unauthorized disclosures is ultimately necessary. And if the government finally intends to get serious about leaks, it should judiciously employ 18 U.S.C. Section 798 the next time a newspaper publishes classified information about the cryptographic or communications intelligence activities of the United States.

These observations should not oversimplify the potential difficulties (legal, policy, and public relations) that would attend any effort to criminally prosecute the press for publication of information protected by Section 798, and examining those difficulties in detail is beyond the scope of this chapter. Perhaps the courts will prove inhospitable to efforts to use the Espionage Laws against the press for the publication of unauthorized disclosures, in which case the need for new, more tailored legislation can be evaluated. In certain circumstances, the extraordinary sensitivity of classified cryptographic or communications intelligence information will foreclose its use in a public legal proceeding; although, the Classified Information Procedures Act is specifically designed to ameliorate those problems and, if it proves unsuitable to that purpose, legislative amendment may be warranted. Should the available statutory tools remain unemployed against unauthorized disclosures, however, the reality is that the government has effectively abdicated its responsibility to secure classified information. Still worse, without mounting even the semblance of an effort to ascertain the effectiveness of currently available statutory provisions in preventing the damaging publication of national security secrets, the losses attributable to such disclosures—in both dollars and intelligence capabilities—will continue unabated.

7
Watchdogs in the Digital Age: Digital Surveillance, Information Security, and the Evolution of Journalist-Confidential Source Relationships

Deborah L. Dwyer

I. Introduction

What would American democracy look like today if Deep Throat had been too afraid to help the press expose former President Richard Nixon's crimes against the American public?

A different outcome for the Watergate scandal in modern times is conceivable, especially if the potential source was aware of current and emerging surveillance technologies. Bob Woodward and Carl Bernstein's typewriters are the laptops and e-tablets of today, capturing a staggering amount of information about an individual's web search history, emails, texts, chat communications, online financial transactions, and more. The rotary phone's modern replacement, as well as text communications, "ping" off cell phone towers that can approximate the user's physical location. Even if electronic communication is avoided, meeting in person is riskier than before: public security cameras have proliferated, satellite technology monitors the on-road guidance systems (such as OnStar) in cars, and smart watches and fitness trackers collect data on each step millions of individuals take each day. Additional data systems related to workplace security, transit systems, and street cameras track the actions of individuals, adding complexity to the landscape of potential opportunities for information about journalists and their sources to be obtained unknowingly.

Government surveillance was thrust into public consciousness in 2013 when *The Guardian* reported on the National Security Agency's (NSA's) pressuring telecommunications giant Verizon to turn over data on millions of Americans' phone records.[1]

---

[1] Glenn Greenwald, "NSA Collecting Phone Records of Millions of Verizon Customers Daily," *The Guardian*, June 5, 2013, https://www.theguardian.com/world/2013/jun/06/nsa-phone-records-verizon-court-order (accessed April 8, 2018).

Deborah L. Dwyer, *Watchdogs in the Digital Age: Digital Surveillance, Information Security, and the Evolution of Journalist-Confidential Source Relationships* In: *National Security, Journalism, and Law in an Age of Information Warfare*. Edited by: Marc Ambinder, Jennifer R. Henrichsen, and Connie Rosati, Oxford University Press. © Oxford University Press 2024. DOI: 10.1093/oso/9780197756621.003.0007

A subsequent *Washington Post* article revealed the NSA's PRISM surveillance initiative had obtained private citizens' data from a variety of companies,[2] and a few days later, former NSA employee and whistle-blower Edward Snowden provided more details about the agency's widespread surveillance.[3] This began a more than year-long public dialogue among the media, government agencies, private corporations, national intelligence experts, and privacy advocates about the tenuous balance between privacy and national security, as well as the positive change—and significant damage—those who leak information to the press can do.[4] Arguments regarding the appropriate balance between national security and surveillance is one fraught with sound points on both sides; those responsible for national defense argue that "privacy is historically a nation-based privilege" and takes a back seat to protecting citizens, while opponents maintain that "privacy is an essential ingredient in a democracy, as privacy acts to safeguard political pluralism and serves as fuel for dissent and a check on power."[5] Passionate debates regarding journalism's role in society, protecting a source's privacy, and the media's basic need to rely on confidential sources to perform its watchdog function were prominent in public discourse.

Interestingly, however, journalists—and their organizations as a whole—have demonstrated lukewarm efforts to protect the information that flows through their digital systems and mobile devices.[6] This lackluster response is particularly perplexing in the wake of numerous documented instances of state-led cybersecurity breaches—just a few of which targeted major news organizations, including the *New York Times*, *Wall Street Journal*, and *Washington Post*,[7] and

---

[2] Barton Gellman & Laura Poitras, "U.S., British Intelligence Mining Data from Nine U.S. Internet Companies in Broad Secret Program," *Washington Post*, June 7, 2013, https://www.washingtonpost.com/investigations/us-intelligence-mining-data-from-nine-us-internet-companies-in-broad-secret-program/2013/06/06/3a0c0da8-cebf-11e2-8845-d970ccb04497_story.html?utm_term=.438793e75106 (accessed April 4, 2018).

[3] Glenn Greenwald, Ewen MacAskill, & Laura Poitras, "Edward Snowden: The Whistleblower behind the NSA Surveillance Revelations," *The Guardian*, June 11, 2013, https://www.theguardian.com/world/2013/jun/09/edward-snowden-nsa-whistleblower-surveillance (accessed April 8, 2018).

[4] Risto Kunelius et al. (eds.), *Journalism and the NSA Revelations: Privacy, Security and the Press*, Reuters Institute for the Study of Journalism (Bloomsbury Publishing, 2017).

[5] *Id.* at 3.

[6] Robert Mahoney, "Securing the Newsroom: CPJ, Journalists, and Technologists Commit," *Committee to Protect Journalists* (blog), June 25, 2015, https://cpj.org/blog/2015/06/securing-the-newsroom-cpj-journalists-and-technolo.php (accessed April 8, 2018); Jesse Holcomb & Amy Mitchell, "Investigative Journalists and Digital Security," Pew Research Center, February 5, 2015, https://www.journalism.org/2015/02/05/investigative-journalists-and-digital-security/ (accessed April 8, 2018).

[7] Nicole Perlroth, "Hackers in China Attacked the Times for Last 4 Months," *New York Times*, January 31, 2013, http://www.nytimes.com/2013/01/31/technology/chinese-hackers-infiltrate-new-york-times-computers.html (accessed April 8, 2018); Nicole Perlroth, "Washington Post Joins List of News Media Hacked by the Chinese," *New York Times*, February 2, 2013, http://www.nytimes.com/2013/02/02/technology/washington-posts-joins-list-of-media-hacked-by-the-chinese.html?_r=0 (accessed April 8, 2018).

the more recent targeting of journalists covering immigration on the US-Mexico border.[8] Even more perplexing are findings from a 2014 survey of 671 journalists that found two-thirds believed that the American government probably collected information from their electronic communications, and 80 percent believed being a journalist increased their chances of being surveilled.[9] Better equipping journalists and news organizations to defend themselves and their sources through strategic and consistent information security strategies may hold the power to reshape the dynamics between reporters and the sources often critical to investigative reporting, especially related to the actions of government.

A. Conceptualizing Surveillance

Conceptualizations of surveillance have evolved along with the technology that enables it. Maša Galič, Tjerk Timan, and Bert-Jaap Koops[10] identify three phases of theoretical development beginning with Michel Foucault's[11] architectural approach described as Panopticism, a social framework in which those being surveilled assist in their own monitoring for the benefit of those in power. With the rise of global mediatization and advanced technological capabilities, conceptions of surveillance have evolved to better reflect the convergence of multiple data-collection systems encountered in all aspects of modern life. The coalescence of multiple systems, or "surveillance assemblage,"[12] increases the information's collective capabilities and power via its networked infrastructure.[13]

The complexities inherent in networked infrastructures and digital information ecologies manifests itself in the language used to describe technological concepts as well. In particular, experts debate the distinctions and hierarchies among terms such as cybersecurity, data security, and information security.[14]

---

[8] Tom Jones, Mari Payton, & Bill Feather, "Source: Leaked Documents Show the U.S. Government Tracking Journalists and Immigration Advocates through a Secret Database," *NBC 7*, March 6, 2019, https://www.nbcsandiego.com/news/local/Source-Leaked-Documents-Show-the-US-Government-Tracking-Journalists-and-Advocates-Through-a-Secret-Database-506783231.html (accessed November 15, 2019); Linda Moon, "103 Organizations Demand Border Agencies End Surveillance, Targeting of Journalists," *Reporters Committee for Freedom of the Press*, May 1, 2019, https://www.rcfp.org/103-organizations-demand-border-agencies-end-surveillance-targeting-of-journalists/ (accessed November 15, 2019).
[9] Holcomb & Mitchell, *supra* note 6.
[10] Maša Galič, Tjerk Timan, & Bert-Jaap Koops, "Bentham, Deleuze and Beyond: An Overview of Surveillance Theories from the Panopticon to Participation," *Philosophy & Technology*, 30 (2017), 9–37.
[11] Michel Foucault, *Discipline and Punish: The Birth of the Prison* (S.L: Penguin Books, 1975).
[12] Kevin D. Haggerty & Richard V. Ericson, "The Surveillant Assemblage," *British Journal of Sociology*, 51, no. 4 (December 2000), 605–22, doi: 10.1080/00071310020015280.
[13] David Lyon, "The Search for Surveillance Theories," *Theorizing Surveillance* (2006), 3–20; Galič, Timan, & Koops, *supra* note 10.
[14] McDermott Will & Emery, "Trendy 'Cybersecurity' versus Traditional 'Information Security' Two Sides of the Same Security Coin," *JDSupra* (blog), April 24, 2014, https://www.jdsupra.com/

This chapter uses information security as an overarching concept, defined by the National Institute of Standards and Technology as "the protection of information and information systems from unauthorized access, use, disclosure, disruption, modification, or destruction in order to provide confidentiality, integrity, and availability." Therefore, information security encompasses online and offline information.[15]

Although this chapter focuses on surveillance of journalists and sources by government entities domestic and abroad, acknowledgment of the breadth and depth of security risks from all areas of society is warranted, including "analog" threats taking place offline. The necessary considerations are complex and ever emerging, making it difficult to identify them all. One breach might be perpetrated by an individual bad actor with an axe to grind; another might be orchestrated by a foreign government. Activist groups may also attack the media, as was the case when the Syrian Electronic Army hijacked the *Chicago Tribune* and CNBC.[16] This illustrates the point that that not all digital threats directed at journalists are directly from government officials or agencies. In cases tracked by the Committee to Protect Journalists,[17] many of the bad actors are "unconnected, 'patriotic' troublemakers who perceive opposition or foreign media as legitimate targets."[18]

While questions of surveillance and cybersecurity must broadly consider the actors, targets, goals, and tactics involved both at the individual and organizational levels,[19] this chapter narrows its focus to the manageable level of the changing nature of the journalist-confidential source relationship in response to threats of surveillance and cybersecurity breaches. Therefore,

---

legalnews/trendy-cybersecurity-versus-traditiona-45143/ (accessed April 8, 2018); Tim Ufer, "Cyber Security vs. Information Security—Is There a Difference?," *GW Cybersecurity Online* (blog), May 24, 2021, https://onlinecybersecurity.seas.gwu.edu/news/cyber-security-vs-information-security/ (accessed June 10, 2023); "Cyber Security versus Information Security," *NoVA Infosec* (blog), May 5, 2014, https://www.novainfosec.com/2014/05/05/cyber-security-versus-information-security/?doing_wp_cron=1572553665.7646379470825195312500 (accessed April 8, 2018).

[15] Information security, "National Institute of Standards and Technology's Computer Security Resource Center Glossary," https://csrc.nist.gov/glossary?index=I (accessed November 15, 2019).

[16] Joshua Barrie, "Syrian Hackers Are Attacking the World's Media," *Business Insider* (blog), November 27, 2014, https://www.businessinsider.com/the-independent-newspaper-and-cnbc-have-been-hacked-2014-11 (accessed April 8, 2018).

[17] "Technology Security: Understanding the Threat," Committee to Protect Journalists, https://cpj.org/reports/2012/04/technology-security.php#planning (accessed March 15, 2018).

[18] Reporters Committee for Freedom of the Press, "The Limits of Promising Confidentiality," *Digital Journalists Legal Guide* (blog), para. 17, https://sunshineweek.rcfp.org/browse-media-law-resources/digital-journalists-legal-guide/limits-promising-confidentiality-0 (accessed March 15, 2018).

[19] Susan E. McGregor, Franziska Roesner, & Kelly Caine, "Individual versus Organizational Computer Security and Privacy Concerns in Journalism," *Proceedings on Privacy Enhancing Technologies*, 2016, no. 4 (October 1, 2016), 418–35, https://doi.org/10.1515/popets-2016-0048 (accessed March 15, 2018).

information security here is focused on safeguarding personal data of journalists and protecting the identity and safety of confidential sources and whistle-blowers.

B. Government Surveillance and the News Media: A Growing Threat

Former US State Department security expert Stephen Jin-Woo Kim learned the hard way how collected data could be used against him when he was charged with espionage and ultimately imprisoned for speaking with Fox News reporter James Rosen about a classified report on North Korea. The Federal Bureau of Investigation (FBI) used simple metadata from Rosen's phone calls as well as digital logs of Kim's entry and exit from his office building to prosecute Kim.[20] Kim's arrest for disclosing information—in this case, information that was already commonly known by the public—exemplified by Barack Obama administration's efforts to identify and punish those who leaked government information to the news media.

Several additional incidents specific to media organizations illustrate the threats cybersecurity vulnerabilities pose. In the months leading up to the 2016 US presidential election, a cyberattack by suspected Russian hackers targeting *New York Times* reporters was investigated by the FBI.[21] Several years earlier, the US Justice Department secretly acquired phone records for more than twenty separate telephone lines used by the Associated Press, including the work and personal phone records of individual reporters.[22] AP president and chief executive officer Gary Pruitt denounced the action, saying:

> There can be no possible justification for such an overbroad collection of the telephone communications of The Associated Press and its reporters. These records potentially reveal communications with confidential sources across all of the newsgathering activities undertaken by the AP during a two-month period, provide a road map to AP's newsgathering operations and disclose

---

[20] Peter Maass, "Destroyed by the Espionage Act: Stephen Kim Spoke to a Reporter. Now He's in Jail. This is His Story," *The Intercept*, February 18, 2015, https://theintercept.com/2015/02/18/destroyed-by-the-espionage-act/ (accessed April 8, 2018).

[21] Reuters Staff, "New York Times Says Suspected Russian Hackers Targeted Moscow Bureau," *Reuters* (blog), August 23, 2016, https://www.reuters.com/article/us-usa-cyber-media/new-york-times-says-suspected-russian-hackers-targeted-moscow-bureau-idUSKCN10Y21I (accessed April 8, 2018).

[22] "Gov't Obtains Wide AP Phone Records in Probe," *Bozeman Daily Chronicle*, May 14, 2013, https://www.ap.org/ap-in-the-news/2013/govt-obtains-wide-ap-phone-records-in-probe (accessed April 8, 2018).

information about AP's activities and operations that the government has no conceivable right to know."[23]

The US government disclosed other instances of surveillance not sanctioned by current approved protocols. In August 2008, for example, FBI director Robert Mueller apologized to the editors of the *Washington Post* and the *New York Times* for collecting four reporters' phone records during the course of a national security investigation that did not follow US Department of Justice policies designed to limit subpoenas of journalists' records.[24]

Broadly, evidence indicates government surveillance is on the rise, and the flow of information via government-press relations is strained. A case in point: a recent Google Transparency Report indicated that from July to December 2017, the government made 48,877 requests for information on the highest number of user accounts ever (87,263).[25] During that same time period, 66 percent of global requests were at least partially granted; the number rises to 82 percent for requests only within the United States. Of those requests, 12,263 were filed for national security reasons—almost seven times the number of the second-ranked category (defamation).

More specifically of concern to journalists are the National Security Letter (NSL) requests filed by the FBI.[26] NSLs allow the government to request data such as users' (including journalists') names, addresses, lengths of service, and long-distance toll billing records, as was the case in 2014 when *Washington Post* reporter Barton Gellman was conducting investigations related to the Snowden revelations.[27] However, the reporting regarding NSLs is not fully transparent. Google reports somewhere between the sizeable range of 1 to 499 requests from July to December 2017.[28] This reporting period marked the largest number of users/accounts affected by NSLs (1,500–1,999) since the company began tracking this data in 2009.

---

[23] *Id.*, para. 5.
[24] Carrie Johnson, "FBI Apologizes to Post, Times," *Washington Post*, August 9, 2008, http://www.washingtonpost.com/wp-dyn/content/article/2008/08/08/AR2008080803603.html (accessed April 8, 2018).
[25] "Google Transparency Report," Google, December 2017, https://transparencyreport.google.com/ (accessed January 4, 2017).
[26] Cora Currier, "Secret Rules Make It Pretty Easy for the FBI to Spy on Journalists," *The Intercept* (blog), January 31, 2017, https://theintercept.com/2017/01/31/secret-rules-make-it-pretty-easy-for-the-fbi-to-spy-on-journalists-2/ (accessed April 8, 2017).
[27] Darren Samuelsohn, "Barton Gellman Aware of Legal Risks," *Politico*, February 25, 2014, https://www.politico.com/blogs/media/2014/02/barton-gellman-aware-of-legal-risks-183998 (accessed April 8, 2018).
[28] Google, "Requests for User Information Visible Changes—Transparency Report Help Center," *Transparency Report Help Center* (blog), December 2016, https://support.google.com/transparencyreport/answer/7381458?hl (accessed January 4, 2017).

In tandem, the number of government leaks is rising. In the report on leaks and the media from the US Senate Committee on Homeland Security and Governmental Affairs (2017),[29] Chairman Sen. Ron Johnson claimed that during President Donald Trump's first 126 days in office, the "leak frenzy" totaled about one leak a day—up to seven times that of the Obama and George W. Bush administrations.[30] In turn, the White House publicly condemned anonymity in news reporting on numerous occasions.[31]

Government representatives have made recent statements reinforcing this point, claiming news organizations are primary targets for cyberterrorism and surveillance because of reporters' contacts and access to sensitive information.[32] There is evidence to support that statement: security and privacy, vigilance within personal networks, and preparing for increased leaking to the media are highlighted as key challenges in a recent trends report on the journalism industry.[33] The intersection of increased risk due to the rising number of whistle-blowers combined with modern-day technologies (and vulnerabilities) has raised sensitivities among government and media organizations regarding journalists' safeguards for confidential sources.[34]

Heightened Threats in the Era of Trump

Even the Obama administration's aggressiveness toward whistle-blowers was no match for the White House administration that followed it. Just one year after his inauguration, US President Donald Trump's Justice Department had three times more open investigations into government leaks to the press,[35] and former FBI

[29] Committee on Homeland Security and Governmental Affairs United States Senate, "State Secrets: How an Avalanche of Media Leaks Is Harming National Security, Committee on Homeland Security and Governmental Affairs of the United States Senate," July 6, 2017, http://static.politico.com/96/11/b983b9fd465a852a7db95550650c/2017-07-06-state-secrets-report.pdf (accessed April 8, 2018).

[30] *Id.*, 1.

[31] Associated Press, "Trump Condemns Anonymous Sources as Staff Demands Anonymity," *Fortune* (blog), February 25, 2017, http://fortune.com/2017/02/25/trump-anonymous-media-sources/ (accessed April 8, 2017).

[32] Christopher Soghoian & Sid Stamm, "Certified Lies: Detecting and Defeating Government Interception Attacks against SSL (Short Paper)" (International Conference on Financial Cryptography and Data Security), *in* G. Danezis (ed.), *Financial Cryptography and Data Security* (Springer, 2012), 250–59, https://legacy.cs.indiana.edu/ftp/techreports/TR684.pdf (accessed June 28, 2024).

[33] "The 2017 Global Survey on Journalism's Futures," *Future Today Institute* (blog), https://futuretodayinstitute.com/global-survey-on-journalisms-futures/ (accessed April 8, 2018).

[34] Steve Coll, "Source Protection in the Age of Surveillance," *in* Emily Bell & Taylor Owen (eds.) with Smitha Khorana and Jennifer R. Henrichsen, *Journalism After Snowden: The Future of the Free Press in the Surveillance State* (Columbia University Press, 2017), 85–96; Michael M. Grynbaum & John Koblin, "After Reality Winner's Arrest, Media Asks: Did 'Intercept' Expose a Source?," *New York Times*, June 7, 2017, https://www.nytimes.com/2017/06/06/business/media/intercept-reality-winner-russia-trump-leak.html (accessed March 1, 2018).

[35] Charlie Savage & Eileen Sullivan, "Leak Investigations Triple under Trump, Sessions Says," *New York Times*, August 4, 2017, https://www.nytimes.com/2017/08/04/us/politics/jeff-sessions-trump-leaks-attorney-general.html (accessed March 1, 2018).

director James Comey testified that Trump had suggested he imprison reporters who published classified information.[36]

During the Trump presidency, White House rhetoric about the news media was ruthless.[37] Trump regularly blasted the press with scorching criticism, proclaiming reporters and news organizations are "crooked," "scum," "disgusting," "the enemy of the people," and the now-infamous "fake news."[38] Trump's threats to the news media during his presidency extended far beyond verbal attacks, however; other intimidation tactics included ejecting reporters from campaign events, revoking White House press access, abandoning regular official press briefings, threatening to revoke broadcasting licenses, and (falsely) promising to make it easier to sue the press for libel.[39] Although several of those threats go beyond presidential authority, industry advocates warn that the Trump era's tenuous state of press–White House relations harkened to that of former President Nixon's Watergate era.[40] In 2017, more than 90 percent of Americans were aware of the feud. Even more surprising in such a polarized political environment, more than three-fourths of Democrats (88%) and Republicans (78%) agreed that the relationship between the president and the media was "unhealthy." In addition, 83 percent of all Americans said the conflicts restrict the public's ability to access political news.[41]

Concerns about government surveillance of journalists heightened again in early 2018 when privacy advocates decried the White House's decision to sign into law a six-year extension of Section 702 of the Foreign Intelligence Surveillance Act (FISA) that permits the incidental collection of unknown amounts of American data—a practice many privacy advocates argue violates the US Constitution and does not exclude journalists from being surveilled.[42] In 2019, privacy and civil liberty organizations called for reforms to Section

---

[36] Michael S. Schmidt, "Comey Memo Says Trump Asked Him to End Flynn Investigation," *New York Times*, May 16, 2017, https://www.nytimes.com/2017/05/16/us/politics/james-comey-trump-flynn-russia-investigation.html?module=inline.

[37] Alex Shephard, "Paper Tiger," *New Republic* (blog), December 11, 2017, https://newrepublic.com/article/145904/paper-tiger (accessed March 15, 2018).

[38] *Id.*

[39] Tatiana Serafin, "President Trump's Plans for Libel Laws," *First Amendment Watch* (blog), March 21, 2018, https://firstamendmentwatch.org/donald-trumps-plans-libel-laws/ (accessed April 8, 2018).

[40] David Smith, "'Enemy of the People': Trump's War on the Media Is a Page from Nixon's Playbook," *The Guardian*, September 7, 2019, https://www.theguardian.com/us-news/2019/sep/07/donald-trump-war-on-the-media-oppo-research (accessed November 15, 2019); Tom Brokaw, *The Fall of Richard Nixon* (Random House, 2019).

[41] Michael Barthel, Jeffrey Gottfried, & Amy Mitchell, "Most Say Tensions between Trump Administration and News Media Hinder Access to Political News," *Pew Research Center* (blog), April 4, 2017, https://www.pewresearch.org/journalism/2017/04/04/most-say-tensions-between-trump-administration-and-news-media-hinder-access-to-political-news/ (accessed April 8, 2017).

[42] Dustin Volz, "Trump Signs Bill Renewing NSA's Internet Surveillance Program," *Reuters* (blog), January 19, 2018, https://www.reuters.com/article/us-usa-trump-cyber-surveillance/trump-signs-bill-renewing-nsas-internet-surveillance-program-idUSKBN1F82MK (accessed April 8, 2018).

215 of the USA PATRIOT Act granting the NSA the authority to gather "Call Detail Records" from a target and all people two degrees away from that target.[43] The NSA improperly used this power twice before to collect 600 million call records.[44]

The Trump administration made good on the promise of more investigations. The first known instance of the Justice Department seizing a journalist's communications emerged in June 2018 with the arrest of a former US Senate Intelligence Committee aide. Prosecutors alleging leaks of classified information secretly obtained from Google and Verizon several years of telephone and email metadata for a *New York Times* reporter.[45] In 2009, the Justice Department charged a Defense Intelligence Agency counterterrorism analyst with leaking top-secret information about foreign weapon systems to journalists from CNBC and NBC.[46] In addition to exceeding the number of leaks investigated by other presidential administrations, Trump administration authorities secured the two longest prison sentences for leakers and created a related FBI counterintelligence.[47] In May 2019, the US Justice Department unsealed eighteen criminal charges against WikiLeaks founder Julian Assange, including three under the Espionage Act for which he could face up to 175 years in jail—an event whistleblower Edward Snowden called a "dark moment for press freedom."[48]

---

[43] CDR Program, "Civil Society Letter to HJC on CDR Program," August 14, 2019, https://s3.amazonaws.com/demandprogress/letters/2019-08-14_Civil_Society_letter_to_HJC_on_CDR_Program.pdf (accessed November 1, 2019).

[44] ACLU, "New Documents Reveal NSA Improperly Collected Americans' Call Records Yet Again," *Press Releases* (blog), June 26, 2019, https://www.aclu.org/press-releases/new-documents-reveal-nsa-improperly-collected-americans-call-records-yet-again (accessed November 1, 2019); Tim Starks, "Coalition Presses to Change Surveillance Law," *Politico* (blog), August 14, 2019, https://www.politico.com/newsletters/morning-cybersecurity/2019/08/14/coalition-presses-to-change-surveillance-law-716898 (accessed November 1, 2019).

[45] Adam Goldman, Nicholas Fandos, & Katie Benner, "Ex-Senate Aide Charged in Leak Case Where Times Reporter's Records Were Seized," *New York Times*, June 7, 2018, https://www.nytimes.com/2018/06/07/us/politics/times-reporter-phone-records-seized.html?hp&action=click&pgtype=Homepage&clickSource=story-heading&module=first-column-region&region=top-news&WT.nav=top-news (accessed November 15, 2019).

[46] Paul M. Duggan, Justin Jouvenal, & Matt Zapotosky, "Defense Intelligence Agency Employee Charged with Leaking Classified Information to Journalists," *Washington Post*, October 9, 2019, https://www.washingtonpost.com/local/legal-issues/defense-intelligence-agency-employee-charged-with-leaking-classified-information-to-journalists/2019/10/09/6fbd1050-eaa6-11e9-9306-47c b0324fd44_story.html (accessed November 1, 2019); Erik Wemple, "Reporters at CNBC and NBC News Become Tangled in Leak Investigation," *Washington Post*, October 10, 2019, https://www.washingtonpost.com/opinions/2019/10/10/reporters-cnbc-nbc-news-become-tangled-leak-investigation/ (accessed November 15, 2019).

[47] Savage & Sullivan, *supra* note 35; Reporters Committee for Freedom of the Press, "Federal Cases Involving Unauthorized Disclosures to the News Media, 1778 to the Present," *Protecting Sources and Materials* (blog), May 21, 2019, https://www.rcfp.org/resources/leak-investigations-chart/ (accessed November 1, 2019).

[48] Edward Snowden (@Snowden), "Images of Ecuador's Ambassador Inviting the UK's Secret Police into the Embassy to Drag a Publisher of—Like It or Not—Award-Winning Journalism out of the Build," *Twitter*, April 11, 2019, https://twitter.com/Snowden/status/1116288726601277440?s=20 (accessed November 1, 2019).

Proof of the White House's strategic approach to quelling media sources emerged with a groundbreaking government report entitled "State Secrets: How an Avalanche of Media Leaks Is Harming National Security" that urged the attorney general to increase investigations into those who served as unauthorized government sources for the media.[49] The report listed 125 news articles that included leaked government information to argue that the journalistic practice interfered with national security efforts. Particularly distressing was the report's claim that "all such revelations are potential violations of federal law, punishable by jail time."[50] And in April 2018, the US Department of Homeland Security announced it would seek a contractor to compile a database of journalists, bloggers, and other "media influencers," as well as monitor 290,000 news sources worldwide—including the "sentiment" of coverage about the agency.[51] Although there have been no official government statements regarding the project's intent, one media law reporter for *Forbes* stated, "Anyone else just pull their blanket up over them a little more tightly? Just me?"[52]

Although overall the White House administration–press relationship has been unhealthy, at times the press does prevail in pushing back on additional government pressure. In November 2019, the federal Massachusetts District Court ruled on behalf of eleven travelers—several of whom were journalists—declaring that US customs protection and enforcement agencies could not conduct border searches without cause and that suspicionless seizures of digital devices such as smart phones violate the Fourth Amendment. And the Electronic Frontier Foundation noted that its high-profile dispute with the NSA over the surveillance of AT&T customers' data, waiting in 2019 to be heard on appeal, has survived numerous attempts by the government to derail the case.[53]

---

[49] Committee on Homeland Security and Governmental Affairs United States Senate, "State Secrets: How an Avalanche of Media Leaks Is Harming National Security, Committee on Homeland Security and Governmental Affairs of the United States Senate," 2017, http://static.politico.com/96/11/b983b9fd465a852a7db95550650c/2017-07-06-state-secrets-report.pdf (accessed March 1, 2018).

[50] *Id.*, 1.

[51] U.S. Department of Homeland Security, "Media Monitoring Services Request for Information," *SAM.gov*, April 3, 2018, https://www.fbo.gov/index?s=opportunity&mode=form&id=22aa793f75ce05efd160cfa36d7a8acc&tab=documents&tabmode=form&tabid=d670a11f6fe1ba66358ff1c777dcb3b9&subtab=core&subtabmode=list&= (accessed November 1, 2019).

[52] Michelle Kaminsky, "Department of Homeland Security Compiling Database of Journalists and 'Media Influencers,'" *Forbes*, April 6, 2018, para. 11, https://www.forbes.com/sites/michellefabio/2018/04/06/department-of-homeland-security-compiling-database-of-journalists-and-media-influencers/#3fb626996121 (accessed April 4, 2018).

[53] Aaron Mackey, "Judge Dodges Legality of NSA Mass Spying, Citing Secrecy Claims," *Electronic Frontier Foundation*, April 26, 2019, https://www.eff.org/deeplinks/2019/04/judge-dodges-legality-nsa-mass-spying-citing-secrecy-claims (accessed November 1, 2019); Basma Humadi, "Mass Surveillance Threatens Reporting That Relies on Confidential Sources," *Reporters Committee for Freedom of the Press* (blog), September 30, 2019, https://www.rcfp.org/nsa-mass-surveillance-against-journalist/ (accessed November 15, 2019).

While the strained relationship between the American media and the Trump administration blatantly exacerbated the effects of journalist surveillance activities by the government, the increased surveillance scope, capability, and power has been acknowledged across the globe. A report on the impact of mass surveillance on writers in fifty countries found that the fear of surveillance and resulting changes in behaviors in democratic countries are almost as high as those in nondemocratic states that are accustomed to widespread government surveillance.[54] Ubiquitous data collection and retention has resulted in the rise of "surveillance societies"[55]—ones in which many consider the loss of privacy and autonomy useless to combat.[56] Because valuable information from a confidential source is typically unobtainable through other channels—and in some cases, proves wrongdoing by governments and other institutions of power—the stakes are high for not only journalists and sources but also for democratic societies at large.

II. The Role of Confidential Sources in News Work

A source is any document, individual, or other entity a journalist uses to attribute information, typically identified for the audience. Historical conceptions of media sources depict sources as playing a critical role in defining reality, then assisting journalists in mediating the communication of that reality to the public via credible professional norms.[57] The act of granting anonymity to a source is an agreement between the journalist and individual to shield the source's identity—typically an agreement reserved for information that cannot be obtained through more transparent channels.[58]

Journalists use confidential, or veiled,[59] sources as a tool to support the profession's fundamental role as the watchdog of government, most often employed when there is a need to circumvent traditional power structures that

---

[54] "Global Chilling: The Impact of Mass Surveillance on International Writers," *PEN America*, 2015, https://pen.org/wp-content/uploads/2022/08/globalchilling_2015.pdf (accessed January 4, 2017).

[55] Lyon, *supra* note 13.

[56] Lina Dencik, "The Advent of Surveillance Realism," *Cardiff University, Journalism, Media and Culture* (blog), January 23, 2015, http://www.jomec.co.uk/blog/the-advent-of-surveillance-realism-2 (accessed January 4, 2017).

[57] Matt Carlson, *On the Condition of Anonymity: Unnamed Sources and the Battle for Journalism* (University of Illinois Press, 2011).

[58] Matt Carlson, "Review of Whither Anonymity? Journalism and Unnamed Sources in a Changing Media Environment," *in* Bob Franklin & Matt Carlson (eds.), *Journalists, Sources, and Credibility: New Perspectives* (Routledge, 2010), 37–48.

[59] Hugh M. Culbertson, "Veiled News Sources—Who and What Are They?," *ANPA News Research Bulletin No. 3*, Internet Archive, May 1975, https://archive.org/details/ERIC_ED130266 (accessed January 4, 2017).

challenge the press' ability to inform the public. Many journalists claim they simply could not break important news without using confidential sources, especially in cases related to national security.[60] In fact, a former editor of the *Los Angeles Times* deemed leaks and anonymous forces "very much in the fabric of American journalism."[61] The ability to protect one's privacy in this regard "acts to safeguard political pluralism and serve" as fuel for dissent and a check on power."[62] The Reporters Committee for Freedom of the Press asserts "without confidentiality between journalists and sources, groundbreaking reporting on stories like Watergate, the Panama Papers or the use of 'enhanced' interrogation techniques on terrorism suspects by the U.S. would not have been possible."[63]

For the purposes of this chapter, the terms "confidential" and "veiled" source are used to identify individuals who work with journalists under the promise of confidentiality. "Leaker" is another term used to identify those who aim to release information to the press under the condition of anonymity.[64] Whistle-blowers, a specific type of confidential source, are "employees who discover and disclose evidence of serious abuses of public trust."[65] The Government Accountability Project, an advocacy organization dedicated to the protection of whistle-blowers, describes the power whistle-blowers can have in society: whistle-blowers "can take down a corrupt CEO or corporation, drive significant legislative and agency reforms, save lives from contaminated food, prevent nuclear accidents, and prompt the impeachment of a President."[66] The types of confidential sources described here differ from the more general category of unnamed sources (such as "a company spokesperson") whose identities are often omitted by journalists because they are not considered critical to the news report.

It is important to situate this discussion within the normative journalistic principle that quality reporting requires judicious and sparing use of sources that cannot be identified for the public.[67] The practice has been criticized by

---

[60] David Greene, Mary Louise Kelly, & Dana Priest, "Why the Media Use Anonymous Sources," *Morning Edition* (podcast), December 16, 2016, https://www.npr.org/2016/12/16/505811892/why-the-media-uses-anonymous-sources (accessed January 4, 2017).

[61] Norm Pearlstine, Interview Norm Pearlstine, interview by PBS Frontline, Transcript, 2006, para. 15, https://www.pbs.org/wgbh/pages/frontline/newswar/interviews/pearlstine.html (accessed November 1, 2019).

[62] Kunelius et al., *supra* note 4, at 3.

[63] Humadi, *supra* note 53.

[64] Richard B. Kielbowicz, "Leaks to the Press as Communication within and between Organizations," *Newspaper Research Journal*, 1, no. 2 (February 1980), 53–58, doi: 10.1177/073953298000100209.

[65] "Working with Whistleblowers: A Guide for Journalists," Government Accountability Project, http://www.whistleblower.org/sites/default/files/whistleblowerguidejournalism.pdf (accessed November 1, 2019).

[66] *Id.*, 1.

[67] Carlson, *supra* note 57.

professionals and researchers for practical and ethical reasons.[68] Use of unidentified sources can threaten journalistic credibility; readers are highly skeptical when journalists withhold source identification, reducing transparency in the reporting process.[69] Additionally, some confidential sources are working as strategic government propaganda tools—political actors who partner with journalists to advance the government's political agenda versus acting as a "parajournalist"[70] or whistle-blower.[71] Research has also suggested that contrary to what might be expected, journalists use anonymous sources less often in "high stakes" coverage such as times of war.[72] Anonymous sources also have led to false accusations in news coverage, at times due to a reporter's lack of diligence—or worse, deliberate use to bolster an otherwise lackluster news item or sensationalize a story.[73]

In spite of concerns about audience perceptions, journalists maintain that important stories cannot be told without the prospect of veiling sources—especially when the government attempts to curtail media access to information in the public interest.[74] In its 2009 report on the information needs of communities, the Knight Commission outlined the societal importance:

> Key democratic institutions are under obvious stress—public service journalism perhaps most of all. Access to news and information is critical to democracy. Journalists serve as watchdogs over public officials and institutions, as well as over the private and corporate sector. They provide information for citizens to run their lives, their communities, and their country. News organizations also foster civic understanding, engagement, and cohesion. When they

---

[68] Matt J. Duffy & Carrie P. Freeman, "Unnamed Sources: A Utilitarian Exploration of Their Justification and Guidelines for Limited Use," *Journal of Mass Media Ethics* 26, no. 4 (October 19, 2011), 297–315, doi: 10.1080/08900523.2011.606006.

[69] Hugh M. Culbertson & Nancy Somerick, "Cloaked Attribution--What Does It Mean to News Readers?," *ANPA News Research Bulletin*, no. 1, May 1976, https://eric.ed.gov/?id=ED141817 (accessed November 1, 2019).

[70] Michael Schudson, *The Sociology of News* (W.W. Norton & Co., 2003), 3.

[71] W. Lance Bennett, "Toward a Theory of Press-State Relations in the United States," *Journal of Communication*, 40, no. 2 (June 1, 1990), 103–27, doi: 10.1111/j.1460-2466.1990.tb02265.x; Schudson, *supra* note 70; John Hatcher, "Unnamed and Anonymous Sources: Did They Shape the Debate over Invading Iraq?," *Global Media Journal*, 10 (Fall 2010), 17, http://www.globalmediajournal.com/open-access/unnamed-and-anonymous-sources-did-they-shape-the-debate-over-invading-iraq.pdf (accessed January 4, 2017).

[72] Meghan R. Sobel & Daniel Riffe, "Newspapers Use Unnamed Sources Less Often in High-Stakes Coverage," *Newspaper Research Journal*, 37, no. 3 (September 2016), 299–311, doi: 10.1177/0739532916664377.

[73] Carlson, *supra* note 57.

[74] Liz Spayd, "The Risk of Unnamed Sources? Unconvinced Readers," *New York Times*, February 18, 2017, https://www.nytimes.com/2017/02/18/public-editor/the-risk-of-unnamed-sources-unconvinced-readers.html (accessed January 4, 2017).

work well, they help make communities open, officials accountable and publics engaged.[75]

To achieve this goal, the Commission stressed the need for government transparency and the public's need for credible information in order to self-govern. It is where these two issues intersect that confidential sources often come into play.

Industry norms such as those depicted in the Society of Professional Journalists Code of Ethics ([SPJ], 2019) and the United Kingdom's National Union of Journalists Code of Conduct (2013) advise journalists to only withhold the identity of a source in cases in which the source may be in danger or face retribution if their identity was revealed. Both codes suggest explaining to readers why a source was granted anonymity. Although confidential sources are often considered crucial to support the marketplace of ideas,[76] news organizations such as the *New York Times* have cautioned reporters about granting sources anonymity—a request that could be motivated by ulterior motives and, if used irresponsibly or arbitrarily, can lead to a loss of audience trust.[77] Proper attribution is preferred as a standard characteristic of transparent reporting practices; identifying sources supports reader credibility.[78] However, research has shown the public *can* respect journalism that relies on unnamed sources, such as news coverage of the Watergate scandal.[79]

Sources' motivations for speaking to a reporter under the condition of anonymity vary. *Washington Post* national security reporter Mary Louise Kelly[80] acknowledged that some confidential sources act as third parties to "unofficially" share information the government wants circulated; at other times, they may be attempting to protect the public, serving as whistle-blowers to reveal wrongdoing or corruption. There are likely a multitude of personal and professional motivations somewhere in between, adding to the complexity of the culture surrounding anonymous sources.[81]

---

[75] Knight Commission, *Informing Communities: Sustaining Democracy in the Digital Age. Report of the Knight Commission on the Information Needs of Communities in a Democracy* (The Aspen Institute, 2009), 3, https://knightfoundation.org/wp-content/uploads/2019/06/Knight_Commission_Report_-_Informing_Communities.pdf (accessed April 4, 2018).

[76] William B. Blankenburg, "The Utility of Anonymous Attribution," *Newspaper Research Journal*, 13, no. 1–2 (January 1992), 10–23, doi: 10.1177/073953299201300103.

[77] Carlson, *supra* note 57.

[78] Reporters Committee for Freedom of the Press, *supra* note 18.

[79] Alex S. Edelstein & Diane P. Tefft, "Media Credibility and Respondent Credulity with Respect to Watergate," *Communication Research*, 1, no. 4 (1974), 426–39, https://ourarchive.otago.ac.nz/bitstream/handle/10523/4616/KabirShahMNJ2014PhD.Pdf.txt;jsessionid=97AE4EA0AFA33AADF80FA81783E82B5A?sequence=3 (accessed January 4, 2017); Carl Bernstein & Bob Woodward, *All the President's Men: The Greatest Reporting Story of All Time* (Simon & Schuster, 1974).

[80] Greene, Kelly, & Priest, *supra* note 60.

[81] Carlson, *supra* note 57.

A. Risks to Sources and Journalists

A source's request to remain anonymous may be driven by a host of factors, including fear of being fired from a job or otherwise being subjected to retribution. Government sources with security clearances are regularly polygraphed, Kelly said, "and one of the questions that is routinely asked is, have you had any unauthorized contact with the media? These people are risking their jobs, their pensions to speak to us."[82]

Regardless of motivation, confidential informants face significant risks if identified. Consequences range from personal embarrassment to a prison sentence or worse. Individual bad actors attempting to use data against someone have different disciplinary tools at their disposal—such as public shaming on social media—than the government, which wields the power of prosecution and imprisonment.

Consequences related to working with confidential sources and running afoul of the government can be dire for media professionals as well, including criminal charges and a potential prison sentence. In March 2018, the US Department of Justice under President Trump furthered its efforts to silence government sources and whistle-blowers when it used the Espionage Act to charge Terry Albury, a former FBI special agent, with leaking information to the media. He ultimately pleaded guilty to two accounts.[83] Stories such as Albury's are not uncommon, nor is a belief by industry advocates that the government demonstrates a more vindictive streak when it disciplines leakers who specifically engage with the press.[84]

B. Legal Risks and Protections

Many governments identify journalism as a profession of specific concern because of journalists' work with sensitive information, government leakers, and whistle-blowers. This professional vulnerability is exacerbated by the "surveillance authority" the American government has through a variety of statutory provisions for data collection.[85]

---

[82] Greene, Kelly, & Priest, *supra* note 60, at para. 21.

[83] Trevor Timm, "The Accused FBI Whistleblower Indicted by Trump's DOJ Allegedly Leaked Secret Rules for Spying on Reporters," *Freedom of the Press Foundation* (blog), 2018, https://freedom.press/news/accused-fbi-whistleblower-indicted-trumps-doj-allegedly-leaked-secret-rules-spying-reporters/ (accessed November 1, 2019).

[84] Trevor Timm, "David Petraeus Receives No Jail Time for Leaking, While Whistleblowers Face Decades in Jail," *Freedom of the Press Foundation* (blog), 2015, https://freedom.press/news/david-petraeus-receives-no-jail-time-for-leaking-while-whistleblowers-face-decades-in-jail/ (accessed January 4, 2017).

[85] Jennifer Henrichsen & Hannah Bloch-Wehba, "Electronic Communications Surveillance: What Journalists and Media Organizations Need to Know" (Reporters Committee for Freedom of the

Legally, the US Supreme Court has protected journalists when they publish information of public concern, even if they are aware that the source obtained it unlawfully, as long as the journalist did not participate in the illegal act.[86] However, the government has other prosecutorial tools at its disposal, such as the previously mentioned Espionage Act of 1917.[87] In total, First Amendment scholar Mary-Rose Papandrea considers the legal defenses for journalists and sources largely ineffective compared to the power the government wields, especially against government claims about risks to national security.[88]

Ubiquitous digital communication and its related risks such as mass surveillance place traditional conceptions of journalistic legal protections in question, however. Operating in the Digital Age increases the potential for a source to be exposed, and First Amendment scholars have raised concerns about a source's potential legal recourse.[89] The US Supreme Court has ruled that journalists have no First Amendment protection against such claims by sources.[90]

Extending beyond a violation of individual rights, and although state shield laws provide limited protection to journalists pressured to reveal their sources, a surveillance culture has other pervasive negative consequences. Some surveillance authorities voluntarily provide the government information that could be used to identify sources, sidestepping the need for a subpoena or warrant.[91] In addition, the legal protections for journalists when a court attempts to compel disclosure are a complex and often-confusing blend of First Amendment protections, state constitutions and statues, common law, and procedural rules; in addition, they vary by state and are by no means ironclad.[92] Attempts to pass a shield law at the federal level have failed, and the US Supreme Court has ruled that journalists can be compelled to testify in front of grand juries when subpoenaed.[93] The increased risks have prompted media attorney and scholar

Press, 2017), 8, https://www.rcfp.org/wp-content/uploads/2017/05/Electronic_Communications_Surveillance_2017.pdf (accessed April 4, 2018).

[86] Reporters Committee for Freedom of the Press, *supra* note 18.
[87] Alexandria Ellerbeck, "How US Espionage Act Can Be Used against Journalists Covering Leaks," *Committee to Protect Journalists* (blog), May 20, 2017, https://cpj.org/blog/2017/05/how-us-espionage-act-can-be-used-against-journalis.php (accessed April 4, 2018).
[88] Mary-Rose Papandrea, "Lapdogs, Watchdogs, and Scapegoats: The Press and National Security Information," *Indiana Law Journal*, 83 (2008), 233.
[89] Reporters Committee for Freedom of the Press, *supra* note 18; J. Posetti, *Protecting Journalism Sources in the Digital Age* (UNESCO, 2017), https://unesdoc.unesco.org/ark:/48223/pf0000248054 (accessed April 4, 2018).
[90] *Cohen v. Cowles Media Co.* (U.S. 1991).
[91] Henrichsen & Bloch-Wehba, *supra* note 85.
[92] Jonathan Peters, "Shield Laws and Journalist's Privilege: The Basics Every Reporter Should Know," *Columbia Journalism Review*, August 22, 2016, https://www.cjr.org/united_states_project/journalists_privilege_shield_law_primer.php (accessed January 4, 2017); Henrichsen & Bloch-Wehba, *supra* note 85.
[93] *Branzburg v. Hayes* (U.S. 1972).

Jonathan Peters to remind journalists that "protecting sources today is as much about technology and electronic security as it is about the law."[94]

An increased chance of exposure, even in cases when both journalist and source are attempting to shield one another, has led to concerns that a surveillance culture has created a "chilling effect" on the journalist-confidential source relationship[95] and a reduction in journalists' ability to inform the public.[96] At a National Press Club event, Associated Press chief executive Gary Pruitt stated that "[s]ome of our long-trusted sources have become nervous and anxious about talking to us—even on stories that aren't about national security."[97] The pervasive effects are evident in *New York Times* investigative reporter David Barstow's statement after he learned of NSA surveillance practices in 2013: "[I]t creeps in every day into my thought process, into my work, into every phone all I make, into every e-mail I write."[98]

III. Information Security as the New Source Protection

As early as 1996, trade organizations expressed concern about digital surveillance of journalists and suggested proactive measures for protection.[99] However, multiple research studies indicate industry response has been slow, even as

---

[94] Peters, *supra* note 92, at para. 28.

[95] David McCraw & Stephen Gikow, "The End to an Unspoken Bargain: National Security and Leaks in a Post-Pentagon Papers World," *Harvard Civil Rights—Civil Liberties Law Review*, 48, no. 1 (2013), 473, http://harvardcrcl.org/wp-content/uploads/2011/09/CRCL_McCraw-Gikow_printversion.pdf (accessed April 4, 2018); Paul Lashmar, "No More Sources? The Impact of Snowden's Revelations on Journalists and Their Confidential Sources," *Journalism Practice*, 11, no. 6 (2017), 665–88, https://doi.org/10.1080/17512786.2016.1179587 (accessed November 1, 2019).

[96] Reporters Committee for Freedom of the Press, *supra* note 18; Rachel Smolkin, "Under Fire: Journalists Have Been Barraged by a Spate of Subpoenas to Identify Confidential Sources and Court Decisions Ordering Them to Comply. Investigative Reporting Could Suffer If More Ensue. Can the Media Fight Back? Does the Public Care?," *American Journalism Review*, 27, no. 1 (2005), 18–26, https://go.gale.com/ps/i.do?id=GALE%7CA129357612&sid=googleScholar&v=2.1&it=r&linkaccess=abs&issn=10678654&p=AONE&sw=w&userGroupName=anon%7Ef2959d57&aty=open-web-entry (accessed November 1, 2019); Posetti, *supra* note 89; Lokman Tsui & Francis Lee, "How Journalists Understand the Threats and Opportunities of New Technologies: A Study of Security Mind-Sets and Its Implications for Press Freedom," *Journalism*, 22, no. 6 (2021), 1317–39, doi: 10.1177/1464884919849411; Anthony Mills, "Now You See Me—Now You Don't: Journalists' Experiences With Surveillance," *Journalism Practice*, 13, no. 6 (July 3, 2019), 690–707, doi: 10.1080/17512786.2018.1555006.

[97] Lindy Royce-Bartlett, "Leak Probe Has Chilled Sources, AP Exec Says," *CNN* (blog), June 19, 2013, para. 2, https://www.cnn.com/2013/06/19/politics/ap-leak-probe/index.html (accessed January 4, 2017).

[98] Jamie Schuman, "The Shadows of the Spooks: NSA Surveillance Efforts Affect Investigative Reporting on a Daily Basis," *The News Media & The Law*, Fall 2013 (2013), para. 3, https://www.rcfp.org/wp-content/uploads/2019/01/Fall_2013.pdf (accessed April 4, 2018).

[99] Whit Andrews, "Surveillance in Cyberspace," *American Journalism Review*, 18, no. 2 (1996), 13, https://link.gale.com/apps/doc/A18105875/AONE?u=tel_oweb&sid=googleScholar&xid=e233884c (accessed April 4, 2018).

organizations have adopted new technologies in other areas of news production. It seems illogical to assume that a media organization that does not prioritize information security would expect its newsroom staff to be well equipped to combat cyber vulnerabilities—especially when there were clear signals that digital defenses should be an organizational priority. After the September 11, 2001, terrorist attack in the United States, advances in technology combined with an aggressive extension of the US government's counterterrorism powers led some to describe the climate as a "surveillance society."[100] Yet in a 2014 study, half of the journalists surveyed said their organizations had not taken appropriate steps to combat surveillance and hacking. Even more interestingly, 42 percent were unsure if their company had taken any proactive security steps at all. And a Research and Analysis of Media survey conducted at the annual International News Media Association World Congress noted that out of 285 media executives, not one identified cybersecurity as a "very important issue" nor an "absolutely critical priority."[101]

The continued misalignment of organizational and individual priorities was apparent in findings from another survey of 2,700 newsroom managers and journalists: journalists listed cybersecurity as one of their top three desired digital training needs, but the topic did not top the list for managers.[102] A year later, a global study of 1,100 media IT professionals found although 82 percent believed their organization will experience a data breach, only 36 percent indicated cybersecurity was a priority for their executive leadership.[103] Overall, pervasive unpreparedness in proportion to heightened risks seems common in media outlets across the globe, yet security practices in American newsrooms lag among the laggards.[104] In fact, the Future Today Institute's (FTI) 2017 Global Survey on Journalism's Futures report made a bleak pronouncement regarding journalism in the technological age: "Almost no one is actively building long-term scenarios for the intersection of news, technology and democracy."[105] The following year's report was only slightly more positive, stating that media outlets

---

[100] Adam L. Penenberg, "The Surveillance Society," *Wired*, December 1, 2001, http://www.wired.com/wired/archive/9.12/surveillance.html (accessed January 4, 2017); Karin Wahl-Jorgensen et al., "Introduction: Journalism, Citizenship and Surveillance," *Digital Journalism*, 5, no. 3 (March 16, 2017), 256–61, doi: 10.1080/21670811.2016.1266134.

[101] "Worst Practices in Cybersecurity," *Newscycle*, June 3, 2015, http://www.newscyclesolutions.com/worst-practices-in-cybersecurity/ (accessed January 4, 2017).

[102] "The State of Technology in Global Newsrooms," Survey, International Center for Journalists, 2019, https://www.icfj.org/sites/default/files/2019-10/2019%20Tech%20Survey-Exec%20Summary.pdf (accessed November 1, 2019).

[103] "2018 Study on Global Megatrends in Cybersecurity," Ponemon Institute Research, 2018, https://www.raytheon.com/sites/default /files/2018-02/2018_Global_Cyber_Megatrends.pdf (accessed November 1, 2019).

[104] "The State of Technology in Global Newsrooms," *supra* note 102.

[105] "The 2017 Global Survey on Journalism's Futures," *supra* note 33, at 6.

"are starting to develop secure drops for would-be leakers."[106] And at least one study has found better alignment among individual and organizational priorities. Susan E. McGregor, Franziska Roesner, and Kelly Caine identified some shared computer security concerns—including source protection—among news organizations and individual journalists, although how those concerns were reflected in professional practices diverged significantly.[107] While these findings are positive, another study found that newsrooms were still not investing in enough technical staff or training for their employees. New hires were found significantly lacking in cybersecurity skills, and employees still want additional training in cybersecurity.[108]

Sluggish attempts to address digital security for news agencies is perplexing, especially in the wake of cautionary tales by their peers. Industry experts pointed out organizational vulnerabilities in the wake of disclosures regarding domestic and foreign surveillance by NSA contractor Edward Snowden, identifying it as a wake-up call for news agencies to strengthen information security practices.[109] A lack of preparedness was apparent when the *New York Times* exposed an NSA agent's name and an agency target by failing to effectively redact a PDF uploaded to its website.[110] To emphasize, it was a *failure to redact the document appropriately*; the error indicated a lack of technical knowledge, not intent or effort. Also during the Snowden revelations, editors of the *New York Times* and *The Guardian* used unencrypted telephone lines to discuss classified information obtained by WikiLeaks, even after the *New York Times* reported that the US government illegally surveilled Americans via international phone conversations.[111] More recently, *The Intercept*'s outing of former NSA contractor Reality Winner exposed the woman after she leaked documents revealing Russian tampering in the 2016 US presidential election.[112] Although the FBI identified Winner, who ultimately confessed to the leak, through other channels, one security expert pointed out that *The Intercept*'s lack of understanding of a document's identifying attributes could have brought about the same result. The uploaded PDF contained a digital

---

[106] "2018 Tech Trends for Journalism and Media," Annual Tech Report, Future Today Institute, 2018, at 58, https://futuretodayinstitute.com/2018-tech-trends-for-journalism-and-media/ (accessed November 1, 2019).

[107] McGregor, Roesner, & Caine, *supra* note 19.

[108] "The State of Technology in Global Newsrooms," *supra* note 102.

[109] Ron Deibert, "Digital Threats against Journalists," *in* Emily Bell & Taylor Owen (eds.), *Journalism after Snowden: The Future of the Free Press in the Surveillance State* (Columbia University Press, 2017), 240–57.

[110] Tim Cushing, "New York Times Suffers Redaction Failure, Exposes Name of NSA Agent and Targeted Network in Uploaded PDF," *Techdirt*, January 28, 2014, https://www.techdirt.com/articles/20140128/08542126021/new-york-times-suffers-redaction-failure-exposes-name-nsa-agent-targeted-network-uploaded-pdf.shtml (accessed January 4, 2017).

[111] Christopher Soghoian, "When Secrets Aren't Safe with Journalists," *New York Times*, October 27, 2011, https://nyti.ms/2zbZN3Q .(accessed January 4, 2017).

[112] Grynbaum & Koblin, *supra* note 34.

watermark: almost undetectable yellow dots used to capture NSA printer activity by individual.[113]

Prioritizing information security is a critical first step. Implementing it effectively, however, is another matter. Technologies are not one-size-fits-all solutions; a tool's implementation does not guarantee it will be appropriate or effective to achieve the desired security goal. The *Washington Post* discovered this after launching a "secure" web-based portal for confidential sources in May 2011—only to later discover the initial platform was rife with vulnerabilities and posed a danger to trusting sources using it.[114] Today, the *Post* uses the open-source whistle-blower submission system SecureDrop managed by the Freedom of the Press Foundation and used by more than fifty organizations worldwide.

Incidents such as these gave credence to experts claiming that one of the most prevalent barriers to journalists' adoption of appropriate cybersecurity measures is a dual "deep technology gap" at the organizational and individual levels.[115] Some outlets, however, such as the controversial website WikiLeaks, were ahead of the curve. WikiLeaks demonstrated its technological savvy by protecting whistle-blowers through the use of servers in undisclosed locations (many, however, known to be in Sweden, where the press enjoys freedom from government intervention), not retaining computer logs, encrypting internal chat communications, and using military-grade encryption. This type of "bulletproof hosting"[116] is one of many reasons WikiLeaks founder Julian Assange characterized the website as an "uncensorable system for untraceable mass document leaking and public analysis."[117]

Regardless of the reasons behind the lack of preparedness, the fact is plain: when it comes to cybersecurity, journalists come up short. News professionals are often found to have limited digital skill sets. An annual survey found that out of twenty-three digital skills assessed, only four were typically used with consistency—none of which were related to cybersecurity.[118] This led the 2017 State of Technology in Global Newsrooms survey report to bluntly state: "Our survey sought to answer a critical question: Are journalists keeping pace with the digital revolution? Despite great strides in leveraging new technologies, we conclude that the answer is no."[119]

---

[113] Robert Graham, "How the Intercept Outed Reality Winner," *Errata Security* (blog), June 5, 2017, https://blog.erratasec.com/2017/06/how-intercept-outed-reality-winner.html (accessed April 4, 2018).

[114] Soghoian, *supra* note 111.

[115] "The State of Technology in Global Newsrooms," *supra* note 102.

[116] Dan Goodin, "Wikileaks Judge Gets Pirate Bay Treatment," *The Register* (blog), February 21, 2008, para. 9, https://www.theregister.co.uk/2008/02/21/wikileaks_bulletproof_hosting/ (accessed January 4, 2017).

[117] Raffi Khatchadourian, "What Does Julian Assange Want?," *New Yorker*, May 31, 2010, para. 4, https://www.newyorker.com/magazine/2010/06/07/no-secrets (accessed January 4, 2017).

[118] "The State of Technology in Global Newsrooms," *supra* note 102.

[119] *Id.* 2.

A case in point: the Center for International Media Assistance found that 83 percent of journalists were not encrypting their mobile devices, 70 percent were not encrypting their overall communications, and 60 percent were not regularly using security tools.[120] A year later, a staggering 54 percent of journalists and 52 percent of news organizations continued use of unsecured email communications. A 2019 study by another organization found more encouraging results, indicating that the number of American journalists securing their communications had doubled from those surveyed two years prior.[121] However, the scope of adoption was light, limited to encrypted messaging apps such as WhatsApp, Telegram, and Signal. A quarter of respondents or fewer were likely to adopt anything more substantial, such as VPN or phone call encryption. Industry advocates acknowledge one of the barriers to appropriate implementation is simply the inconvenient disruption to established work routines—put simply, new ways of doing things raise the inconvenience factor.[122]

Evidence has shown that major partnerships among journalists at multiple organizations have been able to overcome typical obstacles such as inconvenience in highly sensitive investigations such as the *Panama Papers*.[123] In that case, more than 100 journalists from around the globe successfully adopted the digital tools developed for the project and successfully protected the leaker of the documents. Even those with limited digital security knowledge reported they adopted the tools instead of working around them, a result partially attributed to the participants' sense of community and group responsibility. As Susan E. McGregor and Elizabeth Anne Watkins point out, more exploration into journalists' "mental models" such as those uncovered in the *Panama Papers* study are key to determining why the profession on the whole does not seem to prioritize information security.[124]

Ultimately, developing a comprehensive information security strategy can be daunting and must be comprised of efforts on many fronts to be effective. Jennifer R. Henrichsen's interviews with journalists, developers, and digital security trainers pointed to five key issues that must be addressed: a lack of understanding about the risks for individuals and the newsroom; the absence of a

---

[120] Javier Garza Ramos, *Journalist Security in the Digital World: A Survey*, Center for International Media Assistance, 2016, https://www.cima.ned.org/resource/journalist-security-in-the-digital-world/ (accessed April 4, 2018).
[121] "The State of Technology in Global Newsrooms," *supra* note 102.
[122] "Technology Security: Understanding the Threat," *supra* note 17.
[123] Susan E. McGregor et al., "When the Weakest Link Is Strong: Secure Collaboration in the Case of the Panama Papers," 2017, at 505–22, https://www.usenix.org/conference/usenixsecurity17/technical-sessions/presentation/mcgregor (accessed April 4, 2018).
[124] Susan E. McGregor & Elizabeth Anne Watkins, "Security by Obscurity: Journalists' Mental Models of Information Security," *#ISOJ*, 6, no. 1 (April 14, 2016), https://isojjournal.wordpress.com/2016/04/14/security-by-obscurity-journalists-mental-models-of-information-security/ (accessed April 4, 2018).

"security culture"; a perception that only government sources need protection; uncertainty regarding the effectiveness of security tools; and sources' lack of knowledge about technology.[125]

A. A Focus on Digital Security and Sources

While the inconvenience factor may be high, the benefits of cybersecurity investments cannot be overstated if organizations wish to maintain relationships with critical sources, evidenced by US security informatics scholar Christopher Soghoian's recommendation that leakers provide information to organizations such as WikiLeaks instead of mainstream journalists.[126] Soghoian leveled his criticism directly at individuals in the newsroom, describing reporters as uninterested in employing even the most accessible and user-friendly tools available. He warned that "the safety of anonymous sources will depend not only on journalists' ethics, but on their computer skills."[127] Real harms due to journalists' lack of implementing cybersecurity practices were demonstrated when a *Vice* photographer uploaded of a photo with geolocation metadata intact, subsequently leading to the arrest of US eccentric and businessman John McAfee in Guatemala.[128]

The long-term effects of poor information security practices such as these could seriously weaken journalists' ability to fully inform the public—damage that could be widespread considering 13 percent of journalists in 2014 said digital security concerns prohibited them from reaching out to certain sources of information.[129] A staggering 64 percent said they believed the government had likely collected data from their phones and computers.[130] Former journalist Silkie Carlo tied quality reporting with source protection: "Information security is source protection in the digital age, and journalists who show an awareness, willingness and ability to adopt digital security behaviours will attract valuable sources and stories."[131]

---

[125] Jennifer R. Henrichsen, "Breaking Through the Ambivalence: Journalistic Responses to Information Security Technologies," *Digital Journalism*, 8, no. 3 (March 15, 2020), 328–46, doi: 10.1080/21670811.2019.1653207.
[126] Soghoian, *supra* note 111.
[127] *Id.*, A31.
[128] Mat Honan, "How Trusting in Vice Led to John Mcafee's Downfall," *Wired* (blog), December 6, 2012, https://www.wired.com/2012/12/how-vice-got-john-mcafee-caught/ (accessed January 4, 2017).
[129] Michael Barthel, "5 Key Takeaways about How Investigative Reporters View Their Digital Security," *Pew Research Center* (blog), February 5, 2015, http://www.pewresearch.org/fact-tank/2015/02/05/ire-takeaways/ (accessed January 4, 2017).
[130] Holcomb & Mitchell, *supra* note 6.
[131] Silkie Carlo, "Under Surveillance: Journalists Urged to Safeguard Their Data," *International News Safety Institute* (blog), January 22, 2016, para. 9, https://newssafety.org/safety/advisories/

The perspectives of former sources support Carlo's statement, warning that others may not communicate with journalists unless they have significantly protected their computers and phones. In fact, whistle-blowers have said they worry less about finding reporters who can *keep* a secret and more about finding reporters with the *means* to keep that secret.[132] There seems good reason for the concern; a 2017 survey of journalists in the United Kingdom found a staggering percentage took no steps to protect their communications and meetings with sources. In fact, only one journalist acknowledged using a messaging encryption tool.[133]

Even with the knowledge to use security tools effectively, there may be other reasons users have for not adopting the technology. In the wake of the Snowden leaks, for example, journalists said some government sources were refusing to use encrypted email because it indicated they were engaged in unauthorized communications.[134] This speaks to the need to better educate all actors on both sides of the reporting process to ensure appropriate use of unnamed sources can continue.

IV. Recommendations: Forging New Relationship Norms

The threats of digital surveillance at all levels of journalism organizations and the threats to the personal freedom and professional livelihood of confidential sources argue for a new approach to journalist-confidential source dynamics, protocols, and understanding. Stephenson Waters' qualitative study of national security journalists found a widespread and ongoing "Big Brother feeling" that disrupted established practices surrounding source protection.[135] The fact that journalists are adjusting their behaviors, at least to some extent, based on their

---

safety-advisory/detail/under-surveillance-journalists-urged-to-guard-their-data-1685/ (accessed January 4, 2017).

[132] Amy Zhang, "Whistleblowers to Journalists: Protect Your Data," *The News Media & The Law*, Summer 2013, at 6, https://www.rcfp.org/wp-content/uploads/2019/01/Summer_2013.pdf (accessed January 4, 2017).

[133] Paul Bradshaw, "Chilling Effect: Regional Journalists' Source Protection and Information Security Practice in the Wake of the Snowden and Regulation of Investigatory Powers Act (RIPA) Revelations," *Digital Journalism*, 5, no. 3 (March 16, 2017), 334–52, doi: 10.1080/21670811.2016.1251329.

[134] Reporters Committee for Freedom of the Press, "Journalists, Technologists Discuss Encryption at Conference on Digital Security after Snowden," *Newsgathering* (blog), November 11, 2014, https://www.rcfp.org/journalists-technologists-discuss-encryption-conference-digital-secu/ (accessed January 4, 2017).

[135] Stephenson Waters, "The Effects of Mass Surveillance on Journalists' Relations with Confidential Sources: A Constant Comparative Study," *Digital Journalism*, 6, no. 10 (November 26, 2018), 1294–1313, doi: 10.1080/21670811.2017.1365616.

belief that source communications are surveilled are a confirmation of Foucault's Panopticism at work—and a signal that change is required to protect the media's watchdog function and protect free speech more broadly.[136]

What does this new relationship entail, and how do journalists and sources settle into a new dynamic based on an increased need to protect one another? While detailed considerations are too numerous to exhaust here, ten broad areas of focus are proposed.

1. Awareness is key. Numerous industry assessments have found that although there are a multitude of applications, platforms, and procedures available to protect journalists—and, therefore, their sources—from potential threats, most newsroom professionals are simply not aware that these tools exist.[137] Even more concerning is a false sense of security: for example, journalists often point to face-to-face communications as secure,[138] seemingly discounting the ever-growing public data-collection measures such as beacon devices and biometric scanners. Even the most prominent digital tools being adopted by newsrooms such as the digital collaboration platform Slack come with their own weaknesses that need to be understood. Although Slack has become a common tool used in newsrooms, the Electronic Frontier Foundation reminds journalists that "that data is not end-to-end encrypted, which means Slack can read it, law enforcement can request it, and hackers—including the nation-state actors highlighted in Slack's S-1—can break in and steal it."[139]

Awareness must extend beyond the newsroom, however, to encourage sources to collaborate with journalists and serve the public interest. Efforts such as the *New York Times*' "CryptoParty" event for subscribers offering a look inside the organization's security procedures and sharing best practices with the public are models for increased transparency and knowledge sharing.[140]

2. Greater technical knowledge and skills must be obtained—and kept current. Journalists have indicated their jobs are made more difficult by the challenge cybersecurity and digital surveillance places on their work processes and procedures, even if they possess higher levels of technical knowledge.[141] Technical knowledge does, however, translate into a higher utilization of digital security tools, even though the savvier journalists acknowledged their struggles

---

[136] Mills, *supra* note 96.
[137] Mahoney, *supra* note 6; Ramos, *supra* note 120.
[138] Waters, *supra* note 135.
[139] Gennie Gebhart, "What If All Your Slack Chats Were Leaked?," *New York Times*, July 1, 2019, para. 4, https://www.nytimes.com/2019/07/01/opinion/slack-chat-hackers-encryption.html (accessed November 15, 2019).
[140] Insider Staff, "Live Event: Discussing Data Protection at a New York Times 'CryptoParty,'" *New York Times*, July 28, 2017, https://www.nytimes.com/2017/07/28/insider/events/cryptoparty-data-security-new-york-times.html?rref=collection%2Ftimestopic%2FComputer%20Security%20 (accessed March 1, 2018).
[141] Waters, *supra* note 135.

to effectively implement various tools. It can be assumed that conflicting priorities and tight budgetary and time restraints make a serious investment in cybersecurity training difficult for many organizations, yet it offers an opportunity for redefining collaborations among individuals and "competitors" in the industry.

To be fair, the myriad information and tools related to cybersecurity for journalists is diffuse, spread across a multitude of organizations interested in assisting reporters in protecting themselves and their sources.[142] In some cases, this important issue seems muted among other priorities for even prominent journalism advocacy groups; for example, Poynter's News University—a partnership among the Poynter Institute, the American Press Institute, and the Knight Foundation—offered 124 courses on its website in November 2019, but none of them were focused on digital security.[143] Another organization's Whistleblowing Survival Tips do not specifically identify cybersecurity or the use of data privacy tools as something whistle-blowers should consider,[144] and a recent FTI media report does not specifically identify individual journalist cybersecurity as one of its seventy-six tech trends to watch.[145]

As previously stated, the lack of solid information security practices across all media is a significant concern for individuals and organizations on both sides of the journalist-source partnership. However, this should not discount the efforts to bolster the awareness, understanding, and skills of individual journalists and the media outlets that employ them. A portion of the advances in cybersecurity practices has come from the efforts of media outlets and tech-savvier journalists themselves; however, those efforts are rightfully cloaked in secrecy and therefore much more difficult to document than those incidents in which transgressions occur.[146] Professional organizations dedicated to journalism and free speech protections often fill the gap, offering a wide assortment of support including online reference materials, security, checklists, technological applications, and personal training.[147]

Although journalists might be late adopters to digital security tools, there are those who understand the threats and are sharing their expertise with others. Jorge Luis Sierra, a reporter and Knight Fellow with the International Center

---

[142] Adam Marshall, "Sidebar: The Tools of Data Security," *The News Media & The Law*, Fall 2014, https://www.rcfp.org/wp-content/uploads/2019/01/Fall_2014.pdf (accessed January 4, 2017).

[143] "Digital Tools Catalog," *Poynter Institute* (blog), https://www.newsu.org/resources/digital-tools?search=&type%5B%5D=436 (accessed November 15, 2019).

[144] Tom Devine, "Whistleblowing Survival Tips," *Government Accountability Project* (blog), 2009, https://www.whistleblower.org/whistleblowing-survival-tips (accessed January 4, 2017).

[145] "2018 Tech Trends for Journalism and Media," *supra* note 106.

[146] Waters, *supra* note 135.

[147] "Digital Security Archives," Journalist's Toolbox, *Society of Professional Journalists*, June 3, 2018, http://www.journaliststoolbox.org/category/digital-security-and-privacy/ (accessed November 15, 2019).

for Journalists, created an app, Salama, that helps identify security risks for journalists.[148] Sierra reported that as of February 2017, more than 130 news organizations have used the app—several of which found security vulnerabilities.[149] Organizations including the Electronic Frontier Foundation,[150] Google's Project Shield,[151] and Outline[152] are developing tools marketed specifically for journalists and media organizations.

It should not be overlooked that a foundational element of prioritizing enhanced security measures is overcoming a sense of futility many journalists have about their ability to effectively defend themselves against such widespread and veiled surveillance.[153] Empowering journalists and sources may, in some instances, be mandatory before basic changes in professional practices are possible.

3. Organizations should take the lead. It is worth re-emphasizing that organizations should not expect individual journalists to conduct the necessary research, vetting, implementation, and consistent application of appropriate digital security measures on their own—especially in light of shrinking newsrooms and budget cuts across the industry. Organizations must match a cultural commitment to maintain healthy information security practices with significant financial investment. As a component of more comprehensive efforts to improve technological adoption in all aspects of news reporting and presentation, protecting the very origin of critical advocacy journalism must command more attention and be considered an investment rather than an expense.[154] And although the implementation of systems and practices required for healthy information security is a good start, experts remind organizations that the investment is ongoing; a report from global digital consulting firm Accenture found that effective cyber resilience requires that organizations change their security approaches regularly to stay ahead of bad actors.[155] Ongoing efforts should

---

[148] Alexandra Ludka, "'Salama' App Aims to Keep Journalists Safe," *International Center for Journalists* (blog), July 23, 2015, https://www.icfj.org/news/salama-app-aims-keep-journalists-safe (accessed January 4, 2017).

[149] "The State of Technology in Global Newsrooms," Survey, International Center for Journalists, 2017, https://www.icfj.org/sites/default/files/2018-04/ICFJTechSurveyFINAL.pdf (accessed April 4, 2018).

[150] "Security Scenarios: Assessing Your Risks," *Surveillance Self-Defense* (blog), Electronic Frontier Foundation, https://ssd.eff.org/en/playlist/journalist-move#assessing-your-risks (accessed April 4, 2017).

[151] "Project Shield," https://projectshield.withgoogle.com/public/ (accessed November 15, 2019).

[152] "Introducing Outline: Making It Safer to Break the News," *Outline*, March 21, 2018, https://www.getoutline.org/en-GB/ (accessed April 4, 2018).

[153] Waters, *supra* note 135; Lashmar, *supra* note 95.

[154] Charo Henriquez, "Training Is an Investment, Not an Expense," *Nieman Lab* (blog), 2017, http://www.niemanlab.org/2017/12/training-is-an-investment-not-an-expense/ (accessed April 4, 2018).

[155] "Resiliency in the Making," Accenture Security, https://www.accenture.com/content/dam/accenture/final/capabilities/cross-service-group/iconic-thought-leadership/document/Resiliency-in-the-making-report.pdf (accessed October 22, 2023).

include a focus on hiring individuals with better digital security skill seta as well as the investment in—and continuous promotion of—better training for employees across the organization.

4. **Technical knowledge must be shared with sources—and vice versa.** Even if newsrooms are providing the knowledge and technological tools journalists need to protect themselves, it is crucial to keep in mind that communication is a two-way process. Sources are often unaware of the reporter's use of security tools to protect their communications. Therefore, sources—not only journalists—must employ appropriate information security to fully protect their interactions.[156] According to *New York Times* investigative reporter Scott Shane, data were obtained through vulnerabilities on the source's end: "In almost every leak case, an electronic trail led from the source to the reporter that the FBI could file."[157] Some organizations seem to attempt to educate potential sources; the *New York Times* maintains a web page for confidential informants that lists five tools they can use to communicate with the news organization. The same page includes a reminder that no communication system is completely secure.[158] Other journalists, however, have followed advice from their intelligence sources knowledgeable of effective security tools.[159] In one study, Chilean journalists using the WhatsApp messaging platform reported higher levels of relationship dynamics including intimacy, trust, and camaraderie with sources.[160]

5. **Collaboration must be a new industry norm.** If journalists are not receiving adequate information security training from their employers, one would hope the industry as a whole could contribute to an increase in tech savvy. However, there is an understandable trend to keep cyberattacks or revelations about surveillance quiet—including the protective measures that were used, and whether they were effective. After an accusation that Russia had hacked several newspapers in 2016, the *New York Times* responded with a veiled public statement: "There are a variety of approaches we take up to and including working with outside investigators and law enforcement. We won't comment on any specific attempt to gain unauthorised access to The Times."[161]

---

[156] Zhang, *supra* note 132.
[157] Joel Simon & Alexandra Ellerbeck, "The President's Phantom Threats," *Columbia Journalism Review* (blog), Winter 2018, https://www.cjr.org/special_report/president-threats-press.php (accessed November 15, 2019).
[158] "Got a Confidential News Tip?," *New York Times*, December 14, 2016, http://www.nytimes.com/tips.
[159] Tshepo Tshabalala, "How To: Staying Safe Online for Journalists," *Jamlab* (blog), July 21, 2017, https://medium.com/jamlab/how-to-staying-safe-online-for-journalists-32a63785c2ac (accessed April 4, 2018).
[160] Tomás Dodds, "Reporting with WhatsApp: Mobile Chat Applications' Impact on Journalistic Practices," *Digital Journalism*, 7, no. 6 (July 3, 2019), 725–45, doi: 10.1080/21670811.2019.1592693.
[161] Charlie Peat, "Has Putin Hacked US Newspapers? FBI Launches Probe into Security Hack," *Express.Co.Uk*, August 24, 2016, https://www.express.co.uk/news/world/703269/Vladimir-Putin-US-newspaper-New-York-Times-Barack-Obama-FBI-probe-hackers-cyber (accessed January 4, 2017).

Because journalists are often secretive about their digital security practices, the natural knowledge sharing that might occur among peers is less likely to occur.[162] Researchers have experienced this same reluctance when conducting qualitative interviews with journalists about surveillance.[163] Overcoming this obstacle will not only increase understanding of the scope of risk and offer increased efficiencies within the industry, but would likely partially alleviate challenges related to investment costs related to technological development and implementation as well.

6. **Technological disruption and evolution must be anticipated.** Technological innovation is a continuous process, as is the public's understanding of and reaction to it. What challenges will the increased use of drones, artificial intelligence, augmented reality, machine learning, and other emerging technological capabilities pose to the ways journalists and confidential sources interact? As technology becomes more sophisticated, new vulnerabilities arise alongside increased opportunities to collect data. The majority of Americans already believe their personal data is tracked daily by the government and are "concerned, confused, and feeling lack of control over their personal information."[164] Again, collaboration will likely be key to ensuring news organizations not only address any existing deficits related to cybersecurity but also proactively develop strategies in anticipation of what is to come.

7. **Career migrations from the technology sector must be welcomed into the profession.** Experts predict a shift in the industries tech workers seek, potentially in a search for more meaningful, creative opportunities.[165] If received warmly by a profession known to protect its boundaries, especially in an age where the question of who is a journalist looms, an answer to a newsroom's technical challenges may walk through its door.

A closer working relationship with the technology sector should also address general usability issues and difficulties implementing security measures within existing processes and procedures within newsrooms, which are often primary obstacles to successful cybersecurity practices.[166]

---

[162] Michael Fitzgerald, "Burn after Reading: Surveillance Technologies Make It More Important for Journalists Abroad to Protect Sources," *Nieman Reports*, 68, no. 4 (Fall 2014), 29–37, https://niemanreports.org/wp-content/uploads/2014/12/NiemanReportsFall2014.pdf (accessed January 4, 2017).

[163] Waters, *supra* note 135.

[164] Brooke Auxier et al., "Americans and Privacy: Concerned, Confused and Feeling Lack of Control Over Their Personal Information," United States of America: Pew Research Center: Internet, Science & Tech, November 15, 2019, para. 1, https://policycommons.net/artifacts/616499/americans-and-privacy/1597152/ (accessed October 22, 2021).

[165] Rodney Gibbs, "Tech Workers Turn to Journalism," *NiemanLab Predictions for Journalism 2018* (blog), December 2017, https://www.niemanlab.org/2017/12/tech-workers-turn-to-journalism/ (accessed April 4, 2018).

[166] McGregor, Roesner, & Caine, *supra* note 19.

8. **"Rebelpreneurs" must be met with open minds.** Matter Ventures cofounder Corey Ford predicts the continued rise of what he identified as Rebelpreneurs, or "courageous entrepreneurs who made the leap to build ventures that speak truth to power" and bolster the defense of the media industry.[167] Amazon mogul Jeff Bezos' $250 million purchase of the *Washington Post* in 2016 is an example of an industry outsider injecting significant capital into the media sector to ensure the survival of quality journalism, especially regarding the enhancements and development of technology.[168] The rewards have been a sense of optimism and excitement at what is possible being restored to the newsroom, as well as increased readership and revenues.[169] Of course, not all purchases of news outlets are as positive, exemplified by Sheldon Adelson's highly controversial purchase of the *Las Vegas Review Journal*. Experts warn that "potential hazards arise when news outlets increasingly rely on private capital and billionaires' largess."[170]

9. **A commitment to re-establishing (and redefining, if necessary) core ethical values is crucial.** Revisiting the ethical foundation of the use of confidential sources is key, including clear establishment of how confidentiality is to be tactically maintained, when confidentiality agreements must be terminated, identification of instances in which disclosures may be unavoidable, and whether sources remain veiled after death.[171] Calls for stronger contracts that mirror professional commitments between doctors and patients or lawyers and their clients seek a journalistic privilege "as near to an absolute as it is possible to achieve—part of the cultural, political and ethical DNA of all journalists, police officers, lawyers, judges and politicians."[172]

However, others warn that the only ethical practice is to simply acknowledge to sources that news organizations cannot guarantee anonymity in today's

---

[167] Corey Ford, "The Empire Strikes Back," *NiemanLab* (blog), 2017, para. 1, http://www.niemanlab.org/2017/12/the-empire-strikes-back/ (accessed April 4, 2018).

[168] Harry McCracken, "The Washington Post Is a Software Company Now," *Fast Company* (blog), November 17, 2017, https://www.fastcompany.com/40495770/the-washington-post-is-a-software-company-now (accessed March 15, 2018).

[169] Eugene Kim, "How Amazon CEO Jeff Bezos Reinvented The Washington Post, the 140-Year-Old Newspaper He Bought for $250 Million," *Business Insider* (blog), May 15, 2016, https://www.businessinsider.com/how-the-washington-post-changed-after-jeff-bezos-acquisition-2016-5 (accessed January 4, 2017).

[170] Rodney Benson & Victor Pickard, "The Slippery Slope of the Oligarchy Media Model," *The Conversation* (blog), August 11, 2017, para. 4, http://theconversation.com/the-slippery-slope-of-the-oligarchy-media-model-81931 (accessed March 1, 2018).

[171] Tim Crook, "Is Your Source Ever Really Safe?," *British Journalism Review*, 14, no. 4 (December 2003), 7–12, doi: 10.1177/0956474803144002.

[172] Tim Crook, "Political Attack on Journalists' Sources Undermines Democracy and Must Be Stopped," *The Conversation* (blog), October 7, 2014, para. 17, http://theconversation.com/political-attack-on-journalists-sources-undermines-democracy-and-must-be-stopped-32537?utm_source (accessed January 4, 2017).

technological environment. The most technologically astute journalist cannot offer an absolute on this point.[173]

10. Greater transparency about the reporting process—especially the use of anonymous sources—can instill confidence in readers. Although it may seem ironic, "radical transparency" is key when the identity of sources is withheld from readers, who use sources to gauge credibility of information from news organizations.[174] Greater exposure of the reporting process is likely an even greater need given the spread of dis- and misinformation and the lack of media literacy thrust into public consciousness during the 2016 US presidential election.[175]

Ultimately, it will take a pervasive and continuous commitment among all actors in the production and dissemination of vital information to defend the investigative reporting abilities of news organizations. Media companies, individual journalists, and the sources reporters work so diligently to cultivate all have an important role to play—and must act quickly en force if the industry hopes to retain the powerful responsibilities related to alerting the public to government impropriety, social injustice, and myriad other critical aspects of modern life. The consequences of inaction—or ineffective action—extend far beyond even the most serious instance of injury to a single journalist or source. The due diligence of those responsible for defending the freedom of the press is the only antidote for an ailing democracy.

---

[173] Peter Suciu, "Are Newspapers at Risk from Cyber Attack?," *Editor & Publisher* (blog), October 2, 2017, http://www.editorandpublisher.com/feature/are-newspapers-at-risk-from-cyber-attack/ (accessed March 1, 2018).

[174] Sally Lehrman, "Trust Comes First," *NiemanLab* (blog), 2018, http://www.niemanlab.org/2017/12/trust-comes-first/ (accessed November 15, 2019).

[175] Raney Aronson-Rath, "Transparency Is the Antidote to Fake News," *Nieman Lab* (blog), 2018, https://www.niemanlab.org/2017/12/transparency-is-the-antidote-to-fake-news/ (accessed November 15, 2019).

8
Charging Journalists under the Espionage Act: Have We Reached a Tipping Point?

Barry J. Pollack and Brian J. Fleming[*]

I. Introduction

The Espionage Act was passed in 1917, shortly after the United States entered World War I, to prohibit the unauthorized transmission or retention of national defense information. Historically, the US Department of Justice has refrained from prosecuting journalists under the Espionage Act. As recently as 2014, then Attorney General Eric Holder pledged that "no journalist will be prosecuted or go to prison for performing ordinary news gathering activities."[1] The Justice Department's policy represents an attempt to strike a balance between its mandate to enforce the law and protect national security, on the one hand, and First Amendment principles intended to protect free speech and the free press, on the other.

By the letter of the Espionage Act, however, journalists that receive national defense information[2] from sources and/or publish national defense information are at risk of being prosecuted. For individuals unauthorized to possess

---

[*] The authors were both formerly members at Miller & Chevalier Chartered in Washington, D.C. Mr. Pollack is a partner with the law firm of Harris St. Laurent & Wechsler in Washington, D.C. Pollack served as counsel to Jeffrey Sterling in the case detailed in the authors' contribution to this volume and has defended other clients being investigated or charged under the Espionage Act. Fleming is a partner at Steptoe & Johnson in Washington, D.C., and focuses his practice on matters at the intersection of national security and international trade, with an emphasis on economic sanctions, export controls, and foreign direct investment. Fleming formerly worked in the Justice Department's National Security Division, where his responsibilities included investigating and prosecuting matters arising under the Espionage Act, such as media leaks. The authors would like to thank Miller & Chevalier Associate Nina Gupta for her substantial contributions to this chapter.

[1] Charlie Savage, "Holder Hints Reporter May Be Spared Jail in Leak," *New York Times*, May 27, 2014, https://www.nytimes.com/2014/05/28/us/holder-hints-reporter-may-be-spared-jail-in-leak.html (accessed November 7, 2023).

[2] "National defense information" is not a defined term under the Espionage Act, but it has been defined through the case law. In *Gorin v. United States*, the Supreme Court held that the term "national defense" is a "generic concept of broad connotations, referring to the military and naval establishments and the related activities of national preparedness." 312 U.S. 19, 28 (1941). This "generic concept" has been limited to information that the government has taken steps to keep secret. *United States v. Heine*, 151 F.2d 813, 817 (2d Cir. 1945). Classified information is often a useful proxy for national defense information, although the terms are not co-extensive and national defense information can be unclassified. *See, e.g., United States v. Awwad*, Case No. 14-cr-00163 (E.D. Va.

national defense information, like journalists, the Espionage Act criminalizes the willful communication or transmission, as well as the willful retention of such information.[3]

During the Barack Obama era, it was written often in the mainstream press that the administration was waging a "war on leaks."[4] That appellation was the result of a string of high-profile leak prosecutions undertaken by President Obama's Justice Department. Notably, the defendants in each of those leak cases were current or former government employees or contractors who either publicly disclosed national defense information themselves or through an intermediary, such as a journalist.[5]

The Donald Trump administration seemed poised to take the "war on leaks" one step further by going after journalists themselves. President Trump has declared that the media "is the enemy of the American People."[6] Senior administration officials, including former Attorney General Jeff Sessions, have put the news media on notice that there are limits to the First Amendment–based deference they will be accorded.

In an effort to determine whether we have reached a tipping point that could lead to the prosecution of a journalist under the Espionage Act, this chapter first examines two cases from the Obama administration—one that typifies the more aggressive approach of the Justice Department during President Obama's first term (*United States v. Stephen Kim*) and one that illustrates the somewhat more restrained approach taken during Obama's second term (*United States v. Jeffrey Sterling*). Next, we examine public statements by President Trump and senior administration officials to assess whether threats lobbed at the news media—both explicit and implicit—should be taken seriously or disregarded as mere rhetoric. Finally, we look holistically at the recent cases, the current political climate, the legal and structural impediments to charging journalists for conduct related to their newsgathering and reporting activities, and certain external

2015) (defendant pleaded guilty to attempted espionage based upon transmittal of documents that were unclassified).

[3] 18 U.S.C. § 793(e) (2012).
[4] Leonard Downie Jr., "In Obama's War on Leaks, Reporters Fight Back," *Washington Post*, October 4, 2013, https://www.washingtonpost.com/opinions/in-obamas-war-on-leaks-reporters-fight-back/2013/10/04/70231e1c-2aeb-11e3-b139-029811dbb57f_story.html?utm_term=.bb2947ce5903 (accessed November 7, 2023).
[5] Peter Sterne, "Obama Used the Espionage Act to Put a Record Number of Reporters' Sources in Jail, and Trump Could Be Even Worse," *Freedom of the Press Foundation*, June 21, 2017, https://freedom.press/news/obama-used-espionage-act-put-record-number-reporters-sources-jail-and-trump-could-be-even-worse/ (accessed November 7, 2023).
[6] Donald J. Trump (@realDonaldTrump), Twitter (February 17, 2017, 4:48 PM), https://twitter.com/realDonaldTrump/status/832708293516632065?ref_src=twsrc%5Etfw&ref_url=http%3A%2F%2Fthehill.com%2Fhomenews%2Fadministration%2F320168-trump-the-media-is-the-enemy-of-the-american-people (accessed November 7, 2023).

factors that could ultimately determine whether this hypothetical scenario ever becomes reality.

II. *United States v. Stephen Kim*: The Reporter as Co-Conspirator

In August 2010, Stephen Jin-Woo Kim, a former State Department contractor, was indicted for unauthorized disclosure of national defense information and making false statements.[7] The indictment alleged that in June 2009, Kim possessed a top-secret intelligence report and disclosed national defense information contained in the report to an unnamed reporter for a national news organization.[8] Kim then allegedly denied having any contact with the reporter when questioned by the Federal Bureau of Investigation (FBI).[9] On the day that the intelligence report was released, Fox News reporter James Rosen published an article containing information from the report.[10] The article prompted an FBI investigation, which determined that the classified national defense information was first made available to a limited number of members of the intelligence community, including Kim, and that Kim had called and met with Rosen on the day the classified intelligence report was released. On February 7, 2014, Kim entered a guilty plea to a single felony count of disclosing classified national defense information to an unauthorized person.[11] Kim was ultimately sentenced to a thirteen-month prison term.

Before Kim was indicted, in May 2010, the government filed under seal an application for a search warrant to search the Gmail account of Rosen, who was identified in an accompanying affidavit only as "the Reporter."[12] The affidavit in support of the application for a search warrant stated that there was probable cause to believe that "the Reporter has committed or is committing a violation of section 793(d), as an aider and abettor and/or co-conspirator."[13] In support of this assertion, the affidavit stated that the published article reflected the reporter's

---

[7] Indictment, *United States v. Kim*, 808 F. Supp. 2d 44 (D.D.C. 2011) (No. 1:10-cr-00225-CKK), ECF No. 3.
[8] *Id.* at 1.
[9] *Id.* at 2.
[10] James Rosen, "North Korea Intends to Match U.N. Resolution with New Nuclear Test," *Fox News*, June 11, 2009, http://www.foxnews.com/politics/2009/06/11/north-korea-intends-match-resolution-new-nuclear-test.html (accessed November 7, 2023).
[11] Signed Plea Agreement, *United States v. Kim*, 808 F. Supp. 2d 44 (D.D.C. 2011) (No. 1:10-cr-00225-CKK), ECF No. 274.
[12] Application for a Search Warrant, No. 1:10-mj-00291-AK (D.D.C. Nov. 7, 2011), ECF No. 20; Affidavit in Support of Application for Search Warrant at 2, No. 1:10-mj-00291-AK (D.D.C. November 7, 2011), ECF No. 20-1.
[13] Affidavit in Support of Application for Search Warrant at 3, No. 1:10-mj-00291-AK (D.D.C. November 7, 2011), ECF No. 20-1.

knowledge that he had received intelligence information, the disclosure of which could be harmful to the United States, but he nevertheless published an article containing this information.[14] The affidavit also stated that the reporter "asked, solicited and encouraged" Kim to disclose sensitive information, and the reporter did so "by employing flattery and playing to Mr. Kim's vanity and ego."[15] The reporter also allegedly instructed Kim on a plan to facilitate their communication, and the reporter and Kim used aliases in their email communication.[16] After publishing the article, the reporter allegedly provided Kim with news articles in advance of publication and continued to contact him as a source.[17] Based on these facts, the government argued that there was probable cause to believe that the reporter had committed a violation of the Espionage Act as an aider, abettor, and/or co-conspirator of Kim, and his email account should therefore be seized and searched.[18]

On May 19, 2013, after obtaining the affidavit, the *Washington Post* identified James Rosen as the reporter to whom Kim allegedly disclosed national defense information.[19] The *Washington Post* detailed how the Justice Department had monitored Rosen's activities, traced the timing of his calls, and obtained a search warrant for his personal emails.[20] At a time when the Obama administration was under scrutiny for leak investigations, the *Washington Post* noted that this case raised concerns "about the possible stifling effect of these investigations on a critical element of press freedom: the exchange of information between reporters and their sources."[21] The revelations in the *Washington Post* article led to outrage from the press and other critics, who said that calling Rosen a "co-conspirator" threatened to criminalize and chill press freedoms protected by the First Amendment.[22] Fox News immediately defended Rosen and said it was "downright chilling" that the government named him a criminal co-conspirator for simply doing his job.[23] The *New Yorker* similarly called it "unprecedented" for

[14] *Id.* at 26.
[15] *Id.*
[16] *Id.*
[17] *Id.* at 27.
[18] *Id.*
[19] Ann E. Marimow, "A Rare Peek into a Justice Department Leak Probe," *Washington Post*, May 19, 2013, https://www.washingtonpost.com/local/a-rare-peek-into-a-justice-department-leak-probe/2013/05/19/0bc473de-be5e-11e2-97d4-a479289a31f9_story.html?utm_term=.1e125059fbeb (accessed November 7, 2023).
[20] *Id.*
[21] *Id.*
[22] Ann E. Marimow, "Justice Department's Scrutiny of Fox News Reporter James Rosen in Leak Case Draws Fire," *Washington Post*, May 20, 2013, https://www.washingtonpost.com/local/justice-departments-scrutiny-of-fox-news-reporter-james-rosen-in-leak-case-draws-fire/2013/05/20/c6289eba-c162-11e2-8bd8-2788030e6b44_story.html?utm_term=.56442ab48908 (accessed November 7, 2023).
[23] "Justice Department Affidavit Labels Fox News Journalist as Possible 'Co-conspirator,'" *Fox News*, May 20, 2013, http://www.foxnews.com/politics/2013/05/20/justice-department-obtained-records-fox-news-journalist.html (accessed November 7, 2023).

the government to accuse a reporter of breaking the law for reporting on government secrets.[24]

The Justice Department responded that it had abided by "all applicable laws, regulations, and longstanding Department of Justice policies intended to safeguard the First Amendment interests of the press."[25] The Justice Department added that no reporter had been charged in Kim's case, and they did not anticipate bringing additional charges against anyone.[26] The US Attorney's Office for the District of Columbia also asserted that the government "exhausted all reasonable non-media alternatives for collecting the evidence" before seeking a search warrant.[27] The Justice Department's actions, however, appeared to be in tension with statements from President Obama, who stated during his administration: "Journalists should not be at legal risk for doing their jobs. Our focus must be on those who break the law."[28]

Shortly after the backlash, the Justice Department pledged to review its policies relating to the use of criminal process and other investigative tactics in connection with members of the news media. At President Obama's direction, Attorney General Holder held meetings with news media stakeholders, First Amendment academics and advocates, and members of Congress.[29] In July 2013, the Justice Department published a "Report on Revised Media Guidelines."[30] Notably, the report stated that news media would receive advance notice whenever the Justice Department is seeking to access their records, and the Justice Department would require the attorney general's approval for search warrants and court orders directed at members of the news media.[31] In February 2014, Attorney General Holder signed new rules to revise the media guidelines,[32] and in January 2015, Attorney General Holder announced expanded revisions to the media guidelines to "strike an appropriate balance between law enforcement's need to protect the American people, and the news media's role in ensuring the

---

[24] Ryan Lizza, "The D.O.J. Versus James Rosen," *New Yorker*, May 20, 2013, https://www.newyorker.com/news/news-desk/the-d-o-j-versus-james-rosen (accessed November 7, 2023).

[25] Marimow, *supra* note 19.

[26] Marimow, *supra* note 22.

[27] "Justice Department," *supra* note 23.

[28] Washington Post Staff, "Text of President Obama's May 23 Speech on National Security (Full Transcript)," *Washington Post*, May 23, 2013, https://www.washingtonpost.com/politics/president-obamas-may-23-speech-on-national-security-as-prepared-for-delivery/2013/05/23/02c35e30-c3b8-11e2-9fe2-6ee52d0eb7c1_story.html?utm_term=.e68c95f32b65 (accessed November 7, 2023).

[29] Department of Justice, "Report on Review of News Media Policies" (July 12, 2013), https://www.justice.gov/sites/default/files/ag/legacy/2013/07/15/news-media.pdf (accessed November 7, 2023).

[30] *Id.*

[31] *Id.* at 2–3.

[32] "Holder Signs Final Rules Regarding Obtaining Information from Journalists," *JD Journal*, February 24, 2014, https://www.jdjournal.com/2014/02/24/holder-signs-final-rules-regarding-obtaining-information-from-journalists/ (accessed November 7, 2023).

free flow of information."[33] The revisions included an expansion of high-level review by the attorney general for the use of certain law enforcement tools when the Justice Department is seeking information from the news media related to newsgathering activities.[34]

III. *United States v. Jeffrey Sterling*: No Reporter's Privilege

Another case from the Obama administration reflects a contrast to the approach taken in *Kim*. Jeffrey Alexander Sterling, a former CIA employee, was convicted of violating the Espionage Act for revealing national defense information to journalist James Risen. In December 2010, Sterling was indicted for unlawful retention and unauthorized disclosure of national defense information, mail fraud, unauthorized conveyance of government property, and obstruction of justice.[35] The indictment alleged that Sterling stole classified documents and shared classified information with an unnamed author in retaliation for the handling of an employment discrimination case he filed against the CIA.[36] Sterling allegedly provided the author information regarding a clandestine CIA program that attempted to impede certain countries' weapons capabilities.[37] In 2006, Risen published a book, *State of War: The Secret History of the CIA and the Bush Administration*, which described the CIA program and characterized it as a mismanaged mission.[38]

In May 2011, the government subpoenaed Risen to testify at Sterling's trial and reveal his journalistic sources. The government argued that there is no First Amendment or common law reporter's privilege that would shield a reporter from his obligation to testify, even if the testimony reveals confidential sources. Alternatively, the government argued to the extent there is an applicable privilege, it is a qualified one and that the government's need for the testimony outweighed any interest in keeping it confidential.[39] Risen and his attorneys argued to the contrary and moved the court to quash the subpoena with an accompanying

---

[33] Press Release, Department of Justice, Attorney General Holder Announces Updates to Justice Department Media Guidelines, January 14, 2015, https://www.justice.gov/opa/pr/attorney-general-holder-announces-updates-justice-department-media-guidelines (accessed November 7, 2023).

[34] *Id.*

[35] Indictment, *United States v. Jeffrey Alexander Sterling*, No. 1:10-cr-00485-LMB (E.D. Va. December 22, 2010), ECF No. 1.

[36] *Id.* at 7-8.

[37] *Id.* at 8, 13.

[38] James Risen, *State of War: The Secret History of the CIA and the Bush Administration* (Simon & Schuster, 2006), 197, 210-11; Affidavit of James Risen, *United States v. Jeffrey Alexander Sterling*, 1:10-cr-00485-LMB, at ¶¶ 16-17 (E.D. Va. June 21, 2011), ECF No. 115-2.

[39] Government Motion In Limine to Admit the Testimony of James Risen, *United States v. Jeffrey Alexander Sterling*, No. 1:10-cr-00485-LMB (E.D. Va. May 23, 2011), ECF No. 105.

CHARGING JOURNALISTS UNDER THE ESPIONAGE ACT   161

affidavit from Risen in which he asserted his refusal to testify and disclose his confidential sources.[40] The US District Court for the Eastern District of Virginia granted in part and denied in part Risen's motion to quash the government's subpoena, holding that if a reporter presents evidence that he obtained information under a confidentiality agreement or that the subpoena's goal was to harass or intimidate the reporter, then the reporter has a qualified privilege against testifying in a criminal proceeding.[41] The court found that Risen had a confidentiality agreement with his source, and the government could not demonstrate that the information it sought from Risen was unavailable from other sources or that Risen's testimony was necessary to prove Sterling's guilt beyond a reasonable doubt.[42] Thus, Risen was only required to testify to authenticate the accuracy of his journalism.[43]

In July 2013, the US Court of Appeals for the Fourth Circuit reversed the district court's order granting Risen's motion to quash the government's subpoena.[44] The Fourth Circuit held that no First Amendment or common law reporter's privilege exists, and therefore no privilege protected Risen from responding to the government's subpoena and testifying at trial.[45] Although Risen sought review from the US Supreme Court, the Court declined to hear the case, keeping the Fourth Circuit's ruling in place.

Although the Fourth Circuit's ruling has broad implications for reporters and potentially gives prosecutors a powerful tool to force journalists to reveal their sources, the government elected not to call Risen to testify during Sterling's trial. Because Risen had indicated publicly and in court filings that he would not reveal his sources at trial, he likely would have been exposed to a criminal charge for contempt.

Attorney General Holder first suggested that the Justice Department might not call Risen to testify at trial during a meeting with journalists to discuss press-freedom issues in May 2014.[46] While Risen was not cited specifically, Attorney General Holder said that no journalist would be prosecuted or go to jail for doing his job.[47] Given the immense pressure placed upon the Obama administration by the news media at that time—in the wake of *Kim* and other leak cases—and

---

[40] Notice of Motion of James Risen to Quash Subpoena and/or for Protective Order, *United States v. Jeffrey Alexander Sterling*, 1:10-cr-00485-LMB (E.D. Va. June 21, 2011), ECF No. 115; Affidavit of James Risen, *United States v. Jeffrey Alexander Sterling*, 1:10-cr-00485-LMB (E.D. Va. June 21, 2011), ECF No. 115-2.
[41] Memorandum Opinion, *United States v. Jeffrey Alexander Sterling*, 1:10-cr-00485-LMB (E.D. Va. July 29, 2011), ECF No. 146.
[42] *Id.* at 32–32.
[43] *Id.* at 32.
[44] *United States v. Sterling*, 724 F.3d 482 (4th Cir. 2013).
[45] *Id.* at 499.
[46] Savage, *supra* note 1.
[47] *Id.*

the fact that the Justice Department was in the midst of reviewing and revising its media guidelines, the administration may have wanted to take a more cautious approach and refrain from exposing Risen to a contempt charge. Holder has said that one of his biggest regrets was labeling Rosen as a criminal "co-conspirator" in connection with the *Kim* case, and this may have been an attempt to make amends.[48]

Sterling was ultimately convicted without Risen's testimony and without any direct evidence that Sterling had provided information to Risen. Despite the Justice Department's decision not to call Risen to testify, there is now Fourth Circuit precedent that allows future administrations to force journalists to testify regarding their confidential sources.

IV. The Trump Administration: A Declaration of War against the "Enemy of the American People"?

The Trump administration has been vocal about its displeasure with the proliferation of media leaks and, in particular, the role that journalists have played in that perceived trend. During his August 4, 2017, press conference, Attorney General Sessions condemned leaks of classified information and discussed the Justice Department's efforts to investigate and prosecute people who unlawfully disclose classified information.[49] Sessions noted that since January 2017, the Justice Department has more than tripled the number of active leak investigations compared to the number pending at the end of the Obama administration.[50] He also confirmed that the Justice Department is reviewing its internal policies governing leak investigations, such as those related to the issuance of subpoenas and other legal process directed at media members and media entities.[51] These are the very same policies that were reviewed and revised under the direction of former Attorney General Holder just a few short years ago. Attorney General Sessions further stated that the Justice Department "will give [journalists] respect, but it is not unlimited."[52] He emphasized that the role of the press must be balanced with protecting national security.[53]

---

[48] Matt Apuzzo, "Times Reporter Will Not Be Called to Testify in Leak Case," *New York Times*, January 12, 2015, https://www.nytimes.com/2015/01/13/us/times-reporter-james-risen-will-not-be-called-to-testify-in-leak-case-lawyers-say.html?mcubz=3 (accessed November 7, 2023).

[49] Press Release, Department of Justice, Attorney General Jeff Sessions Delivers Remarks at Briefing on Leaks of Classified Materials Threatening National Security, August 4, 2017, https://www.justice.gov/opa/pr/attorney-general-jeff-sessions-delivers-remarks-briefing-leaks-classified-materials (accessed November 7, 2023).

[50] *Id.*
[51] *Id.*
[52] *Id.*
[53] *Id.*

Two days after the press conference, Deputy Attorney General Rod Rosenstein appeared to change course and clarified that the Justice Department does not prosecute journalists for doing their job and that the Department is after the leakers rather than the press.[54] He did emphasize, however, that "there might be a circumstance where" reporters who publish information are committing a crime.[55]

Meanwhile, President Trump routinely has called major news organizations such as CNN, NBC, and the *New York Times* "fake"[56] and has labeled journalists as "dishonest" and "sick" people who "don't like our country."[57] The president's hostile remarks about the press even prompted an op-ed in the *New York Times* titled, "We're Journalists, Mr. Trump, Not the Enemy."[58]

V. Now That We Seem to Have Reached the Precipice, What Is Next?

With the White House setting the tone, many believe that the government's open hostility toward journalists during the Trump Administration has never been worse. Score-settling and vendettas have been the order of the day, with journalists caught in the crossfire. The situation seems especially fraught, considering that journalists have been protected from government interference through the years by a system of First Amendment–related customs and norms. Given the Trump administration's distaste for customs and norms of all varieties, it has been an open question whether this bulwark will hold.

Moreover, as *Kim* and *Sterling* demonstrate, the traditional barriers protecting journalists may have begun to crumble during the Obama administration. At a minimum, some of the investigative tactics directed at journalists during the Obama administration could be deployed more aggressively in the coming

---

[54] Noah Weiland, "Reporters Not Being Pursued in Leak Investigations, Justice Dept. Says," *New York Times*, August 6, 2017, https://www.nytimes.com/2017/08/06/us/politics/trump-leaks-deputy-attorney-general-journalists.html?mcubz=0 (accessed November 7, 2023).

[55] *Id.*

[56] Donald J. Trump (@realDonaldTrump), Twitter (Oct. 4, 2017, 9:47 AM), https://twitter.com/realDonaldTrump/status/915589297096536065; Donald J. Trump (@realDonaldTrump), Twitter (Sept. 27, 2017, 8:36 AM), https://twitter.com/realDonaldTrump/status/913034591879024640 (accessed June 14, 2024).

[57] Donald J. Trump (@realDonaldTrump), Twitter (July 4, 2016, 6:42 AM), https://twitter.com/realdonaldtrump/status/749961528422625281?lang=en (accessed June 14, 2024). Daniel Victor, "Trump, Calling Journalists 'Sick People,' Puts Media on Edge," *New York Times*, August 23, 2017, https://www.nytimes.com/2017/08/23/business/media/trump-rally-media-attack.html?mcubz=3 (accessed November 7, 2023).

[58] Nicholas Kristof, "We're Journalists, Mr. Trump, Not the Enemy," *New York Times*, August 24, 2017, https://www.nytimes.com/2017/08/24/opinion/trump-journalists-enemy.html?mcubz=3 (accessed November 7, 2023).

years.[59] Moreover, the notion that the newsgathering function of journalists should afford them special rights or special treatment—that is, that their constitutionally protected purpose permits them to operate outside of the law—has been criticized sharply and publicly, particularly among policymakers and law enforcement officials.

It seems safe to assume that the former Trump administration would be willing to, at the very least, seriously consider taking the unprecedented step of prosecuting a journalist under the Espionage Act for newsgathering activities. There are, however, significant legal and prudential obstacles that could prevent it from doing so.

Because charging a journalist under the Espionage Act would be a first-of-its-kind case, there is significant litigation risk attached. Should such a case be brought, it likely will face every legal challenge imaginable, whether those challenges are rooted in the First Amendment or otherwise.

Focusing solely on the First Amendment aspect of this issue, it is difficult to anticipate how courts would analyze Espionage Act charges brought against a journalist for newsgathering activities. Despite case law analyzing the limits of First Amendment protections enjoyed by journalists in the context of, for example, grand jury or trial subpoenas, those cases address the issue of protecting journalistic sources. Just as in *Sterling*, those cases invariably wrestled with the question of whether journalists should be compelled to testify and reveal their sources and, should they refuse to comply, the related question of whether they are entitled to any First Amendment–based protections to shield them from punishment for being held in contempt of court.[60]

Not surprisingly, there is no case law examining a First Amendment–based defense for journalists charged under the Espionage Act. Over the years, several cases have addressed, at least in passing, potential First Amendment–based defenses to Espionage Act charges raised by nonjournalist defendants, but none were successful.[61] Of course, should a journalist defendant raise a First Amendment–based challenge to an Espionage Act charge, it is difficult, if not impossible, to predict how a court might react. The Fourth Circuit's holding in *Sterling* might suggest that courts could be hostile to claims of First Amendment protections for journalists in this context. However, if confronted with a

---

[59] James Risen, "If Donald Trump Targets Journalists, Thank Obama," *New York Times*, December 30, 2016, https://www.nytimes.com/2016/12/30/opinion/sunday/if-donald-trump-targets-journalists-thank-obama.html (accessed November 7, 2023).

[60] *See, e.g., In re Grand Jury Subpoena, Judith Miller*, 397 F.3d 964 (D.C. Cir. 2005).

[61] *See, e.g., Kim*, 808 F. Supp. 2d 44 (rejecting an as applied unconstitutional vagueness challenge and a First Amendment content-based restriction challenge to 18 U.S.C. § 793); *United States v. Steven Rosen*, 445 F. Supp. 2d 602 (E.D. Va. 2005) (rejecting an as applied constitutional vagueness challenge to 18 U.S.C. § 793); *United States v. Morison*, 844 F.2d 1057 (4th Cir. 1988) (rejecting an as applied constitutional vagueness challenge to 18 U.S.C. § 793).

journalist defendant who argues, in essence, that he or she was charged under the Espionage Act for doing his or her job, then such an argument could resonate more powerfully and alter the legal analysis.

Courts could also be forced to reckon with content-based challenges to Espionage Act charges against journalists. It is well established that content-based discrimination against particular speech is unconstitutional.[62] Moreover, depending upon how it is applied, a law, such as the Espionage Act, could be considered an impermissible content-based regulation even if it is facially neutral.[63]

For example, let's assume a reporter published an article that was critical of Trump administration policy and was later charged under the Espionage Act in connection with disclosing classified information in that very same story. Depending upon the circumstances, that reporter may consider arguing that he or she has been subjected to impermissible content-based discrimination under the First Amendment. If that same reporter works for the *New York Times*, the *Washington Post*, or CNN—that is, media outlets that have been harshly criticized by the Trump administration for the substance of their reporting—then the argument would seem to be even stronger. Furthermore, if a Fox News reporter published a story containing substantially similar classified information, but that story was not critical of the Trump administration and that reporter was never subsequently charged under the Espionage Act, then that would seem to lend even more weight to the allegations of content-based discrimination.

Another major factor not to be overlooked is the potential influence that the news media itself could have on this issue. As described earlier, in the context of both *Kim* and *Sterling*, many mainstream journalists were outraged by the investigative and courtroom tactics employed by the Justice Department. Accordingly, there were numerous advocacy pieces produced by print and television journalists across the country decrying the perceived overreach by the government and the potential chilling effect that such actions could have on press freedom, specifically, and free speech, generally.[64] With recent precedent for public outcry to influence policymakers with respect to the government's treatment of journalists, one can only imagine the reaction of the mainstream news media if a journalist were to be charged under the Espionage Act. Due to the current administration's well-documented interest in public perception (and approval), this phenomenon could potentially provide a protective buffer for journalists.

---

[62] *See Reed v. Town of Gilbert, Ariz.*, 135 S. Ct. 2218, 2227, 192 L. Ed. 2d 236 (2015).
[63] *See Ward v. Rock Against Racism*, 491 U.S. 781, 791, 109 S. Ct. 2746, 105 L. Ed. 2d 661 (1989).
[64] "The Obama Administration and the Press: Leak Investigations and Surveillance in Post-9/11 America," *Committee to Project Journalists*, October 10, 2013, https://cpj.org/reports/2013/10/obama-and-the-press-us-leaks-surveillance-post-911.php (accessed November 7, 2023).

Given the highly polarized nature of US politics, however, it is an open question whether that same attitude will spill over into the news media. Should we expect that Fox News will lend its support and influence to the *Washington Post*, and vice versa? In connection with James Risen's appeal in the Fourth Circuit Court of Appeals on the reporter's privilege issue, most major media organizations—liberal and conservative—filed amicus curiae briefs in support of Risen's position. One wonders whether that same unified support would be present in a future case, especially if there is sentiment among the news media that certain organizations are being targeted or protected by the government.

Finally, there is always the prospect that state and federal legislators could step in and increase protections for journalists. At present, forty-nine states and the District of Columbia have some form of media shield or common law protection, which recognizes the reporter's privilege. Not surprisingly, those protections vary in scope and quality.[65] In recent years, there also has been discussion of potential federal legislation to enact a media shield law.[66] Notably, there are no current proposals in Congress to enact such legislation, and, of course, prior legislation was focused on the reporter's privilege issue, not on the protection of journalists from other criminal charges in connection with their newsgathering activities. Would the prosecution of a journalist under the Espionage Act be an inciting event that leads Congress to take up the issue once again and pursue more comprehensive legislation? Only time will tell how the next, critical chapter of this story will unfold.

VI. Conclusion

Journalists have been protected from prosecution in connection with their newsgathering activities by a discretionary policy choice rooted in respect for the First Amendment and the free press. Now, it appears more likely than ever that the government may be ready to jettison that policy and test the limits of the First Amendment by prosecuting a journalist under the Espionage Act in connection with its crackdown on media leaks. As discussed earlier, it is difficult to predict whether such criminal charges, if brought, could withstand judicial scrutiny. Nevertheless, one could imagine some theoretical set of factual allegations that even a sympathetic court would be hard-pressed to deny the government the chance to present its case to a jury.

---

[65] *See, e.g.,* New York Civil Rights Law Article 7, Section 79-h (absolute privilege for reporters with respect to confidential sources); North Carolina General Statutes Section 8-53.11 (qualified privilege for reporters with respect to confidential or nonconfidential information).

[66] *See, e.g.,* Free Flow of Information Act of 2013 (H.R. 1962).

Regardless of the prospect of success in the courtroom, the more interesting question may be whether an administration openly hostile to the news media is prepared to deal with the complex repercussions of such a momentous decision (should it choose to make it). Those repercussions are troubling and difficult to imagine; the potential responses of the administration are even more so.

9
Using UK Law to Investigate Misuse of Data during the 2016 US Election: Cambridge Analytica and the Internationalization of Voter Analytics

David R. Carroll

I. Introduction: A Personal Narrative

The Cambridge Analytica story, told in fragments as it unfolded, felt like a watershed moment of the information age. Depending on who you ask, Cambridge Analytica might be understood as a footnote to the tumultuous 2016 US presidential campaign, having been overhyped by media coverage into yet another moral panic about inconvenient truths about free online services. Others understand the scandal as a seismic wake-up call to the practices of newly powerful industries built upon the collection and monetization of personal data at scale. Most people associate Cambridge Analytica with a Facebook data privacy scandal that triggered new attitudes about social impact and justifications for new regulations. Somehow though, the image of swashbuckling data consultants surreptitiously collecting Facebook data to target voters with disinformation based on their personality caused a tipping point, regardless of whether it could ever be proven. Others understand Cambridge Analytica through lenses of national security, data rights, and new forms of wielding power that could be called digital colonialism. This view attempts to confront the privatization of the military industrial complex which resulted in a situation where British aristocrats teamed up with American oligarchs to exploit nations with lax and nonexistent data protections in elaborate and, in certain contexts, unlawful attempts to influence electorates.

When I started my own quest in January of 2017 to recover my personal data from the company in the United Kingdom, I had no idea how far down a rabbit hole I would fall, nor did I have a sense of how consequential this effort could become. As I sat on my kitchen table on the morning of March 27, 2017, checking my email over coffee, an incoming message caught my attention. A letter from Cambridge Analytica had arrived and, with it, a spreadsheet of my voter profile.

My impulse was to publish it to Twitter, capturing my initial reactions. At this point, only a few people had an interest in the company. It would be another year before it became a household name around the world.

II. The Transnational Impetus for a Legal Challenge

Curiosity in Cambridge Analytica began in 2015 as political reporters covered the Senator Ted Cruz campaign for US president during the primary season. Republicans, eager to catch up and leapfrog the Obama digital machine, made for intriguing campaign analysis. The company resurfaced in the summer of 2016, as the Donald Trump digital campaign was covered by news outlets including *Bloomberg*, *Forbes*, *The Intercept*, and VICE's *Motherboard*. However, it wasn't until March 17, 2018, that the peculiar narrative culminated with an announcement by Facebook that it was suspending Cambridge Analytica from its platform. That same day, unrelated, I filed a claim in the High Court in London against Cambridge Analytica and its affiliates SCL Elections Ltd. and SCL Group Limited under the UK Data Protection Act, seeking full disclosure of my voter file. That weekend, three news outlets, *The Guardian/Observer*, the *New York Times*, and the UK Channel 4, launched an explosive series of reports of the mysterious company that included whistle-blowing and undercover videos. Almost immediately, the scandal was roiling the world, as dozens of nations realized their elections had also been managed by a shadowy set of British-based companies engaged in unethical activity at minimum, but the potential for unprosecuted criminal activities loomed large.

At this stage, we might have understood a strange new kind of colonialism emerging, one built upon a newly troubling practice of data laundering, exploiting laissez-faire privacy regulations in often fragile democracies. For the first time in the United States, political campaigns had hired an internationalized entity that worked across jurisdictions, employed foreign nationals, and processed Americans' voter data abroad. This included subcontracting software to an obscure firm in British Columbia called AggregateIQ from an entity within SCL Group, based in the United Kingdom, itself a company with security clearance and subject to weapons export controls by the British government. When the dust settled from the tumultuous aftermaths of the Brexit referendum and the election of Trump, as well as elections in other nations including Kenya and Philippines, citizens began a collective introspection into the new methods of data-driven profiling and microtargeting on social media platforms. As people realized that their personal data might have been used against them without their knowledge or consent, an awakening had been triggered. As former SCL Group Chief Operations Officer, Julian Wheatland, quips in a documentary about the scandal, "There was always going to be a Cambridge Analytica. It just sucks for me that it was Cambridge Analytica."

Data laundering now appears to be an inevitable complement to money laundering among white-collar miscreants, organized crime, and the international plutocratic oligarchy in Russia, the United Kingdom, and the United States. As it were, the American hedge fund "mad scientist" Robert Mercer and his daughter Rebekah Mercer, who champion conservative causes at all levels of government, having recognized the power of data and computation to manipulate both markets and electorates, conscripted the aspiring propagandist Steve Bannon to wage a new transnational culture war to unravel the postwar world order. Robert Mercer's skills and success at using massive data sets to predict and move financial markets would allegedly be used to attempt to sway voters, lurching the culture rightward in the process. Despite mounting a campaign rooted in White supremacy rebranded as "economic nationalism," the Mercer-Bannon machine would be forced to draw data science talent from Britain, Canada, and Italy. It would brazenly collaborate across nations, attempting to support the campaign to convince Britons to leave the European Union. What might have been previously understood as inappropriate election interference and meddling was refashioned into an oxymoronic platform of internationalized nationalist populism. EU member states with strong records of data protection enforcement, including France and Germany, discouraged SCL's sales team from winning contracts there.

III. Marketing Military Methods and "Big Data" Academia Leads to Scandal

In public, the British executives of the SCL Group once touted their ability to win the hearts and minds of jihadists and squelch the scourge of violent extremism as well as they could manage elections for prestigious politicians. In private, these old Etonians at the helm of this psychological operations (PSYOPs) shop proffered KGB-style operations including kompromat attacks, cyberoperations, disinformation, and other dirty tricks. The Mercers and Bannon formally constructed their partnership with the British military contractor SCL officially in 2014, when they formed Cambridge Analytica in an effort to rebrand the firm for use in elections in America and beyond. Mutually eager to expand the firm's practice into data analytics, SCL Elections CEO Alexander Nix teamed up with Rebekah Mercer and Bannon to create Cambridge Analytica across multiple entities, including a secret Delaware-based LLC to stash the Mercer investment funds and a UK-based Cambridge Analytica (UK) Ltd., renamed from SCL USA Ltd.

Meanwhile, in 2014, Nix, Mercer, and Bannon had contracted a Cambridge University lecturer, Aleksander Kogan and his postdoc student Joseph Chancellor at the Psychometrics Centre. To win the contract from SCL, Kogan and Chancellor were instructed to form Global Science Research Ltd. for the express purpose of harvesting a vast database of Facebook likes using a deceptive personality quiz that did not explicitly disclose the extent of data harvesting, which included siphoning it from users' friends. The deceptive quiz misappropriated data by failing to disclose to users that the data would be used for political purposes. Facebook failed to vet rogue developers on its platform during this period of freewheeling growth-at-all-costs. This posture came back to haunt Facebook in the spring of 2018, as the company's most challenging scandal erupted from whistle-blowing and considerable journalistic investigation. This early attempt to build a Cambridge Analytica data warehouse exposed Facebook to congressional and parliamentary inquiries, a stock sell-off, and a sudden drop in user trust by 66 percent according to surveys. Nix and Kogan would later settle with the Federal Trade Commission for deceptive practices involving misleading those who took the original quizzes. Facebook hired Chancellor from GSR and then dismissed him without explanation after specific inquiries from Congress and Parliament about his role in the scandal.

On March 17, 2018, I attended PutinCon, convened by chess grandmaster turned activist Garry Kasparaov. A tight operation, secured for the guest dissidents, the Hell's Kitchen location in New York City was only disclosed to attendees the morning of the event. I kept having to get up out of my seat and leave the theater. My lawyer in Britain, Ravi Naik, kept calling me on Signal, an encrypted messaging app. He was finalizing my claim against Cambridge Analytica. We were shooting to get the filing to the court and served to SCL Group in London, a year in the making, on my ultra-secure Swiss VPN over the PutinCon Wi-Fi, making final approvals on my iPhone. I bumped into Natasha Bertrand from *The Atlantic* and Issie Lapowsky from *Wired*, tipping them on the news. The staffer who served SCL's papers at their offices said that it seemed like SCL knew we were on our way. Later that night, Facebook announced they were suspending Cambridge Analytica and SCL in attempt to front-run the pending headlines in the *New York Times* and *The Guardian/Observer* about Christopher Wiley.

If you had told me in 2015 that I'd be at a conference about Russia, paranoid about my secure comms to my British lawyer, who was finalizing a lawsuit against Donald Trump's voter data shop, which turned out was tightly intertwined with a military-grade psychographic PSYOPS shop, funded by a mad scientist far-right billionaire for his alt-right culture war, I would not have believed you. When people ask me how I got here, they ask me if I was ever concerned for my safety. There was only one occasion when SCL employees attempted to mount a disruption on my school's campus for a shakedown to get me to drop my lawsuit.

IV. Transnational Regulatory Arbitrage in Enforcing Data Protection Rights

Back when I was just sitting at the kitchen table, enjoying my morning coffee, checking my email, it arrived from data.compliance@sclgroup.cc with the subject line "Next steps in your request" dated March 27, 2017. When I started the process to request my data from the Trump campaign's data analytics firm, Cambridge Analytica, that January, I did so out of an academic curiosity, researching intersections between the advertising industry's use of data and technology and its impact on civil society, especially journalism. I did not expect to end up as a witness presenting evidence to Members of the British Parliament in Washington, D.C., as part of their inquiry into propaganda and electoral irregularities. Nor did I expect to learn the difference between a solicitor and a barrister and other significant differences between the American and British legal systems. Shortly after publishing my Cambridge Analytica data on Twitter, I became a client of a formidable legal team in the United Kingdom eager to represent me in a landmark data protection case challenging the completeness of the firm's disclosure and respect of the rights afforded to American citizens who had their voter registration files enriched with their commercial behavior data by this weird military contractor in London, a company embroiled in multiple international investigations into election interference across the United States, Great Britain, Canada, Kenya, and beyond.

Cambridge Analytica and its disgraced and banned CEO made misleading statements to the press and Parliament while in the limelight, many easily refuted. The company adamantly and falsely insisted it had no Facebook data. The whistle-blower, Christopher Wylie, working with Carole Cadwalladr at *The Guardian* to expose their illicit data operation, the day after I filed my claim in British court, vividly described how the company's models and algorithms originated from Facebook. Issie Lapowsky reported that her sources close to the company saw Facebook data at Cambridge Analytica in 2017, well past the firm's claim of deletion. The letter signed by Alexander Nix to Facebook certifying deletion of illicitly harvested data was itself fraudulent.

During public sessions, Nix did not always demonstrate a sterling grasp of English law. For example, while before the House of Commons, when asked by an MP if an American citizen requested their data, would they be presented with all 4,000–5,000 data points assembled into their profile, Nix seemed to think that the UK Data Protection Act did not apply to American citizens. The following week, Nix's regulator, Information Commissioner Elizabeth Denham, was asked by committee chair Damian Collins why she had jurisdiction over my case. She clearly asserted that because Cambridge Analytica processed my data in the United Kingdom, the Data Protection Act applies, regardless of citizenship. The Information Commissioner released to the press a remarkable tidbit from her engagement with SCL. They asserted to her that I had no more rights to my data than a member of the Taliban sitting in a cave in the remotest corner of Afghanistan. In that statement, attempting to troll their data protection regulator, their mask came off. To them, there is no real difference between a terrorist and a voter, if neither enjoys data protection rights and enforcement.

V. Crucial Collaboration Supporting the Private Action

Long before I started admiring the intricacies of Nix's signature subterfuge, I knew deep down exactly what had happened over the summer of 2016. In the immediate aftermath of the election, as the fallout dissipated, I found myself connecting with Jonathan Albright, the data forensics specialist working out of a basement office at Columbia Journalism School. He was collecting huge data sets, scraping gigantic portions of the internet into his own data analytics operation. He was mapping the "disinfoscape" by visualizing how sites link to each other. His maps revealed the vast scale of the right-wing media ecosystem and how sites like the Mercers' Breitbart News, RT.com, YouTube, and WikiLeaks served as crucial nodes in the amplification networks. He honed in on the adtech trackers on hyperpartisan hoax sites. We chatted over Signal late nights about what he was revealing and the disturbing implications. The privacy Death Star looked like an infection, engulfing establishment media, choking it. Facebook and Google's microtargeting of business model and algorithms appeared to be getting gamed, helping to explain why misinformation flooded feeds and autocomplete search bars.

Paul-Olivier Dehaye, the Swiss-based mathematician, was requesting data from companies under EU law before it was de rigueur. He had recovered his Uber data well before the "Greyballing" controversies erupted as Apple CEO Tim Cook demanded that then founder CEO Travis Kalanick quit using device fingerprinting and cloaking techniques prohibited by App Store policy. This data sovereignty entrepreneur was independently researching that SCL Group and its dodgy dealings and PYSOPs-as-a-service business model well before any intrepid journalists had broken a big enough story to start attracting the trust of whistle-blowers.

Dehaye not only taught me how to request my data from Cambridge Analytica in the Winter of 2017 but had his startup PersonalData.IO donate the £10 fee that was required to seek my data from SCL Elections Ltd. That was the first clue that for some strange reason, Rebekah Mercer, Bannon, and Nix decided to store and process their voter data and models in the United Kingdom instead of the United States. They did this after seeking advice from former New York Mayor Rudy Giuliani's firm warned them about the dangers of using an international political data and "election management" firm. We know this because Christopher Wylie, the former research director at Cambridge Analytica's early days, provided the memo to the press, after carefully and methodically piercing his nondisclosure agreement over the course of a year of coverage, mostly led by Cadwalladr from *The Guardian/Observer*.

VI. Confronting the Power of Insolvency and Bankruptcy

I knew the day would come. I just didn't know how big it would be. Serving as a source for Cadwalladr since the start of her investigation, I knew that a whistleblower existed. But I didn't know his name, or any substance to his story. I was wisely protected from him during the process. I had no idea about the Channel 4 undercover work catching Nix and colleagues in the act of boasting about entrapment schemes. Watching them was a moment of vindication that my original worries were absolutely justified. It was also a nightmarish vision of our worst fears. Nix would later receive his punishment of being banned from directorships by the UK Insolvency Service for his conduct of professionalized deception.

According to Cambridge Analytica's official statement, I was "wasting other people's money" with my "spurious" action against them. Indeed, the SCL Group companies were eventually and successfully liquidated into the Mercer family's holding company called Emerdata Ltd. by the joint administrators led by the firm Crewe. My data protection challenge against the companies was thwarted by the moratorium triggered by going into administration in the United Kingdom and filing for bankruptcy in the United States. A strong data-protection case on behalf of every registered voter in the 2016 presidential elections suddenly shifted our legal strategy as the Cambridge Analytica companies employed a drastic exit strategy.

What started as a data-protection application to the court under the Data Protection Act of 1998 evolved into a filing against the joint administrators under the Insolvency Act alleging bias against me as a contingent creditor, a unique status I enjoyed from filing the data protection claim, put under moratorium. While I did win court-ordered documents about the SCL Group companies in liquidation that were inappropriately withheld from a creditor like myself, proving such bias, and vindicating other concerns about the company's failure to respect UK law in connection to US elections, I ultimately lost my case against the companies through the joint administrators. The judge presiding over the case decided that the remediation of my complaint would involve reassigning the administration of the SCL Group companies to the secretary of state. We had arranged for a new administrator from the accounting firm KPMG to volunteer to take on work for state in the event of that outcome. KPMG had pledged to directly address outstanding data protection issues, whereas the Crowe firm flatly refused. Instead, the judge likened the data protections to sanitation violations even though they were described by the Information Commissioner's Office report as breaching a key principle of the Data Protection Act of 1998 by unfairly creating political profiles of US voters in connection with the 2016 presidential election without their consent or associated data rights.

VII. Conclusion: Regulatory Failure and the Journalistic Failsafe of Leaks

Instead of releasing a detailed forensic report as suggested in earlier parliamentary subcommittee hearings, the Information Commissioner (ICO) sent a finalizing letter to the chair of the House of Commons Digital, Culture, Media and Sport Committee. The letter hinted at various loose ends while dithering on larger questions. Depending on one's prior views of the scandal, the letter confirmed one's biases. For skeptics, the company was indeed selling "snake oil" because internal communications examined by the ICO's forensic team suggested that employees used industry standard tools and methods for data analytics. For alarmists, the ICO's letter to the Digital Culture, Media, and Sport (DCMS) Committee proved that the company was dangerous because forensics revealed how it was in the process of moving its operations offshore to evade further accountability. Either way, US voters were not offered a narrative as to how their data was assembled by and with various data brokers and then processed by SCL in Britain, even though UK law entitled the public to this information precisely because Cambridge Analytica was a thin façade for SCL, and ultimately a UK operation.

In the lead-up to the 2020 presidential election in the United States, the UK broadcaster Channel 4 News produced another exposé related to the Trump 2016 campaign operation. An unknown source leaked the entire 2016 voter database to Channel 4, whose broadcasters proceeded to approach individual voters in battleground districts in Wisconsin and Florida, showing them their voter files on digital tablets. When a Black woman voter in Milwaukee is shown her file that marks her for a deterrence campaign designed by Cambridge Analytica that disproportionately targeted Black voters in her district, she replied that knowing this made her want to voter even more. In that moment, the power of a voter profile was neutralized through its transparency. Also significantly, it took a follow-up act of journalism to achieve my full data rights. An unknown whistle-blower, having leaked the Trump campaign's 2016 database to reporters, achieved what the Information Commissioner's Office could not. Channel 4 delivered my complete voter profile from Trump's 2016 campaign from the leak, which contained all the data points I always expected, and far more disclosure than originally provided by SCL in 2017. Of course, it included a blend of data-brokered files from firms such as Axciom, Aristotle, InfoGroup, DataTrust, and LL2, all matching Cambridge Analytica's own marketing materials boasting of its commercial data sourcing. A personality score was also included in my file provided by Channel 4 News. This was despite repeated denials by the company and campaign staff about the Trump campaign's use of psychographics.

10
Digital Shackles: The Political Economy of Surveillance Technologies and the Emergence of Transnational Surveillance Fascism

Jennifer R. Henrichsen

I. Introduction

Journalists are facing increasing physical and digital attacks around the globe as they strive to carry out their work. These attacks include physical and digital surveillance; hacking of their devices and accounts; online harassment, doxing, and mob censorship; and physical assault, arrest, and murder.[1] An area of significant concern for journalists globally is the increasing sophistication, availability, and ubiquity of unregulated spyware technologies that are sold to governments ostensibly for fighting terrorism, but which are increasingly being used to target journalists and activists in countries around the world.[2]

Over the last several years, numerous journalists and news organizations globally have reported incidents in which their communications have been hacked, intercepted, or retrieved.[3] The use of surveillance against journalists occurs even in countries where freedom of the press is enshrined in law. For example, in the United States, surveillance programs and an aggressive Department of Justice have reduced the flow of information from government sources to journalists.[4]

---

[1] Jennifer R. Henrichsen, Michelle Betz, & Joanne Lisosky, *Building Digital Safety: A Survey of Key Issues* (UNESCO, 2015); Julie Posetti et al., "The Chilling: Global Trends in Online Violence Against Women Journalists," UNESCO, 2021, https://en.unesco.org/publications/thechilling (accessed January 19, 2024).

[2] Siena Anstis et al., "The Dangerous Effects of Unregulated Commercial Spyware," *Citizen Lab*, June 24, 2019, https://citizenlab.ca/2019/06/the-dangerous-effects-of-unregulated-commercial-spyware/ (accessed January 19, 2024).

[3] Stephanie Kirchgaessner et al., "Revealed: Leak Uncovers Global Abuse of Cyber-Surveillance Weapon," *The Guardian*, July 18, 2021, https://www.theguardian.com/world/2021/jul/18/revealed-leak-uncovers-global-abuse-of-cyber-surveillance-weapon-nso-group-pegasus (accessed January 19, 2024).

[4] "With Liberty to Monitor All: How Large-Scale US Surveillance Is Harming Journalism, Law, and American Democracy," Human Rights Watch and American Civil Liberties Union, July 2014,

---

Jennifer R. Henrichsen, *Digital Shackles: The Political Economy of Surveillance Technologies and the Emergence of Transnational Surveillance Fascism* In: *National Security, Journalism, and Law in an Age of Information Warfare*. Edited by: Marc Ambinder, Jennifer R. Henrichsen, and Connie Rosati, Oxford University Press.
© Oxford University Press 2024. DOI: 10.1093/oso/9780197756621.003.0010

Surveillance and metadata of the communications prevents government sources from remaining anonymous, making them less likely to be in contact with journalists about background information that may be sensitive but is not necessarily classified. In response to their shrinking source pool, journalists have felt the need to adopt steps to protect their sources from metadata that reveals their identity or relationship. This, in turn, reduces the efficiency of the reporting enterprise, resulting in fewer stories and less accountability.[5] In response to this more challenging and restrictive environment, journalists are taking longer to piece together information on key aspects of government, including the intelligence community, national security, and law enforcement.[6]

Journalists' concerns about surveillance also have led journalists and writers to self-censor. A 2013 PEN America report[7] found that 24 percent of writers have avoided certain topics of conversation over phone or email because of concerns about surveillance and how it might cause them future trouble. Writers also avoided conducting research on certain topics because they were concerned about how their search terms on these topics might be interpreted. In addition, approximately 93 percent of journalism professionals reported being "very concerned" about government efforts that sought to compel journalists to reveal sources who had provided classified information.[8] Indeed, writers in liberal democratic countries are engaging in self-censorship at levels similar to writers in nondemocratic countries, indicating that "mass surveillance has badly shaken writers' faith that democratic governments will respect their rights to privacy and freedom of expression."[9]

The expansion and use of secret surveillance technologies against journalists, writers, and activists have troubling implications for freedom of expression, despite international legal agreements designed to ensure its protection. Article 12 of the UN Universal Declaration of Human Rights (UDHR), for example, seeks to protect individuals from arbitrary targeting. It states, "No one shall be subjected to arbitrary interference with his privacy, family, home, or correspondent, nor to attacks upon his honour and reputation. Everyone has the right to the protection of the law against such interference or attacks."[10] Article 19 of the UDHR mandates, "Everyone has the right to freedom of opinion and

---

https://www.hrw.org/sites/default/files/reports/usnsa0714_ForUPload_0.pdf (accessed January 19, 2024).

[5] Id.
[6] Id.
[7] "Chilling Effects: NSA Surveillance Drives U.S. Writers to Self-Censor," FDR Group and PEN America, 2013, as of December 12, 2016, http://www.pen.org/chilling-Effects.
[8] Id.
[9] Id. 5.
[10] "Universal Declaration of Human Rights," United Nations, 1948, http://www.un.org/en/universal-declaration-human-rights/ (accessed November 25, 2023).

expression; this right includes freedom to hold opinions without interference and to seek, receive and impart information and ideas through any media and regardless of frontier."[11] Additionally, international legal obligations, as identified in the UN Guiding Principles on Business and Human Rights, indicate that "companies have a responsibility to respect human rights wherever they operate in the world" and must "take proactive steps to ensure that they do not cause or contribute to human rights abuses within their global operations and respond to any human rights abuses when they do occur."[12] These declarations and principles are aimed at ensuring nation-states implement and respect fundamental human rights.

Additionally, and more specifically, there are several international legal agreements that seek to regulate dual-use technologies (i.e., technologies that are used for military and civilian purposes). One of the most important agreements pertaining to dual-use technologies is the Wassenaar Arrangement, which includes forty-two members. Wassenaar is a voluntary, multilateral export control agreement that stipulates countries must follow certain rules when allowing companies to sell surveillance technologies. States that have signed on to this arrangement have agreed to have national export controls on certain items such as munitions (e.g., small arms, light weapons, tanks) and dual-use goods and technologies such as computers, telecommunications systems, and information security systems.[13] The countries associated with the Wassenaar Arrangement have certain responsibilities, including to report on transfers and denials of specified controlled items to destinations not listed in the arrangement, and to exchange information on dual-use technologies and goods which are considered sensitive. These countries also must follow agreed-upon "Best Practices, Guidelines, and Elements" as declared in the arrangement.[14] Finally, the countries carry out national export controls on listed items through the implementation of national legislation.[15]

Although intended to originally limit weapons (such as landmines), the Wassenaar Arrangement was updated in 2013 to include "intrusion software" (like FinFisher) and Internet Protocol (IP) monitoring to its list of export-controlled goods as a result of reports linking the sale of surveillance technologies to regimes with abuses.[16] This was a significant achievement and the result of

---

[11] *Id.*
[12] Sam Biddle & Fahad Desmukh, "Phone-Cracking Cellebrite Software Used to Prosecute Tortured Dissident," *The Intercept*, December 8, 2016, https://theintercept.com/2016/12/08/phone-cracking-cellebrite-software-used-to-prosecute-tortured-dissident/ (accessed January 19, 2024).
[13] "About Us," Wassenaar, 2016, last modified September 18, 2023, http://www.wassenaar.org/about-us/ (accessed January 19, 2024).
[14] *Id.*
[15] *Id.*
[16] *Id.*

research on the harms that surveillance technologies can pose to activists and journalists and advocacy initiatives to mitigate them. Despite this, the majority of technologies that can be used for repression are still unregulated, such as undersea fiber-optic cable taps and monitoring centers.[17] Ultimately, the success of the Wassenaar Arrangement depends on its member states implementing the export controls, and it remains to be seen how successful it will be for limiting the sale of surveillance technologies to certain governments.

Alongside the Wassenaar Arrangement is the Organisation for Economic Cooperation and Development (OECD). The OECD is a forum where thirty-seven democratic countries with market-based economies work with one another and with other nonmember countries' economies to promote sustainable development, economic growth, and prosperity.[18] As such, it has some power in overseeing the sale of technologies by its members. Human rights groups like Privacy International have filed complaints to member countries' OECD representatives arguing that the sale of surveillance technologies by companies within OECD member countries to countries with poor human rights records is in violation of OECD guidelines.

II. Bahrain: A Case Study

This chapter uses the case study of Bahrain because press freedom and journalistic norms are neither well established nor respected in the country.[19] Government officials have used sophisticated surveillance technologies to spy on journalists' and activists' communications and then arrest them for comments that do not portray the ruling party in a positive light.[20] Bahrain officials also regularly bar foreign reporters based in Bahrain from receiving licenses to work in the country, thereby limiting news and knowledge about human rights abuses occurring on the ground.[21]

---

[17] "An Open Letter to the Members of the Wassenaar Arrangement," Human Rights Watch, December 1, 2014, https://www.hrw.org/news/2014/12/01/open-letter-members-wassenaar-arrangement (accessed January 19, 2024).
[18] "The Organization for Economic Cooperation and Development (OECD)," U.S. Department of State, https://www.state.gov/the-organization-for-economic-co-operation-and-development-oecd/ (accessed January 19, 2024).
[19] "Bahrain," Reporters Without Borders, 2023, https://rsf.org/en/country/bahrain (accessed January 19, 2024).
[20] "Bahrain Government Must Cease Judicial Harassment of Faisal Hayyat and Other Bahraini Journalists," Fédération Internationale des Ligues des Droits de l'Homme, November 29, 2016, https://www.fidh.org/en/region/north-africa-middle-east/bahrain/bahrain-government-must-cease-judicial-harassment-of-faisal-hayyat (accessed January 19, 2024).
[21] "Bahrain: Put an End to the Systematic Surveillance Practices on Activists and Human Rights Defenders," Bahrain Center for Human Rights, August 18, 2014, https://bahrainrights.net/?p=6544 (accessed January 19, 2024).

Bahrain is a small Arab monarchy located in the Persian Gulf, which became independent from the United Kingdom in 1971. Formerly the State of Bahrain, it became the Kingdom of Bahrain in 2002 and is considered a constitutional monarchy.[22] Bahrain has a high internet penetration rate, with more than 99 percent of the population using the internet.[23] In 2011, following the Arab uprisings in nearby countries, Bahrain cracked down on activists and others supporting pro-democracy and reform efforts.[24] Censorship, especially related to political content, is widespread. Once websites are blocked, they largely remain inaccessible to users, forcing users to move to social media platforms like YouTube, Facebook, and Twitter/X. Numerous news organizations, including the independent Bahraini news outlet *Awal Online* and Qatari outlets *Al-Sharq, Al-Raya*, and *Al-Jazeera* have been blocked from 2017 or 2018.[25] The Bahrain Center for Human Rights, Alualua TV's website, and the news site, the *Bahrain Mirror*, also remain blocked.[26]

A. The Political Economy of Surveillance Technologies in Bahrain

The global trade in communication surveillance technologies is big business with an estimated worth of $5 billion dollars every year and a 20 percent increase annually.[27] According to the online database the Surveillance Industry Index, more than 528 companies are involved in the surveillance technology industry.[28] Countries that house the most surveillance companies include the United States (122), the United Kingdom (104), France (45), Germany (41), and Israel (27).[29] These countries are also within the top ten countries which export the highest number of conventional arms.[30]

---

[22] "History," Bahrain, as of October 27, 2017, http://www.bahrain.com/en/about-bahrain/pages/history.aspx.

[23] "Freedom on the Net: Bahrain," Freedom House, 2022, https://freedomhouse.org/country/bahrain/freedom-net/2022 (accessed January 19, 2024).

[24] Arch Puddington, "Essay: The Arab Uprisings and Their Global Repercussions," 2012, as of October 27, 2017, https://freedomhouse.org/report/freedom-world-2012/essay-arab-uprisings-and-their-global-repercussions.

[25] Freedom House, *supra* note 23.

[26] *Id.*

[27] "Coalition Against Unlawful Surveillance Exports (CAUSE)," Amnesty International, April 4, 2014, https://www.amnesty.org/en/latest/news/2014/04/questions-and-answers-coalition-against-unlawful-surveillance-exports-cause/ (accessed January 19, 2024).

[28] Privacy International, "The Global Surveillance Industry: A Report by Privacy International."

[29] *Id.*

[30] *SIPRI Yearbook 2015: Armaments, Disarmament and International Security* (Stockholm International Peace Research Institute, 2015), https://www.sipri.org/sites/default/files/2016-03/YB-15-Summary-EN.pdf (accessed January 19, 2024).

Bahrain has purchased a number of different surveillance systems from companies over the years, with documentation indicating these purchases occurred as early as the late 1990s. Surveillance companies which have sold their products to Bahrain include Trovicor (Germany and the UAE), Gamma (Germany and the United Kingdom), Nokia Siemens (Finland), Micro Systemation/MSAB (Sweden), Blue Coat (United States), Hacking Team (Italy), Cellebrite (Israel), and NSO Group (Israel).[31] This section will examine a few of these companies (Trovicor, Gamma, Hacking Team, Cellebrite, and NSO Group) in more detail.

Trovicor (Germany and the UAE)

Trovicor is a former subsidiary of Nokia Siemens. Siemens divested from Trovicor following protests about Trovicor's role in supplying surveillance systems to Iran after the 2009 election.[32] Perusa Partners Fund 1LP (based in Germany) then bought Trovicor. In 2019, Boss Industries purchased Trovicor and remains the owner today.[33] Trovicor is one of the most prolific mass surveillance companies, having sold spy technology to twelve countries in the Middle East and North Africa and believed to have operated in Bahrain since the late 1990s.[34] Trovicor has been linked to installing and maintaining sophisticated monitoring centers in Bahrain which have been used to surveil activists' communications. Nearly twenty-four political prisoners have testified that they have been shown transcripts of their communications while being beaten and interrogated.[35] According to *Bloomberg News*, Trovicor confirmed the sale of its surveillance technologies to Bahrain.[36] Despite this public assertion, a complaint

---

[31] "Surveillance Industry Index," as of December 10, 2016, https://sii.transparencytoolkit.org/search?utf8=%E2%9C%93&q=Bahrain; Biddle & Desmukh, *supra* note 12; Stephanie Kirchgaessner, "Phones of Nine Bahraini Activists Found to Have Been Hacked with NSO Spyware," *The Guardian*, August 24, 2021, https://www.theguardian.com/world/2021/aug/24/phones-of-nine-bahraini-activists-found-to-have-been-hacked-with-nso-spyware (accessed January 19, 2024).

[32] Trevor Timm, "Spy Tech Companies and Their Authoritarian Customers, Part II: Trovicor and Area SpA," Electronic Frontier Foundation, February 21, 2012, https://www.eff.org/deeplinks/2012/02/spy-tech-companies-their-authoritarian-customers-part-ii-trovicor-and-area-spa (accessed January 19, 2024).

[33] "Clairfield Advises Boss Industries on the Acquisition of Dubai-based Company Trovicor," *Clairfield*, December 17, 2019, https://www.clairfield.com/clairfield-advises-boss-industries-on-the-acquisition-of-dubai-based-company-trovicor/ (accessed January 19, 2024); "The Predator Files: Caught in the Net," Amnesty International, October 9, 2023, https://www.amnesty.org/en/documents/act10/7245/2023/en/ (accessed January 19, 2024).

[34] Timm, *supra* note 32; "Enemies of the Internet 2014: Entities at the Heart of Censorship and Surveillance," Reporters Without Borders, November 3, 2014, last modified January 25, 2016, https://rsf.org/en/news/enemies-internet-2014-entities-heart-censorship-and-surveillance.

[35] Timm, *supra* note 32.

[36] Trevor Timm & Jillian York, "Surveillance Inc: How Western Tech Firms Are Helping Arab Dictators," *The Atlantic*, March 6, 2012, https://www.theatlantic.com/international/archive/2012/03/surveillance-inc-how-western-tech-firms-are-helping-arab-dictators/254008/ (accessed January 19, 2024).

filed by human rights groups with the OECD, which alleged Trovicor breached the OECD Guidelines for Multinational Enterprises (relating to human rights), was rejected by the German National Contact Point because of insufficient evidence.[37] In recent years, Trovicor has argued that it carefully assesses human rights risks before issuing contracts to governments.[38]

Gamma (Germany and the United Kingdom)

The company Gamma created FinFisher, a sophisticated spyware suite sold to governments ostensibly for law enforcement and intelligence purposes. FinFisher has been used by Bahrain's government to monitor, harass, and intimidate journalists, activists, and opposition leaders.[39] The spyware suite gives the user complete access to the target's communications via their phone and computer.[40] The software can also record keystrokes, Skype conversations, and mobile phone conversations.[41] Gamma claimed it never sold FinFisher to Bahrain. Yet, in 2014, WikiLeaks published information that showed communications between officials in Bahrain and tech support from Gamma about problematic glitches in the software.[42] The evidence from WikiLeaks shows that authorities in Bahrain were using FinFisher in 2010, during the Arab Spring and the uprisings in Bahrain.[43] The spyware has also been linked to the arrest, detainment, and torture of activists in Bahrain who then sought asylum in the United Kingdom.

Human rights groups, including the Bahrain Center for Human Rights, Bahrain Watch, the European Center for Constitutional and Human Rights (ECCHR), Privacy International, and Reporters Without Borders, also filed a complaint against Gamma with the OECD's UK National Contact Point (NCP). In the complaint, the nongovernmental organizations (NGOs) accused the companies of selling surveillance technologies and providing technical support to Bahrain, which then used these technologies to monitor activists, leading to

---

[37] "German OECD National Contact Point Unwilling to Investigate Role of Germany Company in Human Rights Abuse in Bahrain," Privacy International, 2013, as of November 5, 2017, https://www.privacyinternational.org/node/478.

[38] Trovicor, "Annual Report of the Ethical Committee 2021," 2021, https://trovicor.com/wp-content/uploads/ethical-committee-report-2021.pdf.pdf (accessed January 19, 2024).

[39] Fahad Desmukh, "Bahrain Government Hacked Lawyers," BahrainWatch, April 7, 2014, https://bahrainwatch.org/blog/category/amantech/ (accessed May 16, 2024).

[40] Adriana Edmeades, "How Bahrain Spies on British Soil," Open Democracy, November 4, 2014, http://www.opendemocracy.net/opensecurity/adriana-edmeades/how-bahrain-spies-on-british-soil (accessed January 19, 2024).

[41] Reporters Without Borders, *supra* note 34.

[42] Kim Zetter, "Bahraini Activists Hacked by Their Government Go After UK Spyware Maker," *Wired*, October 13, 2014, https://www.wired.com/2014/10/bahraini-activists-go-after-spyware-source/ (accessed January 19, 2024).

[43] *Id.*

their arrest, imprisonment, and torture.[44] The OECD's UK NCP investigated and told Gamma that it should make changes to its business practices to ensure it respects the human rights of those affected by its technologies. This is the first time that the OECD found a company selling surveillance technologies to be in violation of human rights guidelines, and thus this was considered a win by advocacy groups, although tangible outcomes from the criticism remain ambiguous.[45] In addition, Privacy International filed a complaint with OECD's German National Contact Point; however, the German NCP's rejected the complaint, citing insufficient evidence.[46]

Privacy International also filed an official complaint with the United Kingdom's National Crime Agency against Gamma to investigate the unlawful surveillance of activists in the United Kingdom who were surveilled using FinFisher.[47] The complaint argues that the hacking by Bahraini officials violated the United Kingdom's Regulation of Investigatory Powers Act of 2000. Since Gamma, which has offices in the United Kingdom, helped Bahrain implement the surveillance, Privacy International claims Gamma "is liable as an accessory under the Accessories and Abettors Act of 1861 and is also guilty of encouraging and assisting the unlawful activity," which is considered a crime according to the Serious Crime Act of 2007.[48]

Hacking Team (Italy)

Hacking Team, originally based in Italy, sold technology to Bahrain through an intermediary known as MidworldPro, a Dubai-based IT company.[49] The technology that was sold was a one-year pilot program of Hacking Team's Remote Control System, which allows the user to spy on the target's communications. A cyberattack against Hacking Team and the subsequent leak of millions of internal documents, published in a searchable database by WikiLeaks, exposed the sale.[50] Although Hacking Team has claimed it "goes to great lengths" to not sell its technologies to repressive regimes, it sold its technology via an intermediary to Bahrain. The Hacking Team company hired a legal team to write a report examining whether there were limitations under Italian law preventing Hacking

---

[44] "UK Rebukes German-British Software Company Gamma," European Center for Constitutional and Human Rights, 2015, https://www.ecchr.eu/en/our_work/business-and-human-rights/surveillance-technology.html (accessed January 19, 2024).
[45] *Id.*
[46] *Id.*
[47] "NCA Bahrain Hacking," Privacy International, October 13, 2014, https://privacyinternational.org/legal-action/nca-bahrain-hacking (accessed January 19, 2024).
[48] Zetter, *supra* note 42.
[49] Reda Al-Fardan, "How the Government of Bahrain Acquired Hacking Team's Spyware," Bahrain Watch, 2015, as of December 11, 2016, https://bahrainwatch.org/blog/2015/11/13/how-the-government-of-bahrain-acquired-hacking-teams-spyware/.
[50] *Id.*

Team from selling its surveillance systems to Bahrain. The report found that there were no legal restrictions at the time of the sale.[51]

The hack and leak operation against Hacking Team contributed to a public relations scandal, lost customers, and a diminished bottom line. Despite this, a financial backer believed to be from Saudi Arabia helped to ensure the company didn't go under. A few years later, in 2019, Hacking Team was purchased by InTheCyber and renamed Memento Labs.[52] The transition was difficult for several reasons, and in 2020, the former CEO of Hacking Team, David Vincenzetti, claimed on LinkedIn that "Hacking Team is dead."[53] In 2023, Vincenzetti was arrested for attempted murder.[54]

Cellebrite (Israel)

Israel's Cellebrite software system was found to have been used by Bahrain's government against activists. Israel-based Cellebrite is owned by a Japanese software conglomerate and is a subsidiary of Japan's Sun Corporation.[55] Bahrain has used Cellebrite's technology to identify dissidents and then arrest and torture them.[56] Yet neither Bahrain nor Cellebrite would go on the record confirming the relationship, despite public evidence to the contrary.[57] Cellebrite officials stated they sell their products to government-operated law enforcement agencies around the world, although they would not confirm they sold technologies to repressive countries.[58]

NSO Group (Israel)

The Israeli cyber-intelligence firm, NSO Group, is well known for its spyware technologies, including Pegasus, in part because of large-scale investigations in

---

[51] *Id.*

[52] Joseph Cox, "Current and Ex-Employees Describe the Situation Inside Memento Labs, Which Formed after a Vigilante Hacker Targeted Hacking Team," *Motherboard*, March 31, 2020, https://www.vice.com/en/article/xgq3qd/memento-labs-the-reborn-hacking-team-is-struggling (accessed January 19, 2024).

[53] Lorenzo Franceschi-Bicchierai, "Hacking Team Founder: 'Hacking Team Is Dead,'" *Motherboard*, May 26, 2020, https://www.vice.com/en/article/n7wbnd/hacking-team-is-dead (accessed January 19, 2024).

[54] Lorenzo Franceschi-Bicchierai, "Founder of Spyware Maker Hacking Team Arrested for Attempted Murder: Local Media," *TechCrunch*, November 29, 2023, https://techcrunch.com/2023/11/29/founder-of-spyware-maker-hacking-team-arrested-for-attempted-murder-local-media/ (accessed January 19, 2024).

[55] Biddle & Desmukh, *supra* note 12; "Surveillance Company Cellebrite Finds a New Exploit: Spying on Asylum Seekers," Privacy International, April 3, 2019, https://privacyinternational.org/long-read/2776/surveillance-company-cellebrite-finds-new-exploit-spying-asylum-seekers (accessed January 19, 2024).

[56] *Id.*

[57] *Id.*

[58] *Id.*

recent years by civil society groups and academic institutions.[59] The Bahraini government is believed to have bought NSO Group's Pegasus spyware in 2017, and it is believed to have been used against Bahraini activists sometime before 2019.[60] Citizen Lab researchers observed a significant increase in Pegasus activity globally, including in Bahrain, in the summer of 2020.[61] NSO Group's Pegasus spyware has been used to successfully hack Bahraini activists' iPhones between June 2020 and February 2021. Four of the activists were hacked by a Pegasus operator that Citizen Lab researchers attribute with high confidence to the government of Bahrain, while the forensic analysis of five activists' devices is ongoing.[62]

III. The Use of Surveillance Technologies against Activists and Journalists in Bahrain

Freedom of information and expression has been under threat for more than a decade in Bahrain.[63] The government has created a news blackout and denied licenses to foreign journalists based in Bahrain so that they cannot write or publish information about the ongoing abuses in the country.[64] In addition, Bahrain has conducted widespread surveillance, harassment, arrests, and prosecutions of activists, bloggers, journalists, and netizens.[65] According to Reda Al-Fardan, from the NGO Bahrain Watch, digital attacks and emails containing malware have increased steadily since March 2012.[66] Malware can be disseminated through phishing attempts sent electronically through email and social media. This malware can compromise sensitive information, including the IP addresses of activists and journalists who might be critical of the regime.

Between mid-2012 and mid-2013, at least fifteen activists and netizens were arrested and/or convicted of crimes in Bahrain.[67] These crimes involved netizens writing anonymous tweets that called Bahrain's king a dictator. The government claimed that these tweets were against the law, which prohibits "offending the

---

[59] Bill Marczak et al., "From Pearl to Pegasus: Bahraini Government Hacks Activists with NSO Group Zero-Click iPhone Exploits," Citizen Lab, August 24, 2021, https://citizenlab.ca/2021/08/bahrain-hacks-activists-with-nso-group-zero-click-iphone-exploits/ (accessed January 19, 2024).
[60] *Id.*
[61] *Id.*
[62] *Id.*
[63] Reporters Without Borders, *supra* note 19.
[64] Bahrain Center for Human Rights, *supra* note 21; Reporters Without Borders, *supra* note 34.
[65] "World Report 2023: Bahrain, Events of 2022," Human Rights Watch, 2022, https://www.hrw.org/world-report/2023/country-chapters/bahrain (accessed January 19, 2024); Reporters Without Borders, *supra* note 34.
[66] Reporters Without Borders, *supra* note 34.
[67] "An Interactive Timeline of Netizens Being Arrested and Harassed Because of Their Tweets," Bahrain Watch, https://bahrainwatch.org/ipspy/ (accessed December 12, 2016).

Amir."[68] The government was able to identify these anonymous Twitter accounts by sending malicious links that impersonated well-known opposition leaders. Once an activist clicked on the links, they inadvertently revealed their IP address. The government then required the internet service provider to give the real address and name of the individual.[69] During interrogations of activists, officials often demanded activists' passwords to their social media and email accounts to better conduct network analysis and obtain evidence that could be used against them.[70]

A. Surveillance Technologies in Action against Journalists

Unregulated spyware technologies used by governments against members of civil society can have serious repercussions. Bahraini journalist Mohammed "Moosa" Abd-Ali was tortured, raped, beaten, and repeatedly imprisoned for his antigovernment activism over the years. He fled to London in 2005 after a particularly vicious attack by government authorities. He was granted asylum and became a cameraman for a news agency and an unofficial archivist of protests in Bahrain, which he has broadcast on YouTube.[71]

Abd-Ali has been repeatedly targeted with spyware over the years. In 2011, he opened Facebook Messenger on his iPhone and saw someone else typing to a fellow activist friend using his name and probing for information. Someone also impersonated Abd-Ali to solicit his Facebook friends for sex—potentially to blackmail or defame him because Bahrain is a conservative country. What Abd-Ali was witnessing was the government's commandeering of his entire digital existence by infecting his phone and computer with a sophisticated type of spyware.[72]

In fact, Abd-Ali was digitally attacked by government officials in Bahrain who used the sophisticated surveillance software known as FinFisher to compromise his devices and accounts.[73] The spyware became known to the public when it was published on WikiLeaks in late 2011. The spyware suite was created by Gamma, which has offices in Germany and the United Kingdom. The surveillance technologies involve remote listening and monitoring, a type of spyware

---

[68] *Id.*
[69] *Id.*
[70] Reporters Without Borders, *supra* note 34.
[71] Amar Toor & Russell Brandom, "A Spy in the Machine: How a Brutal Government Used Cutting-Edge Spyware to Hijack One Activist's Life," *The Verge*, January 21, 2015, https://www.theverge.com/2015/1/21/7861645/finfisher-spyware-let-bahrain-government-hack-political-activist (accessed January 19, 2024).
[72] *Id.*
[73] *Id.*

that normally would be considered as something worthy of export control restrictions.[74] A massive data leak in 2014 revealed that Gamma sold FinFisher to Bahrain's government, in violation of export laws in the United Kingdom and Germany, where Gamma is based, and also worked with Bahraini officials to remotely monitor computers and smartphones of activists.[75] Abd-Ali continues his activism and journalism despite being beaten and arrested while protesting the maltreatment of activists in Bahrain.[76]

Another example of a Bahraini citizen targeted by surveillance technologies is Dr. Saeed Shehabi, a journalist, commentator, and activist from Bahrain who was sentenced in absentia in 2011 to life in prison for his human rights activism.[77] He became a British citizen in 2002.[78] Shehabi is long affiliated with the Bahrain Freedom Movement, which aims to achieve human rights and democracy in Bahrain. He has also been the director of the Abrar Institute and presented a weekly program on Alaalam TV.[79] Shehabi's computer was hacked by Bahraini government officials who used Gamma's FinFisher spyware suite. The spyware allows officials to remotely monitor web traffic and Skype calls, log passwords, and turn on microphones to record.[80]

Bahrain Watch, which has strong ties to Bahraini activists, received several malicious files and sent them in a protected attachment to Morgan Marquis-Boire, a researcher formerly associated with Citizen Lab, who has experience identifying and reverse-engineering malware. Marquis-Boire was able to identify the malware as FinFisher and also trace it to the activists.[81] Marquis-Boire published his findings in papers for Citizen Lab[82] while Bahrain Watch was able to publish new evidence showing the connection to the activists through the data leak affecting Gamma.[83] This evidence was then used by advocacy groups, including Privacy International, to file complaints on the activists' behalf and to

---

[74] *Id.*

[75] *Id.*

[76] "They Tried to Throw Me Off the Roof of the Bahraini Embassy," *Vice News*, April 15, 2021, https://www.youtube.com/watch?v=p19gErE6CTA (accessed January 19, 2024).

[77] Cora Currier, "Privacy Group Targets British Spyware Company over Bahrain Surveillance," *The Intercept*, October 13, 2014, https://theintercept.com/2014/10/13/privacy-group-targets-british-spyware-company-bahrain-surveillance/ (accessed January 19, 2024).

[78] Dominic Dudley, "Bahrain Fails in Bid To Claim State Immunity Over Alleged Hacking of Dissidents," *Forbes*, February 8, 2023, https://www.forbes.com/sites/dominicdudley/2023/02/08/bahrain-fails-in-bid-to-claim-state-immunity-over-alleged-hacking-of-dissidents/?sh=5b4dcc863030 (accessed January 19, 2024).

[79] Saeed Shehabi, "About," https://saeedshehabi.wordpress.com/about/ (accessed November 25, 2023).

[80] Currier, *supra* note 77.

[81] Toor & Brandom, *supra* note 71.

[82] Morgan Marquis-Boire & Bill Marczak. "From Bahrain With Love? FinFisher's Spy Kit Exposed?," Citizen Lab, July 25, 2012, https://citizenlab.ca/2012/07/from-bahrain-with-love-finfishers-spy-kit-exposed/ (accessed January 19, 2024).

[83] Toor & Brandom, *supra* note 71.

press for reform. Prior to these disclosures, the closest evidence Shehabi had that he was being targeted was when his Twitter account began following more and more people, his daughter's travel plans were disclosed to government officials in Bahrain, and his home was the target of an arson attack.[84]

Abd-Ali and Shehabi sued Bahrain for the 2011 infection of their devices with the FinSpy surveillance software. In February 2023, London's High Court in the United Kingdom ruled that it has jurisdiction to hear the claim. In doing so, the UK court disagreed with the Bahraini government's argument that the kingdom had state immunity and that the case should be thrown out. The court proceedings are not yet scheduled.[85]

IV. The Emergence of Transnational Surveillance Fascism

This chapter has used the case study of Bahrain to reveal how spyware technologies are being used by the government to silence journalists and activists. The use of surveillance technologies by repressive regimes is increasingly commonplace and widespread. Surveillance technologies can be used by states to strengthen their power over citizens, intrude into individuals' private lives, and enforce the law.[86] These manifestations of power have a symbiotic relationship––the greater the intrusion, the more data that is collected, and the greater ability of the state to enforce the law.[87]

While Information and Communication Technologies (ICTs) and interconnected networks were heralded as a way to restructure and reshape traditional power dynamics between citizens and their governments, states and corporations can reassert the status quo and maintain control of populations through the use of these technologies in a capitalistic society.[88] As Toshimaru Ogura notes,[89] capitalism and the nation-state work together to create a climate of surveillance and management of the population: "The intention of surveillance

---

[84] Owen Bowcott, "UK Police Asked to Investigate Alleged Bahraini Hacking of Exiles' Computers," *The Guardian*, October 13, 2014. https://www.theguardian.com/technology/2014/oct/13/uk-police-investigate-alleged-bahraini-hacking-exiles-computers (accessed January 19, 2024).

[85] Dania Akkad, "High Court Rules UK-Based Bahrain Activists' Case Against Kingdom Can Proceed," *Middle East Eye*, February 7, 2023, https://www.middleeasteye.net/news/uk-bahrain-activist-case-can-move-forward-court-rules (accessed January 19, 2024).

[86] Kat Hadjimatheou, "Ethics and Surveillance in Authoritarian and Liberal States," Surveillance: Ethical Issues, Legal Limitations, and Efficiency Collaborative Project, European Union's Seventh Framework Programme, April 30, 2013, https://surveille.eui.eu/wp-content/uploads/sites/19/2015/04/D4.4-Ethics-and-surveillance-in-authoritarian-and-liberal-states.pdf (accessed January 19, 2024).

[87] *Id.*

[88] Toshimaru Ogura, "Electronic Government and Surveillance-Oriented Society," *in* David Lyon (ed.), *Theorizing Surveillance* (Willan, 2006), 270–95.

[89] *Id.*

in modern capitalist society is to control and mobilize each individual as labour power and to integrate various subject identities into a national identity."[90] In other words, surveillance in society reinforces the status quo of those who are in power by serving the interest of government and corporate bureaucracies.[91] This political and economic symbiosis shows no sign of lessening in a post-9/11 world where nation-states have expanded their surveillance powers considerably in the name of fighting terrorism, although these same technologies have been used to silence dissent from human rights activists and journalists.

The interconnection of communication technologies and the monetization of attention have led to the emergence and intensification of Shoshana Zuboff's notion of *surveillance capitalism*. Surveillance capitalism is "an emergent logic of accumulation in the networked sphere," which challenges "democratic norms and departs in key ways from the centuries-long evolution of market capitalism."[92] Computer-mediated transactions, including "data extraction and analysis," "new contractual forms due to better monitoring," "personalization and customization," and "continuous experiments," are the computer-mediated foundations for the "implicit logic of surveillance capitalism."[93] This global framework of surveillance capitalism produces new distributions and expressions of power that "exile persons from their own behavior while producing new markets of behavioral prediction and modification."[94]

Zuboff's articulation of surveillance capitalism is a good starting point for understanding the development of *transnational surveillance fascism*. Scholars have long struggled with how to define fascism. It has been conceptualized as "independent hyper-nationalist movements or as an international movement defined by a fairly rigid set of criteria."[95] Scholars have defined fascism as "the state and large corporations working together to promote corporate interests and a state preoccupied with militarism, secrecy, propaganda, and surveillance."[96] Fascist regimes may aim to overthrow current systems of government and persecute political rivals[97] while fascist leaders tend to espouse extreme nationalism, cultivate

---

[90] *Id.*, 277.

[91] Oscar Gandy, *The Panoptic Sort: A Political Economy of Personal Information* (Westview Press, 1993).

[92] Shoshana Zuboff, "Big Other: Surveillance Capitalism and the Prospects of an Information Civilization," *Journal of Information Technology*, 30, no. 1 (2015), 75, https://doi.org/10.1057/jit.2015.5 (accessed January 19, 2024).

[93] *Id.* at 75.

[94] *Id.* at 75.

[95] Samuel Huston Goodfellow, "Fascism as a Transnational Movement: The Case of Inter-War Alsace," *Contemporary European History*, 22, no. 1 (2013), 87, https://www.cambridge.org/core/journals/contemporary-european-history/article/abs/fascism-as-a-transnational-movement-the-case-of-interwar-alsace/AC8B472B62511CC03A346A5AED2C344E (accessed January 19, 2024).

[96] Robert McChesney, *Digital Disconnect: How Capitalism is Turning the Internet Against Democracy* (New York: The New Press, 2013), 171.

[97] "What Is Fascism?" Council on Foreign Relations, April 14, 2023, https://world101.cfr.org/contemporary-history/world-war/what-fascism (accessed January 19, 2024).

images of themselves as figures to be loved, and demand popular mobilization of the people.[98] Typically, fascism is justified by a government's reference to an internal enemy that cannot otherwise be controlled except by extraordinary means. Amidst these criteria, scholars have also argued that fascism is better understood as a transnational movement because it helps us "to understand the connections and similarities across a wide range of movements"[99]

Drawing from these conceptual elements, I argue that transnational surveillance fascism is the collusion between governments and corporations working together in service of commercial interests and a government's interest in controlling the population. The close cooperation of the state and corporations in the development, selling, and purchasing of surveillance technologies is emblematic of concentrated power relationships that promote the agendas of the state and big business. Transnational surveillance fascism involves the development of surveillance technologies, the selling of these technologies, a secret relationship between the state and corporations around the purchasing of these technologies, and the use of these technologies to surveil, censor, and otherwise control members of the population that are deemed a threat to the governing regime.

V. Conclusion

This chapter examined the companies that develop spyware technologies and sell them to the Bahraini government, which then has used them to target journalists and activists within Bahrain and transnationally. Companies in democratic countries create many of the sophisticated surveillance systems which are used by governments against journalists and activists in violation of international laws and norms, thus facilitating the rise of transnational surveillance fascism.

The dual-use nature of these technologies makes them difficult to regulate because companies can claim they are selling them to legitimate, government-operated law enforcement agencies which intend to use them for lawful means. The classification of such technologies as "lawful intercept" devices is, on the one hand, accurate for governments which use them in responsible ways, but illegitimate for governments that buy them under this designation and then use them to crack down on dissenting voices.

Voluntary agreements such as the Wassenaar Arrangement, which restrict what types of technologies and munitions companies can sell to other

---

[98] *Id.*
[99] Goodfellow, *supra* note 95.

governments, are not particularly effective as companies can evade scrutiny by maneuvering around these restrictions. Companies can and have publicly claimed that they do not sell their technologies to human rights–abusing countries, but rather that their technologies were stolen or otherwise used without their knowledge. Other times, companies and governments that buy their products refuse to comment, citing confidentiality agreements. The secrecy and duplicity of the political economy around surveillance technologies is one reason for their endurance.

Another source of the strength of surveillance technologies is the billion-dollar industry of communication technologies. The global trade of communication technologies is big business and increasing in monetary value. The capitalistic rewards for the creation and sale of these technologies appear to outweigh adherence to international legal frameworks and norms despite agreements by countries and companies to uphold them. The collusion between companies and governments in the selling and purchasing of surveillance technologies is facilitating the rise of transnational surveillance fascism despite export control mechanisms and international legal principles that nation-states are obliged to follow.

Yet recent developments in certain countries suggest the possible mitigation of transnational surveillance fascism. In 2020, the US Department of Commerce's Bureau of Industry and Security amended the Export Administration Regulations "to require the consideration of the human rights implications of licensing the export of any controlled item."[100] In 2021, the United States, Australia, Denmark, and Norway worked together to create a new initiative known as the Export Controls and Human Rights Initiative, which aims to "stem the tide of authoritarian government misuse of technology and promote a positive vision for technologies anchored by democratic values."[101] Additional countries, including Canada, France, the Netherlands, and the United Kingdom, later joined the initiative. The countries worked to establish a voluntary, nonbinding written code of conduct that countries could pledge to follow, which aims to prevent the proliferation of technologies that are used to facilitate serious abuses

---

[100] Christopher A. Casey, "Export Controls—International Coordination: Issues for Congress," Congressional Research Service, September 8, 2023, at 27, https://crsreports.congress.gov/prod uct/pdf/R/R47684 (accessed January 19, 2024); see also "Amendment to Licensing Policy for Items Controlled for Crime Control Reasons," Federal Register, 85, no. 63007, Bureau of Industry and Security, U.S. Department of Commerce, October 6, 2020, https://www.federalregister.gov/docume nts/2020/10/06/2020-21815/amendment-to-licensing-policy-for-items-controlled-for-crime-cont rol-reasons (accessed January 19, 2024).

[101] "Joint Statement on the Export Controls and Human Rights Initiative," White House, December 10, 2021, 1, https://www.whitehouse.gov/briefing-room/statements-releases/2021/ 12/10/joint-statement-on-the-export-controls-and-human-rights-initiative/ (accessed January 19, 2024).

of human rights.[102] Twenty-five countries[103] have endorsed the code and began discussions in the summer of 2023 on how to implement the commitments in the code of conduct.[104] It remains to be seen whether and to what extent this code of conduct will reduce the intensity, ubiquity, and pernicious nature of transnational surveillance fascism.

---

[102] *Id.*

[103] Countries that have endorsed the code include Albania, Australia, Bulgaria, Canada, Costa Rica, Croatia, Czechia, Denmark, Ecuador, Estonia, Finland, France, Germany, Japan, Kosovo, Latvia, The Netherlands, New Zealand, North Macedonia, Norway, Republic of Korea, Slovakia, Spain, the United Kingdom, and the United States.

[104] "Export Controls and Human Rights Initiative Code of Conduct Released at the Summit of Democracy," US Department of State, March 30, 2023, https://www.state.gov/export-controls-and-human-rights-initiative-code-of-conduct-released-at-the-summit-for-democracy/ (accessed January 19, 2024).

11
Digital Surveillance and Its Impact on Media Freedom: Navigating the Legal Landscape

Jennifer R. Henrichsen, Hannah Bloch-Wehba, Gabe Rottman, Grayson Clary, and Emily Hockett*

I. Introduction

The practice of journalism has never been more global than it is today. Reporters use Zoom and other video chat services to communicate with sources halfway around the world. Newsrooms rely on cloud storage to share documents among far-flung teams working on global stories. Individuals and organizations increasingly turn to cutting-edge technologies to break important news.

At the same time, new applications and services can pose risks to the security and integrity of communications. Journalists and news media organizations have increasingly been the targets of hacking. Edward Snowden's revelations about global surveillance brought to the fore the broad reach of US surveillance programs both domestically and abroad. Subsequent disclosures by the intelligence community and government oversight bodies have provided additional visibility into federal surveillance capabilities and claimed authorities.

---

* The first edition of this guide—published by the Reporters Committee for Freedom of the Press in 2017—was written by Henrichsen, a former First Look Media Technology Fellow at the Reporters Committee, and Bloch-Wehba, a former Stanton Foundation National Security Fellow at the Reporters Committee. See Jennifer R. Henrichsen & Hannah Bloch-Wehba, "Electronic Surveillance: What Reporters Should Know About the Law," Reporters Committee for Freedom of the Press, May 11, 2017, https://perma.cc/9C5C-DB5F (accessed November 5, 2023). Selina MacLaren also provided invaluable assistance with that edition. This edition was revised in 2023 by Rottman, Technology & Press Freedom Project Director at the Reporters Committee; Clary, a staff attorney at the Reporters Committee; and Hockett, Technology & Press Freedom Project Fellow at the Reporters Committee, to reflect intervening changes in the law. The authors also thank Joshua Lustig and Bre de Vera for their careful and thorough research assistance. Henrichsen and Elizabeth Chambers also provided additional editing assistance on this newer version.

Jennifer R. Henrichsen, Hannah Bloch-Wehba, Gabe Rottman, Grayson Clary, and Emily Hockett, *Digital Surveillance and Its Impact on Media Freedom: Navigating the Legal Landscape* In: *National Security, Journalism, and Law in an Age of Information Warfare*. Edited by: Marc Ambinder, Jennifer R. Henrichsen, and Connie Rosati, Oxford University Press. © Oxford University Press 2024. DOI: 10.1093/oso/9780197756621.003.0011

Responding to the shift from the analog world to the world of electronic communications, foreign intelligence entities like the National Security Agency (NSA) have developed programs to collect, analyze, and retain these communications. Sometimes these programs have swept up data from a large number of Americans in bulk, either purposefully or as a result of "incidental" acquisitions obtained while surveilling individual targets of an investigation. Bulk surveillance of communications—whether collected "incidentally" under Section 702 of the Foreign Intelligence Surveillance Act (FISA) Amendments Act of 2008,[1] through the procedures set out in the amended Section 215 program,[2] or under Executive Order 12333[3]—implicates reporters' rights in myriad ways. These programs may collect information that can reveal details of confidential communications between reporters and their sources. Because this information is not always gleaned directly from reporters, however, journalists are uncertain about the extent to which their communications are exposed. The inability to know whether and to what extent communications are being monitored creates fear and uncertainty concerning what the government considers lawful surveillance, chills speech, and impedes the exercise of First Amendment rights, including free association and free expression.

Both journalists and sources have stated that bulk surveillance and increased leak investigations make them more reluctant to communicate with each other, even if the information at issue is not classified.[4] The "chilling effect" of mass surveillance has been documented in several reports by organizations including PEN America, Human Rights Watch, and the American Civil Liberties Union, among others.[5]

But bulk surveillance is not the only threat; other national security requests have also been directed at journalists without a warrant. Even apart from foreign intelligence surveillance, the ubiquity of digital communications in the twenty-first century can facilitate government access to information about

---

[1] 50 U.S.C. § 1881a.
[2] 50 U.S.C. § 1861.
[3] Executive Order 12333.
[4] Leonard Downie Jr., "The Trump Administration and the Media: Attacks on Press Credibility Endanger US Democracy and Global Press Freedom," Committee to Protect Journalists, April 16, 2020, https://cpj.org/reports/2020/04/trump-media-attacks-credibility-leaks/ (accessed November 5, 2023); Leonard Downie Jr., "Leak Investigations and Surveillance in Post 9-11 America," Committee to Protect Journalists, October 10, 2013, https://cpj.org/reports/2013/10/obama-and-the-press-us-leaks-surveillance-post-911/ (accessed November 5, 2023).
[5] "Global Chilling: The Impact of Mass Surveillance on International Writers," PEN America, January 5, 2014, https://pen.org/research-resources/global-chilling/ (accessed November 5, 2023); see also "With Liberty to Monitor All: How Large-Scale US Surveillance Is Harming Journalism, Law and American Democracy," Human Rights Watch and ACLU, 2014, https://www.hrw.org/sites/default/files/reports/usnsa0714_ForUPload_0.pdf (accessed November 5, 2023).

private communications, including the emails, phone calls, messaging logs, and browsing histories of journalists and sources. The ability of governments, corporations, and other nonstate actors to obtain information, target searches, and store vast amounts of data for indeterminate periods of time can pose a threat to the traditional journalist-source relationship, especially when a source seeks to remain anonymous. In recognition of this fact, and following revelations of secret subpoenas and court orders in 2020 demanding records of eight journalists across three news outlets, in three separate investigations into the unauthorized disclosure of national defense information, the US Department of Justice issued in 2022 a significantly revised set of "News Media Guidelines," 28 C.F.R. Section 50.10, that governs when and how elements of the department can seek information from or of members of the news media.[6] The revised guidelines now bar legal process completely when journalists are acting within the scope of newsgathering (as defined by the policy). Most government agencies, other than the Justice Department, however, have not disclosed the policies and procedures, if any, they use to ensure that surveillance does not tread on the First Amendment rights of journalists and media organizations.[7]

The behavior of journalists and sources adds to the challenge. Both communities are often unaware of the risks of communicating electronically, or if they are aware of the risks, they may not know how to determine what steps are necessary to protect their communications.

Email encryption, secure messaging, and anonymous web browsing can be helpful tools, but can also be difficult to implement.

This chapter has two aims. First, in light of the Justice Department's revised news media guidelines, we attempt to clarify the scope of US government authority to obtain information about journalists' communications. The new guidelines, where they apply, appear to provide robust protection from legal process in federal criminal investigations, though they do not explicitly address whether the department may seek process when journalists affirmatively solicit information in a way that, nominally, could support an inchoate criminal charge

---

[6] *See* Bruce D. Brown & Gabe Rottman, "The Nuts and Bolts of the Revised Justice Dept. News Media Guidelines," *Lawfare*, May 23, 2023, https://www.lawfaremedia.org/article/the-nuts-and-bolts-of-the-revised-justice-dept.-news-media-guidelines (accessed November 5, 2023).

[7] At a federal level, at least two other agencies—Immigration and Customs Enforcement at the Department of Homeland Security and the Securities and Exchange Commission—have policies governing the use of legal process vis-à-vis the media, though neither is as protective as the revised News Media Guidelines at the Justice Department. *See* Gabe Rottman, "ICE Enacts New Policy Protecting Media from Legal Demands," *Lawfare*, June 29, 2009, https://www.lawfaremedia.org/article/ice-enacts-new-policy-protecting-media-legal-demands; "Securities and Exchange Commission v. Covington & Burling LLP," Reporters Committee for Freedom of the Press, https://www.rcfp.org/briefs-comments/sec-v-covington-burling/ (accessed November 5, 2023).

like conspiracy.[8] Furthermore, the 2022 guidelines revisions, like all previous iterations, do not apply to foreign intelligence surveillance tools, including national security letters. As such, this chapter attempts to provide a broad overview of the main statutes authorizing the government to conduct communications surveillance in the foreign intelligence, national security, and criminal justice settings, and how they interface with the new "News Media Guidelines," 28 C.F.R. Section 50.10 policy (or not).

Second, we outline how some common journalism tools expose reporters and sources to risks in light of this framework. It is our hope that a better understanding of the legal architecture that facilitates government access to communications records will help journalists make informed decisions about the types of security tools they use.

II. Legal and Regulatory Protections for Journalists

In the United States, journalists have constitutional, statutory, common law, and regulatory protections that help ensure their ability to gather and report the news without government interference. Two of the most important legal protections available to US journalists include the First Amendment and state shield laws. In the regulatory sphere, the aforementioned updated protections in Justice Department guidelines prohibit the use of legal process to seek records from or of journalists acting within the scope of newsgathering, as defined by the guidelines, with limited exceptions.[9]

A. Constitutional Protection: The First and Fourth Amendments

The First Amendment to the US Constitution guarantees freedom of expression by, among other things, prohibiting any law that infringes the freedom of the press or the rights of individuals to speak freely. The First Amendment affords broad protection to journalists and news organizations engaged in the gathering

---

[8] *See* Bruce D. Brown & Gabe Rottman, "How the New Justice Dept. Media Guidelines Might Work in Close Cases," May 30, 2023, https://www.lawfaremedia.org/article/how-the-new-justice-dept.-media-guidelines-might-work-in-close-cases (accessed November 5, 2023).

[9] *See generally* 28 C.F.R. § 50.10. As discussed *infra* section II, the revised guidelines clarify that "newsgathering" includes the "mere receipt, possession, or publication by a member of the news media of Government information, including classified information, as well as establishing a means of receiving such information, including from an anonymous or confidential source." *Id.* at 50.10(b)(2)(ii). The guidelines are "less clear on how it would apply to the explicit solicitation of information from a source." Brown & Rottman, *supra* note 8.

and dissemination of news, and a core purpose of the First Amendment is the fostering of robust and uninhibited debate on public issues.[10] For example, in *Bartnicki v. Vopper*,[11] the US Supreme Court held that the First Amendment protected a news organization from liability for the publication of information of public interest that had been obtained unlawfully by a source. The use of subpoenas to compel journalists to identify sources also presents serious First Amendment concerns: several federal circuits have recognized a qualified reporters' privilege under the First Amendment in both civil and criminal cases to protect journalists from compelled disclosure of their sources.[12]

Along with First Amendment protections, Fourth Amendment protections are among the most crucial constitutional safeguards of newsgathering in the context of government investigations. The Fourth Amendment provides that "[t]he right of the people to be secure in their persons, houses, papers, and effects, against unreasonable searches and seizures, shall not be violated, and no warrants shall issue, but upon probable cause."[13] The prohibition on unreasonable searches of "papers" and the use of "general warrants" arose from a long list of abusive colonial-era practices, many of which targeted printers and publishers of dissenting publications for seditious libel.

Under the Fourth Amendment, a "search" occurs only when the person searched has a "reasonable expectation of privacy" in the place or thing to be searched.[14] What a person "knowingly discloses" to a third party is generally not the subject of Fourth Amendment protections, and government requests for such information typically do not require a warrant or probable cause. For instance, because a telephone subscriber "knowingly discloses" dialed numbers to the telephone company, courts have held that the use of a subpoena or court order to obtain that information does not implicate the Fourth Amendment.[15] The Supreme Court has recently held, however, that this "third-party doctrine" does not extend to historical cell-site location information because of its revealing

---

[10] RCFP's First Amendment Handbook provides a primer on how the First Amendment protects journalists in a range of contexts, including from libel and defamation charges, privacy torts, and prior restraints. *See* "First Amendment Handbook," https://www.rcfp.org/wp-content/uploads/imported/FAHB.pdf (accessed November 5, 2023); *see also* Reporters Committee for Freedom of the Press, "Digital Journalists Legal Guide."

[11] 532 U.S. 514 (2001).

[12] *See, e.g., von Bulow by Auersperg v. von Bulow*, 811 F.2d 136, 142 (2d Cir. 1987) (reasoning that "the process of newsgathering is a protected right under the First Amendment, albeit a qualified one," and that "[t]his qualified right . . . results in the journalist's privilege"); *Miller v. Transamerican Press, Inc.*, 621 F.2d 721, 725 (5th Cir. 1980) (recognizing a qualified privilege not to disclose confidential informants in civil cases); *United States v. LaRouche Campaign*, 841 F. 2d 1176, 1181–83 (1st Cir. 1988). For more information, *see* "The Reporters Privilege," Reporters Committee for Freedom of the Press, https://rcfp.org/reporters-privilege (accessed November 5, 2023).

[13] U.S. Const. amend. IV.

[14] *Katz v. United States*, 389 U.S. 347, 360 (1967) (Harlan, J., concurring).

[15] *See, e.g., Smith v. Maryland*, 442 U.S. 735, 741–46 (1979).

nature,[16] and lower courts have continued to grapple with that decision's relevance for other forms of surveillance.[17] What's more, in challenges to the constitutionality of the government's bulk collection of telephone metadata, discussed in more detail later, federal courts have expressed "strong reasons to doubt" that the third-party doctrine extends to large-scale collection activity as distinct from individual surveillance orders.[18]

Nevertheless, the third-party doctrine continues to have significant ramifications for the protection of electronic communications. For example, electronic communications service providers necessarily have access to metadata such as telephone numbers, email to/from addresses, IP addresses of websites visited, and other addressing data that users are aware "is provided to and used by Internet service providers for the specific purpose of directing the routing of information."[19] This metadata can be obtained through many types of legal process. On the other hand, although the content of emails, instant messages, and text messages are often accessible by service providers as well, courts that have addressed the issue have found that individuals retain a reasonable expectation of privacy in the substance of their communications.[20] As a result, the government may *not* obtain the content without a search warrant.[21]

As a practical matter, however, many surveillance authorities permit the government to obtain information that law enforcement can use to identify sources without using formal process such as subpoenas or warrants, compelling testimony, or giving notice to a journalist whose communications may be secretly monitored or seized. Reporters whose records are obtained pursuant to national security processes such as national security letters, directives, or orders under FISA, or, when available, delayed-notice warrants or subpoenas under criminal investigative authorities, would likely not be notified or have an opportunity to try to quash the request. Indeed, it is unlikely that reporters would ever be aware that foreign intelligence authorities had been used to obtain their records. This

---

[16] See Carpenter v. United States, 138 S. Ct. 2206, 2220 (2018).

[17] See generally Matthew Tokson, "The Aftermath of Carpenter: An Empirical Study of Fourth Amendment Law, 2018–2021," Harvard Law Review, 135 (2022), 1790 (collecting cases).

[18] United States v. Moalin, 973 F.3d 977, 990 (9th Cir. 2020).

[19] United States v. Forrester, 512 F.3d 500, 510 (9th Cir. 2008).

[20] See, e.g., United States v. Warshak, 631 F.3d 266, 288 (6th Cir. 2010); Forrester, 512 F.3d at 511; cf. United States v. Hambrick, 225 F.3d 656, 2000 WL 1062039, at *2 (4th Cir. 2000) (per curiam) (finding no reasonable expectation of privacy in noncontent information provided to an ISP). See also Orin S. Kerr, "The Next Generation Communications Privacy Act," University of Pennsylvania Law Review, 162 (2014), 373, 399–400 (noting that "several lower courts have ruled that the Fourth Amendment fully protects the contents of emails held by third party providers" and "Warshak has been adopted by every court that has squarely decided the question"); cf. Carpenter, 138 S. Ct. at 2222 (suggesting that the third-party doctrine "does not apply to the modern-day equivalents of an individual's own papers or effects" (citation and quotation marks omitted); id. at 2230 (Kennedy, J., dissenting) (same (citing Warshak, 631 F.3d at 283–88))).

[21] To the extent the Stored Communications Act appears to permit warrantless acquisition of content data, it violates the Fourth Amendment. See, e.g., Warshak, 631 F.3d at 288.

uncertainty has been an impediment to journalists wishing to challenge surveillance practices that impact their own newsgathering processes.[22]

In the national security context, the Fourth Amendment's application is complex. The Fourth Amendment's protections apply domestically and to US persons abroad, but do not apply to noncitizens abroad.[23] There are no protections under the US Constitution for noncitizens abroad who are affected by foreign intelligence investigations. As a result, surveillance of non-US persons abroad is outside the scope of the Fourth Amendment. However, because some of the surveillance authorities used to collect the communications of non-US persons abroad sweep up many communications belonging to US persons as well, courts have considered whether those programs are "reasonable" under the Fourth Amendment.[24]

B. Statutory and Common Law Protections: State Shield Laws, Testimonial Privileges, and the Privacy Protection Act

The vast majority of states recognize a reporter's privilege based on state law.[25] Forty states and the District of Columbia have statutory shield laws, which give media varying degrees of protection for confidential source information.[26] Some shield laws protect reporters from forced disclosure of their sources. Other shield laws provide qualified or absolute protection that varies depending on the type of legal proceeding (civil or criminal), the scope of the statute's definition of "journalists," whether material is confidential and/or published, and whether the journalist is a defendant or an independent third party. No federal shield law exists, despite several efforts to enact such statutory protections by legislators at the national level.[27] In addition, some judges have argued

---

[22] *See, e.g., ACLU v. NSA*, 493 F. 3d 644, 662–65 (6th Cir. 2007) (noting that the journalists' injury involved "purely speculative fears" and a "personal subjective chill" that was not sufficiently concrete, actual, or imminent to establish standing for a First Amendment cause of action).

[23] *See United States v. Verdugo-Urquidez*, 494 U.S. 259, 274–75 (1990) (holding that Fourth Amendment did not apply to a citizen and resident of Mexico where the search occurred in Mexico).

[24] *See* Mem. Op. and Order at *28–29, FISC (Oct. 3, 2011) (J. Bates), http://www.dni.gov/files/documents/0716/October-2011-Bates-Opinion-and%20Order-20140716.pdf (accessed November 5, 2023).

[25] *See, e.g., O'Neill v. Oakgrove Construction Inc.*, 71 N.Y.2d 521, 524 (1988) (recognizing a reporter's privilege under state constitution).

[26] *See* "Introduction to the Reporters Privilege Compendium," Reporters Committee for Freedom of the Press, last updated November 5, 2021, https://perma.cc/8WT8-EUU7 (accessed November 5, 2023). The ten states that do not have shield laws include Hawaii, Idaho, Iowa, Massachusetts, Mississippi, Missouri, New Hampshire, Utah, Virginia, and Wyoming. These states—with the exception of Wyoming—recognize a reporter's privilege either as a matter of state common law or pursuant to court rules. *See id.*

[27] *See* "Reporters Privilege Compendium," Reporters Committee for Freedom of the Press, https://www.rcfp.org/reporters-privilege/ (accessed November 5, 2023).

that federal common law establishes a qualified reporter's privilege in certain settings.[28]

In recognition of the importance of safeguarding journalists and newsrooms from improper searches and seizures by law enforcement, federal law offers additional protections from searches and seizures beyond those afforded by the First and Fourth Amendments. The Privacy Protection Act of 1980 (PPA)[29] prohibits searches for certain types of materials related to newsgathering and publishing activities, except under limited circumstances. Generally speaking, the PPA prevents the government from searching or seizing work product or documentary materials possessed by a person "in connection with a purpose to disseminate to the public a newspaper, book, broadcast, or other similar form of public communication" unless there is probable cause to believe that the person has committed or is committing a criminal offense related to the materials.[30] The PPA also permits the government to search for work product or documentary materials if there is reason to believe that the immediate seizure of the materials is necessary to prevent death or serious bodily injury to any human being, and further permits searches of documentary materials if there is reason to believe that issuing a subpoena would result in the destruction, alteration, or concealment of such materials.[31] As such, the PPA goes a step beyond the Fourth Amendment in granting additional protections to journalists' work product and documentary materials, but still provides considerable latitude to government investigators, particularly in the context of national security investigations.

C. Regulatory Protection: The Department of Justice's Media Subpoena and Search Warrant Guidelines

As mentioned earlier, the Department of Justice has issued guidelines governing the use of certain law enforcement tools to obtain records of or pertaining to the news media.[32] The guidelines have gone through several iterations and date back to the Richard Nixon administration. Initially limited to just subpoenas, the

---

[28] *See, e.g., Riley v. City of Chester*, 612 F.2d 708 (3d Cir. 1979) (concluding that "journalists have a federal common law privilege, albeit qualified, to refuse to divulge their sources" outside the grand jury setting); *In re Grand Jury Subpoena Miller*, 397 F.3d 964 (D.C. Cir. 2005) (J. Tatel, concurring), *opinion superseded by* 438 F.3d 1141 (D.C. Cir. 2006); *New York Times Co. v. Gonzales*, 459 F.3d 160 (2d Cir. 2006) (Sack, J., dissenting).

[29] 42 U.S.C. §§ 2000aa *et seq.*

[30] *Id.* at § 2000aa(a), (b). The suspected criminal offense must be something other than merely receiving, possessing, communicating, or withholding the materials, unless, however, the offense concerns certain specified crimes against minors or violations of national security laws, including the Espionage Act.

[31] 42 U.S.C. §§ 2000aa(a)(2); 2000aa(b)(2); 2000aa(b)(3).

[32] 28 C.F.R. § 50.10.

guidelines were significantly revised in 2014 and 2015 to cover search warrants and court orders for electronic metadata.[33] It is important to note at the outset that the guidelines can be amended at the Justice Department's discretion and cannot be enforced in court.

In 2021, the Justice Department notified CNN, the *New York Times*, and the *Washington Post* that officials had authorized secret subpoenas and court orders for telephone and email records for eight reporters across those three outlets, all in national security "leak" investigations.[34] In the case of the *Times* and CNN, the email demands came with nondisclosure orders under 18 U.S.C. Section 2705(b) that had the effect of barring in-house counsel from notifying the newsroom of their existence.

Following those revelations, Attorney General Merrick Garland then reconvened the News Media Dialogue Group, a collection of senior media representatives and Justice Department officials created in advance of the 2014–2015 reforms (which the Reporters Committee assists in coordinating), to discuss further modifications to the guidelines. In July 2021, Attorney General Garland released a memorandum featuring a significant change to the department's policy. Previously, the guidelines implemented a "balancing test," where prosecutors' need for the information would be weighed against the equities on the press side.

Finding that that approach "may fail to properly weight the important national interest in protecting journalists from compelled disclosure of information revealing their sources, sources they need to apprise the American people of the workings of their government," the Garland memorandum replaced it with a bright line rule that the department "will no longer use compulsory legal process for the purpose of obtaining information from or records of members of the news media acting within the scope of newsgathering activities...."[35]

The Justice Department then promulgated a revised version of the 50.10 guidelines implementing this directive in October 2022. First, the 2022 guidelines confirm that they apply to subpoenas, search warrants, court orders issued pursuant to the Stored Communications or Pen-Register Acts (18 U.S.C. §§ 2703(d) and 3123, respectively), interception orders issued pursuant to 18 U.S.C. Section 2518, civil investigative demands, and mutual legal assistance

---

[33] Brown & Rottman, *supra* note 6.
[34] Bruce D. Brown & Gabe Rottman, "Everything We Known About the Trump-Era Records Demands from the Press," *Lawfare*, July 6, 2021, https://www.lawfaremedia.org/article/everything-we-know-about-trump-era-records-demands-press (accessed November 5, 2023).
[35] "Memorandum from the Attorney General Regarding the Use of Compulsory Process to Obtain Information From, Or Records Of, Members of the News Media, 1," July 19, 2021, https://www.justice.gov/opa/pr/doj-formally-adopts-new-policy-restricting-use-compulsory-process-obtain-reporter-information (accessed November 5, 2023).

treaties, regardless of whether they are issued directly to a member of the news media or to a third-party service provider.[36]

The guidelines then draw the line of protection around a definition of "newsgathering." That term is defined as the "process by which a member of the news media collects, pursues, or obtains information or records for the purposes of producing content intended for public dissemination."[37] Moreover, and importantly, the guidelines confirm that newsgathering includes the "mere receipt, possession, or publication by a member of the news media of Government information, including classified information, as well as establishing a means of receiving such information, including from an anonymous or confidential source."[38]

The guidelines caution, however, that except as provided in the section quoted directly preceding, "newsgathering does not include criminal acts committed in the course of obtaining information or using information, such as: breaking and entering; theft; unlawfully accessing a computer or computer system; unlawful surveillance or wiretapping; bribery; extortion; fraud; insider trading; or aiding or abetting or conspiring to engage in such criminal activities, with the requisite criminal intent."[39]

That language is significant in that the Justice Department has long held that, for instance, the Espionage Act of 1917 applies to journalists and could apply to the solicitation of a violation of the act (asking a source to disclose classified information) or to the publication of that information.[40] Accordingly, while the Justice Department has not changed its position on that front, it has expressly limited its ability to use process based on the receipt, possession, or publication of classified (and other government) information. The second clause regarding "establishing a means of receiving such information" confirms that efforts to protect a confidential source's identity—moving, for instance, to encrypted communications—cannot be characterized as an inchoate crime by the journalist, such as accessory after the fact, in order to justify the issuance of process.[41]

For conduct that fits on the "newsgathering" side of the bright line, there are only very limited exceptions: authentication of published information (with the authorization of a deputy assistant attorney general (DAAG) for the Criminal Division), obtaining records with the consent of the member of the news media (also with DAAG's approval), and exigency (with attorney general approval).[42]

---

[36] 28 C.F.R. § 50.10(b)(2)(i).
[37] Id. § 50.10(b)(2)(ii).
[38] Id. § 50.10(b)(2)(ii)(A).
[39] Id. § 50.10(b)(2)(ii)(B).
[40] Brown & Rottman, supra note 6.
[41] Id.
[42] 28 C.F.R. § 50.10(c). The exigency provision does not include a broad exception for national security that had appeared in previous versions.

For conduct that is on the other side of the line, the guidelines establish a different set of exceptions and procedures. Process that targets certain non-newsgathering activity—for instance, subpoenaing purely commercial or financial records or basic subscriber information—can be authorized under 28 C.F.R. Section 50.10(d)(ii)–(vi). Such subpoenas, however, still come with certain protections, such as advance notice requirements. The main exception here, however, is under Section (d)(1)(i), where the department seeks "information or records of a member of the news media who is not acting within the scope of newsgathering... when the member of the news media is the subject or target of an investigation and suspected of having committed an offense." Such process can be authorized by a DAAG at the Criminal Division and, while notice is permissible in such cases, it is not required.[43] Additionally, in February 2024, the Justice Department published a revised section of the "Justice Manual," a deskbook for prosecutors, providing direction for DOJ personnel on implementing the news media guidelines.[44] The revised section includes an important clarification of the scope of the (d)(1)(i) exception. "Subject" is a term of art in the department and broadly refers to a person "whose conduct is within the scope of the grand jury's investigation."[45] The Justice Manual revision clarifies that the phrase "suspected of having committed an offense" modifies "subject" as well, meaning that the (d)(1)(i) exception cannot be used to issue legal process "to a member of the news media whose conduct falls within the scope of the early stages of a grand jury investigation, but who is not yet suspected of criminal wrongdoing."[46]

The 2022 guidelines include additional guardrails that appear intended to prevent improper circumvention of the bright line. Searches of the "premises of a news media entity" requires attorney general approval.[47] Additionally, when there is a "close or novel" question as to whether someone qualifies as a member of the news media, the assistant attorney general (AAG) for the Criminal Division must make the determination.[48] And, crucially, when there is a close or novel question about whether a member of the news media is acting within the *scope of newsgathering*, that determination must be made by the AAG and, if there is "genuine uncertainty," then by the attorney general personally.[49]

The revised 2022 guidelines include several other notable provisions for journalists—including approval requirements for compelled testimony or

---

[43] *Id.* § 50.10(j)(5).
[44] *See* Justice Manual, § 9-13.400.
[45] *Id.* § 9-11.151.
[46] *Id.* § 9.13-400; *see also* Gabe Rottman, "DOJ Revises Prosecutors' Manual on News Media Guidelines," *Reporters Committee for Freedom of the Press*, February 20, 2024, https://www.rcfp.org/doj-revises-justice-manual/ (accessed June 28, 2024). It includes the same clarification for process in civil matters as well.
[47] 28 C.F.R. § 50.10(d)(2)(ii).
[48] *Id.* § 50.10(e)(1).
[49] *Id.* § 50.10(e)(2).

voluntary questioning and new guidelines on Stored Communication Act gag orders—and they can be complicated to navigate. *Lawfare* has published two lengthy posts breaking down the guidelines in detail.[50] And, as noted above, in February 2024, the Justice Department published a revised section of the "Justice Manual," which offers additional guidance on the scope and meaning of specific provisions in the policy.[51] Readers may want to consult with legal counsel when facing uncertainty under the guidelines.

Finally, as discussed later, the 2022 guidelines do not apply to process under foreign intelligence authorities, including national security letters.

III. Electronic Communications Surveillance Authorities

Journalists in the United States face numerous challenges when striving to protect their sources. These challenges include, but are not limited to, collection and interception of communications by the US government and prosecutors' aggressive pursuit of sources for government leaks. Combined, these factors greatly challenge journalists' ability to communicate securely with sources, assure sensitive sources that the communications will be confidential, and gather news vital to the public interest.

There are a number of reasons reporters might be concerned about the scope of "surveillance authority"—our shorthand term for a variety of statutes that enable the government to request and obtain information about stored or real-time communications. Government agents may use surveillance authority to gain access to the content of reporters' communications, as well as to obtain certain records related to those communications. For example, agents might use a trap and trace order to obtain a list of telephone numbers dialed by the reporter, or use a national security letter to obtain a user's web browsing history or historical location information.

While the Department of Justice's news media guidelines and the Privacy Protection Act, discussed previously, partially protect journalists' records from search and seizure by the Justice Department, foreign intelligence surveillance authorities are outside the scope of these statutory and regulatory protections, as the chart in Appendix A indicates. Although many national security authorities permit the government to collect and use the same type of communications metadata that they may otherwise obtain using a standard subpoena, the regulatory limits on subpoenas do not apply to these national security authorities. Certain national security processes allow the government to request and obtain

---

[50] Brown & Rottman, *supra* note 6; Brown & Rottman, *supra* note 8.
[51] Justice Manual, § 9-13.400.

Table 11.1 Content and Metadata at Rest or in Transit

	At rest	In transit
Content	Search warrant (Fed. R. Crim. Proc. 41) SCA search warrant (18 U.S.C. § 2703(a)) SCA court order (18 U.S.C. § 2703(d)) Subpoena (grand jury, administrative, or trial) FISA search warrant	Wiretap Section 702 directive
Metadata	SCA court order (18 U.S.C. § 2703(d)) Subpoena (grand jury, administrative, or trial) National Security Letter Section 215 order	Pen Register/Trap and Trace (PR/TT) FISA PR/TT

journalists' records if the material is merely relevant to an authorized investigation, even if the target is not suspected of a crime.

The wide array of legal mechanisms available to obtain information regarding communications can be overwhelming. Unfortunately, the overlapping and complex legal architecture for communications surveillance, coupled with widespread secrecy about government policies and capabilities, makes it difficult to understand how and under what circumstances the government can use its authority.

Understanding the risks posed by communications surveillance requires knowledge of two key concepts. First, surveillance authorities tend to distinguish between communications *content* and *metadata*. Second, statutes providing surveillance authority tend to distinguish between stored data, or information *at rest*, and real-time surveillance of information *in transit*. As a result, different requirements apply to the acquisition of real-time content or metadata than to stored content or historical metadata, and different statutes, outlined in Table 11.1 and described in more detail later, authorize the acquisition of each type of information.

A. Electronic Surveillance Authorities: Criminal Investigations

Journalists seeking to protect confidential sources need to be aware of the full range of legal authorities for surveillance in the context of criminal investigations as well as national security investigations. For example, government investigations of unauthorized leaks may use both criminal and national security investigative tools. Three of the most significant information-gathering authorities in the criminal context are the Stored Communications Act, the Pen Register Act, and the Wiretap Act.

Stored Communications Act, Codified at 18 U.S.C. §§ 2701–2712

The Stored Communications Act (SCA) authorizes the government to require providers of electronic communications services to disclose both the substantive *contents* of stored communications as well as the *metadata* records associated with those communications (e.g., email dates, times, and header information, including "to" and "from" addresses).

The SCA does not always require a warrant based on probable cause. Under Section 2703(a) of the act, if a communication has been in storage for 180 days or less, the government must get a warrant in order to obtain the communications. Under Section 2703(b), if a communication has been in storage for more than 180 days, the government may obtain communications using an administrative subpoena or a court order based on "specific and articulable facts" showing that the communications are relevant to a criminal investigation if the government provides notice to the subscriber. Alternatively, it always remains the case that the government may obtain communications without providing notice if it obtains a traditional search warrant based on probable cause.[52]

Legislation has repeatedly been proposed that would require law enforcement to obtain a search warrant when it seeks the contents of communications, regardless of how long the communications have been in storage.[53] In addition, one federal appellate court has held that a warrant is required for the government to acquire communications content under the SCA,[54] and it is the policy of some internet companies to disclose communications content only pursuant to a search warrant.[55] In 2018, Congress adopted legislation to clarify that service providers in the United States must respond to legal process under the SCA even if the data sought is stored on servers outside the United States.[56]

Under 18 U.S.C. Section 2703(d), the government may obtain noncontent subscriber records without notice using an administrative subpoena or a court

---

[52] *See also* "Searching and Seizing Computers and Obtaining Electronic Evidence in Criminal Investigations," https://www.justice.gov/file/442111/download (accessed November 5, 2023).

[53] *See, e.g.*, Email Privacy Act, H.R. 699, 114th Cong. (2016); David Ruiz, "Email Privacy Act Comes Back, Hopefully to Stay," Electronic Frontier Foundation, May 29, 2018, https://perma.cc/R8FH-YNJD (accessed November 5, 2023).

[54] *Warshak*, 631 F.3d at 288 ("[T]o the extent that the SCA purports to permit the government to obtain such emails [stored with a commercial ISP] warrantlessly, the SCA is unconstitutional.").

[55] *See, e.g.*, "Requests for User Information FAQs," https://www.google.com/transparencyreport/userdatarequests/legalprocess/#whats_the_difference(accessed November 5, 2023); *see also* "Written Testimony of Richard Saldago, Director, Law Enforcement and Information Security at Google, Inc., Senate Judiciary Subcommittee on Privacy, Technology and the Law, Hearing on 'The Surveillance Transparency Act of 2013,'" November 13, 2013, http://www.judiciary.senate.gov/imo/media/doc/11-13-13SalgadoTestimony.pdf (accessed November 5, 2023).

[56] Clarifying Lawful Overseas Use of Data (CLOUD) Act, Pub. L. No. 115-141, 132 Stat. 1213-25 (2018).

order based on "specific and articulable facts" showing that the records are relevant to a criminal investigation.[57] As discussed previously, the Supreme Court has held that that authority may not constitutionally be used to obtain historical cell-site location information in particular.[58]

In 2010, the US Attorney for the District of Columbia sought and obtained a search warrant under 18 U.S.C. Section 2703(a) for the personal email account of James Rosen, a Fox News reporter, in connection with an investigation of unauthorized disclosure of classified information that Rosen had published in a 2009 article. In that case, the government obtained a warrant for the disclosure of "any and all communications" between Rosen's email address and three specified email addresses, in addition to "any and all communications" to or from Rosen's email address on the two days following the publication of Rosen's article. In the probable cause affidavit in support of its warrant application, the government argued that Rosen had conspired with his source to violate the Espionage Act and that the search was therefore permissible under the "suspect exception" to the Privacy Protection Act.[59] In addition, the Justice Department took the position that email search warrants obtained under the SCA did not require notice to customers and subscribers whose accounts were searched.[60] According to press accounts, Rosen did not learn of the search until nearly three years later.[61] At the time of the Rosen search, the attorney general's policy on obtaining records of members of the news media did not specifically apply to search warrants, although news reports indicate that then Attorney General Eric Holder nonetheless personally approved the warrant.[62] Today, the Department of Justice media subpoena guidelines apply to search warrants as well as to court orders issued under Section 2703(d) of the SCA and bar the use of such tools for members of the news media acting within the scope of newsgathering, as defined, with only limited exceptions.

Section 2705 of the SCA, which permits the government to apply for a gag order when executing warrants pursuant to Section 2703, has been the subject of repeated legal challenges.[63] The Section 2705 gag order prevents companies from telling their customers that their records were searched. In 2016, Microsoft

---

[57] The government may also obtain basic subscriber and session information using an administrative subpoena, trial subpoena, or grand jury subpoena. *See* 18 U.S.C. § 2703(c)(2).
[58] *See Carpenter*, 138 S. Ct. at 2221.
[59] *See* Dep't of Justice Report on Review of News Media Policies, *supra* section I.
[60] *See* Ryan Lizza, "How Prosecutors Fought to Keep Rosen's Warrant Secret," *New Yorker*, May 24, 2013, http://www.newyorker.com/news/news-desk/how-prosecutors-fought-to-keep-rosens-warrant-secret (accessed November 5, 2023).
[61] *Id.*
[62] *Id.*
[63] *See* Complaint, *Microsoft Corp. v. U.S. Dept. of Justice*, Case No. 2:16-cv-00538-JLR (W.D. Wash. June 17, 2016).

filed a lawsuit in federal district court in Seattle arguing that these gag orders violate both the First Amendment and the Fourth Amendment. The court denied the government's motion to dismiss Microsoft's First Amendment claims, but granted the motion as to the Fourth Amendment claims, concluding that Microsoft lacked standing to assert its customers' Fourth Amendment rights.[64] Microsoft ultimately dropped the case after the Department of Justice adopted new internal policies limiting the use of SCA gag orders.[65] Recent proposed legislation, the Non-Disclosure Order (NDO) Fairness Act, would impose further statutory restrictions on the practice.[66]

Pen Registers and Trap and Trace Devices, Codified at 18 U.S.C. §§ 3121–3127

The so-called "Pen/Trap" statute regulates the collection of noncontent information related to electronic communications in real time. Pen registers and trap and trace (PR/TT) orders authorize the government to obtain communications metadata, such as the phone numbers associated with incoming and outgoing calls, or the email addresses of a sender and recipient.[67] The Pen Register Act requires a federal court to "enter an ex parte order authorizing the installation and use of a pen register or trap and trace device" on a facility or other service belonging to a wire or electronic communication service provider.[68] In order to obtain the order, the government must certify that "the information likely to be obtained by such installation and use is relevant to an ongoing criminal investigation."[69] PR/TT orders are sealed pending further order of the court and accompanied by a gag order directing the communication service provider not to disclose the existence of the order. The Justice Department policy on obtaining records of members of the news media applies to PR/TT orders.

Wiretap Act, Codified at 18 U.S.C. §§ 2510–2522

The Wiretap Act authorizes the government to make an application to a federal judge for an order—often referred to as a "Title III" order given the placement of the Wiretap Act in the 1968 omnibus crime legislation—authorizing the real-time interception of wire, oral, or electronic communications. The act requires the government to demonstrate probable cause to believe that an individual is

---

[64] See *Microsoft Corp. v. U.S. Dep't of Justice*, 233 F. Supp. 3d 887 (W.D. Wash. 2017).
[65] See Brad Smith, "DOJ Acts to Curb the Overuse of Secrecy Orders. Now It's Congress's Turn," *Microsoft*, October 23, 2017, https://perma.cc/KQ2Z-DVWB (accessed November 5, 2023).
[66] See Greg Nojeim & Jessie Miller, "Congress Needs to Make Surveillance Gag Orders Fair and Rare," Center for Democracy and Technology, August 5, 2022, https://perma.cc/LU5C-A7N6 (accessed November 5, 2023).
[67] 18 U.S.C. § 3127.
[68] 18 U.S.C. § 3123(a).
[69] *Id.*

committing a criminal offense, and that the places where the interception is to occur—for example, the phone line or online account—"are being used, or are about to be used, in connection with the commission" of that offense.[70] The 2022 news media guidelines do apply to applications under the act, and the act itself requires advance departmental review and approval before applications for certain types of electronic surveillance may be submitted to a court. Specifically, 18 U.S.C. Section 2516(1) requires that the attorney general review and approve such applications, but the attorney general may delegate this authority to certain enumerated high-level Justice Department officials, such as the Deputy Assistant Attorneys General for the Criminal Division. Moreover, the government must minimize the interception of communications not otherwise subject to interception under the order, and minimize the duration of the interception by terminating the surveillance once the conversation sought is seized.[71] Interception periods must be no longer than thirty days, but the court may extend this period under certain circumstances.[72]

B. National Security Letters

National security letters (NSLs) are warrantless requests issued by high-ranking FBI officials and directed at third parties for *noncontent* records. The FBI may issue an NSL compelling disclosure of subscriber records—that is, metadata—if it certifies that the records sought are relevant to an authorized investigation to protect against international terrorism or clandestine intelligence activities. Unless the recipient challenges the NSL, the request is not subject to judicial review.

Four statutes authorize the use of NSLs to obtain subscriber information from third parties, such as telephone companies, internet service providers, financial service providers, and credit institutions.[73] By far the most commonly used NSL authority is a provision in the Electronic Communications Privacy Act (ECPA), which enables the FBI to request the "local and long distance toll billing records" of any person from a "wire or electronic communication service provider."[74] As amended by the USA FREEDOM Act, each request must be based on "a term

---

[70] 18 U.S.C. § 2518.
[71] *See* 18 U.S.C. § 2518(5); *see also Nixon v. Administrator of General Services*, 433 U.S. 425, 463 (1977); *Berger v. New York*, 388 U.S. 41, 55 (1967).
[72] *See* 18 U.S.C. § 2518(5).
[73] These statutes are the Electronic Communications Privacy Act (18 U.S.C. § 2709), the National Security Act (50 U.S.C. § 3162), the Right to Financial Privacy Act (12 U.S.C. § 3414), and the Fair Credit Reporting Act (15 U.S.C. §§ 1681u, v).
[74] 18 U.S.C. § 2709.

that specifically identifies" a particular person, account, and so forth to avoid bulk collection.[75]

By some estimates, over 90 percent of NSLs are issued with gag orders prohibiting the third party from informing the subscriber that the government requested the subscriber's information.[76] The FBI may accompany an NSL with a gag order if "otherwise there *may* result a danger to the national security of the United States, interference with a criminal, counterterrorism, or counterintelligence investigation, interference with diplomatic relations, or danger to the life or physical safety of *any* person."[77] The gag orders typically have no expiration date. The Reporters Committee filed an amicus brief in a constitutional challenge to the ECPA's NSL provision, arguing that the gag orders are unconstitutional prior restraints and that the atmosphere of secrecy surrounding NSLs obscures surveillance efforts by the government and chills reporter-source communications.[78] That case was remanded to the lower court in light of 2015 reforms to the NSL statute pursuant to the 2015 USA FREEDOM Act. These reforms required the attorney general to adopt new procedures for NSL gag orders that require "review at appropriate intervals" and termination of nondisclosure obligations if they are no longer necessary.[79] Under these NSL procedures, when an investigation ends, the gag order must be lifted unless the FBI makes a determination that one of a number of statutory standards for nondisclosure is satisfied.[80] The FBI is also required to review the gag order three years after the investigation begins to determine whether one of the statutory exceptions applies.[81] While publicly available information casts doubt on the practical impact of those reforms,[82] the US Court of Appeals for the Ninth Circuit has rejected a First Amendment challenge to the statute as amended.[83]

---

[75] 18 U.S.C. § 2709(b); 12 U.S.C. § 3414(a)(2); 15 U.S.C. § 1681u(a); 15 U.S.C. § 1681v(a).

[76] *See* Office of the Inspector General, "A Review of the Federal Bureau of Investigation's Use of National Security Letters: Assessment of Corrective Actions and Examination of NSL Usage in 2006 124," March 2008 ("Of the 375 NSLs we examined in our random sample, 365, or 97 percent imposed the non-disclosure and confidentiality obligation established in the Patriot Reauthorization Act. Based on that result, we projected that of the 15,187 NSLs the FBI issued from March 10, 2006, through December 31, 2006, 14,782 NSLs imposed the non-disclosure and confidentiality obligations."), https://oig.justice.gov/reports/2014/s1410a.pdf (accessed November 5, 2023).

[77] 18 U.S.C. § 2709(c)(1)(B).

[78] *See, e.g.*, Amicus Br. in Support of Petitioner-Appellant, *Under Seal v. Holder* et al., Nos. 13-15957, 13-16731 (9th Cir. filed April 9, 2014), https://rcfp.org/sites/default/files/2014-06-10-in-re-national-security-letter.pdf (accessed November 5, 2023).

[79] "Termination Procedures for National Security Letter Nondisclosure Requirement," https://www.fbi.gov/file-repository/nsl-ndp-procedures.pdf/view (accessed November 5, 2023).

[80] *Id.* at 2.

[81] *Id.*

[82] *See* Andrew Crocker & Aaron Mackey, "The Failed Fix to NSL Gag Orders: How the Majority of National Security Letter Recipients Remain Gagged after USA FREEDOM," Electronic Frontier Foundation, December 13, 2019, https://perma.cc/L8BF-854X (accessed November 5, 2023).

[83] *See In re National Security Letter*, 33 F.4th 1058, 1076 (9th Cir. 2022).

The FBI has used NSLs to compel electronic communications service providers to disclose data including web browsing history and online purchases.[84] Because of the pervasive secrecy surrounding NSL procedures, it remains unconfirmed whether the FBI has obtained communications records of journalists using NSLs. However, several incidents of abuse implicating reporters' rights have come to light in recent years regarding similar instruments. These incidents involved processes that, like NSLs, were not subject to judicial review.

In 2007, during the first review of NSL usage by the Office of the Inspector General for the Department of Justice (OIG), the OIG found that the FBI had frequently sought telephone toll billing records or subscriber information by using an "exigent letter," an informal request, rather than NSLs or grand jury subpoenas.[85] The OIG identified three leak investigations in which journalists' records had been requested using methods that did not comply with the Department of Justice guidelines.[86] Under the version of the guidelines then in place, the attorney general was required to approve the issuance of subpoenas for reporters' records. The OIG found that by using an "exigent letter," the FBI was functionally circumventing the guidelines' requirement to seek attorney general approval.

In one instance, the FBI obtained phone records for *Washington Post* reporters Ellen Nakashima and Alan Sipress, *Washington Post* researcher Natasha Tampubolon, and *New York Times* reporters Raymond Bonner and Jane Perlez using an exigent letter that claimed a grand jury subpoena was forthcoming; none was. In response to the exigent letter, the phone provider produced twenty-two months of records for Ellen Nakashima, and twenty-two months of records for the *Washington Post* bureau in Jakarta.[87] The OIG report called this production of materials "a complete breakdown in the required Department [of Justice] procedures for approving the issuance of grand jury subpoenas for reporters' toll billing records."[88] While the OIG did not address the availability of NSL practice in this instance or the others involving journalists, its concerns about the abuse of exigent letters could not have been more clear or emphatic.

[84] Dustin Volz, "U.S. Government Reveals Breadth of Requests for Internet Records," *Reuters*, December 1, 2015, https://www.reuters.com/article/us-usa-cybersecurity-nsl-idUSKBN0TJ2PJ20151201 (accessed November 5, 2023).

[85] *See* Office of the Inspector General, "A Review of the Federal Bureau of Investigation's Use of National Security Letters 86–97," March 2007, https://oig.justice.gov/reports/2014/s1410.pdf (accessed November 5, 2023).

[86] *See* Office of the Inspector General, "A Review of the Federal Bureau of Investigation's Use of Exigent Letters and Other Informal Requests for Telephone Records 89–121," January 2010, https://www.oversight.gov/sites/default/files/oig-reports/s1001r.pdf (accessed November 5, 2023).

[87] *Id.* at 95–97.

[88] *Id.* at 103.

The Department of Justice and the FBI have taken the position that the guidelines do not apply to NSLs.[89] And, while the guidelines may not apply to NSLs, there have been reports about other policies at the Justice Department that may apply. In 2016, *The Intercept* published a classified appendix to the FBI's Domestic Investigations and Operations Guide, which required certain approvals for NSLs implicating members of the news media.[90] Specifically, if the NSL is seeking telephone toll records of a member of the news media or a news organization and the purpose is to identify confidential sources, the FBI's general counsel and the executive assistant director of the National Security Bureau (EAD-NSB), in consultation with the assistant attorney general for the National Security Division at the Justice Department, must approve.[91] If the NSL is seeking records of a member of the news media or news organization and the purpose is other than to identify confidential sources, or if the NSL is targeting a nonmedia person but is intended to reveal confidential sources, the EAD-NSB and the FBI's general counsel must approve.[92] And, if the NSL is seeking telephone records of an individual who is a member of the news media or a news organization that is a suspected or known intelligence officer, affiliated with a news organization that is associated with a foreign intelligence service, or is otherwise acting on behalf of a foreign power, and a purpose is to identify confidential news media sources, the same officials must approve.[93] Note that it is possible this policy has been changed.

C. Electronic Surveillance Authorities: Foreign Intelligence

In foreign intelligence and national security investigations, the government has additional statutory authorities that enable it to conduct electronic communications surveillance. While the government may use ordinary wiretaps and pen registers in investigations touching on national security, it also possesses expanded authority under provisions of the FISA as well as the USA PATRIOT Act. The scope and secrecy of FISA-related surveillance has

---

[89] *See* DIOG App. § G.12 ("The [28 C.F.R. § 50.10] regulation concerns *only* grand jury subpoenas, not National Security Letters (NSLs) or administrative subpoenas."); Amicus Brief at 7–8, *Freedom of the Press Foundation v. Dep't of Justice*, No. 15-cv-3503-HSG (N.D. Cal. June 10, 2016), ECF No. 36, https://www.rcfp.org/wp-content/uploads/imported/2016-06-10-freedom-of-the-press-foundatio.pdf (accessed November 5, 2023).
[90] *See* DIOG App. § G.12; Cora Currier, "Secret Rules Make It Pretty Easy for the FBI to Spy on Journalists," *The Intercept*, January 31, 2017, https://theintercept.com/2017/01/31/secret-rules-make-it-pretty-easy-for-the-fbi-to-spy-on-journalists-2/ (accessed November 5, 2023).
[91] *Id.*
[92] *Id.*
[93] *Id.*

raised particular concerns that digital newsrooms could be searched using a FISA court order.

Foreign Intelligence Surveillance Act: Overview

FISA authorizes electronic and physical surveillance of foreign powers and agents of foreign powers for the purpose of collecting "foreign intelligence information." FISA was originally enacted in 1978 primarily to regulate the collection of foreign intelligence information within the United States.[94] Until 2001, FISA permitted electronic and physical surveillance of "foreign powers" and "agents of foreign powers" if foreign intelligence collection was "the purpose" of the activity. In 2001, the USA PATRIOT Act amended FISA to allow searches if foreign intelligence collection was a "significant purpose."

"Foreign intelligence information" is a broad term and includes information that pertains to a variety of dangers related to "foreign powers" as well as "information with respect to a foreign power or foreign territory that relates to, and if concerning a United States person is necessary to—(A) the national defense or the security of the United States; or (B) the conduct of the foreign affairs of the United States."[95] In addition, the PATRIOT Act relaxed the standards for acquiring metadata through PR/TT orders and for orders compelling production of business records or "tangible things" relevant to an investigation to obtain foreign intelligence information. This authority, known as Section 215, was the statutory authority for the bulk telephony metadata collection program disclosed by former NSA contractor Edward Snowden in 2013. As discussed later, the USA FREEDOM Act ended the government's bulk collection of telephone records in November 2015, and Congress failed to reauthorize Section 215 in 2020, causing FISA's business-records authority to revert to its pre–PATRIOT Act scope.[96]

Beginning in 2007, Congress enacted a series of amendments to FISA intended to broaden its scope to authorize electronic surveillance of foreigners abroad.[97] In 2007 and 2008, Congress enacted further amendments to FISA that created statutory authority to conduct programmatic surveillance on non-US persons outside the United States with the compelled assistance of service providers in the United States. This provision, commonly known as Section 702, is the statutory authority for some of the other activities disclosed by Snowden.[98]

---

[94] 50 U.S.C § 1801(f) (defining "electronic surveillance" for purposes of FISA).
[95] 50 U.S.C. § 1801.
[96] USA FREEDOM Act of 2015, Pub. L. 114-23, Sec. 107 (2015).
[97] *See* Protect America Act of 2007, Pub. L. 110-55 (2007); FISA Amendments Act of 2008, Pub. L. 110-261 (2008).
[98] *See* "NSA Slides Explain the PRISM Data-Collection Program," *Washington Post*, June 6, 2013, http://www.washingtonpost.com/wp-srv/special/politics/prism-collection-documents/ (accessed November 5, 2023).

In April 2024, as described in more detail later, Congress reauthorized Section 702 for two years with minor amendments after heated debate over whether officials should be required to obtain a warrant before sifting through communications collected under the authority for information on US persons.[99]

Traditional FISA: Electronic and Physical Searches, Codified at 50 U.S.C. §§ 1801–1829

"Traditional" FISA primarily governs electronic and physical surveillance within the United States, as well as intentional targeting of US persons wherever located, of targets who are foreign powers or agents of foreign powers.[100] Electronic surveillance includes the acquisition of communications content. (Acquisition of communications metadata, under the FISA definition, is generally not "electronic surveillance"; rather, domestic metadata collection is governed by FISA's business-records provision and pen register authority, discussed later.)

Traditional FISA orders require the government to identify a specific target for surveillance and to demonstrate probable cause to believe that the target of surveillance is a foreign power or an agent of a foreign power.[101] In addition, FISA's electronic surveillance provision requires the attorney general to adopt "minimization procedures" that are designed "to minimize the acquisition and retention, and prohibit the dissemination, of non-publicly available information concerning unconsenting United States persons."[102] Each application is reviewed by a judge on the Foreign Intelligence Surveillance Court (FISC).

FISA PR/TT Orders, Codified at 50 U.S.C. §§ 1841–1846

The government may obtain a FISA PR/TT order in an "investigation to obtain foreign intelligence information not concerning a United States person or to protect against international terrorism or clandestine intelligence activities."[103] FISA PR/TTs may be used to monitor telephone calls and electronic communications.

---

[99] 50 U.S.C. § 1801(n) (defining "contents"). Because FISA's definition of "contents" includes "any information concerning the identity of the parties to such communication," some information that would likely be characterized as metadata for other purposes—such as the to- or from- fields in an email header—may nevertheless be "contents" for purposes of FISA.

[100] 50 U.S.C. § 1801 (defining "foreign power," "agent of a foreign power," and "electronic surveillance"). The provisions of FISA governing the surveillance of US persons outside the United States are known as Section 703 (if the collection takes place inside the United States) and Section 704 (if the collection takes place abroad). 18 U.S.C. §§ 1881b–c. Because the substantive rules governing each form of surveillance are similar to classic FISA orders, the three are often referred to together as "traditional FISA" or "probable-cause FISA."

[101] 50 U.S.C. § 1805 (requiring probable cause for electronic surveillance); 50 U.S.C. § 1824 (requiring probable cause for physical surveillance).

[102] *Id.* at (a)(3), (c)(2)(A); 50 U.S.C. § 1801(h) (defining minimization procedures).

[103] 50 U.S.C. § 1842(a)(1).

FISA PR/TT requests do not require the government to demonstrate probable cause that the target is a foreign power or an agent of a foreign power. Rather, the government must certify that the information at issue is "relevant" to an authorized investigation.[104] However, under the USA FREEDOM Act of 2015, the government is required to use a "specific selection term" (SST) to identify a person, account, device, or other personal identifier as the basis for use of the PR/TT device and to ensure that the PR/TT provision is not used for impermissible bulk collection.[105]

Section 702 of the FISA Amendments Act, Codified at 50 U.S.C. § 1881a

Like FISA's traditional electronic surveillance provision, Section 702 of the FISA Amendments Act of 2008 authorizes the collection of communications content, but the provision's procedures and safeguards differ dramatically from traditional FISA. Section 702 is intended to permit electronic foreign intelligence surveillance of non-US persons located abroad with the assistance of US service providers, regardless of whether there is probable cause to believe that those persons are foreign powers or agents of foreign powers and without judicial review of individual targeting decisions.

Accordingly, Section 702 grants authority for the government to obtain directives compelling electronic communication service providers to enable surveillance of communications of non-US persons located abroad, without mandating that the government identify a specific target to the FISC. Instead, Section 702 requires the government to annually provide to the FISC a written, sworn certification attesting that there are "targeting procedures" in place that are "reasonably designed" to ensure that surveillance is "limited to targeting persons reasonably believed to be located outside the United States" and to avoid "intentional acquisition" of communications when the sender and all recipients are known to be located in the United States.[106]

Because Section 702 authorizes "electronic surveillance," it also requires the attorney general and the Director of National Intelligence to adopt minimization procedures. The minimization and targeting procedures required by Section 702 are subject to judicial review and approval by the FISC. It is unclear, however, whether the minimization procedures comport with the Privacy Protection Act's statutory ban on newsroom searches.[107]

Perhaps Section 702's most controversial feature is that the statute allows officials to query information collected under the authority for intelligence on US persons who could not lawfully have been targeted directly. After amendments to Section 702 in 2018, the attorney general must now adopt "querying procedures" in

[104] *Id.* at (c)(2).
[105] USA FREEDOM Act of 2015, Pub. L. 114-23, Sec. 201.
[106] 50 U.S.C. § 1881a(d).
[107] *See supra* section II.B.

consultation with the Director of National Intelligence that are consistent with the Fourth Amendment to the US Constitution.[108] The 2018 amendments to Section 702 also required the FBI to obtain an order from the FISC before querying information acquired pursuant to Section 702 using US person identifiers "in connection with a predicated criminal investigation ... that does not relate to the national security of the United States."[109] As of this writing, the FBI has never sought such an order but has identified cases in which analysts conducted queries for which a court order should have been required.[110] While the full impact of Section 702 surveillance on journalists' rights remains unclear, a review of Section 702 compliance incidents declassified in 2022 documented an unknown number of improper "batch queries" in which the identifiers of US "journalists" and "political commentators" were used as query terms.[111] In connection with the statute's reauthorization in 2024, Congress added a further requirement that the deputy director of the FBI approve "sensitive queries," including the use of any query term "reasonably believed to identify ... a United States media organization or a United States person who is a member of such organization."[112]

Section 702 has historically involved two approaches to surveillance: "upstream" collection, in which telecommunications providers assist in collecting communications to or from a target directly from the Internet backbone, and "downstream or "PRISM" collection, in which Internet service providers offering, for instance, email services produce communications to or from a targeted account.[113] In 2022, the FISC also authorized pursuant to Section 702 a third, "highly sensitive" collection technique whose exact nature remains classified.[114] In connection with the 2024 reauthorization of the statute, Congress expanded the class of service providers who can be compelled to assist in 702 surveillance to include "any other service provider who has access to equipment that is being used or may be used to transmit or store wire or electronic communications," with exceptions for hotels, restaurants, and homes.[115] While reportedly intended to

---

[108] 50 U.S.C. § 1881a(f)(1)(A).

[109] 50 U.S.C. § 1881a(f)(2)(A).

[110] *See* Privacy & C.L. Oversight Bd., "Report on the Surveillance Program Operated Pursuant to Section 702 of the Foreign Intelligence Surveillance Act at 103," 2023.

[111] Justice Department and Office of the Director of National Intelligence, "Semiannual Assessment of Compliance with Procedures and Guidelines Issued Pursuant to Section 702 of the Foreign Intelligence Surveillance Act, Reporting Period: December 1, 2018 through May 31, 2019, at 60," 2021, https://perma.cc/9SBA-X6E8 (accessed November 5, 2023).

[112] 50 U.S.C. § 1881a(f)(3)(d)(ii)(I).

[113] *See* James Ball, "NSA's Prism Surveillance Program: How It Works and What It Can Do," *The Guardian*, June 8, 2013, https://www.theguardian.com/world/2013/jun/08/nsa-prism-server-collection-facebook-google (accessed November 5, 2023).

[114] Off. of the Dir. of Nat'l Intel., "Release of Two FISC Decisions Authorizing Novel Intelligence Collection," May 19, 2023, https://www.intel.gov/ic-on-the-record-database/results/1259-release-of-two-fisc-decisions-authorizing-novel-intelligence-collection (accessed November 5, 2023).

[115] 50 U.S.C. § 1881(b)(4).

address data centers that provide cloud computing services, the new definition's plain language is broad enough, according to one US Senator, that it "could be used to conscript someone with access to a journalist's laptop to extract communications between that journalist and a hypothetical foreign source."[116]

Organizations have repeatedly challenged the constitutional and statutory basis of bulk surveillance. In 2008, the Electronic Frontier Foundation filed a lawsuit, *Jewel v. National Security Agency*, challenging "upstream" surveillance (as well as other bulk collection activities) on behalf of AT&T customers whose communications and telephone records were collected by the NSA. In 2019, the district court in that case refused to allow it to proceed, finding that it would be impossible to do so without revealing state secrets.[117] The US Court of Appeals for the Ninth Circuit affirmed, and the Supreme Court declined to review the case.[118]

In addition, Wikimedia, PEN American Center, and the *Nation Magazine*, among other organizations, filed a lawsuit challenging "upstream" surveillance of online communications, raising both First Amendment and Fourth Amendment arguments. The Wikimedia plaintiffs claimed that upstream surveillance impeded their journalism, advocacy, and publishing activities, but the plaintiffs were barred from litigating on the merits after the Fourth Circuit ruled that the state secrets privilege applied in the case.[119] The Supreme Court likewise declined to hear that dispute.

FISA's Business-Records Provision and Section 215 of the PATRIOT Act, Codified at 50 U.S.C. §§ 1861 et seq.

Since 1998, FISA has allowed the government to seek a court order for the production of certain business records in national security investigations. As expanded by Section 215, the statute provided authority for the government to obtain "tangible things" relevant to an investigation to obtain foreign intelligence information not concerning a US person or to protect against international terrorism or clandestine intelligence activities.[120] Section 215 was the authority under which the government maintained the bulk telephony metadata program, which had collected all domestic calling records without suspicion on an ongoing basis.[121]

---

[116] Charlie Savage, "Secret Rift over Data Center Fueled Push to Expand Reach of Surveillance Program," *The New York Times*, April 16, 2024, https://www.nytimes.com/2024/04/16/us/fisa-surveillance-bill-program.html (last accessed May 23, 2024).

[117] *Jewel v. NSA*, No. C 08-04373, 2019 WL 11504877 (N.D. Cal. April 25, 2019), *aff'd*, 856 F. App'x 640 (9th Cir. 2021), *cert. denied*, 142 S. Ct. 2812 (2022).

[118] *See* Cindy Cohn, "EFF's Flagship Jewel v. NSA Dragnet Spying Case Rejected by Supreme Court," Electronic Frontier Foundation, June 13, 2022, https://www.eff.org/deeplinks/2022/06/effs-flagship-jewel-v-nsa-dragnet-spying-case-rejected-supreme-court (accessed November 5, 2023).

[119] *Wikimedia Foundation v. NSA*, 14 F.4th 276, 304 (4th Cir. 2021), *cert. denied*, 143 S. Ct. 774 (2023).

[120] 50 U.S.C. § 1861(a)(1).

[121] *See, e.g.*, Glenn Greenwald, "NSA Collecting Phone Records of Millions of Verizon Customers Daily," *The Guardian*, June 6, 2013, https://www.theguardian.com/world/2013/jun/06/nsa-phone-records-verizon-court-order (accessed November 5, 2023).

In 2015, Congress reauthorized Section 215 but ended the government's bulk collection of telephone records.[122] The revised statute required the government to use an SST to identify a person, account, device, or other personal identifier as the basis for production of call detail records. Under that framework, rather than collecting the call detail records itself, the government requested records pertaining to a specific selector from a telephone carrier.

On March 15, 2020, Section 215 expired; as of this writing, Congress has not reauthorized it.[123] As a result, the authority has reverted to its 1998 scope. As operative now, the provision reaches only specific classes of businesses—"a common carrier, public accommodation facility, physical storage facility, or vehicle rental facility"—and requires the government to show "specific and articulable facts giving reason to believe that the person to whom the records pertain is a foreign power or an agent of a foreign power."[124]

Executive Order 12333

In addition to the other authorities discussed previously, the intelligence community also conducts communications surveillance activities that take place abroad and target non-US persons abroad under Executive Order 12333 (EO 12333),[125] a 1981 presidential order setting out general contours and guidelines for intelligence-gathering. EO 12333 places constraints on the use of these surveillance programs to target communications of US persons.[126] However, some have argued that collection activities are so broad and sweeping that any constraints are relatively trivial.[127] EO 12333 appears to permit the collection of actual communications content—not just metadata—of US citizens so long as the communications are collected "incidentally" to authorized activities. Moreover, many of the minimization procedures[128] that constrain government use of information collected pursuant to EO 12333 remain classified, and the limited information that is publicly available only gives vague guidance as to protections in place for

---

[122] USA FREEDOM Act of 2015, Pub. L. 114-23, Sec. 107.

[123] *See* India McKinney & Andrew Crocker, "Yes, Section 215 Expired. Now What?," Electronic Frontier Foundation, April 16, 2020, https://perma.cc/XZ99-W8X3 (accessed November 5, 2023).

[124] 50 U.S.C § 1862(a)–(b).

[125] Exec. Order No. 12333, United States Intelligence Activities, 46 Fed. Reg. 59941 (December 4, 1981) (as amended at 73 Fed. Reg. 45325 (2008)), https://www.archives.gov/federal-register/codification/executive-order/12333.html (accessed November 5, 2023).

[126] *Id.* at 59950.

[127] *See, e.g.*, John Napier Tye, "Meet Executive Order 12333: The Reagan Rule That Lets the NSA Spy on Americans," *Washington Post*, July 18, 2014, https://www.washingtonpost.com/opinions/meet-executive-order-12333-the-reagan-rule-that-lets-the-nsa-spy-on-americans/2014/07/18/93d2ac22-0b93-11e4-b8e5-d0de80767fc2_story.html (accessed November 5, 2023).

[128] "Status of Attorney General Approved U.S. Person Procedures Under E.O. 12333," Civil Liberties and Privacy Office of the Office of the Director of National Intelligence, May 16, 2017, https://www.dni.gov/files/CLPT/documents/Chart-of-EO-12333-AG-approved-Guidelines_May-2017.pdf (accessed November 5, 2023).

First Amendment activity. Likewise, many of the programs conducted under EO 12333 are secret as well.

Beyond 12333, there may be other executive branch regulations that restrict the use of foreign surveillance tools to target journalists. Notably, in 2018, the Knight First Amendment Institute at Columbia University and the Freedom of the Press Foundation obtained documents in a Freedom of Information Act lawsuit including a memorandum for the National Security Division from the attorney general on procedures for FISA process targeting known media entities or known members of the news media.[129] According to the memorandum, all FISA applications for electronic surveillance, physical searches, PR/TT orders, business records, and surveillance targeting certain US persons located outside the United States (but not Section 702 surveillance) must be presented to the attorney general or deputy attorney general for approval prior to submission to the FISC, but, at the direction of the attorney general or deputy attorney general, any such applications may be referred to the assistant attorney general for the National Security Division for disposition.[130] The memorandum also requires attorney general or deputy attorney general notice or review if circumstances change or if an existing FISA target is subsequently assessed to be a media entity or member of the news media.[131] As with the National Security Letter Domestic Investigations and Operations Guide (NSL DIOG) section, it is not known if this policy is still operative.

IV. Conclusion

Understanding the variety of legal authorities and mechanisms that the government relies upon in conducting surveillance is crucial to assessing the relative risks to journalists and sources who use these electronic communications technologies. The chart in Appendix A summarizes key aspects of legal and policy protections in the context of these authorities. Journalists concerned about securing their communications or interested in adopting technical measures to enhance privacy or confidentiality may be interested in exploring how their newsgathering practices might implicate information at rest and in transit, as well as how they might protect their content and metadata. Appendix B offers a number of resources for journalists and reporters interested in experimenting with and implementing secure communications protocols themselves.

---

[129] "Revealed: The Justice Dept's Secret Rules for Targeting Journalists with FISA Court Orders," September 17, 2018, https://freedom.press/news/revealed-justice-depts-secret-rules-targeting-journalists-fisa-court-orders/ (accessed November 5, 2023).
[130] Id.
[131] Id.

APPENDIX A

Type of process	Standard	Type of information sought	Issued by	Covered by Guidelines	Covered by PPA
Subpoena (administrative, grand jury, or trial)	Relevance to a lawful purpose	Communications content (opened, sent, or older than 180 days) (only with notice); basic subscriber and session information	Agency (administrative subpoena) or with court oversight (grand jury or trial subpoena)	Yes	Yes (if content); no (if subscriber/session information)
Search Warrant	Probable cause	Communications content, metadata, and/or basic subscriber and session information	Court	Yes	Yes
2703(d) Order	"Specific and articulable facts showing that there are reasonable grounds to believe that the contents of a wire or electronic communication, or the records or other information sought, are relevant and material to an ongoing criminal investigation"	Communications content (opened, sent, or older than 180 days) (only with notice); basic subscriber and session information; communications metadata	Court	Yes	Yes (if content); no (if metadata or subscriber/session information)

PR/TT	Government certification "that the information likely to be obtained by such installation and use is relevant to an ongoing criminal investigation"	Dialing, routing, addressing, or signaling information	Court	Yes	No
Wiretap (Title III)	Probable cause that an individual is committing or has committed an enumerated offense; probable cause "that particular communications concerning that offense will be obtained through such interception; normal investigative procedures have been tried and have failed or reasonably appear to be unlikely to succeed if tried or to be too dangerous; the facilities from which, or the place where, the wire, oral, or electronic communications are to be intercepted are being used, or are about to be used, in connection with the commission of such offense"	Communications content	Court	Yes	Yes

(continued)

Type of process	Standard	Type of information sought	Issued by	Covered by Guidelines	Covered by PPA
FISA warrant	Probable cause to believe that the target "is a foreign power or an agent of a foreign power, except that no United States person may be considered an agent of a foreign power solely upon the basis of activities protected by the first amendment to the Constitution of the United States," and the place or thing to be searched "is being used, or is about to be used, by a foreign power or an agent of a foreign power"	Communications content and metadata	FISA Court	No	Yes
FISA PR/TT	Relevance to "any investigation to obtain foreign intelligence information not concerning a United States person or to protect against international terrorism or clandestine intelligence activities, provided that such investigation of a United States person is not conducted solely upon" the basis of First Amendment activities	Dialing, routing, addressing, or signaling information	FISA Court	No	No

	Standard	Information collected	Who approves	Notice to the target	Suppression remedy
FISA business-records order (post-Section 215)	Specific and articulable facts giving reason to believe that the records pertain to whom the person is a foreign power or an agent of a foreign power	Records of a "common carrier, public accommodation facility, physical storage facility, or vehicle rental facility"	FISA Court	No	No
FISA Section 702	Targeting persons reasonably believed to be located outside the United States to acquire foreign intelligence information while employing approved minimization procedures	Communications content and metadata	FISA Court	No	No
NSL	Relevance to an "open, predicated national security investigation," provided that "such an investigation of a United States person is not conducted solely upon the basis of" First Amendment activities	Communications metadata; subscriber information	FBI	No	No

APPENDIX B

Digital Security Resources

1. Committee to Protect Journalists, "Journalist Security Guide," https://cpj.org/wp-content/uploads/2020/05/guide.pdf (accessed November 5, 2023)
2. Digital Defenders Project, "The Digital First Aid Kit," https://digitalfirstaid.org/en/ (accessed November 5, 2023)
3. Electronic Frontier Foundation, "Surveillance Self-Defense," https://ssd.eff.org/ (accessed November 5, 2023)
4. Free Software Campaign, "Email Self-Defense Guide," https://emailselfdefense.fsf.org/en/ (accessed November 5, 2023)
5. Tactical Technology Collective, "The Holistic Security Manual," https://holistic-security.tacticaltech.org/ (accessed November 5, 2023)
6. Tactical Technology Collective and Front Line Defenders, "Security In-A-Box," https://securityinabox.org/en/ (accessed November 5, 2023)

Legal Reports

Privacy and Civil Liberties Oversight Board, "Report on the Surveillance Program Operated Pursuant to Section 702 of the Foreign Intelligence Surveillance Act," September 28, 2023, https://documents.pclob.gov/prod/Documents/OversightReport/054417e4-9d20-427a-9850-862a6f29ac42/2023%20PCLOB%20702%20Report%20(002).pdf (accessed November 5, 2023).

Privacy and Civil Liberties Oversight Board, "Report on the Surveillance Program Operated Pursuant to Section 702 of the Foreign Intelligence Surveillance Act," July 2, 2014, https://documents.pclob.gov/prod/Documents/OversightReport/ba65702c-3541-4125-a67d-92a7f974fc4c/702-Report-2%20-%20Complete%20-%20Nov%2014%202022%201548.pdf (accessed November 5, 2023).

Privacy and Civil Liberties Oversight Board, "Report on the Telephone Records Program Conducted under Section 215 of the USA PATRIOT Act and on the Operations of the Foreign Intelligence Surveillance Court," January 23, 2014, https://www.govinfo.gov/content/pkg/GOVPUB-PREX29-PURL-gpo45397/pdf/GOVPUB-PREX29-PURL-gpo45397.pdf (accessed November 5, 2023).

PART III
NATIONAL SECURITY, JOURNALISM, AND THE DIGITAL MEDIA ECOSYSTEM

12
Enemies Foreign *and Domestic*: America's Media Ecosystem and the Externalization of Domestic Threats

Christopher J. Fuller

I. Introduction

The year 2016's bad tempered and divisive presidential election campaign exposed many of the deep-set divisions and fissures which have been undermining the well-being of the American body politic for decades. Such a traumatic episode should have been the nadir which triggered a period of reflection and rejuvenation—an enduring aspect of American political life which the nation has been through many times in the past. But this was prevented from happening. Instead of forcing necessary critical introspection a distracting narrative took hold—an account which allowed those individuals and sectors which played key roles in dividing the United States so grievously to externalize the blame. A Russian propaganda campaign became the primary focus, with stories of Kremlin-sponsored fake news, misinformation spread through armies of Russian bots, and compromising material held by Vladimir Putin himself taking up a disproportionate amount of commentary and time. Doubtless Russian intervention is a serious matter deserving of attention. But that attention was so disproportionate compared to the Kremlin's likely influence on the election that it diverted debate from more significant discussions that needed to take place regarding the culpability of the political elite, Silicon Valley's social media platforms, and America's media ecosystem.

Russian information warfare is not new. There is a long history of the state employing such techniques, first developed for domestic use to influence individuals and shape narratives, and eventually utilized outside of its borders. In his famous "Long Telegram," setting out perceived Soviet motivations in 1946, the State Department Russianist George Kennan described early Soviet propaganda efforts beyond their domestic sphere as "basically negative and destructive," and thus "relatively easy to combat [. . .] by any intelligent and really

---

Christopher J. Fuller, *Enemies Foreign* and Domestic: *America's Media Ecosystem and the Externalization of Domestic Threats* In: *National Security, Journalism, and Law in an Age of Information Warfare.* Edited by: Marc Ambinder, Jennifer R. Henrichsen, and Connie Rosati, Oxford University Press. © Oxford University Press 2024. DOI: 10.1093/oso/9780197756621.003.0012

constructive program."[1] Despite efforts to improve the sophistication and impact of their output throughout the Cold War, the Kremlin's propaganda campaigns—orchestrated largely by the KGB's Service A—proved largely ineffective. Leninist clichés and improbable tales of Soviet superiority failed to gain traction with American citizens. Alongside the unconvincing exaggeration of life under communist rule ran two more surreptitious and connected forms of information warfare. The first, "kompromat," involved the use of covertly acquired sensitive information to discredit political opponents, while "dezinformatsiya" referred to the placing of Kremlin-penned news stories and selective information into the public domain. From a Western perspective these activities—dubbed "active measures" by the US intelligence community—involved the spreading of politically motivated lies. But for the Soviet bloc propagandists, these campaigns were more than mere disinformation. The topics were carefully selected with varying degrees of truth at their core to highlight what the authors perceived as the real nature of the United States and life under capitalism.[2] The overt racism of the Jim Crow South, for example, provided ample grist to the Soviet propagandist's mill by undermining American's "land of the free" rhetoric. However, ultimately the progress of the civil rights movement in the 1950s and 1960s, combined with the USSR's blatant oppression of those living behind the Iron Curtain, helped maintain the West's sense of moral superiority.

What is vital to understand as fear and paranoia over the increased sophistication of the Kremlin's twenty-first-century active measures becomes commonplace is that the key tenets of Russian information warfare have not changed. The Kremlin's propagandists employed the exact same methods of kompromat and dezinformatsiya in the run-up to the 2016 presidential election as they did during their less successful Cold War years. Changes in technology have provided Russia's agents with new forms of dissemination, but the central principles of the method remained unchanged. This begs the question: If the Kremlin's foreign propaganda methods have barely changed since the fallow years of the twentieth century, what has made them so effective in the twenty-first century? The answer, in short, is that it is not that the Russian approach that has become more effective but that the United States has become more vulnerable. This chapter reveals how shifts in the domestic political landscape, developments in the digital space, and changes in the media ecosystem amplified the power of traditional Russian information warfare while simultaneously increasing the United States'

---

[1] Telegram, George Kennan to James Byrnes ["Long Telegram"], February 22, 1946. Elsey Papers, Harry S. Truman Administration File. Foreign Relations—Russia, at 16, <https://www.trumanlibrary.org/whistlestop/study_collections/coldwar/documents/index.php?documentid=6-6&pagenumber=18> (accessed July 13, 2018).

[2] Thomas Boghardt, "Soviet Bloc Intelligence and Its AIDS Disinformation Campaign," *Studies in Intelligence*, 53, no. 4 (December 2009), 2.

vulnerability to such nefarious tactics. In doing so, it not only serves to challenge the dominant narrative around Russian interference but highlights areas of vulnerability which could be addressed to better protect the United States from such information warfare in the future.

II. "WikiLeaks! I Love WikiLeaks!" The Rise and Fall of Political Consensus

In a packed convention center in Wilkes-Barre, Pennsylvania, during one of his many campaign rallies, the Republican presidential candidate Donald J. Trump waved a sheet of paper in the air declaring: "Now this just came out... WikiLeaks, I love WikiLeaks!"[3] The compliment, relating to one of the tens of thousands of emails stolen from the account of Hillary Clinton's campaign chairman John Podesta and those of Democratic National Committee staffers, was the first of many. Despite cybersecurity experts promptly linking the data breach to a hacking group affiliated with Russian intelligence services, and WikiLeaks' constant and selective drip-feeding of stolen material over October and November clearly representing an act of external political sabotage, Trump continued to cite the material, often inaccurately, a further 163 times before election day.[4] A presidential candidate's embrace of such a controversial organization, which six years earlier had been responsible for the largest leak of classified government documents and whose founder, Julian Assange, was a fugitive from the American justice system, was controversial enough.[5] But WikiLeaks' well-documented association with the Kremlin made the actions all the more contentious.[6] Indeed six months later, Trump's then director of the Central Intelligence Agency, Mike Pompeo, described the organization as a "non-state hostile intelligence service" which was "often abetted by state actors like Russia."[7] In principle, a presidential candidate's cozying up to an antagonistic foreign organization posed such a direct challenge to the traditional prioritization of American national security that

---

[3] Presidential Candidate Donald J. Trump, Wilkes-Barre, Pennsylvania, October 10, 2016.

[4] Gabrielle Healy, "Did Trump Really Mention WikiLeaks over 160 Times in the Last Month of the Election Cycle?," *PolitiFact*, April 21, 2017, <http://www.politifact.com/truth-o-meter/statements/2017/apr/21/jackie-speier/did-trump-really-mention-wikileaks-over-160-times-/> (accessed September 16, 2019).

[5] Inderjeet Parmar, "Obama, WikiLeaks, and American Power," in Inderjeet Parmar et al. (eds.), *Obama and the World: New Directions in U.S. Foreign Policy*, (Routledge, 2014), 243.

[6] Kathryn Watson, "How Did WikiLeaks become Associated with Russia," *CBS News*, November 15, 2017, <https://www.cbsnews.com/news/how-did-wikileaks-become-associated-with-russia/> (accessed September 18, 2019).

[7] "Director Pompeo Delivers Remarks at CSIS," *CIA.gov*, April 13, 2017, <https://www.cia.gov/news-information/speeches-testimony/2017-speeches-testimony/pompeo-delivers-remarks-at-csis.html> (accessed September 16, 2019).

it should have triggered staunch bipartisan opposition, prompting calls for a cessation of the behavior, or the party's withdrawal of support for a candidate whose lack of patriotism should have rendered them unelectable. Between Congress and the electorate, the Founders believed accountability would hold American politicians in check. But in the hyperpartisan political domain of contemporary America, electoral campaigns are fought with such a win-at-all-costs attitude that there is no space to reprimand a candidate for such actions, especially if they cause political harm to the opponent. These intense political divisions have festered and deepened over the preceding decades, aggravated and accelerated by a media that has become increasingly divisive.

The United States' ascendancy to superpower status and subsequent ideological contest with the Soviet Union following the end of the Second World War transformed the nation's politics. It created a need for America to demonstrate how capitalism could provide peace, prosperity, and progress for all citizens, not just those who were wealthy or White. On the left, a form of international socialism inspired by Henry Wallace's vision of a "Peoples' Century" was ascendant, but his talk of wealth redistribution was deemed dangerously close to communism by his own party's leadership. On the right, the small-minded parochialism of the isolationist "America First" movement had been shattered by Franklin D. Roosevelt's national security rhetoric, Japan's surprise attack, and the global impact of the world war.[8] A new form of policymaking emerged to bridge these two visions, rooted in the domestic reforms of Roosevelt's New Deal and tempered Wilsonianism abroad. Liberalism, as this approach came to be known, positioned itself as the "vital center," its advocates balancing a belief in the government's responsibility to ensure national security and the basic welfare of Americans, with strong support for free enterprise. They rejected ideas of "rugged individualism" and laissez-faire governance, seeking to regulate the market in ways that protected citizens, strengthened capitalism, and ultimately enhanced democracy. While Harry Truman was not a charismatic candidate, the broad appeal of liberalism's non-ideological policies delivered a convincing victory in 1948's election. Progressive domestic reforms and a muscular foreign policy which saw the United States directly confront the perceived existential threat posed by the USSR proved popular enough to sweep up Republicans and corporate leaders alike, prompting a remarkable era of sustained bipartisan agreement about the nature of politics and government.[9]

Scholars have since challenged just how tolerant, harmonious, and inclusive the "liberal consensus" really was, and revisionist histories have argued

---

[8] Andrew Preston, "Monsters Everywhere: A Genealogy of National Security," *Diplomatic History*, 38, no. 3 (2014), 477–500, 497–98.

[9] Jenifer Delton, "Why the American Center Held—And Then Fell Apart," *Current History* (November 2017), 297.

convincingly that matters of race, class, gender, and sexuality, not to mention the extremes of McCarthyism, reveal a less progressive period than the term suggests.[10] However, when viewed in the light of the polarization that followed in subsequent decades, there is a case for considering the areas of consensus which did exist. Liberal policies such as pro-union legislation and employment stabilization gained support from both Democrats and Republicans seeking to demonstrate the benefits afforded to workers by free market capitalism. Bipartisan legislation such as the Serviceman's Readjustment Act of 1944 (GI Bill) was a political and economic success, giving millions of veterans access to college education and training programs, which significantly boosted social mobility and contributed to America's deep stock of human capital, helping sustain the nation's long-term economic growth. Government-subsidized mortgages and new mass-production housing techniques stimulated a housing boom which allowed more citizens to own a piece of the American dream, prompting the expansion of the suburbs. These government-inspired settlement patterns impacted growth in other ways, too. The automobile industry quadrupled in size from 1946 to 1955, and businesses and retail expanded to meet the new demand. Where there had been just eight commercial shopping malls at the end of the Second World War, there were 3,840 by 1960.[11] The political coalition that enabled this domestic revolution held firm for more than two decades, transforming America's previously hard-up workers into a burgeoning consumerist middle class. Collectively, the bipartisan cooperation and pragmatic policies of this consensus period contributed to the most sustained period of economic growth the United States had ever experienced, with gross national product increasing from $300 million in 1950 to $500 million by 1960, consolidating America's position as the world's richest country.[12]

Just as veteran care and workers' conditions aligned matters of national security with the ideals of a progressive liberal agenda, so too did America's racial politics. As Cold War competition expanded into the developing world, Russian propagandists publicized every lynching, riot, and the racial injustice of Jim Crow in the United States in efforts to attract support from the decolonizing peoples. Presidents and policymakers were forced to act to address the gulf between America's rhetoric of freedom, individual rights, and cultural tolerance, and its system of White supremacy. Collectively 1954's *Brown v. Board of Education*, the 1964 Civil Rights Act, 1965 Voting Rights Act, and the 1965 Immigration

---

[10] Gary Gerstle, "Race and the Myth of the Liberal Consensus," *Journal of American History*, 82, no. 2 (September 1995), 579–86, 579.

[11] "The Postwar Economy: 1945–1960," "Country Studies/Area Handbook," Federal Research Division, Library of Congress, 1998, <http://countrystudies.us/united-states/history-114.htm> (accessed September 16, 2019).

[12] *Id.*

and Nationality Act moved the United States toward being a more heterogeneous society.[13] To reflect these changes, the Democratic Party sought to reform its membership to include a new generation of minority and female leaders—a process that required a new "political correctness," focused upon race, identity, and difference, as well as, eventually, a new sensitivity about language and representation. A huge progressive step forward in terms of racial justice, these changes challenged the established order in emotive and divisive ways, their passage marking the first phase of a fraught and ongoing process of inclusion and integration. The political backlash against Liberals' support for civil rights saw key Democrat figures in the South leave the party, while in the North a significant number of working-class union men, feeling displaced by their party's new focus upon inclusivity, drifted away, uprooting the social homogeneity of the liberal consensus voter base. By the end of the 1960s the pursuit of racial progress, combined with the economic impact of recession and deindustrialization, and contentious debates over the direction of America's foreign policy had deeply divided American society. The conditions that had fostered political cooperation disintegrated and the vital center collapsed, setting the stage for the hostile polarization that characterizes contemporary American politics.

In the political realignment which took place in the following decades, the Republican Party exploited the divisions within the Democrat voter base by making opposition to the new "political correctness" and progressive politics a central cause, especially in the South. While race was certainly a significant factor for voters, the party's espousal of more traditional positions on a range of other matters such as taxes, moral values, Second Amendment gun rights, national security, abortion, and opposition to the counterculture all contributed to the rise of the political Right, culminating in Ronald Reagan's two electoral victories in the 1980s and that of his chosen successor, George H.W. Bush, for a further term.[14] While Bill Clinton won two successive terms from 1993, and his Vice President Al Gore came within a Supreme Court decision of securing victory in 2000, his election did not mark a period of national unity. Clinton's 1993 victory was secured by a mere 43 percent of the popular vote—a smaller portion of citizens than those who voted for 1988's unpopular Democratic candidate, Michael Dukakis. He was aided by the negative impact of a short but severe economic recession upon Bush's popularity, combined with the significant portion of the Republican voter base siphoned off by the independent candidacy

---

[13] Delton, *supra* note 9, at 300.
[14] Sean Trende, "Misunderstanding the Southern Realignment," *Real Clear Politics*, September 9, 2010, <https://www.realclearpolitics.com/articles/2010/09/09/misunderstanding_the_southern_realignment_107084.html> (accessed July 23, 2018).

of the billionaire Ross Perot.[15] And while Clinton maintained a hold on the White House for the second term, the 1990s saw the continued drift of a significant portion of the population to the political and cultural Right, deepening national divides and having a catastrophic impact upon the Democrats at state and local levels. A wave of conservatism and aggressive partisan politics saw the Republican Party, having consolidated its structures across the South, win the region in 1994 and with it the House of Representatives for the first time since 1952. It was the worst political performance by the Democrats since the 1920s.[16]

III. "It Is a Cultural War..." The Dividing of the Media Ecosystem

Key to the so-called Republican Revolution was the party's wholehearted commitment to identity politics, coupled with the transformation of the way citizens received news and opinions which purposefully blurred the lines between the two.[17] This agenda had first emerged as the Republican Party's opposition to the counterculture and emergent "political correctness" in the 1960s, but expanded into a full-blown culture war, as declared by Patrick Buchanan in a fiery speech at the 1992 Republican National Convention. Buchanan warned that "[t]here is a religious war going on in our country for the soul of America. It is a cultural war, as critical to the kind of nation we will one day be as the cold war itself."[18] The alarmist rhetoric epitomized widespread concerns among many social conservatives regarding what they perceived as the decline of the traditional American national identity, as economic changes, continued immigration, and ongoing racial integration transformed America's social landscape. The conflict was stoked by combatants galvanized by dramatic changes to the nation's media ecosystem, which become ideally suited to the divisive and opinion-based arguments which characterized debates around such sensitive and subjective topics as immigration, race relations, gun control, gay rights, and same-sex marriage. A range of factors contributed to the emergence of this new information

---

[15] Russell Riley, "Bill Clinton: Campaigns and Elections: The Campaign of 1992," Miller Center, University of Virginia, <https://millercenter.org/president/clinton/campaigns-and-elections> (accessed August 8, 2019).

[16] Philip Jenkins, *Rethinking a Nation: The United States in the 21st Century* (Red Globe Press, 2019), 18.

[17] Adam Clymer, "The 1994 Elections: Congress the Overview; G.O.P. Celebrates Its Sweep to Power; Clinton Vows to Find Common Ground," *New York Times*, November 10, 1994, <https://www.nytimes.com/1994/11/10/us/1994-elections-congress-overview-gop-celebrates-its-sweep-power-clinton-vows.html> (accessed August 28, 2019).

[18] Patrick Buchanan, "Address to the Republican National Convention," Houston, Texas, August 17, 1992, <https://www.americanrhetoric.com/speeches/patrickbuchanan1992rnc.htm> (accessed August 28, 2019).

environment, but central among these was the sustained reduction in legislation and regulation that would otherwise have limited the expression of views.

Key among the repeal of regulations was the striking down of the Fairness Doctrine in 1987, the removal of which permitted media outlets to engage in discussions related to popular culture war themes with a new vehemence, coarseness, and bias. Introduced in 1949, the Fairness Doctrine required holders of broadcast licenses to discuss controversial issues of public importance and to do so in a manner that was—in the view of the Federal Communications Commission (FCC)—honest, equitable, and balanced. The primary purpose was to ensure that American citizens were exposed to a diversity of viewpoints, a principle that was attacked as "misguided government policy" in a 1985 report issued under the leadership of FCC chairman Mark Fowler, a communications attorney who had worked on Reagan's 1976 and 1980 campaigns. The report questioned whether the doctrine was "constitutionally permissible under current marketplace conditions and First Amendment jurisprudence" and argued that in operation the doctrine had a "'chilling' effect on free expression and ideas."[19] "We should reverse course, and head ballistically toward liberty of the press for radio and television," concluded Fowler."[20] Swayed by the argument, Congress directed the FCC to look for alternative methods of regulation, and in August 1987, the Committee abolished the doctrine.

The removal of the Fairness Doctrine and the shift in the news values it embodied was as much a symbolic change to America's media landscape as it was directly impactful.[21] The rise of the vital center and Washington's period of consensus politics had coincided with and been aided by a media which predominantly shared broad journalistic values of truth, accuracy, and integrity. The paucity of choice of news outlets, combined with the sense of duty the doctrine represented ensured that news reporting was, in the main, concerned with the impartial representation of events. Conservative publications, however, believing themselves marginalized by their more popular liberal rivals, had begun to challenge the concept that journalism should be impartial. In the early 1960s, *Human Events*, a right-wing newsweekly founded in 1944 to champion conservative and Christian values, defined its reporting as "objective" while at the same time not being "impartial." The publication's editors described their mission as looking at events "through eyes that are biased in favour of limited

---

[19] "Fairness Doctrine Report," Before the Federal Communications Commission, Washington D.C., August 23, 1985, at 145, <https://archive.org/stream/FairnessReport/102Book1FCC2d145#page/n107>.
[20] *Id.* 252.
[21] Dan MacGuill, "Did Ronald Reagan Pave the Way for Fox News?," *Snopes*, January 26, 2018, <https://www.snopes.com/fact-check/ronald-reagan-fairness-doctrine/> (accessed August 28, 2019).

constitutional government, private enterprise, and individual freedom."[22] As the communications historian Nicole Hemmer has argued, by distinguishing between objectivity and impartiality, the conservative media sought to create a news environment in which "bias" was an acceptable journalistic value which worked in tandem with objectivity to publish "facts" they believed other outlets purposefully overlooked due to their own liberal biases.[23] Despite the rise of conservative material through the 1950s and 1960s, with publications such as *National Review*, publishing houses such as Regency and Devin-Adair, and broadcasters like the *Manion Forum* and *Dan Smooth Report* all emerging to represent right-wing positions, conservatives retained a sense that they could not break what they perceived as the stranglehold of a liberal media. The removal of the Fairness Doctrine sent the message that informing the citizenry was no longer the responsibility of a news outlet, marking a transformative period in the quality and nature of what passed for political commentary.

One of the first conservative commentators to benefit from the change in the way political issues could be discussed—and a symbol of how dramatically the news environment transformed post–Fairness Doctrine—was the radio talk show host Rush Limbaugh, whose show went nationwide in 1988. Limbaugh's staunch disapproval of abortion, controversial statements regarding African Americans and welfare, rejection of climate science, belief in "Feminazis," anti-Latino immigration stance, and attacks upon the LGBTQ community promptly established the bombastic broadcaster as a forceful and influential voice of a political right twisted by the culture wars. Within just two years, Limbaugh's show had amassed over twenty million listens, and his success inspired many more political and social commentators to express hardline views and opinions which were well to the right of the mainstream political discourse at the time.[24] The demonization or mockery of political opponents became common practice, as did the broadcast of purposefully inflammatory divisive content, and the dissemination of conspiracy theories. As audience numbers increased, commentators prioritized engagement over information, adopting the format of infotainment. The embrace of these false narratives not only transformed news and political commentary but also warped the relationship between reality and fiction. In 1994, Fairness and Accuracy in Reporting (FAIR), a left-leaning media watchdog established in 1986, published a report highlighting fifty instances of inaccurate

---

[22] Nicole Hemmer, *Messengers of the Right: Conservative Media and the Transformation of American Politics* (University of Pennsylvania Press, 2016).
[23] Nicole Hemmer, "The Conservative War on the Liberal Media Has a Long History," *The Atlantic*, January 17, 2014, <https://www.theatlantic.com/politics/archive/2014/01/the-conservative-war-on-liberal-media-has-a-long-history/283149/> (accessed August 9, 2019).
[24] Ze'ev Chafets, *Rush Limbaugh: An Army of One* (Sentinel, 2010), 53; Jenkins, *supra* note 16, at 25.

or distorted commentary on Limbaugh's show to advance his political agenda.[25] PolitiFact's scorecard for the radio personality, a man who promoted himself as "America's Truth Detector," recorded 82 percent of his political statements ranked as false.[26] The blurring of news, opinion, entertainment, fiction, and reality was accelerated by the proliferation of cable news channels, which offered choice beyond the original three networks. Like the talk radio stations that proceeded them, these channels were often avowedly partisan with Fox News, launched in 1996, catering for the political right, and MSNBC, established in the same year, targeted at a more liberal-minded audience.

IV. "You Guys Love Breaking News, and You Did It, You Broke It." The Economics of Objective Bias

The purposeful use of bias in news reporting was not just of ideological benefit to policymakers and proponents of the culture clash but also presented valuable business opportunities for the moguls who owned the emergent broadcasts, as well as their shareholders.[27] Most notable among these was Rupert Murdoch, who hired the former Republican Party media consultant Roger Ailes to serve as the CEO of his new channel, Fox News. While liberals railed against Fox's overt favoritism and bias, Ailes' network capitalized upon the United States' increasingly divided society to amass a mature viewer base united around conservative and Christian values. The network overtook CNN as the most watched cable TV news channel in January 2002 and has remained in that position ever since.[28] Not only has this given Fox significant political influence, but it also provides an identifiable consumer base to sell to advertisers, generating massive profits at considerable cost to the bedrock of a successful democracy and a healthy body politic.[29] Other news networks followed suit, providing their own bias interpretations of the news in order to appeal to alternative viewer bases, consolidating a new era in television news. While sensationalism was nothing new in America's media, the lack of regulation, focus upon entertainment at the expense of traditional journalism, and hosts' embrace of overblown demagoguery meant citizens were able to access extreme and divisive content, broadcast with a coarse vulgarity

---

[25] FAIR, "The Way Things Aren't," Fairness and Accuracy in Reporting (FAIR), March 8, 1992, <https://fair.org/extra/the-way-things-arent/> (accessed August 28, 2019).
[26] Jenkins, *supra* note 16, at 26.
[27] "Michelle Wolf Complete Remarks at 2018 White House Correspondents' Dinner," *C-SPAN*, April 29, 2018, <https://www.youtube.com/watch?v=DDbx1uArVOM> (accessed August 9, 2019).
[28] Mike Allen, "How Fox News Stayed on Top," *Politico*, <https://www.politico.com/story/2012/02/how-fox-news-stayed-on-top-072253> (accessed August 13, 2019).
[29] Tara Lachapelle, "The New Fox Shows What Outrage Is Worth," *Bloomberg*, <https://www.bloomberg.com/opinion/articles/2019-03-28/fox-news-shows-what-outrage-is-worth> (accessed August 13, 2019).

more akin to tabloids than mainstream newscasting, with a breadth of choice that ensured viewers could find content that satisfied their own ideological and social preconceptions.

The deliberate confirmation bias of each network developed a strong sense of viewer loyalty, locking audiences into the selective realities each network constructed for its audience. During 2016's presidential campaign for example, 40 percent of Trump voters listed Fox as their primary source of campaign news. The network provided consistently positive reporting on candidate Trump, while promoting fallacies and conspiracy theories related to his opponent Hillary Clinton, such as the Uranium One nuclear "scandal," false accusations of incompetence linked to the Benghazi attack, and constant suggestions of ill health and poor mental fitness. On the other side of the political spectrum, barely any Clinton voters watched Fox, with only 3 percent claiming it was their main source for campaign news. Instead, those of a more left-wing persuasion relied upon CNN (18%) and the left-leaning MSNBC (9%) as part of a slightly more varied media diet, which in a similar way to its rival fed its viewers stories which reaffirmed their negative views of Trump, although often with greater validity.[30] Even when voices from opposing political camps were invited onto the news networks, the interviews were often acts of theater as opposed to any serious effort to broaden viewers' understanding, with hosts berating guests for their views and opinions, at times even cutting them off before their segment has finished for added entertainment value and dramatic effect.[31] The fragmentation of political discourse, and with it the electorate, has been incredibly detrimental to the practice of political compromise and has undermined the chances of workable political solutions on a whole range of challenges facing the United States. For a democracy to be successful, some degree of partisanship is necessary, even desirable. But when that partisanship comes to blindly overwhelm all other critical thought, empathy evaporates and the political process breaks down.[32] Reason and argument give way to a blind tribal loyalty, transforming those who oppose a viewpoint from fellow citizens to enemies. It is this hyperpartisan and hostile environment that enabled a presidential nominee to openly employ kompromat provided by a hostile foreign actor to smear his political opponent without political repercussions.

---

[30] Amy Mitchell, Jeffrey Gottfried, & Michael Barthel, "Trump, Clinton Voters Divided in Their Main Source for Election News," Pew Research Center, January 18, 2017, <https://www.journalism.org/2017/01/18/trump-clinton-voters-divided-in-their-main-source-for-election-news/> (accessed August 9, 2019).

[31] Jon Stewart, *Crossfire*, October 15, 2004, <https://www.youtube.com/watch?v=aFQFB5YpDZE> (accessed September 19, 2019).

[32] Jamie Bartlett, *The People vs Tech: How the Internet Is Killing Democracy (And How We Save It)* (Edbury Press, 2018), 54–55.

Rather than reflecting upon the internal weakness caused by America's own media ecosystem, the Director of National Intelligence's (DNI's) report into Russia's interference in the 2016 presidential election perfectly highlighted the American tendency to externalize threats. Published in January 2017, the intelligence community's assessment attacked RT (formerly Russia Today)—a Kremlin-funded news outlet—for its role in disrupting the political process. Indeed, RT is the most visible face of Russian propaganda within the United States, serving as a conduit for the Kremlin's agenda cloaked as a television news channel. The network's core mission is not journalistic but military, serving as an "information weapon" to support the Russian state.[33] In a process dubbed "airbrushing reality" by the researcher Ben Nimmo, RT seeks to hide Russia's role in international crimes, such as the downing of the airliner MH17, justify aggression like the seizure and annexation of the Crimea, and spin narratives which cast doubt on accurate news reports through the broadcasting of falsified information. To enhance the credibility of its information warfare, RT employs native English speakers, uses modern video techniques, and books guests with some claim of expertise whose views align with the political position the Kremlin wishes to promote.[34] As an extra layer of camouflage for its propaganda, the network also broadcasts shows and produces coverage that is not overtly anti-American or pro-Kremlin.[35] The DNI's report argued that "Russia's state-run propaganda machine [. . .] contributed to the influence campaign by serving as a platform for Kremlin messaging [. . .]." It did this by "consistently cast[ing] President-elect Trump as the target of unfair coverage from traditional U.S. media outlets that they claimed were subservient to a corrupt political establishment"; "denigrat[ing] Secretary Clinton" with segments like "Clinton and ISIS Funded by the Same Money"; and casting doubt on the outcome of the US election with clips like "Trump Will Not be Permitted to Win." According to the report, the channel "substantially expanded its repertoire of programming that highlights criticism of alleged U.S. shortcomings in democracy and civil liberties."[36] Yet what the report fails to acknowledge is that what RT does is no different from Fox and other American news outlets and commentators. RT utilizes

---

[33] Ben Nimmo, "Question That: RT's Military Mission," Digital Forensic Research Lab, Atlantic Council, Medium, <https://medium.com/dfrlab/question-that-rts-military-mission-4c4bd9f72c88> (accessed September 5, 2019).

[34] Ben Nimmo & Jonathan Eyal, "Russia's Information Warfare—Airbrushing Reality," written evidence submitted to UK Parliament Select Committee, March 14, 2016, <http://data.parliament.uk/writtenevidence/committeeevidence.svc/evidencedocument/defence-committee/russia-implications-for-uk-defence-and-security/written/30408.html> (accessed September 5, 2019).

[35] Sarah Oates, "A Perfect Storm: American Media, Russian Propaganda," *Current History*, 116, no. 792 (October 2017), 283.

[36] Background to "Assessing Russian Activities and Intentions in recent US Elections": The Analytic Process and Cyber Incident Attribution, Director of National Intelligence, January 6, 2017, <https://www.dni.gov/files/documents/ICA_2017_01.pdf>

the loosening of journalistic standards and lack of balance news networks in the United States have already normalized. It is the news environment within which RT exists that is America's primary problem, not the network itself.

Ignoring the wider issues poisoning the US media ecosystem, the Justice Department forced RT to register under the US Foreign Agent Registration Act.[37] Despite the government's targeting of RT, research has revealed the broadcaster was not a key element of the Russian misinformation campaign, ranking nineteenth in a list of the top twenty-five sites which produced "news" content shared through Russia's network of social media bots. Instead, most of the content came collectively from right-leaning American networks such as Fox News, Breitbart News, and the Daily Caller. The *Washington Post* and *San Francisco Chronicle* ranked more highly than RT in terms of shared stories, in particular their coverage of the Clinton campaign's stolen emails.[38] The Kremlin did not need to use RT to create false and divisive narratives because they already existed from American media sources. It just elevated the content's distribution.[39] Furthermore, RT's airbrushing of reality is no different from what Fox and its peers do in terms of denigrating political opposition and boosting their preferred candidate, producing loaded content which ignores or excuses legitimate concerns regarding politicians and policies which align with their ideological interests, while misrepresenting and vilifying opposing perspectives. The American public is subjected to information warfare and propaganda as potent and manipulative as anything employed by the Russian state every day of their lives, not a product of the active measures of a hostile intelligence service, but instead a homemade product, spawned from America's fragmented society and the selfish interests of a shallow pool of wealthy citizens, exploiting and exacerbating these conditions for their own gain. These elites, such as Rupert Murdoch, the late Roger Ailes, and the billionaire conservative activist Robert Mercer (who endowed the ultraconservative news site Breitbart News with $11 million in 2011), have no interest in a free press as a critical component of liberal democracy, and instead have utilized media outlets as powerful propaganda tools through which they can influence society, shape the political agenda,

---

[37] Natalka Pisnia, "Why Has RT Registered as a Foreign Agent in the US?," *BBC News*, November 15, 2017, <https://www.bbc.co.uk/news/world-us-canada-41991683> (accessed August 13, 2019).

[38] Jonathan Albright, "Troll Accounts by News Outlet by Tweet Date (11.5k links)," *Columbia University*, February 15, 2018,
https://public.tableau.com/views/r_tweets_org_links/TrollAccountsbyNewsOutletbyTweetDate11_5klinks?:embed=y&:display_count=yes&publish=yes&:showVizHome=no (accessed September 5, 2019).

[39] Craig Timberg, "Russia Used Mainstream Media to Manipulate American Voters," *Washington Post*, February 15, 2018, <https://beta.washingtonpost.com/business/technology/russia-used-mainstream-media-to-manipulate-american-voters/2018/02/15/85f7914e-11a7-11e8-9065-e55346f6de81_story.html?outputType=amp> (accessed September 5, 2019).

and drive their own agendas.[40] This is the polarized information environment in which Russian propaganda is operating, not as the key influencer, but one player in a complex, destructive, and self-serving game. America presents an easy, target-rich environment which grants the opportunity for foreign countries and wealthy individuals alike to influence citizens who are unmoored from objectivity, consuming information which offers ever more distorted versions of the reality their specialized and filtered news feed provides.

V. "Part of What Makes for a Healthy Democracy Is Ensuring You've Got Citizens Who Are Informed..."

One could be forgiven for thinking that a solution to the closing of Americans minds through narrowcast news programming would come from the dramatic increase in citizens' access to the World Wide Web, particularly the hyperconnectivity that came with the rise of social networks in the 2000s.[41] When Fox News launched in 1996, just 16 percent of Americans were internet users. But by the time of the 2016 election, that number had increased to 75 percent, placing a much greater range of information at citizens' fingertips.[42] Yet despite the dramatically expanded scope of information web access offered, the increase in the use of sites such as Facebook and Twitter as primary sources of news consumption did nothing to diminish the deep political divides afflicting the United States. Instead, a combination of legislation and Silicon Valley's business model served to exacerbate and accelerate the divisions talk radio and cable news had been fostering for the previous two decades, creating further opportunities for Russian information warfare to influence the fragmented body politic.

In July 1995, *Time* published a cover story sensationally titled "Cyberporn," with a subheading asking: "Can we protect our kids?"[43] The article reported that 83.5 percent of images on the internet were pornographic. Despite the piece receiving significant criticism from experts within the tech sector for its

---

[40] Max Kutner, "Meet Robert Mercer, the Mysterious Billionaire Benefactor of Breitbart," *Newsweek*, November 21, 2016, <http://www.newsweek.com/2016/12/02/robert-mercer-trump-donor-bannon-pac-523366.html> (accessed September 1, 2019).

[41] President Barack Obama, "Remarks by the President at the Facebook Town Hall," Facebook Headquarters, Palo Alto, California, April 20, 2011, <https://obamawhitehouse.archives.gov/the-press-office/2011/04/20/remarks-president-facebook-town-hall> (accessed August 10, 2019).

[42] "Internet Users in the United States," World Bank Development Indicators, Federal Reserve Economic Data, <https://fred.stlouisfed.org/series/ITNETUSERP2USA> (accessed August 14, 2019).

[43] Philip Elmer-Dewitt, "Cyberporn—Online Erotica: On a Screen Near You," *Time*, July 3, 1995, http://content.time.com/time/magazine/article/0,9171,134361,00.html (accessed August 1, 2019).

inaccuracy, it triggered a moral panic.[44] While the exact percentage of online pornography was questionable, there was no doubt that it was a profitable and expanding industry. By 1993 for example, the Event Horizon message board was grossing over $3.2 million per annum through subscriptions to their adult image forums. The origins of this pornography—uploaded scans from adult magazines—triggered a copyright lawsuit from *Playboy*.[45] Collectively, the sense of an unregulated and unsafe domain prompted the Clinton administration to introduce legislation establishing new rules and protocols for the internet. The Telecommunications Act 1996 was a formative piece of legislation, with one clause playing a huge role in how the World Wide Web evolved. Section 230 C(1) stated: "No provider or user of an interactive computer service shall be treated as the publisher or speaker of any information provided by another information content provider."[46] The removal of responsibility for content from the host allowed a new kind of business to emerge, as social media platforms encouraged users to upload and share content across their sites with the freedom to publish their words, images, and eventually videos without a legal responsibility for that content. Without this permissible environment, mainstream platforms such as Facebook, Twitter, and YouTube, and their more select subculture cousins such as the controversial 8chan and 4chan message boards, would not be able to exist in their current form, as control over material would need to be much stricter.

Far from creating the interconnected global village Silicon Valley CEOs dreamed of, or ushering in the period of a new unified social contract John Perry Barlow's "Declaration of Independence of Cyberspace" alluded to, the users that joined this emergent electronic medium brought with them the standards, expectations, and prejudices already established within the traditional media ecosystem.[47] The web proved itself ideally suited to the continued pursuit of controversial and inflammatory policy positions and perspectives, and far from ending divisions, the internet became the culture war's new front line. These online divisions have been dramatically exacerbated by the business model social media platforms have adopted. Initially, it was unclear to Silicon Valley's entrepreneurs how best to monetize their new sites, but one major innovation transformed the online economy—and American politics. The sites' owners explored how they could exploit the data they collected from their users, sharing

[44] Philip Elmer-Dewitt, "Finding Marty Rimm," *Fortune*, July 1, 2015, <https://fortune.com/2015/07/01/cyberporn-time-marty-rimm/> (accessed August 1, 2019).
[45] Brian McCullough, "A History of Internet Porn," *Internet History*, <http://www.internethistorypodcast.com/2015/01/history-of-internet-porn/> (accessed June 2, 2018).
[46] Telecommunications Act 1996, Section 230, C(1), at 101, <https://transition.fcc.gov/Reports/tcom1996.pdf> (accessed February 5, 2018).
[47] John Perry Barlow, "A Declaration of the Independence of Cyberspace," Electronic Frontier Foundation, February 8, 1996, <https://www.eff.org/cyberspace-independence> (accessed August 14, 2019).

it across platforms to build a picture of what users do on the rest of the internet. They built profiles of user interests to sell to companies for targeted advertising, which the sites themselves could host. To encourage users to spend more time online, thus providing ever more data while also being exposed to more advertising and online retail opportunities, the work of the behavioral scientist Daniel Kahneman was utilized. In a series of meetings with some of Silicon Valley's leading innovators, including Amazon founder Jeff Bezos, Facebook's first president Sean Parker, and the founders of Google, Larry Page and Sergey Brin, Kahneman and his colleagues shared their research on behavioral economics and decision-making. They posited that people make decisions based around one of two different systems of thinking. In the first dichotomy, people act on guesses, hunches, and gut feelings. An emotional decision-making based upon a sense of "I just know." The second, more critical, mindset utilizes analysis, statistical data, and probability. While good for addressing contested and controversial points, this mindset is much less appealing to advertisers, who seek to hook customers through a more emotional connection.[48] Trying to grab the attention of consumers is nothing new, but Silicon Valley's insights into individual users has enabled their platforms to customize and shape online content in personalized ways. In the pursuit of keeping users in the emotional state of mind, Silicon Valley's web giants coded algorithms to filter content and provide more of what they already liked while sifting out opposing opinions, evidence, and perspectives.[49]

While algorithmically curated "filter bubbles" proved enormously profitable by drawing users in for ever-longer periods of online activity, they have been disastrous for critical discourse.[50] Filtering content may be harmless when a user is browsing cat videos or makeup tutorials, but the same automated censorship of content becomes much more ominous when one considers that by 2016 the majority of American adults—62 percent—also used social media to access news.[51] In most instances, the code that governs content on these platforms is so subtle most users have no idea that the information they are consuming can be so drastically different from that other users are experiencing.[52] A combination of the

---

[48] Jamie Bartlett, "The Persuasion Machine," *Secrets of Silicon Valley*, Episode 2, BBC 2, August 13, 2017, <https://computer-literacy-project.pilots.bbcconnectedstudio.co.uk/c6d27ffedcf614232f7bb813d0c6d8b1> (accessed August 14, 2019).

[49] Eli Pariser, *The Filter Bubble: How the New Personalized Web Is Changing What We Read and How We Think* (Penguin, 2011), 9.

[50] "2018 Digital Future Project: Surveying the Digital Future," USC Annenberg School Center for the Digital Future, December 2018, <https://www.digitalcenter.org/wp-content/uploads/2018/12/2018-Digital-Future-Report.pdf> (accessed August 16, 2019).

[51] Elisa Shearer & Jeffrey Gottfried, "News Use Across Social Media Platforms 2016," Pew Research, May 26, 2016, <https://www.journalism.org/2016/05/26/news-use-across-social-media-platforms-2016/> (accessed August 16, 2019).

[52] P.W. Singer, Emerson Brooking, *Like War: The Weaponization of Social Media* (Eamon Dolan, 2018), 122.

preexisting political divisions and the intense segregation of information caused by individuals' filter bubbles has seen the rise of separate online partisan media ecosystems across the United States, where, like their cable news counterparts, political entrepreneurs have been able to further upend politics by establishing their own highly ideological news outlets, feeding into filter bubbles and getting their messages across in the raw and unfiltered manner social media platforms allow. The left-leaning Huffington Post, co-founded and edited by Arianna Huffington, emerged in 2005, establishing itself as a credible news source and becoming the first digital media enterprise to win a Pulitzer Prize in 2012.[53] Two years later, the echo on the political right saw the launch of the aggressive tabloid-style Breitbart News, named after its founder the late conservative commentator Andrew Breitbart. The site quickly attracted the support the billionaire conservative activist Robert Mercer and produces content which, while masquerading as conservative-leaning news, is misogynistic, homo- and transphobic, racist, xenophobic, and Islamophobic, focused upon exploiting pent-up resentment, social divisions, economic hardship, and mistrust in the government.[54]

The dezinformatsiya portion of Russia's influence campaign was designed to take advantage of the partisan, viral, and filtered nature of the social media ecosystem. The normalized hostility, tabloid tone, and conspiratorial content has enabled Russian propaganda to hide in plain sight, masquerading as just another point of view or an alternative source of information.[55] In his indictment of Russian officials identified as being involved in the manipulation of the 2016 presidential election, Special Counsel Robert Mueller described the surreptitious social media campaign as addressing "divisive U.S. political and social issues" with "a strategic goal to sow discord in the U.S. political system, including the 2016 U.S. presidential election." This was done, Mueller, continued, through posting "derogatory information about a number of candidates," "supporting the presidential campaign of then-candidate Donald J. Trump and disparaging Hillary Clinton."[56] During the November 2017 House of Representatives Permanent Select Committee on Intelligence's open hearing with officials from

[53] Yochai Benkler et al., *Network Propaganda: Manipulation, Disinformation, and Radicalization in American Politics* (Oxford University Press, 2018), 81–82.

[54] For example, see: Milo Yiannopoulos, "The Solution to Online 'Harassment' Is Simple; Women Should Log Off," *Breitbart News*, July 5, 2016, <https://www.breitbart.com/social-justice/2016/07/05/solution-online-harassment-simple-women-log-off/>; "Gay Rights Have Made Us Dumber, It's Time to Get Back in the Closet," *Breitbart News*, June 15, 2015, <https://www.breitbart.com/politics/2015/06/17/gay-rights-have-made-us-dumber-its-time-to-get-back-in-the-closet/>; Raheem Kassam, "Young Muslims in the West Are a Ticking Time Bomb, Increasingly Sympathetic with Radicals, Terror," *Breitbart News*, March 22, 2016, <https://www.breitbart.com/europe/2016/03/22/polling-muslims-in-the-west-increasingly-sympathise-with-extremism-terror/> (accessed August 16, 2019).

[55] Oates, *supra* note 35, at 282.

[56] "Internet Research Agency Indictment," Department of Justice, February 16, 2018, <https://www.justice.gov/file/1035477/download> (accessed August 17, 2019).

Facebook, Twitter, and Google concerning their platforms' manipulation by Russian agents, the Ranking Member Adam Schiff echoed Mueller's concerns noting that foreign agents had been "sowing discord in the U.S. by inflaming passions on a range of diverse issues" through the distribution of "politicized content and videos," and calling for the United States to "identify, expose, and defend ourselves against similar covert influence operations in the future."[57]

As with the similarities between RT and Fox, however, to see the manipulation of this online environment to unleash propaganda upon the American public as a predominantly Russian activity is an externalization of the United States' more pressing internal vulnerabilities. First, the idea that it is predominantly Russian agents who utilize social media bots to influence political discourse is naive, with a well-placed Republican National Committee informant confessing that the use of such methods is "a common tactic, in both presidential campaigns and lower down the ladder."[58] Furthermore, revelations concerning Cambridge Analytica, a data analytics and marketing firm funded by the Breitbart News investor Robert Mercer, which leveraged illegally obtained profile information from millions of Facebook users to drive a pro-Trump microtargeting campaign, reveals one does not need to look beyond America's own borders to find those guilty of efforts to subvert America's democracy.[59] Even when one does look at the content shared by the Russian network of bots, it is clear that America's domestic media environment is the most influential component, with links to domestic sites of an ideologically conservative bent being the most prominent.[60] The bot network established by Russia's Internet Research Agency (IRA)—the Kremlin-funded agency charged with overseeing Russia's influence operation—was predominantly geared toward amplifying Indigenous content related to contentious domestic matters, such as race relations, conservative social views, LGBTQ rights, and other long-running facets of the culture wars (this is shown in Figure 12.1). Where the IRA did produce content, such as Facebook and Instagram advertisements, these simply followed themes already established by the domestic sites. The reality is that with the deep political, social, and economic divisions afflicting American society, and the charged and subjective reporting that dominates the media, Russian agents had no need to create false narratives with which to inflame citizens—the abundance of hostile and divisive American-manufactured content that passed as news already

---

[57] Adam Schiff, "Exposing Russia's Efforts to Sow Discord Online: The Internet Research Agency and Advertisements," U.S. House of Representatives Permanent Select Committee on Intelligence, <https://intelligence.house.gov/social-media-content/> (accessed August 16, 2019).

[58] Samuel Wooley et al. (eds.), *Computational Propaganda: Political Parties, Politicians, and Political Manipulation on Social Media* (Oxford University Press, 2019), 195.

[59] Hannes Grassegger & Mikael Krogerus, "The Data That Turned the World Upside Down," *Motherboard*, January 28, 2017, <https://www.vice.com/en_us/article/mg9vvn/how-our-likes-helped-trump-win> (accessed September 10, 2019).

[60] Albright, *supra* note 38.

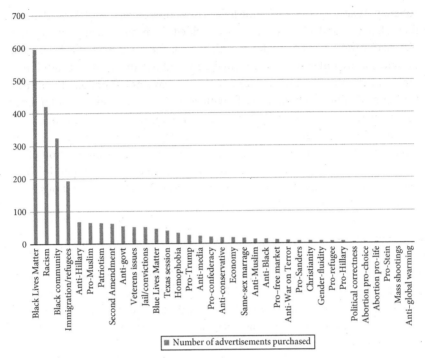

Figure 12.1 Russian Facebook and Instagram advertisements purchased by the Internet Research Agency, Quarter 2, 2015–Quarter 3, 2017.
Source: "Social Media Advertisements," US Permanent Select Committee on Intelligence, https://democrats-intelligence.house.gov/social-media-content/social-media-advertisements.htm.

dominated the airwaves and cyberspace. The Kremlin's agents simply took existing narratives and amplified their distribution.[61] Rather than "fake news" or foreign propaganda, the majority of content linked to the Russian influence campaign can be most accurately understood as domestic disinformation: the purposeful construction of true or partially true pieces of information into a message that is, at its core, misleading, with the express intention of politically aggravating, alarming, and polarizing debate, pushing politically active people away from the center to more ideological extremes.

Over the past four decades, aggressive misinformation, which began on talk radio, expanded onto cable news, and then took root in citizens' online filter bubbles, has turned both left- and right-wing media ecosystems into internally

---

[61] Craig Timberg, "Russia Used Mainstream Media to Manipulate American Voters," *Washington Post*, February 15, 2018, <https://www.washingtonpost.com/amphtml/business/technology/russia-used-mainstream-media-to-manipulate-american-voters/2018/02/15/85f7914e-11a7-11e8-9065-e55346f6de81_story.html> (accessed February 19, 2018).

coherent, relatively insulated knowledge communities, where citizens reinforce their shared worldviews while being shielded from any journalism, opinion pieces, or other forms of evidence which challenge it.[62] Americans have come to hold starkly different sets of factual beliefs about the current condition of their nation, as well as the motives of political actors as a function of their partisanship. Online discussion is rife with fear, paranoia, and unsubstantiated rumors which emerge from and propagate through polarized political discussion networks. The lack of responsible reporting which seeks to raise citizens' awareness in a nonpartisan manner has meant that a significant portion of the American electorate are vulnerable to a widely studied phenomenon in social psychology known as the Dunning-Kruger effect. This is composed of several interrelated phenomena thought to occur because:

> ... individuals vary in their awareness of "known unknowns" (concepts, skills, or experiences that one is aware of but have not yet mastered) relative to unknown unknowns (which fall outside of an individual's cognizance). As a result, low achievers are unaware of the extent of their ignorance because they are lacking in metacognitive skills. This "double burden of incompetence" means that low-performing individuals often overestimate their own objective performance.[63]

Applied to politics, the impact of this ignorance is that "[o]verconfident citizens may become emboldened, making strong political assertions in their social networks and resisting persuasive counterarguments."[64] In the case of the United States, it is not that citizens are ignorant because they refuse to engage with political news, but that the news is so ideologically skewed and filtered that the more intense their engagement, the more ill-informed they are likely to be. It is this phenomenon more than any hostile foreign intervention which has created a media environment in which inaccurate reporting such as that on Clinton's response to the Benghazi attack, lies related to the Uranium One case, and nonexistent conspiracies such as Pizzagate can all come to be seen as credible.[65]

---

[62] Yochai Benkler et al., "Breitbart-Led Right-Wing Media Ecosystem Altered Broader Media Agenda," *Columbia Journalism Review*, March 3, 2017, <https://www.cjr.org/analysis/breitbart-media-trump-harvard-study.php?fbclid=IwAR3N9FJDJ47D2_IYOSUdennhvvaSI2imZWrJjsIvuVXjRQOzOjxeVtUgESA> (accessed August 16, 2019).
[63] Ian Anson, "Partisanship, Political Knowledge, and the Dunning-Kruger Effect," *Political Psychology*, 39, no. 5 (October 2018), 1173–92, 1173–74.
[64] Id.
[65] Lori Robertson, "A False "Corruption" Claim," *FactCheck.Org*, October 25, 2016, <https://www.factcheck.org/2016/10/a-false-corruption-claim/> (accessed August 19, 2019).

VI. "Russia, If You're Listening, I Hope You'll Be Able to Find the 30,000 Emails That Are Missing... I Think You'll Be Rewarded Mightily by Our Press." The Decline of Print Journalism

There are in the body politic, economic and social, many and grave evils, and there is urgent necessity for the sternest war upon them. There should be relentless exposure of and attack upon every evil man, whether politician or business man, every evil practice, whether in politics, business, or social life. I hail as a benefactor every writer or speaker, every man who, on the platform or in a book, magazine, or newspaper, with merciless severity makes such attack, provided always that he in his turn remembers that the attack is of use only if it is absolutely truthful.[66]

In his 1906 speech titled "The Man with the Muck-Rake," Theodore Roosevelt hailed the function of the free press and its investigative journalism within American society, while calling upon it to be undertaken responsibly.[67] The quality press of the fourth estate has long been seen as a watchdog of the American public, ensuring citizens are informed on important matters. For a long time, however, this role did not extend to holding political figures within the federal government to account.[68] Much of the print media's early coverage regarding governmental affairs was bland and deferential, with the journalistic value of objectivity dulling any critical edge, lest it be seen as sensationalist yellow journalism or self-aggrandizing editorializing.[69] The most damaging example of this approach to reporting came during the Red Scare of the 1950s, when these journalistic conventions caused newspapers to legitimize and amplify Senator Joseph McCarthy's false accusations and smears. Following a period of reflection across newsrooms at their failure to hold the powerful to account and motivated by the new competitive threat posed by television—the medium that had played a key role in exposing McCarthy—newspaper editors encouraged their reporters to move beyond factual recitations and begin providing readers opinion, explanation, and critical interpretation. This shift in journalistic values coincided with the end of the "era of trust," as government lies about the Vietnam War exposed through the leaking of the *Pentagon Papers*, the Watergate scandal, and

---

[66] Theodore Roosevelt, "Address of President Roosevelt at the Laying of the Corner Stone of the Office Building of the House of Representatives: The Man with the Muck-Rake," April 14, 1906, <https://voicesofdemocracy.umd.edu/theodore-roosevelt-address-of-president-roosevelt-at-the-laying-of-the-corner-stone-of-the-office-building-of-the-house-of-representatives-april-14-1906-the-man-with-the-muck-rake-14-april/> (accessed August 20, 2019).
[67] Yochai Benkler, "A Free Irresponsible Press: Wikileaks and the Battle over the Soul of the Networked Fourth Estate," *Harvard Civil Rights–Civil Liberties Law Review*, 46 (2011), 311–97, 311, <https://dash.harvard.edu/handle/1/10900863> (accessed September 10, 2019).
[68] Presidential Candidate Donald J. Trump, Miami, Florida, July 28, 2016.
[69] Ted Smyth, *The Gilded Age Press, 1865–1900* (Praeger, 2003), 173.

congressional hearings such as the Church Committee and Tower Commission helped forge a new adversarial style of political journalism, more in keeping with the watchdog role Theodore Roosevelt had advocated.

The late 1960s and 1970s marked a golden age for print journalism, as leading publications adjusted their fundamental relationship with the government and elevated their investigative reporting. By the time *All The President's Men* hit cinemas in 1976, dramatizing the role of journalists in exposing the Watergate conspiracy, the image of the brave reporter challenging political corruption proliferated across the country. But journalists' willingness to take sides also came at a cost. No longer could the press count upon the automatic trust their bland factual reporting guaranteed. As publications challenged politicians and policies, they made enemies. On the right, the likes of Vice President Spiro Agnew attacked reporters for exercising what he argued was undue influence through their left-wing bias. In a 1969 speech, Agnew criticized journalists as a like-minded elite who "live and work in the geographical and intellectual confines of New York," making them "the most unrepresentative community in the entire United States." Preempting the eventual ideological reinforcement of the social media filter bubble, Agnew railed against the "parochialism" of a news community which "read the same newspapers [. . .], draw their political and social views from the same sources" and "talk constantly to one another, thereby providing artificial reinforcement to their shared viewpoints."[70] Viewpoints which, in the eyes of many on the right, were deeply bias against conservative views. Meanwhile, on the left, the intellectual and financial selectivism within the press corps drew a different kind of criticism, with the mainstream media attacked as an extension of the elitist establishment which dominated Washington, D.C.[71]

With powerful enemies, a divided support base, and increasing competition the golden age of journalism was short lived. The removal of the Fairness Doctrine and the dramatic expansion of political commentators and voices that followed—first through the medium of talk radio, then cable news, and finally the expansion of digital and social media—destroyed print media's traditional role as gatekeeper to the news. The sheer variety of voices meant that there were no longer any gates to keep, and the decline in circulation and influence of the quality press can be directly mapped to the rise of the alternative outputs and voices. From peak circulation of over 63 million daily newspapers in 1973, the figure steadily declined, hitting 55.7 million in 2000, and just 28.5 million in 2018. Thus, American print outlets have been in financial and professional crisis

---

[70] Vice President Spiro Agnew, "Television News Coverage," Des Moines, Iowa, November 13, 1969, <https://www.americanrhetoric.com/speeches/spiroagnewtvnewscoverage.htm> (accessed September 11, 2019).

[71] Jacob Weisberg, "Bad News: Can Democracy Survive If the Media Fails?," *Foreign Affairs*, September/October 2019.

for decades as declining sales hit all aspects of the business model. One brief exception was advertising revenue, which initially bucked the trend of decline, increasing steadily from $2.6 million in 1970 to $49.4 million in 2005.[72] However, the emergence of social media platforms shifted both attention and advertising to online forums, deepening the print media's economic woes as people discovered they no longer needed to buy a paper to read the news, and advertisers found more direct ways to target potential customers. Some publications sought to evolve, with *The Guardian* in particular being quick to adopt to a format of online reporting.[73] The rise in visitors to the major newspapers' websites showed some success in this adaptation by the traditional media, with average traffic to the top fifty US newspapers by circulation increasing from 8.2 million in 2014, to 11.6 million in 2018. Furthermore, although digital subscriptions are not included in official circulation figures, financial statements from the *New York Times* and *Wall Street Journal* revealed significant gains in this field between 2017 and 2018. Yet despite the rise of digital consumption, the gains are still not enough to reverse the losses brought on by the continued decline in physical sales and advertising. Even with a shift to producing more online content, traditional press outlets have struggled to capitalize on the new media economy as search companies and social media platforms have cashed in, exempt from the responsibilities of being publishers by the Telecommunications Act of 1996, while at the same time coming to dominate the shifting information landscape. By 2016, just two in ten US adults got their news from the printed press, a figure that had fallen from 27 percent in 2013. This is compared to 57 percent who relied predominantly upon television news, 38 percent online, and 25 percent from the radio.[74]

The final crash of the sector's business model was rapid, giving outlets little time to react and adjust and impacting even the papers of records' ability to report on news across the county. In 2004, the *Washington Post* brought in $143 million in profits. Five years later, the paper posted a loss of $164 million, which, combined with the impact of the global financial crisis, forced rounds of cutbacks, staff buyouts, and layoffs. The decline in income has hit investment significantly, and newsrooms have been shrinking at alarming rates. Newspapers almost everywhere were trimming staff and cutting costs even before the competition posed by social media platforms and digital outlets, but the shift in

---

[72] "State of the News Media 2016," Pew Research Center, June 15, 2016, <https://www.pewresearch.org/wp-content/uploads/sites/8/2016/06/state-of-the-news-media-report-2016-final.pdf> (accessed September 12, 2019).

[73] Weisberg, *supra* note 71.

[74] Michael Barthel, "Pathways to News," Journalism & Media, Pew Research Center, July 7, 2016, <https://www.journalism.org/2016/07/07/pathways-to-news/>; "Newspapers Fact Sheet," *Journalism.org*, July 9, 2019, <https://www.journalism.org/fact-sheet/newspapers/> (accessed August 21, 2019).

citizens' habits of news consumption has accelerated the decline. Despite the vital importance of a free press to the successful functioning of a healthy democracy, the United States is one of the only major world powers that does not have a large state-funded or public broadcaster to occupy the central information space. This means that corporations and individual media outlets are left to uphold standards, training, and reporting, problematically linking the health of the citizens' watchdog to the profitability of the sector. And as profits and audience numbers have declined, so have the influence, impact, and integrity of the fourth estate. According to data from the Bureau of Labor Statistics, the number of staff employed as reporters, editors, photographers, or film and video editors in the newspaper industry in 2018 was 37,900, a drop in the journalistic workforce of 47 percent in a decade.[75] Even for those staff fortunate enough to retain their jobs, the conditions of employment have declined. The *Washington Post*, for example, reduced its journalistic workforce by 7 percent in 2003, before promptly rehiring more than a dozen reporters on precarious temporary contracts, demonstrating how a once prestigious career choice had been pushed into the exploitative gig economy.[76] In 2006, the paper cut a further eighty full-time newsroom jobs, amounting to a further 9 percent shrinkage of its newsroom.[77] By 2018, the median annual income of newsroom employees with a college degree was approximately $51,000—about 14 percent less than the median of all other college-educated workers. Job losses are not purely limited to traditional print journalism either, and while the cuts are not as pronounced among digital-native news outlets, the sector still experienced a 23 percent decline in revenue followed by subsequent layoffs in 2017–2018.[78]

As staff numbers have shrunk, newspapers have shut down domestic reporting bureaus outside of the capital and major metropolitan areas, deepening the disconnect between mainstream journalists and the citizens of the flyover states, dubbed the "forgotten America" by the journalist Sarah Kendzior.[79] In

---

[75] "State of the New Media," Pew Research Center, <https://www.pewresearch.org/topics/state-of-the-news-media/> (accessed August 21, 2019).

[76] T.J. McCue, "57 Million U.S. Workers Are Part of the Gig Economy," *Forbes*, August 31, 2018, <https://www.forbes.com/sites/tjmccue/2018/08/31/57-million-u-s-workers-are-part-of-the-gig-economy/>

[77] https://www.washingtonpost.com/lifestyle/style/the-washington-posts-new-slogan-turns-out-to-be-an-old-saying/2017/02/23/cb199cda-fa02-11e6-be05-1a3817ac21a5_story.html?utm_term=.6956bb2d9e4b; Katherine Q. Seelye, "Washington Post to Cut 80 Newsroom Jobs," *New York Times*, March 11, 2006, <https://www.nytimes.com/2006/03/11/business/media/washington-post-to-cut-80-newsroom-jobs.html> (accessed April 4, 2018).

[78] Elizabeth Grieco, Nami Sumida, & Sophie Fedeli, "About a Third of Large U.S. Newspapers Have Suffered Layoffs Since 2017," Pew Research Center, July 23, 2018, <https://www.pewresearch.org/fact-tank/2018/07/23/about-a-third-of-large-u-s-newspapers-have-suffered-layoffs-since-2017/> (accessed August 20, 2019).

[79] Sarah Kendzior, *The View From Flyover Country: Dispatches from the Forgotten America* (Flatiron Books, 2015), 5.

2018, a Gallup-Knight Foundation survey found that 69 percent of Americans had lost trust in the news media over the past decade, with many feeling a legitimate sense of disconnection from an elite class who were either unaware or disinterested in the issues facing many American citizens across the nation. On the political right, the impact of decades of criticism against the so-called liberal bias of the mainstream print media, combined with the alternative reality offered by the broad and internally coherent right-wing media ecosystem was particularly effective in destroying journalists' credibility, with 94 percent of Republicans declaring their mistrust of the print media.[80]

Along with the reduction in the employment and training of the journalistic workforce and the declining connection between print media and citizens, the sector's reduced financial stability has had a dramatic impact upon the news values of even the most prestigious papers of record. While there should be little doubt journalists still take seriously their responsibility to reliably provide their readership with the material they need to make informed decisions on matters of importance, they cannot ignore the significant financial pressures their sector is functioning under. With a greater need to attract readers to generate advertising revenue, traditional press outlets have embraced increasingly sensationalist reporting and story selection. A detailed study into the news coverage of Hillary Clinton's and Donald Trump's campaigns during the 2016 presidential election by mainstream publications such as the *New York Times*, *Washington Post*, and *Wall Street Journal* revealed these shifting news values. Analyzing an eighteen-month period, the research revealed that when it came to reporting on Hillary Clinton, the papers printed approximately four times as many sentences related to scandals as it did the candidate's policies. In their coverage of Donald Trump, sentences were one-and-a-half times as likely to be about policy as scandal. Given the range of scandals Trump as a candidate was implicated in—sexual assault; the illegal Trump Foundation; the fraudulent Trump University; redlining real-estate developments; attacking a Gold Star family; and numerous instances of misogynistic, racist, and offensive speech—it is striking that journalists devoted more attention to his policies than his personal failings. Even more revealing of the decline in journalistic standards is the fact that coverage related to the various Clinton-related email scandals—her use of a private email server while secretary of state, and the content stolen from the Democratic National Committee (DNC) and campaign manager John Podesta—accounted for more sentences than all of Trump's scandals combined (65,000 compared to 40,000).[81] This

---

[80] "Indicators of News Media Trust," Gallup/Knight Foundation, September 11, 2001, <https://www.knightfoundation.org/reports/indicators-of-news-media-trust> (accessed September 11, 2019).

[81] Duncan Watts & David Rothschild, "Don't Blame the Election on Fake News. Blame It on the Media," *Columbia Journalism Review*, December 5, 2017, <https://www.cjr.org/analysis/fake-news-media-election-trump.php> (accessed August 21, 2019).

was also twice as much content as was devoted to her policy positions. Gossip and sensationalism dominated the pages of the so-called news watchdogs, and it should be noted that these 65,000 sentences were written by professional journalists employed at mainstream American news organizations, not Kremlin propagandists.

That is not to say that Russian propaganda did not play a role in influencing this reporting. It was, after all, a Kremlin-linked hack that gained access to the DNC and Podesta emails, and WikiLeaks that distributed them. But it was the press itself that served as the conduit to bring the emails into mainstream discourse and build the narrative of scandal around them, in exchange for readers and internet traffic. Yes, Americans increasingly consume their news via recommendations, shares, and likes on social media, with crowd interest rather than careful editorial curation dictating which news stories and topics gain the most traction. But the print media's long-standing ability to set the agenda and determine what counts as important news to be shared in the first place remains formidable. That voters mistrusted Clinton as "two-faced," perceived the Clinton Foundation as corrupt, or saw her conduct as secretary of state to have been negligent or criminal can be traced back to stories run in papers of record as opposed to Russian-purchased adverts. Likewise, that voters knew more about these spurious scandals than the difference between Clinton's policy positions and those of her opponent owes more to the questionable reporting of the mainstream press than it does any hostile foreign efforts.

To get a greater sense of the press's complicity in the spread of the Russian kompromat, one can compare the lack of impact a similar Kremlin-sponsored effort had over the French elections the following year. The 2017 French presidential election saw the pro–European Union centrist Emmanuel Macron facing off against the Kremlin-backed far-right candidate, Marine Le Pen. Two days before the French people went to the polls, hackers stole nine gigabytes of emails from the Macron campaign and dumped them online, where they were promptly shared across social media by WikiLeaks and a number of pro–Le Pen right-wing activists.[82] The French Electoral Commission issued a statement urging "the media, but also all citizens—to show responsibility and not to pass on this content, so as not to distort the sincerity of the ballot."[83] The statement was mostly rhetorical, as France is one of a number of countries which imposes a media blackout prior to elections—forty-four hours before polls open in their

---

[82] Mark Scott, "U.S. Far-Right Activists Promote Hacking Attack Against Macron," *New York Times*, May 6, 2017, <https://www.nytimes.com/2017/05/06/world/europe/emmanuel-macron-hack-french-election-marine-le-pen.html> (accessed August 21, 2019).

[83] "French Election: Media Warned Not to Publish Emmanuel Macron's Hacked Emails Ahead of Vote," *ABC News*, May 7, 2017, <https://www.abc.net.au/news/2017-05-06/french-media-warned-not-to-publish-macrons-hacked-emails/8503568> (accessed August 21, 2019).

case. Despite broad public interest in the hack, the media obeyed the ban, publishing nothing in relation to the emails. Much of the reporting in the United States focused upon the media ban, framing it as an infringement upon press freedom and an emergency measure. The media's displeasure at the silence, especially at a time when a foreign power was clearly trying to interfere in the outcome, speaks volumes. As well as being increasingly driven by sensationalism and the pursuit of reader clicks, the US media is hyperactive, creating a constant wall of noise that floods the airwaves, newsstands, and cell phone screens with so much information it denies citizens the opportunity to think for themselves. Election silences are not infringements upon civil liberties and freedoms. They are the opposite. They create time and space for citizens to reflect—a moment in which voters can consider the candidates on their merits and policy positions, as opposed to being influenced by the noise, narrative, and agenda setting of an attention-seeking media that has collectively fallen a long way from its original role as a watchdog and objective informer on matters of public importance.

VII. Conclusion

It is not all bad news in the media sector. Some response and recovery can already be seen, but it is limited and problematic. In 2013, Amazon's founder, Jeff Bezos, purchased the *Washington Post*, and in recent years the paper has seen a return to some semblance of economic health, if not stable profitability. The *New York Times* and several other leading publications have also moved from financial jeopardy to viability in recent years. Ironically, Trump's repeated verbal assaults upon news organizations served to remind audiences of the importance of a free press that readers are willing to pay for.[84] But even within this apparent recovery, the underlying weakness of division remains. The *Washington Post*, for example—a paper which adopted the motto "Democracy Dies in Darkness" in February 2017 to market itself as a panacea to misinformation—is a subscription service. While democracy may die in darkness, it certainly does not thrive behind a paywall, and once again free market capitalism and the pursuit of profit has shown itself to be a poor model to guarantee a healthy news environment. It is too soon to say that the economic crisis of journalism has passed, and the crisis of journalistic values and the truth remains. Furthermore, while the papers of record may show signs of recovery, there still exists no replicable business model that works for local news, which diminishes the accountability of state

---

[84] Weisberg, *supra* note 71.

and metropolitan government and leaves mainstream publications blind to the plight of everyday Americans.[85]

Regarding Russia's propaganda campaign, it is important to note that there is nothing particularly unique in their mission. All major countries seek to broadcast information to citizens in other nations. To protest too strongly would be to expose American hypocrisy to the highest degree. The United States has a long history of engaging in foreign propaganda efforts and covert activities to influence foreign populations, dating back to the emergence of the Cold War and the intelligence establishment in the late 1940s.[86] Beyond covert activity, the United States funds a range of foreign news programming, including Radio Liberty's Russian service and the Current Time (Nastoyashchee Vremya) television network, launched in February 2017. Distributed in twenty-three countries on fifty-nine satellite, cable, and digital distribution outfits and targeted specifically at Russian speakers, the network produces daily news shows which feature reports on business, entrepreneurship, civil society, culture, and corruption, and is the leading distributer of documentaries from independent Russian film makers.[87] In essence, it is a Russian-language alternative to RT and Kremlin-influenced domestic new channels, but in practice there is some difference. While these programs are designed for foreign citizens, they are obliged by US government rules to adhere to accuracy in their programming. Ironically, unlike RT and its own domestic news outlets, the American government's foreign broadcasts must be free of the disinformation and distortion which characterizes so much of America's domestic broadcasting. The US government must produce news, rather than propaganda, to try to win hearts and minds of foreign citizens, while its own benefit from no such protections.[88]

It is an enduring strength of American democracy that whenever the nation has faced a significant domestic crisis such as that of which Trump's election was a symptom, it has triggered the sort of reflection and reform that has enabled

---

[85] Sheelah Kolhatkar, "The Growth of Sinclair's Conservative Media Empire," *New Yorker*, October 15, 2018, <https://www.newyorker.com/magazine/2018/10/22/the-growth-of-sinclairs-conservative-media-empire>; Camila Domonoske, "Video Reveals Power of Sinclair, as Local News Anchors Recite Script in Unison," *National Public Radio*, April 2, 2018, <https://www.npr.org/sections/thetwo-way/2018/04/02/598794433/video-reveals-power-of-sinclair-as-local-news-anchors-recite-script-in-unison?t=1568725732540> (accessed September 17, 2019).

[86] NSC 10/2, "National Security Council Directive on Office of Special Projects," June 18, 1948, *Foreign Relations of the United States, 1945–1950, Emergence of the Intelligence Establishment*, <https://history.state.gov/historicaldocuments/frus1945-50Intel/d292> (accessed September 7, 2019); Stephen Long, "Strategic Disorder, the Office of Policy Coordination and the Inauguration of US Political Warfare against the Soviet Bloc, 1948–1950," *Intelligence and National Security*, 27, no. 4 (August 2012), 459–87.

[87] "The Scourge of Russian Disinformation," Hearing before the Commission on Security and Cooperation in Europe, 115th Congress, September 14, 2017, <https://www.govinfo.gov/content/pkg/CHRG-115jhrg26880/html/CHRG-115jhrg26880.htm> (accessed September 5, 2019).

[88] Oates, *supra* note 35, at 283.

the United States not only to overcome its domestic travails but to adapt and evolve, renewing itself as a stronger, more inclusive, and innovative nation. The Civil War, the social and economic inequalities of the late nineteenth century, the Wall Street Crash and Great Depression, the protests, riots, and violence that accompanied the civil rights movement, and the national malaise that followed Vietnam: in the wake of each instance, the United States found ways to revitalize itself. But not first without a period of reflection, reckoning, and reform. The 2016 election brought to light a domestic challenge as serious as any mentioned here. A bitter and divided body politic made easy pickings for interested parties, foreign and domestic, to manipulate. Split into decreasing segments based on ever-narrower identities created by broadcasters, ideologues, marketeers, and political campaign teams, the fracturing of the American populace by a media ecosystem built around division and microtargeting has grievously harmed America's body politic and rendered the possibility of deliberation, compromise, and collective action—the core tenet of successful democratic rule—implausible. The internal forces discussed in this chapter have succeeded in dividing America in a way the Soviet Union's propagandists could only ever have dreamt of, and unless the United States can work its way back to more universal understandings of human dignity, political choice, and shared values, it is doomed to continuing internal conflict and the gradual breakdown of its democracy.

13
Securing the Digital Media Ecosystem

Susan E. McGregor

I. Introduction

On the evening of Sunday, October 30, 1938, CBS radio began airing its Halloween episode of *The Mercury Theater on Air*, an hour-long drama series meant to bring serious dramatic performance to the airwaves. Halfway through that evening's broadcast, however, CBS supervisor Davidson Taylor received a call demanding that the network interrupt the show.[1] Within minutes, uniformed police officers were in the CBS station rooms, and the show's performers had been corralled into a small office nearby.[2] By then, Paul White, the head of CBS news, had arrived at the station and was personally writing on-air bulletins and answering some of the phone calls that were flooding the station's switchboards[3] about the evening's program.

"Radio Listeners in Panic," read the *New York Times* the next morning. "Fake Radio 'War' Stirs Terror Through U.S.,"[4] read the *New York Daily News*. According to the newspaper headlines, Orson Welles' adaption of the H.G. Wells science fiction classic *The War of the Worlds* had caused a mass panic, leading to riots in the streets across the United States. According to an academic analysis released two years after the event, as many as one million people heard the broadcast and were "frightened," "disturbed," or "excited" by it[5]—sentiments the researchers characterized as "panicked." The immediacy, power—and peril—of radio as a mass medium was established in the popular imagination.

---

[1] John Houseman, *Run Through: A Memoir* (Simon and Schuster, 1st ed., 1972), 404.

[2] Tom Vallance, "Obituary: Stefan Schnabel," *The Independent*, March 25, 1999, https://www.independent.co.uk/arts-entertainment/obituary-stefan-schnabel-1082825.html (accessed July 12, 2023).

[3] Paul W. White, *News on the Air* (Harcourt, Brace, 1947), 47.

[4] "Radio Listeners in Panic; Taking War Drama as Fact," *New York Times*, October 31, 1938, https://upload.wikimedia.org/wikipedia/en/4/4a/WOTW-NYT-headline.jpg (accessed July 12, 2023); "Fake Radio 'War' Stirs Terror Through U.S.," *New York Daily News*, October 31, 1938, http://www.slate.com/content/dam/slate/articles/arts/history/2013/10/131028_HIST_OrsonWellesDailyNews.jpg.CROP.promovar-medium2.jpg (accessed July 12, 2023).

[5] Jefferson Pooley & Michael J. Socolow, "The Myth of the *War of the Worlds* Panic," *Slate*, October 28, 2013, http://www.slate.com/articles/arts/history/2013/10/orson_welles_war_of_the_worlds_panic_myth_the_infamous_radio_broadcast_did.html (accessed July 12, 2023).

Susan E. McGregor, *Securing the Digital Media Ecosystem* In: *National Security, Journalism, and Law in an Age of Information Warfare*. Edited by: Marc Ambinder, Jennifer R. Henrichsen, and Connie Rosati, Oxford University Press.
© Oxford University Press 2024. DOI: 10.1093/oso/9780197756621.003.0013

Modern scholarship, however, suggests this narrative is as apocryphal as it is appealing. Welles' visceral radio drama[6] was a thirteen-week summer fill-in series that had only recently been moved to its Sunday evening slot and was scheduled opposite the long-running and wildly popular *Chase and Sanborn Hour*,[7] raising questions about how many Americans even heard Welles' broadcast that evening. And while firsthand accounts confirm the presence of police and the prevalence of phone calls on the night of the broadcast, communications scholars Jefferson Pooley and Michael J. Socolow suggest that the large-font print headlines the next day were less about the scale of the public response than the desire of a commercially threatened newspaper industry to "discredit radio as a source of news"[8] in order to "prove to advertisers, and regulators, that radio management was irresponsible and not to be trusted."[9] While it no doubt helped springboard Welles' radio and film career, the alleged panic around *The War of the Worlds* broadcast was almost certainly more media sensation than watershed public event.

II. *War of the Worlds* 2.0?

Today,[10] the internet has destabilized traditional news media operations in a way not dissimilar to that of radio programming eighty years ago, with the immediacy and ubiquity of the newer medium upending both the production norms and the business model of legacy news. As in Welles' era, media coverage of the 2016 US presidential election warned readers of the danger of the "psychographic targeting" advertising methods used by companies like Cambridge Analytica,[11] despite scant evidence regarding the true efficacy of such tactics.[12]

Years later, however, the ongoing proliferation and impact of misinformation and disinformation highlights crucial and unresolved vulnerabilities in today's digital media ecosystem. Despite platforms' efforts to characterize

---

[6] Lucille Fletcher, "Squeaks, Slams, Echoes, and Shots," *New Yorker*, April 13, 1940.

[7] "The Chase and Sanborn Hour," *Wikipedia*, https://en.wikipedia.org/wiki/The_Chase_and_Sanborn_Hour (accessed July 12, 2023).

[8] Pooley & Socolow, *supra* note 5.

[9] *Id.*

[10] *Id.*

[11] Paul Wood, "The Brits behind Trump," *The Spectator*, December 3, 2016, https://www.spectator.co.uk/article/the-brits-behind-trump/ (access July 12, 2023); Hannes Grassegger & Mikael Krogerus, "The Data That Turned the World Upside Down," *Vice Motherboard*, January 28, 2017, https://www.vice.com/en_us/article/mg9vvn/how-our-likes-helped-trump-win (accessed July 12, 2023).

[12] Elizabeth Gibney, "The Scant Science Behind Cambridge Analytica's Controversial Marketing Techniques," *Nature*, March 29, 2018, https://www.nature.com/articles/d41586-018-03880-4 (accessed July 12, 2023).

inappropriate—and sometimes illegal[13]—content-targeting as surprising or unforeseeable security exploits, critics have long argued that these dark patterns[14]—such as leveraging profile data about a user's extended network, or targeting advertisements in violation of US employment laws—were explicit and visible design choices of the system.[15] More recently, companies like Facebook have pivoted to openly embracing these practices, publicly declining to enforce longstanding news publishing standards by allowing false claims and targeted political advertising to proliferate on the platform.[16]

The consequences of unchecked misinformation and disinformation were on particular display during the worst of the COVID-19 pandemic, as their impact on health behaviors cost tens of thousands of American lives.[17] All of this suggests that platform-based misinformation, security flaws, and illegal conditions[18] constitute a national information security risk that cannot be left up to platforms to address adequately. Despite nations, think tanks, and companies continually experimenting with information integrity interventions that range from media-literacy campaigns to crowd-sourced labels,[19] little definitive progress has been made in developing policy, pedagogy, or practice in how to defend essential information systems against becoming overwhelmingly polluted with misinformation. In this chapter, I argue that these attacks on the integrity of our

---

[13] Ariana Tobin & Jeremy B. Merrill, "Facebook Is Letting Job Advertisers Target Only Men," *ProPublica*, September 18, 2018, https://www.propublica.org/article/facebook-is-letting-job-advertisers-target-only-men (accessed July 12, 2023); Ava Kofman & Ariana Tobin, "Facebook Ads Can Still Discriminate Against Women and Older Workers, Despite a Civil Rights Settlement," *ProPublica*, https://www.propublica.org/article/facebook-ads-can-still-discriminate-against-women-and-older-workers-despite-a-civil-rights- (accessed July 12, 2023).

[14] "Bringing Dark Patterns to Light," Federal Trade Commission, September 15, 2022, https://www.ftc.gov/system/files/ftc_gov/pdf/P214800%20Dark%20Patterns%20Report%209.14.2022%20-%20FINAL.pdf (accessed July 12, 2023).

[15] Julia Angwin & Terry Parris Jr., "Facebook Lets Advertisers Exclude Users by Race," *ProPublica*, https://www.propublica.org/article/facebook-lets-advertisers-exclude-users-by-race (accessed July 12, 2023); Josh Constine, "Facebook Is Shutting Down Its API for Giving Your Friends' Data to Apps," *TechCrunch*, April 28, 2015, https://techcrunch.com/2015/04/28/facebook-api-shut-down/ (accessed July 12, 2023).

[16] Tony Romm, Isaac Stanley-Becker, & Craig Timberg, "Facebook Won't Limit Political Ad Targeting or Stop False Claims under New Ad Rules," *Washington Post*, January 9, 2020, https://www.washingtonpost.com/technology/2020/01/09/facebook-wont-limit-political-ad-targeting-or-stop-pols-lying/ (accessed July 12, 2023).

[17] Michael A. Gisondi et al., "A Deadly Infodemic: Social Media and the Power of COVID-19 Misinformation," *Journal of Medical Internet Research*, 24, no. 2 (2022), e35552.

[18] Kofman & Tobin, *supra* note 13.

[19] Ben Collins, "Twitter Is Testing New Ways to Fight Misinformation—Including a Community-Based Points System," *NBC News*, February 20, 2020, https://www.nbcnews.com/tech/tech-news/twitter-testing-new-ways-fight-misinformation-including-community-based-points-n1139931 (accessed July 12, 2023); Daniel Funke & Daniela Flamini, "A Guide to Anti-misinformation Actions around the World," *Poynter*, n.d., https://www.poynter.org/ifcn/anti-misinformation-actions/ (accessed July 12, 2023); Darrell M. West, "How to Combat Fake News and Disinformation," *Brookings Institute*, December 18, 2017, https://www.brookings.edu/research/how-to-combat-fake-news-and-disinformation/ (accessed July 12, 2023).

information supply chain can be usefully understood as the result of outdated digital infrastructure designs and that by amending digital publishing norms to support the nonrepudiation qualities typical of mass print publishing, it is possible to create a media ecosystem that allows information consumers to readily judge the quality of information sources and content.

Further, I argue that we have reached a crucial inflection point, beyond which the continued insecurity of digital media threatens not only the current social, political, and economic utility of the internet, but the viability of many next-generation computing technologies. Indeed, while human communities may be able to adapt and recover from the effects of disinformation and misinformation, the current dependence of many cutting-edge computational tools on data sourced from the internet means that an increasingly polluted online environment could actually lead to enormous lost innovation in computational systems in the coming years.

For example, the field of machine learning—the diverse set of computational approaches that drives artificial intelligence tools from natural language processing to image analysis and autonomous vehicles—is fundamentally dependent on high-quality input data to yield accurate results. While the science behind machine learning—which allows computers to "learn" by identifying and replicating patterns present in huge data sets—is now almost six decades old,[20] building real-world machine learning systems has become feasible only recently, as the mass adoption of mobile technologies and an explosion of social media content generated the volume of data required to train such systems effectively. Underpinned by modern processing power,[21] these massive data sources are what make sophisticated machine learning—and the "artificial intelligence" applications it drives—possible.

Yet machine learning systems remain subject to a core axiom of computational systems: "garbage in, garbage out." Machine learning systems trained on poor-quality or inappropriate data make deeply problematic[22]—and even deadly—mistakes. For example, when Microsoft's "Tay" chatbot was released on Twitter in March of 2016, it took less than a day for the users to "teach" the bot not just to repeat but generate highly offensive statements.[23] In 2018, a self-driving car

---

[20] Arthur L. Samuel, "Some Studies in Machine Learning Using the Game of Checkers," *IBM Journal of Research and Development*, 44 no. 1.2 (2000), 206–26.

[21] Tom Simonite, "Moore's Law Is Dead. Now What?," *MIT Technology Review*, May 13, 2016, https://www.technologyreview.com/s/601441/moores-law-is-dead-now-what/ (accessed July 12, 2023).

[22] Jackie Snow, "Google Photos Still Has a Problem with Gorillas," *MIT Technology Review*, January 11, 2018, https://www.technologyreview.com/f/609959/google-photos-still-has-a-problem-with-gorillas/ (accessed July 12, 2023).

[23] Elle Hunt, "Tay, Microsoft's AI Chatbot, Gets a Crash Course in Racism from Twitter," *The Guardian*, March 24, 2016, https://www.theguardian.com/technology/2016/mar/24/tay-microsofts-ai-chatbot-gets-a-crash-course-in-racism-from-twitter (accessed July 12, 2023).

killed a pedestrian because its training data lacked sufficient scope to detect a human walking a bicycle.[24]

Whether the result of intentionally "bad" training data, as in the case of Tay AI,[25] or because of undetected gaps such as those suggested by autonomous vehicle accidents, the reality is that even widely deployed machine learning systems can suffer from poor training data, with unexpected and harmful consequences. For example, in 2018 MIT and Stanford researchers, Joy Buolamwini and Timnit Gebru, published a paper demonstrating that three major commercial facial-recognition programs (Microsoft; IBM; Face++) incorrectly labeled the sex of dark-skinned women as much as 35 percent of the time.[26] As of August 2023, at least half a dozen people—all of them Black, and one eight months pregnant—have been falsely accused of a crime because of facial recognition technologies.[27]

These failures alone threaten the very legitimacy of the nation's core social, political, and legal systems—yet at least, they carry the potential for detection and remedy. Increasingly, however, it is possible to imperceptibly contaminate data in order to undetectably manipulate the outputs of machine learning system. In 2016, for example, researchers created "adversarial" images that that could trick the machine learning algorithm into misclassifying images of digits by changing so few pixels (an average of just 4 percent of pixels)[28] that the changes escaped human detection more than 90 percent of the time.[29] More recently, researchers have demonstrated that stickers or tags on street signs could similarly cause an autonomous vehicle's computer-vision algorithm to misclassify a stop sign as a yield sign, creating nonobvious but deadly security risks.[30] At a moment when the systems used by governments, law enforcement, and private companies increasingly rely on internet-sourced data to function, a polluted digital media ecosystem is both a threat to the country's social and political systems and risks

---

[24] Sam Levin & Julia Carrie Wong, "Self-driving Uber Kills Arizona Woman in First Fatal Crash Involving Pedestrian," *The Guardian*, March 19, 2018, https://www.theguardian.com/technology/2018/mar/19/uber-self-driving-car-kills-woman-arizona-tempe (accessed July 12, 2023).

[25] For example, many users conversing with Tay discovered that it would simply parrot any content that started with "repeat after me."

[26] Joy Buolamwini & Timnit Gebru, "Gender Shades: Intersectional Accuracy Disparities in Commercial Gender Classification," in *Conference on Fairness, Accountability and Transparency* (PMLR, 2018), 77–91.

[27] Kashmir Hill, "Eight Months Pregnant and Arrested after False Facial Recognition Match," *New York Times*, August 6, 2023, https://www.nytimes.com/2023/08/06/business/facial-recognition-false-arrest.html (accessed August 14, 2023).

[28] Nicolas Papernot et al., "The Limitations of Deep Learning in Adversarial Settings," *2016 IEEE European Symposium on Security and Privacy (EuroS&P)*, IEEE (2016), 372–87.

[29] *Id.*

[30] Nicolas Papernot et al., "Practical Black-Box Attacks against Machine Learning," *Proceedings of the 2017 ACM on Asia Conference on Computer and Communications Security* (2017), 506–19; Kevin Eykholt et al., "Robust Physical-World Attacks on Deep Learning Visual Classification," *Proceedings of the IEEE Conference on Computer Vision and Pattern Recognition*, IEEE (2018), 1625–34.

derailing the next generation of innovations that are essential to the future economic growth of the United States.

III. The Limits of Reactive Systems

Thus far, most attempts at improving the quality of online information have focused on post facto interventions, such as professional or crowdsourced identification of misinformation or disinformation. In December of 2016, for example, Facebook announced changes[31] to its content-reporting system that would target "fake news" for fact-checking as a way to mark questionable articles as "disputed"; the platform even went so far as to add an intermediary "Are you sure?" step to sharing articles marked in this way.

Yet barely a year after the announcement, Facebook scrapped the feature,[32] in part because a review of existing research[33] revealed that strong visual markers—like the red "disputed" flag Facebook had selected—may further entrench readers' existing beliefs about the labeled content, hardening their belief in misinformation. Perhaps even more telling was the simple fact that Facebook's system required manual review by at least two fact checkers, a process that was too costly and labor-intensive to keep up with the volume of reported content on the platform.[34]

The sheer volume of misinformation and disinformation online remains a key challenge for any post facto efforts to determine information quality, especially since assessing content quality is time-consuming and equivocal, even for trained professionals. Attempting to screen data for machine learning systems after the fact is even less auspicious. Even where tainted training data can be successfully identified, correcting the problem can be time-consuming and costly. For example, Microsoft designed its second chatbot, Zo, to simply avoid political discussion altogether,[35] but after several months online, Zo was also

---

[31] Adam Mosseri, "Addressing Hoaxes and Fake News," *Facebook Newsroom*, December 15, 2016, https://newsroom.fb.com/news/2016/12/news-feed-fyi-addressing-hoaxes-and-fake-news/ (accessed July 12, 2023).

[32] Catherine Shu, "Facebook Will Ditch Disputed Flags on Fake News and Display Links to Trustworthy Articles Instead," *TechCrunch*, December 21, 2017, https://techcrunch.com/2017/12/20/facebook-will-ditch-disputed-flags-on-fake-news-and-display-links-to-trustworthy-articles-instead/ (accessed July 12, 2023).

[33] Stephan Lewandowsky et al., "Misinformation and Its Correction: Continued Influence and Successful Debiasing," *Psychological Science in the Public Interest*, 13, no. 3 (2012), 106–31.

[34] Jeff Smith, Grace Jackson, & Seetha Raj, "Designing Against Misinformation," *Design at Meta, Medium*, December 20, 2017, https://medium.com/facebook-design/designing-against-misinformation-e5846b3aa1e2 (accessed July 12, 2023).

[35] Mehedi Hassan, "Zo Is Microsoft's Latest AI Chatbot," *MS Power User*, December 4, 2016, https://mspoweruser.com/zo-microsofts-latest-ai-chatbot/ (accessed July 12, 2023).

making strange and problematic connections in its conversations with users.[36] For computer-vision systems like the digit- and sign-recognition algorithms discussed previously, no reliable, scalable method for detecting "adversarial samples" (manipulated input data designed to cause misclassification) has yet been identified.[37]

IV. Corroboration and Accountability

Calibrating the quality of information is, of course, a core activity of traditional news production, where verifying information underlies every step of the reporting process. Technical changes in recent decades have generated the novel journalistic practices needed to verify new information flows, such as user-generated content (UGC). In 2014, for example, media researchers Claire Wardle, Sam Dubberley, Jenni Sargent, and Pete Brown founded "Eyewitness Media Hub" to develop ethical standards of practice around the use of UGC. In 2015, journalist Craig Silverman chronicled some of the challenges newsrooms faced in handling misinformation.[38] In the years since, Wardle, Silverman and others have developed the "Verification Handbook," which offers practical methods to journalists and researchers for verifying digital content.[39] Yet these methods remain constrained in the scale they can achieve, as their methods still rely on human-driven reporting and fact-checking, and their resources are vanishingly compared to social media platforms.

Prophylactic approaches to improving information security and integrity have often looked toward "media literacy" tools, with the goal of "inoculating" information consumers against mis- and disinformation.[40] Yet there is limited evidence to support the efficacy of such interventions, especially in the online space.[41] As the tools for generating real-time "deepfake" audio and video

---

[36] Alex Kantrowitz, "Microsoft's Chatbot Zo Calls the Qur'an Violent and Has Theories about Bin Lade," *BuzzFeed News*, July 3, 2017, https://www.buzzfeed.com/alexkantrowitz/microsofts-chatbot-zo-calls-the-quran-violent-and-has (accessed July 12, 2023).

[37] Papernot et al., *supra* note 28.

[38] Craig Silverman, "Lies, Damn Lies and Viral Content," *Tow Center for Digital Journalism, Columbia University*, 2015, https://academiccommons.columbia.edu/doi/10.7916/D8Q81RHH (accessed July 12, 2023).

[39] "The Verification Handbook," *Datajournalism.com*, http://verificationhandbook.com/book/ (accessed July 12, 2023).

[40] "Knight Prototype Fund Awards $1 Million to 20 Projects to Improve the Flow of Accurate Information," Knight Foundation, June 22, 2017, https://knightfoundation.org/press/releases/knight-prototype-fund-awards-1-million-to-20-projects-to-improve-the-flow-of-accurate-information (accessed July 12, 2023).

[41] S. Mo Jones-Jang, Tara Mortensen, & Jingjing Liu, "Does Media Literacy Help Identification of Fake News? Information Literacy Helps, But Other Literacies Don't," *American Behavioral Scientist*, 65, no. 2 (2021), 371–88.

using commodity hardware and relatively limited training data become commonplace,[42,43,44] it is unlikely that media literacy efforts will be sufficient for combating the spread of the coming deluge of online digital fakes.[45]

Current methods for systematically detecting faked photos and videos at scale are still largely in the prototype phase,[46] and the process of creating and combatting faked media will remain an ongoing arms race. At the same time, both directed and chaos actors are beginning to shift *away* from fully fabricated media and toward the use of partially fabricated or strategically repurposed media in order to leverage what Wardle describes as "the liar's dividend,"[47] which seeks to increase doubts about the veracity and authenticity of *all* information as a means to better obfuscate manipulated media.

V. A Priori Authentication of Information for Enhanced Media Security

Given these challenges, it is essential to develop an approach to misinformation and disinformation that can scale effectively with the increasing volume and quality of fakes and deceptively repurposed media in order to secure the digital media ecosystem and our nation's broader information supply chain. To do this, we must draw on the lessons of journalistic history, which indicates that the most effective way to build and maintain the security and credibility of information in particular is to create a priori indicators of content quality. In the print era, this led to the creation of proprietary typefaces, broadsheet layouts,

---

[42] Justus Thies et al., "Face2face: Real-Time Face Capture and Reenactment of Rgb Videos," *Proceedings of the IEEE Conference on Computer Vision and Pattern Recognition*, IEEE (2016), 2387–95.

[43] James Vincent, "Lyrebird Claims It Can Recreate Any Voice Using Just One Minute of Sample Audio," *The Verge*, April 24, 2017, https://www.theverge.com/2017/4/24/15406882/ai-voice-synthesis-copy-human-speech-lyrebird (accessed July 12, 2023).

[44] Supasorn Suwajanakorn, Steven M. Seitz, & Ira Kemelmacher-Shlizerman, "Synthesizing Obama: Learning Lip Sync from Audio," *ACM Transactions on Graphics (ToG)*, 36, no. 4 (2017), 1–13.

[45] Matt Novak, "29 Viral Photos and GIFs from 2017 That Were Totally Fake," *Gizmodo*, December 20, 2017, https://gizmodo.com/29-viral-photos-and-gifs-from-2017-that-were-totally-fa-1821440079 (accessed July 12, 2023).

[46] Thanh Thi Nguyen et al., "Deep Learning for Deepfakes Creation and Detection: A Survey," *Computer Vision and Image Understanding*, 223 (2022), 103525; Siwei Lyu, "Deepfake Detection: Current Challenges and Next Steps," *2020 IEEE International Conference on Multimedia & Expo Workshops (ICMEW)*, IEEE (2020), 1–6; Shruti Agarwal & Hany Farid, "Photo Forensics from Rounding Artifacts," *Proceedings of the 2020 ACM Workshop on Information Hiding and Multimedia Security* (2020),103–14; Andreas Rossler et al., "Faceforensics++: Learning to Detect Manipulated Facial Images," *Proceedings of the IEEE/CVF International Conference on COMPUTER VISION* (2019), 1–11; Luisa Verdoliva, "Media Forensics and DeepFakes: An Overview," *IEEE Journal of Selected Topics in Signal Processing*, 14, no. 5 (2020), 910–32.

[47] Claire Wardle, "This Video May Not Be Real," *New York Times*, August 14, 2019, https://www.nytimes.com/2019/08/14/opinion/deepfakes-adele-disinformation.html (accessed July 12, 2023).

bylines, datelines, and correction notices in order to establish and maintain both substantive and perceptual measures of information quality. While the rise of internet and social media technologies have effectively "broken" many of these traditional indicators, building such integrity indicators in the digital space is both technically feasible and compatible with current digital publishing mechanisms.

For example, one of the key components of current content verification practices—in both the journalism and computational spaces—is the robust and reliable attribution of source identity or authorship. While journalists do occasionally make use of truly anonymous sources[48] (that is, sources whose identity is unknown even to the journalist), knowing a source's identity often provides important clues about the information they share: Is it likely that this person would have access to the information they are allegedly providing? Might they have ulterior motives? A source's identity can also help journalists select corroborating sources with appropriate discretion.[49] Even for more typical user-generated content, source identity verification remains non-negotiable, and confirming the original source is the first step in the verification process of any type internet-sourced media.[50] As with all source verification processes, this is as much for the protection of the source as that of the news organization; not all individuals who post information online are interested in or adequately prepared for the consequences of having their material shared more broadly.[51].

In the computational space, source attribution is typically operationalized through the use of cryptographic signatures, which are widely used to secure everything from proprietary software to financial transactions. These signatures exist as bits of metadata that allow digital systems to mathematically verify the relationship between a piece of content and an authoring or controlling party in a nearly instantaneous authentication process that requires no additional action on the part of the user. While currently used only rarely to sign human-readable content (such as some digital documents used for legal purposes), cryptographic signatures support a number of additional features that are valuable within the broader media ecosystem: in addition to authenticating authorship, cryptographic signatures can be used to effectively timestamp digital content, making clear not just *who* published *what*, but *when*. Moreover, cryptographic signatures support "non-repudiation": in addition to authenticating authorship, they also make it virtually impossible to *deny* authorship of legitimately signed content.

---

[48] Charles Berret, "Guide to SecureDrop," *Tow Center for Digital Journalism, Columbia University*, 2014, https://academiccommons.columbia.edu/doi/10.7916/D84178B2 (accessed July 12, 2023).

[49] An instructive example here is the case of Reality Winner, whose identity was unknown to journalists at *The Intercept*. Unfortunately, the journalists' verification process resulted in Winner's unintended identification to the FBI.

[50] "The Verification Handbook," *supra* note 39, ch. 4.

[51] "Eyewitness Stories," *Eyewitness Media Hub*, http://eyewitnessmediahub.com/research/user-generated-content/uploader-stories (accessed July 12, 2023).

In many ways, cryptographically "signing" software and other digital artifacts is similar to comparing the signature on a document with someone's photo ID. Yet there are key differences that make the computational approach even more valuable. First, cryptographic signatures are, at any given moment, mathematically impossible to forge contemporaneously.[52] Second, the "signature" on digital content (whether it be a software package, digital photograph, or government report) essentially embeds the content of the signed document into the signature itself. Thus, in addition to confirming that, say, the Centers for Disease Control (CDC) was the source of particular document, the signature can be used to confirm whether the content of the report itself is identical to a reference copy. In this sense, computational authentication via cryptographic signatures goes far beyond the typical analog standard.

VI. Deploying Widespread Content Authentication: The HTTPS Model

While technically simple to execute, effectively deploying digital content–signing systems requires coordination among a number of stakeholders within the information ecosystem, from content creators to software developers and browser manufacturers. While daunting, however, such an effort is not outside the realm of success. In the news and media space, for example, a related effort has proved successful in only the last few years: the deployment of HTTPS connections to major media websites.

Like software signatures, HTTPS connections guarantee that the content you see in your browser is what the website owner actually published; with insecure HTTP-only connections, it's possible to intercept, change, and manipulate this content without the end user ever being aware of it. HTTPS connections also protect website users from prying eyes in general: not only is it impossible for an outside observer to *change* what your computer sends to a website, those messages also cannot be *observed* from the outside either. The work of confirming who actually controls a given website (and therefore which website signatures a device should trust) has long been allocated to so-called certificate authorities (CAs) that, in theory, verify site ownership and track legitimate certificates (a website's certificate is equivalent to a software signature).

Although the HTTPS protocol has been available for nearly thirty years, however, many major websites and service providers began offering HTTPS by

---

[52] As computers become more powerful over time, older signatures do effectively become "weaker" and could potentially be forged. However, contemporaneous forging of appropriately strong cryptographic signatures is unlikely.

default only relatively recently. Facebook, for example, didn't become HTTPS-only until 2013, with YouTube and even email providers like Hotmail not making the switch until 2014.[53] For most providers, a delay in adopting HTTPS was associated with the increased cost and technical overhead—and, quite possibly, the sense that users didn't seem to notice or care whether their connection was HTTPS or not.[54] Thanks to the efforts of the Let's Encrypt project[55]—a nonprofit collaboration that made HTTPS certificates available for free for small websites at the click of a button—HTTPS connections exploded in 2016–2017, with more than half of all internet traffic delivered via an HTTPS connection just a year after its launch.[56]

Let's Encrypt's efforts to encrypt the web succeeded at scale because the project operators identified the major roadblocks to adopting HTTPS: high cost and technical requirements. As of 2014, for example, it cost up to $1,999 per year to offer HTTPS[57]—a prohibitive cost for many organizations, small municipalities, and even government service agencies. Even with sufficient budget, obtaining and installing the certificate correctly was a relatively complex and error-prone process, even for individuals with significant technical expertise.[58]

Through the related nonprofit Internet Security Research Group, Let's Encrypt contributors built an automated protocol for configuring security certificates that verified website control through the uploading of a simple sample file. Sponsorships secured from large companies like Google, Akamai, and others allowed the security certificates to be offered for free, while the open source certificate[59] configuration protocol has been engaged by the Internet Engineering Task Force (IETF), the internet's main standards-development body, helping ensure its continued refinement and adoption in the long term.

In recent years, of course, many certificate authorities—Let's Encrypt not least of all—have come under fire for failing to properly vet the websites for whom they provide security certificates.[60] Yet the value of having increased security

---

[53] David Naylor et al., "The Cost of the 'S' in HTTPS," *Proceedings of the 10th ACM International on Conference on Emerging Networking Experiments and Technologies* (2014), 133140; Jamie Condliffe, "Yahoo Mail Is Switching to HTTPS—Found Years after Gmail," *Gizmodo*, October 15, 2013, https://gizmodo.com/yahoo-mail-is-switching-to-https-four-years-after-gmai-1445475950 (accessed July 12, 2023).

[54] Indeed, a large body of research in computer security has focused on the failure of so-called "certificate warnings" to influence user behavior.

[55] "Let's Encrypt," https://letsencrypt.org/ (accessed July 12, 2023).

[56] Klint Finley, "Half the Web Is Now Encrypted. That Makes Everyone Safer," *Wired*, January 30, 2017, https://www.wired.com/2017/01/half-web-now-encrypted-makes-everyone-safer/ (accessed July 12, 2023).

[57] Naylor et al., *supra* note 53.

[58] Katharina Krombholz et al., "'I Have No Idea What I'm Doing'—On the Usability of Deploying HTTPS," *26th USENIX Security Symposium*, USENIX (2017), 1339–56.

[59] "How It Works," *Let's Encrypt*, https://letsencrypt.org/how-it-works/ (accessed July 12, 2023).

[60] Dan Goodin, "Already on Probation, Symantec Issues More Illegit HTTPS Certificates," *ArsTechnica*, January 20 2017, https://arstechnica.com/information-technology/2017/01/alre

across the many legitimate websites that can now offer HTTPS[61] is hard to overstate. Nonetheless, these controversies highlight the fact that an HTTPS connection is a necessary—but not sufficient—indicator of information integrity on the web. Providing robust information integrity guarantees about digital information requires going one step further, by introducing both content provenance guarantees *and* accountability around what is published online.

VII. Toward a More Secure Information Supply Chain

As already outlined, adjudicating the truth-value of content at internet speed and scale is not actually feasible—either conceptually or technically. More importantly, however, such efforts actually run counter to the core information philosophies of the United States, which was founded precisely upon an open, reputation-based approach to media development, rather than a regulatory one: as the founders knew, regulatory and licensing procedures, no matter how thoughtfully developed or well-intentioned, are always vulnerable to manipulation by the powerful. Moreover, without the backstop of official sanction, rigorous organizations have historically been fierce in maintaining their journalistic standards to retain competitive advantage and avoid liability.[62] While greater transparency around journalistic processes and professional norms is overdue, they have—when coupled with reliable provenance indicators—been instrumental in sustaining a functioning media ecosystem in the United States for the better part of a century. Augmenting digital publishing with stronger authentication and non-repudiation measures is simply a way to implement key analog publishing attributes in the digital space.

Content-level signatures similar to those now used for software—for articles, press releases, photographs, and virtually any other type of digital media on the web—offers an efficient, reliable, and robust way for media consumers to confirm the source, time, and substance of digital media—including the ability to confirm that what they are seeing now is the same as what was published an hour, a week, or a month ago. Adding digital signatures to content would allow media

---

ady-on-probation-symantec-issues-more-illegit-https-certificates/ (accessed July 12, 2023). Ionut Arghire, "Let's Encrypt Wildcard Certificates a 'Boon' for Cybercriminals, Expert Says," *Security Week*, https://www.securityweek.com/lets-encrypt-wildcard-certificates-boon-cybercriminals-expert-says (accessed July 12, 2023).

[61] Josh Aas, "The CA's Role in Fighting Phishing and Malware," *Let's Encrypt*, October 29, 2015, https://letsencrypt.org/2015/10/29/phishing-and-malware.html (accessed July 12, 2023).

[62] David Folkenflik & Mary Yang, "Fox News Settles Blockbuster Defamation Lawsuit with Dominion Voting Systems," *NPR*, April 18, 2023, https://www.npr.org/2023/04/18/1170339114/fox-news-settles-blockbuster-defamation-lawsuit-with-dominion-voting-systems (accessed August 15, 2023).

producers to protect their intellectual property and also demonstrate their commitment to accountability by making it possible for consumers to prove what *was* published, not just what happens to be online at a given moment. Just as a recording of a radio broadcast or a "hard copy" of a newspaper makes it possible for media consumers to access a reliable—and immutable—record of what an organization published, digital signatures could bring that same level of accountability to the digital publishing space.

This type of authentication, moreover, which is already used commercially by streaming services and equipment manufacturers,[63] could be applied across the digital space. Social media platforms could choose to apply digital signatures to user posts, simply by leveraging the information they already employ for digital marketing purposes. In an information ecosystem where the provenance of a digital artifact travels along with it, users of that artifact can obtain instant, passive confirmation about authorship, creation time, and more—and *then* choose whether or not to engage with it.

In a contentious media climate, content authentication via digital signatures offers a robust way to determine what content is being published by whom and when, while avoiding the pitfalls of attempting to define "truth" or infringing on individuals' essential liberty to select which information sources they choose to trust. Instead, it simply allows information publishers of any kind to signal to their audiences that they are willing to be fully transparent and accountable for their work—something the current configuration of web technologies simply does not support.[64]

Even if the use of such cryptographic signatures was confined to government press releases or bulletins, news articles, and other media, the potential benefits are manifold. While research suggests that the assurances offered by such signatures have bipartisan appeal,[65] they would also be invaluable to preserving the historical record in the digital age. Already, for example, the web is a slippery slope of evolving narratives, as illustrated by the relatively mundane example of websites' ever-changing "Terms of Service."[66] In reality, however, most digital

---

[63] Andy Parsons, "Major Steps Forward for the CAI: Partnerships with Leica and Nikon, New Content Credentials Features in Photoshop and Beyond at MAX 2022," *Adobe Blog*, October 18, 2022, https://blog.adobe.com/en/publish/2022/10/18/major-steps-forward-cai-partnerships-leica-nikon-new-content-credentials-features-photoshop-beyond-max-2022 (accessed August 15, 2023).

[64] Susan McGregor, "The 'Huge Issue' with Identifying Original Content from Media Outlets," *Columbia Journalism Review*, July 19, 2017, https://www.cjr.org/tow_center/authentication-digital-articles-fake-news.php (accessed July 12, 2023).

[65] Errol Francis et al., "Transparency, Trust, and Security Needs for the Design of Digital News Authentication Tools," *Proceedings of the ACM on Human-Computer Interaction*, 7, no. CSCW1 (2023), 1–44.

[66] *E.g.*, https://twitter.com/kashhill/status/998710227569557504; Kate Conger, "Google Removes 'Don't Be Evil' Clause from Its Code of Conduct," *Gizmodo*, May 18, 2018, https://gizmodo.com/google-removes-nearly-all-mentions-of-dont-be-evil-from-1826153393 (accessed July 12, 2023).

content is disturbingly susceptible to arbitrarily revisionist practices,[67] or at risk of disappearing altogether.[68]

In other words, digital signatures have the possibility of addressing another threat to our collective information security: the fragility of the digital record.[69] Especially at a time when a large portion of the historical record exists on platforms owned by private companies,[70] important questions exist about not just what should be part of the historical record, but how to identify precisely *which* historical record is actually being preserved. With content authorship already such a resource-intensive task to verify, there is little hope that underresourced institutions like libraries will be able to reliably archive even a fraction of the digital material that might otherwise meet their collection requirements. With digital signatures applied, however, both authorship imprints (i.e., digital signatures) and specific editions of work (i.e., those with the earliest timestamps) could be identified, preserved, distributed, and verified—not just in libraries, but by web users themselves.

Digital signatures could permit publishers to seamlessly allow users and scholars to browse and compare various versions of content, as well as allow digital archives to be built by institutions or even interested groups of individuals. This would enable digital information to better conform to the legal and social norms that have been evolved over hundreds of years of print publication: that news can be archived by the public and in the public interest.

As with any system, of course, such an augmentation of existing digital infrastructure would require the cooperation of many players—from data publishers to browser companies. And yet the incentives for all these actors are not necessarily in opposition. Instead of being forced to adopt expensive post facto verification methods, appending a priori authentication data to digital content would make what is currently a major hurdle in the verification process a given: confirming authorship, temporality, and accountability could be

---

[67] Joseph Cox, "The Wayback Machine Is Deleting Evidence of Malware Sold to Stalkers," *Vice Motherboard*, May 22, 2018, https://motherboard.vice.com/en_us/article/nekzzq/wayback-machine-deleting-evidence-flexispy (accessed July 12, 2023).

[68] Sharon Ringel & Angela Woodall, "A Public Record at Risk: The Dire State of News Archiving in the Digital Age," *Tow Center for Digital Journalism, Columbia University*, March 28, 2019, https://www.cjr.org/tow_center_reports/the-dire-state-of-news-archiving-in-the-digital-age.php (accessed July 12, 2023).

[69] Sean Captain, "The Internet's Future Is More Fragile Than Ever, Says One of Its Inventors," *FastCompany*, July 7, 2016, https://www.fastcompany.com/40437402/the-internets-future-is-more-fragile-than-ever-says-one-of-its-inventors (accessed July 12, 2023); Meredith Broussard, "The Irony of Writing Online About Digital Preservation," *The Atlantic*, November 20, 2015, https://www.theatlantic.com/technology/archive/2015/11/the-irony-of-writing-about-digital-preservation/416184/ (accessed July 12, 2023).

[70] "Federal Court Rules that President Trump's Blocking of Twitter Critics Violates First Amendment," *Knight First Amendment Institute at Columbia University*, May 23, 2018, https://knightcolumbia.org/news/federal-court-rules-president-trumps-blocking-twitter-critics-violates-first-amendment (accessed July 12, 2023).

effectively built in to digital publication systems with the click of a button, much as was previously done for HTTPS certificates. While such features will naturally appeal to reputable information agents, no gatekeeping on the use of these technologies is required—where the content quality is lacking, the mechanisms of accountability will still remain.

Perhaps most crucially at this stage, such an authentication system can be deployed using currently available technologies and infrastructure, and the largest adoption costs will be borne by the same organizations (i.e., publishers) that also have the most to gain from implementing it. The system could even be made backward-compatible, allowing users to enjoy the benefits of signature-bearing content without "breaking" their experience on other media.

Just as the raw immediacy of Orson Welles' *War of the Worlds* radio broadcast touched a nerve for print media publishers more than eighty years ago, the ill effects of misinformation highlight the extent to which the technical defaults of digital publishing have upended expectations about media trust and accountability. Yet the real problem is not that sensationalist, fake, and untrustworthy media *exist*; this has always been the case. Instead, the issue is that many of the credibility indicators associated with trustworthy legacy media were intrinsic properties of the analog format that were unintentionally lost in the digital transition; specifically, the high cost and difficulty of creating and distributing convincing forgeries—along with the near impossibility of destroying all genuine originals. The key to securing the digital information supply chain, then, is to restore some of these key integrity indicators to digital media through cryptographic signatures. By empowering media consumers with the tools to identify accountable, original content, such a system can help restore much-needed confidence in our digital media ecosystem, and help secure it against future attacks.

14
On the Frontlines of the Information Wars: How Algorithmic Gatekeepers and National Security Impact Journalism

Courtney C. Radsch

I. Introduction

Social media are a critical front in geopolitical information wars, strategically important for shaping journalistic coverage, public opinion, and policymaking. They are also the primary platforms for independent and citizen journalism, especially in countries that restrict press freedom or are experiencing violent conflict or human rights abuses.[1] In this increasingly crowded and complex media ecosystem, journalism and fact-based commentary struggle to compete with disinformation and computational propaganda campaigns that drown out authentic speech and require new regulatory efforts to control and combat.[2] In this chapter I argue that social media platforms have become the new gatekeepers and have compelled journalism to adapt to the forcing logic of their algorithms, their terms of service, and their community guidelines, and that this logic, in turn, is influenced by powerful national security interests espoused by the United States and Europe. These companies are based in, and make profits in, the United States and Europe, which exert influential regulatory power, even if often only through the implicit threat of regulation.[3] I focus on two shared national security priorities for the United States and the European Union: countering violent extremist (CVE) and combating weaponized disinformation, particularly by

---

[1] Courtney Radsch, *Cyberactivism and Citizen Journalism in Egypt; Digital Dissidence and Political Change* (Palgrave Macmillan, 2016); Philip Seib, *Real-Time Diplomacy: Politics and Power in the Social Media Era* (Palgrave Macmillan, 2012); Courtney Radsch, "Urgent: Understanding and Responding to Global Emerging News Threats," *Internews*, March 2023, https://papers.ssrn.com/sol3/papers.cfm?abstract_id=4406895.

[2] Courtney Radsch, "AI and Disinformation: State-Aligned Information Operations and the Distortion of the Public Sphere," *#SAIFE, OSCE*, July 2022, https://papers.ssrn.com/sol3/papers.cfm?abstract_id=4192038.

[3] Anu Bradford, *The Brussels Effect: How the European Union Rules the World* (Oxford University Press, 2020), https://doi.org/10.1093/oso/9780190088583.001.0001.

Courtney C. Radsch, *On the Frontlines of the Information Wars: How Algorithmic Gatekeepers and National Security Impact Journalism* In: *National Security, Journalism, and Law in an Age of Information Warfare*. Edited by: Marc Ambinder, Jennifer R. Henrichsen, and Connie Rosati, Oxford University Press. © Oxford University Press 2024.
DOI: 10.1093/oso/9780197756621.003.0014

Russia in the wake of the 2016 US election. I begin with a discussion of the media strategy of the so-called Islamic State, better known as ISIS, and the ensuing effort to counter the terrorist group's influence online, a strategy that became part of the CVE agenda and initially focused almost solely on the Islamist terrorist group until 2019, when it slowly expanded to cover a wider array of White nationalist and populist movements in the wake of a livestreamed attack on two mosques in Christchurch, New Zealand. Following the defeat of ISIS in Syria in 2018, the strategic priority of CVE expanded and, in some ways, shifted to focus on antidemocratic movements, becoming less clearly distinguished from efforts to fight "fake news" and disinformation online.

While an entire book could be written on CVE, I focus on demands US and EU governments made of platforms related to content moderation at key inflection points. I then show how the pressure put by Western policymakers on tech platforms had unintended consequences that negatively impacted the ability of activists, citizen journalists, and alternative information sources to report from Syria and counter the influence of ISIS. In the next section on combating disinformation and computational propaganda campaigns, I provide a brief overview of state-sponsored disinformation campaigns sponsored by Russia prior to its 2022 invasion of Ukraine, and how platforms and policymakers reacted to attempt to restrict the impact of these efforts through a slew of voluntary and regulatory initiatives. I then examine some of the unintended consequences on journalism. In conclusion, I examine how the reaction to the Christchurch massacre and platform-level efforts to counter violent extremism and propaganda online in response to pressure from the United States and Europe has led to censorship of journalistic content, affected citizen journalism from conflict zones, and impacted the ability to use violent imagery in news reporting.

Media have the potential to influence both public opinion and possible policy options, creating narratives that seek to make selective sense of reality by weaving together disparate issues and omitting others in a sequence that suggests causality and solutions to problems that is inherently normative. Journalists and politicians play a significant role in constructing narratives, and if the latter are able to create a consensus about what problems matter, they can garner support for their proposed solutions.[4] As Hannah Arendt observed, "appearances are realities, and that which does not appear is politically insignificant."[5] Thus when propaganda and disinformation drown out facts and truth, journalism falters, an informed citizenry cannot be cultivated, and democratic politics are distorted.

---

[4] Alister Miskimmon, Ben O'Loughlin, & Laura Roselle, *Strategic Narratives: Communication Power and the New World Order* (Routledge, 2013).

[5] Jeffrey C. Goldfarb, *The Politics of Small Things: The Power of the Powerless in Dark Times* (University of Chicago Press, 2007), 14.

But journalists and politicians alike are increasingly competing for visibility and significance on platforms according to rules they can't see or understand, rules that are set by the algorithms, community standards, and terms of service that govern participation, visibility, and amplification on social media and internet platforms. A handful of private companies control the algorithms that determine visibility, amplification, and network viability in the contemporary information ecosystem, and thus compel journalism to adapt to a new logic set by internet platforms, as I discuss in greater detail in this chapter. While much has been written about the power and influence of these technology companies, less understood or analyzed are the political influences that shape platform rules. In this chapter I argue that these platforms have become the new algorithmic gatekeepers that compel journalism to adapt to a new logic undergirded by national security prerogatives, which play an often unseen but influential role in the new media ecosystem. Journalism must navigate complex and shifting logics while competing with coordinated propaganda campaigns and the challenges arising from concern about "fake news" and violent extremism.

II. From Violent Extremism to "Fake News": Weaponizing Social Media Platform Logic

Social media platforms and direct messaging are central to the recruitment strategy and propaganda efforts of extremist groups worldwide. A handful of contemporary conflicts illustrate the weaponization of social media platforms by extremist groups: the beheadings of journalists James Foley and Steven Sotloff by ISIS in Syria in 2014 were posted online and proliferated across the internet; the perpetrator of the mosque attacks in Christchurch, New Zealand, in 2019 were tailor-made for the digital age as the perpetrator livestreamed his seventeen-minute rampage live on Facebook; the 2018 genocide in Myanmar was perpetuated in part through Facebook and WhatsApp groups that played "a determining role in stirring up hatred";[6] the performance artist Alex Jones built his entertainment empire Infowars online to become a leading conspiracy vortex. And Russia has mastered the art of digital propaganda campaigns aimed at undermining and destabilizing democracy,[7] weaponizing the very platforms that just a few years prior had been central to the democratic citizen uprisings in

---

[6] Disinformation and "fake news: Interim Report. House of Commons Digital, Culture, Media and Sport Committee. Fifth Report of Session 2017–19. HC 363. July 29, 2018. P. 22.
[7] "Pillars of Russia's Disinformation and Propaganda Ecosystem," *Global Engagement Center Special Report*. U.S. Department of State, August 2020, https://www.state.gov/wp-content/uploads/2020/08/Pillars-of-Russia%E2%80%99s-Disinformation-and-Propaganda-Ecosystem_08-04-20.pdf.

the Middle East that became known as the Arab Spring.[8] By leveraging the personalization and amplification potential of platforms built on a logic of engagement that favors extremism,[9] these movements, groups, and individuals have helped make visible the forcing function of algorithms that constitute the front lines of contemporary information warfare. Those who can leverage and manipulate the algorithms and terms of service that govern these platforms can control the flow, framing, and amplification of information.

I focus on three platforms: (1) Facebook, because of its size and ubiquity; (2) Google because of its video-sharing and search service YouTube; (3) and Twitter (which changed its name to X in 2023) because of its influential elite, albeit far smaller, audience. These platforms play a significant role in the global media ecosystem as the primary platforms of visibility. A range of other platforms and sites play a role in the media ecosystem, such as Telegram, 4chan, 8chan, Infowars, and Reddit, but the strategies of amplification and journalistic influence depend in part on the three mainstream platforms to bridge the media ecosystem and the public sphere.[10] This chapter shows how the agenda-setting and framing power of algorithms coupled with the terms of service that govern participation on these tech platforms are in many cases reinforced by contemporary journalistic practices that put platform logics at the center of contemporary news production and dissemination.

These algorithms and terms of service are, in turn, underpinned in part by national security priorities of the Western superpowers: combating violent extremism and counteracting disinformation campaigns by foreign adversaries. The major social media platforms profess not to want extremist content, "fake news," or other problematic content on their sites and reflect this is their terms of service and guidelines. Although these interests dovetail in some cases with the companies' own stated interests, I argue that the resources allocated to addressing these priorities indicate that externalities, like government pressure, are a factor shaping the decisions of these private companies.

Countering terrorism and violent extremism online and mitigating the impact of weaponized disinformation campaigns are among the leading national security prerogatives facing the United States and its European allies, according to official documents, statements, and policy processes.[11] Although these issues are

---

[8] Courtney Radsch, *Cyberactivism and Citizen Journalism in Egypt: Digital Dissidence and Political Change* (Palgrave-Macmillan, 2015).

[9] Katherine J. Wu, "Radical Ideas Spread Through Social Media. Are the Algorithms to Blame?," *PBS Nova*, March 28, 2019, https://www.pbs.org/wgbh/nova/article/radical-ideas-social-media-algorithms/.

[10] Rebecca Lewis, "Alternative Influence: Broadcasting the Reactionary Right on YouTube," *Data & Society*, September 18, 2018, https://datasociety.net/library/alternative-influence/.

[11] *See, e.g.*, the National Security Strategy of the United States 2015, http://nssarchive.us/national-security-strategy-2015 (accessed October 23, 2020); Department of State & USAID Joint Strategy on Countering Violent Extremism, May 2016, https://doi.org/2009-2017.state.gov/j/ct/rls/other/257

also critically important to governments around the world, this chapter focuses on national security priorities of the United States and the European Union because of their outsized impact on global internet governance, regulatory efforts, and location of the major internet platforms.[12] A rash of proposals in Western democracies have emerged to try to stave the flow of violent extremism and other "harmful" content online, calling for defensive censorship, expanded government regulation, and more intensive removal coordination across platforms. And the potential for ensnaring journalism and restricting press freedom has become more evident. The challenge, from the journalistic point of view, is how to address these harms without also causing censorship or chilling journalism, which relies on these platforms for source material and the dissemination of information.

When the platforms are pushed by powerful governments like the United States and European Union to integrate national security concerns about the prevention of terrorism and combating ISIS, or xenophobic nationalist groups, or Russian-sponsored disinformation operations, they adjust their algorithms to help them reduce visibility and virality of problematic content or even prevent its upload in the first place. And they adjust their terms of service or community guidelines to allow or disallow categories of content or accounts.

III. The Forcing Logic of Algorithms

The news industry, professional and citizen alike, must increasingly adapt to the logic of the internet and social media platforms that are central to modern journalism.[13] In countries without independent media or which restrict press freedom, these platforms are often the only avenue for independent

---

725.htm; Eric Schmitt, "U.S. Intensifies Effort to Blunt ISIS' Message," *New York Times*, February 17, 2015, https://www.nytimes.com/2015/02/17/world/middleeast/us-intensifies-effort-to-blunt-isis-message.html; Communication from the Commission to the European Parliament, the Council, the European Economic and Social Committee and the Committee of the Regions the European Agenda on Security, https://ec.europa.eu/home-affairs/sites/homeaffairs/files/e-library/documents/basic-documents/docs/eu_agenda_on_security_en.pdf (accessed October 23, 2020), as well as Security Minister James Brokenshire, "Countering Violent Extremism Through Communications," June 27, 2013, https://www.gov.uk/government/speeches/security-minister-james-brokenshire-countering-violent-extremism-through-communications (accessed October 23, 2020).

[12] I exclude China because the dynamics of its media ecosystem and restrictions on independent journalism and its influence on the global platforms that dominate the contemporary system are, for the time being, more limited.

[13] Courtney Radsch, "Platformization and Media Capture: A Framework for Regulatory Analysis of Media-Related Platform Regulations," *UCLA Journal of Law & Technology, Platforms and the Press*, 28, no. 2 (Winter 2023), 175–223. https://uclajolt.com/platformatization-and-media-capture-a-framework-for-regulatory-analysis-of-media-related-platform-regulations/.

or critical reporting, and citizen journalism would be nearly impossible without them.

Journalism is dependent on Facebook, Google, and Twitter: these platforms are where the audience is, where the advertisers are, and they control the means of publishing. According to Reuters Institute Digital News Reports, the growth of social media for news consumption rose steadily until 2017, when more than half of all online users across the thirty-six countries surveyed (54%) said they used social media as a source of news each week.[14] And while people may get news media from a range of traditional and social media, the majority (53%) preferred to use algorithmically driven interfaces such as social media, search engines, or news aggregators to access news, rather than directly visiting new websites, apps, or human-driven interfaces.[15] Most of the audience for news publishers during this period came through Google Search or Facebook referrals.[16]

As a result, journalists must contend with the forcing function of these algorithms and navigate the complex and evolving community standards and terms of service to ensure that they optimize engagement but do not violate the rules. This platformization means Facebook and Google determine what gets seen and according to which rules, giving these companies outsized influence on the news. For example, YouTube's Up Next algorithm generated more than 70 percent of views on the platform.[17] When Facebook decided to prioritize video in 2015, publishers pivoted to video.[18] When the company decided in 2016, and then again in early 2018, to deprioritize media in favor of "meaningful" content from friends, news organizations suffered.[19] Visibility is the oxygen of journalism, yet news media have little control over the machine learning and algorithmic logic of the platforms they depend on.

---

[14] Nic Newman, "Reuters Institute Digital News Reports 2017 through 2019," https://www.digitalnewsreport.org/ (accessed October 3, 2020).

[15] *Id.* Newman DNR 2018. P. 13.

[16] Kevin Tran, "Publishers Are Trying to Navigate Facebook's Algorithm Change," June 27, 2018, https://www.businessinsider.com/publishers-navigate-facebooks-algorithm-change-2018-6; Emily Bell & Taylor Owen, "The Platform Press: How Silicon Valley Reengineered Journalism," *Columbia University Tow Center for Digital Journalism*, 2017, https://www.cjr.org/tow_center_reports/platform-press-how-silicon-valley-reengineered-journalism.php.

[17] AlgoTransparency, https://algotransparency.org/?date=16-07-2019&keyword= (accessed October 23, 2020).

[18] "What the Shift to Video Means for Creators. Facebook Newsroom," January 7, 2015, https://media.fb.com/2015/01/07/what-the-shift-to-video-means-for-creators/; Will Oremus, "The Big Lie Behind the 'Pivot to Video,'" *Slate*, October 18, 2018, https://slate.com/technology/2018/10/facebook-online-video-pivot-metrics-false.html Matt Taibbi, "Who Will Fix Facebook?," *Rolling Stone*, November 26, 2018, https://rollingstone.com/politics/politics-features/who-will-fix-facebook-759916/.

[19] Mark Zuckerberg, January 18, 2018, https://www.facebook.com/zuck/posts/10104413015393571; Lucia Moses, "Uh-oh, Some Publishers See a Drop in Facebook Traffic," *Digiday*, April 8, 2016, https://digiday.com/media/publishers-just-saw-decline-facebook-traffic/.

Algorithms that recommend similar content or suggest what to watch or read next can also end up promoting sites that pirate or manipulate news content at the expense of the original source, ultimately undermining journalistic content in favor of clickbait or disinformation campaigns.[20] On the other hand, algorithms that identify prohibited content have trouble accounting for context. Whether a video showing a terrorist attack constitutes praise, criticism, or straightforward reporting is deeply challenging to decide algorithmically without a human moderator, the former being prohibited while the latter may be allowed. Algorithms are also extremely complicated and increasingly built on neural networks, as with YouTube's Up Next algorithm and Google's search algorithm, that use deep learning but must also incorporate the national security prerogatives of influential governments threatening to regulate them if they don't comply.

The forcing function of algorithms influences those who seek to create and publicize the news in a plethora of ways: how newsrooms allocate budgets or hire personnel (like social media producers and analytics experts); how journalists use their social media personas to gather information and connect with sources; how journalism is reported and disseminated; and how audiences engage with it.

Well-resourced news organizations may hire professional search engine optimization specialists, video producers that cater to Facebook's preference for video, and social media specialists to leverage the latest algorithmic permutation. ISIS also devoted significant resources to propaganda and content production and amplification. ISIS media operatives were reportedly paid up to seven times the salary of regular fighters and provided with training, high-quality equipment, and staff,[21] far more than journalists working at national and local news outlets in the region. The freelancers and citizen journalists trying to cover Syria were poorly paid if they were paid at all, working on a shoestring budget with limited equipment and expertise.[22] These dynamics have profound implications for quality journalism, which must compete to circulate and monetize in the information glut of social media while trying not to be ensnared by terms of service violations or obscure algorithmic decision-making.

---

[20] Caroline O'Donnovan et al., "We Followed YouTube's Recommendation Algorithm Down the Rabbit Hole," *BuzzFeed News*, January 24, 2019, https://www.buzzfeednews.com/article/carolineo donovan/down-youtubes-recommendation-rabbithole (accessed June 28, 2024); Courtney Radsch, "AI and Disinformation: State-Aligned Information Operations and the Distortion of the Public Sphere." #SAIFE. OSCE, July 2022, https://papers.ssrn.com/sol3/papers.cfm?abstract_id=4192038 (accessed June 28, 2024).

[21] Greg Miller & Souad Mekhennet, "Inside the Surreal World of the Islamic State's Propaganda Machine," *Washington Post*, November 20, 2015, https://www.washingtonpost.com/world/national-security/inside-the-islamic-states-propaganda-machine/2015/11/20/051e997a-8ce6-11e5-acff-673 ae92ddd2b_story.html.

[22] Citizen journalist collectives are not well-funded, if their members received any payment for their journalism at all.

IV. Countering Violent Extremism and Weaponized Disinformation as National Security Priorities

Algorithms are not neutral, they embody human agency and are influenced by a range of factors, including political values.[23] And they have been called upon to support national security imperatives, specifically combating ISIS propaganda and mitigating weaponized disinformation campaigns by Russia. Countering violent extremism online and holding social media platforms partially responsible became a major national security priority as ISIS gained territory in Syria, broadcast its 2014 beheadings of journalists James Foley and Steven Sotloff, and instigated the deadly attack on the satirical French newspaper *Charlie Hebdo*.[24] Staving the flow of ISIS propaganda and recruitment online became a major national security priority for the United States, the United Kingdom, and Europe, and officials enlisted social media platforms in their efforts.[25]

Although CVE ostensibly applied to any violent extremist group, it was primarily focused on countering ISIS and affiliated Islamist terrorist groups online, despite the growth of White nationalist groups on social media.[26] When revelations about foreign information operations aimed at influencing the 2016 US elections and UK "Brexit" vote to leave the European Union emerged, pressure on tech platforms to stave Russian propaganda and disinformation

---

[23] T. Gillespie & N. Seaver, "Critical Algorithm Studies: A Reading List," 2016, https://socialmedi acollective.org/reading-lists/critical-algorithm-studies/.

[24] "Charlie Hebdo," *Wired*, January 12, 2015, http://www.wired.co.uk/news/archive/2015-01/12/charlie-hebdo-isp-internet-surveillance; "France Seeks to Sanction Web Companies for Posts Pushing Terrorism," *Bloomberg*, January 27, 2015, http://www.bloomberg.com/news/2015-01-27/france-seeks-to-sanction-web-companies-for-posts-pushing-terror.html; "Senators Introduce Social Media Bill After Terror Attacks," *MSNBC*, http://www.msnbc.com/msnbc/senators-introd uce-social-media-bill-after-terror-attacks.

[25] Courtney Radsch, "Privatizing Censorship in the Fight Against Extremism," Committee to Protect Journalists, October 16, 2015, https://cpj.org/blog/2015/10/privatizing-censorship-in-fight-against-extremism-.php; "Department of State & USAID Joint Strategy on Countering Violent Extremism," U.S. Department of State and USAID, May 2016, https://2009-2017.state.gov/docume nts/organization/257913.pdf.

[26] J.M. Berger, "Nazis vs. ISIS on Twitter: A Comparative Study of White Nationalist and ISIS Online Social Media Networks," September 2016. GW Program on Extremism; Courtney Radsch & Kate Coyer (unpublished manuscript). Countering Violent Extremism Online: Challenges and Opportunities. Vox-Pol. 2018; Julia E. Ainsley, Dustin Volz, & Kristina Cooke, "Exclusive: Trump to Focus Counter-Extremism Program Solely on Islam—Sources." Reuters, February 3, 2017, https://www.reuters.com/article/us-usa-trump-extremists-program-exclusiv-idUSKBN15G5VO (accessed June 28, 2024); Dia Kayyali, "Submission to the Special Rapporteur on Freedom of Religion or Belief for the Report on Countering Islamophobia/Anti-Muslim Hatred to Eliminate Discrimination and Intolerance Based on Religion or Belief: Anti-Muslim Hatred and Discrimination," Office of the High Commissioner for Human Rights, February 25, 2021, https://www.ohchr.org/Documents/Iss ues/Religion/Islamophobia-AntiMuslim/Civil%20Society%20or%20Individuals/DiaKayyali.pdf (accessed June 28, 2024); Courtney Radsch, "GIFCT: Possibly the Most Important Acronym You've Never Heard Of," *Just Security*, September 30, 2020, https://www.justsecurity.org/72603/gifct-possi bly-the-most-important-acronym-youve-never-heard-of/ (accessed June 28, 2024).

increased. Meanwhile, antidemocratic and authoritarian states embraced the CVE and "fake news" framework to clamp down on dissent and criticism online, but have had more limited influence over the design and terms of the major platforms.[27] Until 2019, however, these policy streams and debates over content moderation remained largely distinct.[28] The Christchurch massacre in March 2019 led to a convergence of these previously separate policy priorities, helping to shift the focus of online CVE to include a wider range of extremist groups, including violent White nationalist movements, which were also linked to the policy debate around "fake news" and weaponized disinformation.[29]

The mid-2010s was an inflection point in the government-technology company relationship as the largely hands-off approach focused on voluntary frameworks and commitments shifted to an interventionist approach focused on ensuring that technology companies comply with local policy priorities including through legislation and regulation to compel compliance. The United Kingdom and the European Union created Internet Referral Units (IRUs) to flag extremist content to the platforms for removal under their existing terms of service, which prohibit terrorist content and graphic violence, with great success.[30] Several governmental and UN initiatives calling for the platforms to show greater responsibility toward removing extremist content, preventing recruitment, and combatting radicalization had the effect of propelling content moderation to the forefront of the international agenda.[31] Government

---

[27] Courtney Radsch, "In Fight against Extremism, Press Freedom Must Not Be Compromised." Committee to Protect Journalists, February 20, 2015, https://cpj.org/2015/02/fine-line-between-countering-extremism-and-allowin/ (accessed June 28, 2024).

[28] Between 2015 and 2019 the author took part in more than a dozen consultations, roundtables, and dialogues focused on CVE online held under Chatham House rules with technology platforms, government officials, academics, and civil society.

[29] "European Commission—Fact Sheet. Commission Recommendation on Measures to Effectively Tackle Illegal Content Online," March 1, 2018, http://europa.eu/rapid/press-release_MEMO-18-1170_en.htm.

[30] *See* the EU Internet Referral Unit transparency reports available at https://www.europol.europa.eu/; Brian Chang, "Internet Referral Units to International Agreements: Censorship of the Internet by the UK and EU," *Human Rights Law Review*, 49, no. 2 (Winter 2018), 116–210, http://hrlr.law.columbia.edu/files/2018/07/BrianChangFromInternetRef.pdf.

[31] The US government set up an interagency CVE task force under the leadership of the Department of Home land Security, which is charged with, among other things, coordinating with the tech industry Fact Sheet: DHS FY 2017 Budget, February 9, 2016, https://www.dhs.gov/news/2016/02/09/fact-sheet-dhs-fy-2017-budget (accessed June 13, 2021). The State Department launched the Global Engagement Center and established the Sawab Center, in partnership with the United Arab Emirates, a social media countering message center aimed at refuting ISIS propaganda, in Arabic, and attempting to stop the spread of misinformation, http://www.sawabcenter.org/ (accessed June 3, 2021). In late 2015, the United Kingdom launched a new Commonwealth Counter Extremism Unit to focus on supporting other countries and civil society organizations to counter extremist ideologies and supporting civil society counter narrative programs with more than a million dollars a year for five years. Press release, PM announces £5 million for Commonwealth counter-extremism unit, GOV.UK, November 27, 2015, https://www.gov.uk/government/news/pm-announces-5-million-for-commonwealth-counter-extremism-unit (accessed October 23, 2020). Daniel Boffey, "Britain to Fund Team of Counter-Extremism Experts in Commonwealth,"

officials demanded faster and more proactive removal of terrorist and White supremacist content and "fake news," including the prevention of uploading such content in the first place, as a national security imperative.[32] For example, Germany's 2017 Network Enforcement Act, known as NetzDG, required major online platforms to remove within twenty-four-hours of notification "obviously illegal" content or face fines of up to €50 million. Meanwhile, the UK prime minister called for companies to remove extremist content shared by terrorist groups within two hours of being notified, and to develop technology to prevent it from being shared from the outset, and the Online Safety bill was poised to turn this into law.[33] Meanwhile, policymakers in the United States held numerous hearings on misinformation and "fake news" online and were considering strengthening regulation of social media companies in the wake of the COVID-19 pandemic, the US January 6 insurrection, and the 2022 Russian invasion of Ukraine.[34]

Social media platforms responded to government initiatives by adopting a range of voluntary measures, including updating terms of service and community guidelines, closing accounts, providing aggressive content moderation by both humans and algorithms, industry collaboration, and voluntary codes of conduct. Although all the platforms' rules prohibit terrorist content, and include some type of restrictions on graphic violence, algorithms and human moderators had to be enlisted to interpret how to apply the guidelines to specific pieces of content. In mid-2016, in what appeared to be a response to government pressure and threats to impose regulation, four of the biggest and most influential social networks—Facebook, Microsoft, Twitter, and YouTube—agreed to collaborate on the creation of a shared database of "hashes"—unique digital

---

The Guardian, November 26, 2015, http://www.theguardian.com/politics/2015/nov/27/britain-to-spend-1m-on-counter-extremism-experts. In Europe, the focus of European institutions was getting companies to adopt voluntary codes of conduct to combat illegal or problematic material. See European Commission on Code of Conduct on Countering Illegal Hate Speech Online, May 31, 2016, http://ec.europa.eu/justice/fundamentalrights/ files/hate-speech-codeof_conduct-en.pdf (accessed June 11, 2020).

[32] "The Christchurch Call to Eliminate Terrorist and Violent Extremist Content Online," https://www.christchurchcall.com/ (accessed October 30, 2020).

[33] "Online Harms White Paper: Full Government Response to the Consultation," Command Paper. UK: Department for Digital, Culture, Media & Sport, December 15, 2020, https://www.gov.uk/government/consultations/online-harms-white-paper/outcome/online-harms-white-paper-full-government-response (accessed October 22, 2020).

[34] "Theresa May Will Tell Internet Firms to Tackle Extremist Content," *The Guardian*, September 19, 2017, https://www.theguardian.com/uk-news/2017/sep/19/theresa-may-will-tell-internet-firms-to-tackle-extremist-content (accessed June 3, 2021); Kiran Jeevanjee et al., "All the Ways Congress Wants to Change Section 230," *Slate*, March 23, 2021, https://slate.com/technology/2021/03/section-230-reform-legislative-tracker.html; Dipayan Ghosh, "Are We Entering a New Era of Social Media Regulation?," *Harvard Business Review*, January 14, 2021, https://hbr.org/2021/01/are-we-entering-a-new-era-of-social-media-regulation.

identifiers—of violent terrorist images and videos that they had removed from their services.[35] A year later, the companies created the industry-led Global Internet Forum to Counter Terrorism (GIFCT) aimed at curbing the spread of terrorist content online, and recruited dozens of new company members, enabling better and faster sharing of extremist content deemed unacceptable by the dominant players, but also multiplying potential erroneous designations.[36] Initially officials said that the database only included ISIS propaganda, but expanded in 2019 according to conversations at various convenings held under Chatham House rules that the author attended. The Christchurch video, for example, is included in the database.

The platforms turned to machine learning and artificial intelligence to flag content even as they also hired thousands of new human moderators and engaged in a series of consultations to update its policies affecting content moderation.[37] Facebook said its AI team trained its algorithms to identify extremist images and language, automatically delete new accounts created by banned users, and identify terrorist clusters. In late 2017, Google's trust and safety team spent five months manually reviewing nearly two million videos for violent extremist content to help train the machine learning technology.[38] In the summer of 2017, amid increased pressure from policymakers (and advertisers) to combat terrorist propaganda, YouTube released an advanced machine learning algorithm to detect extremist content.[39] Google specifically recognized the challenge

---

[35] "Partnering to Help Curb the Spread of Terrorist Content Online," December 5, 2016, https://blog.google/topics/google-europe/partnering-help-curb-spread-terrorist-content-online/ (accessed June 13, 2021). *See also* Radsch, *supra* note 26.

[36] Radsch, *supra* note 26.

[37] "Facebook Privacy Scandal Has a Plus: Thousands of New Jobs AI Can't Do," *CNBC*, March 23, 2018, https://www.cnbc.com/2018/03/23/facebook-privacy-scandal-has-a-plus-thousands-of-new-jobs-ai-cant-do.html; "Human Moderators," *Fortune*, March 22, 2018, https://fortune.com/2018/03/22/human-moderators-facebook-youtube-twitter/; Mark Zuckerberg, "A Blueprint for Content Governance and Enforcement," November 15, 2018, https://www.facebook.com/notes/mark-zuckerberg/a-blueprint-for-content-governance-and-enforcement/10156443129621634/ (accessed November 20, 2019).

[38] Emily Dreyfuss, "Facebook's Counterterrorism Playbook Comes into Focus," *Wired*, June 17, 2017, https://www.wired.com/story/facebook-counterterrorism/; Susan Wojcicki, "Expanding Our Work against Abuse of Our Platform," *YouTube Official Blog*, December 5, 2017, https://blog.youtube/news-and-events/expanding-our-work-against-abuse-of-our/ (accessed June 3, 2021).

[39] "An Update on Our Commitment to Fight Terror Content Online," *YouTube Official Blog*, August 1, 2017, https://youtube.googleblog.com/2017/08/an-update-on-our-commitment-to-fight.html (accessed June 3, 2021). "Faster Removals and Tackling Comments—An Update on What We're Doing to Enforce YouTube's Community Guidelines," *YouTube Official Blog*, December 13, 2018, https://youtube.googleblog.com/2018/12/faster-removals-and-tackling-comments.html (accessed June 3, 2021). The transparency report and information on removals can be accessed via https://transparencyreport.google.com/youtube-policy/removals (accessed June 3, 2021). *See also* Amanda Hess, "How YouTube's Shifting Algorithms Hurt Independent Media," *New York Times*, April 17, 2017, https://www.nytimes.com/2017/04/17/arts/youtube-broadcasters-algorithm-ads.html.

of differentiating journalistic coverage and context via machine learning, but the pressure to address CVE priorities outweighed the censorial externalities.[40]

Pressure for platforms to take more rapid action, remove offending content and accounts, and prevent extremist content from being uploaded in the first place resulted in journalistic content being flagged for deletion, the closures of journalistic accounts, and increased hurdles for journalists seeking to counter such propaganda.[41] In late 2016, Facebook revised its community guidelines to allow graphic content that is "newsworthy, significant, or important to the public interest," but such content is regularly removed.[42] Although the European Parliament said that content disseminated for "journalistic" purposes should be protected in its new regulation and that removal should take into account "journalistic standards" in cases "where the content provider holds an editorial responsibility," it provided no guidance on how to algorithmically check for such context.[43] One of the problems with algorithmic content and account removal is that even if such a system was 99.9 percent effective, it would still misidentify tens of thousands of people, among them journalists and news outlets. The cases of citizen journalism in Syria is illustrative.

V. The Impact of CVE on Journalistic Content: The Case of Syria

When the Islamic State (ISIS) took over Raqqa in 2014 and made it the capital of their self-declared Caliphate, media and information were at the heart of its propaganda and recruitment strategy. ISIS had a dual-pronged "media jihad" strategy—controlling access to information in the territories it controlled and

---

[40] Kent Walker, "Google in Europe: Four Steps We're Taking Today to Fight Terrorism Online," June 18, 2017, https://www.blog.google/around-the-globe/google-europe/four-steps-were-taking-today-fight-online-terror/ (accessed June 3, 2021).

[41] Courtney Radsch, "Tweaking a Global Source of News," *Columbia Journalism Review*, February 18, 2018, https://www.cjr.org/special_report/internet-intermediary-news.php/; Courtney Radsch, "Countering Violent Extremism and Media Development; An Uneasy Relationship, a Need for Dialogue," Center for International Media Assistance, October 2016, https://www.cima.ned.org/wp-content/uploads/2016/10/CIMA-CVE-Paper_web-150ppi.pdf; Courtney Radsch, "When Fighting Fake News Aids Censorship," *Project Syndicate*, March 1, 2018, https://www.project-syndicate.org/commentary/fighting-fake-news-leads-to-censorship-by-courtney-c-radsch-2018-03.

[42] "Lost and Found: Syrian Archive's Work on Content Taken down from Social Media Platforms," Syrian Archive, https://syrianarchive.org/en/lost-found (accessed November 20, 2021); Courtney Radsch, "On Christchurch Call Anniversary, a Step Closer to Eradicating Terrorism Online?," *Just Security*, May 21, 2021, https://www.justsecurity.org/76607/on-christchurch-call-anniversary-a-step-closer-to-eradicating-terrorism-online/.

[43] *See* European Parliament website, https://www.europarl.europa.eu/news/en/press-room/20190410IPR37571/terrorist-content-online-should-be-removed-within-one-hour-says-ep; https://www.europarl.europa.eu/doceo/document/TA-8-2019-0421_EN.html (accessed June 3, 2021).

ensuring that information in the public sphere supports the Caliphate project.[44] Social media was central to this strategy.

In late 2014, ISIS was producing between 46,000 to 70,000 tweets per day, and by early 2015, they were circulating 90,000 social media posts per day.[45] ISIS produced an average of three videos and fifteen photographic reports per day, using Hollywood-style production, including subliminal messages and quick frame techniques on par with those of the major satellite television stations in the region, according to one study.[46] Its Amaq News Agency, meanwhile, provided a constant stream of content online and via an Android app that offered footage of ISIS leaders speaking, daily life in occupied territories, beheadings, and other violence, in multiple languages and formats for reuse and remixing to spread the propaganda videos on social media. According to Abdelaziz al-Hamza, founder of the citizen journalist and media activism group Raqqa is Being Slaughtered Silently (RBSS), ISIS propaganda was the only source of information online about his hometown when they established the capital of their Caliphate in Raqqa.[47]

RBSS set out to change this by documenting the atrocities and eventually reporting on the impact of the war more broadly on their hometown. They relied on the tools of citizen journalists everywhere: Facebook, YouTube, and Twitter. Dozens of other news agencies, media collectives, and human rights documentation efforts emerged during the conflict in Syria as important primary information providers and sources for international media, and their reporting on the conflict became even more crucial as journalists were targeted, kidnapped, and murdered.[48] Human rights activists established the Syrian Archive to collect

---

[44] Karim el-Damankhoury (PhD candidate, Georgia State University), conversation with the author, April 7, 2016, Vienna, Austria. *See also* Abu Bakr Naji, "The Management of Savagery: The Most Critical Stage Through Which the Umma Will Pass," Translated by William McCants, May 23, 2006, https://azelin.files.wordpress.com/2010/08/abu-bakr-naji-the-management-of-savagery-the-most-critical-stage-through-which-the-umma-will-pass.pdf (accessed May 2, 2019).

[45] Eric Schmitt, "U.S. Intensifies Effort to Blunt ISIS' Message," *New York Times*, February 17, 2015, http://www.nytimes.com/2015/02/17/world/middleeast/us-intensifies-effort-to-blunt-isis-message.html?_r=0 (accessed June 28, 2024 J.M. Berger & Jonathon Morgan, "The ISIS Twitter Census: Defining and Describing the Population of ISIS Supporters on Twitter," *Brookings Institution* (20), March 2015, http://www.brookings.edu/~/media/research/files/papers/2015/03/isis-twitter-census-berger-morgan/isis_twitter_census_berger_morgan.pdf?la=en.

[46] Charlie Winter, "The Virtual 'Caliphate': Understanding Islamic State's Propaganda Strategy," *Quilliam*, 2015, https://www.quilliamfoundation.org/wp/wp-content/uploads/publications/free/the-virtual-caliphate-understanding-islamic-states-propaganda-strategy.pdf (accessed June 13, 2019). Philippe Abou Zeid (TV producer and reporter) Presentation at Media narratives on violent extremism: media professionals and researchers will discuss local coverage of Daesh media narratives in both online and traditional media session at Countering Violent Extremism and Freedom of Expression conference in Lebanon, April 6, 2016. In 2016, a U.S. Senator, dismissed approaches taken by U.S. government agencies in light of what he said were ISIS' superior capabilities, http://abcnews.go.com/US/senators-suggest-trolling-terrorists-memes-presidential-campaign-staffers/story?id=30876720 (accessed June 5, 2021).

[47] Personal communication with Abdelaziz al-Hamza in November 2015.

[48] Committee to Protect Journalists, database of killed journalists; Naadia Massih, Infographic: Islamic State's assault on the press, Committee to Protect Journalists, June 8, 2016,

and preserve digital documentation of human rights violations in a war that has generated more hours of social media content documenting the conflict than hours in the conflict itself.[49]

These grassroots initiatives by citizen journalist and media activist collectives lacked the resources of ISIS but sought to fight the information war on the virtual battlefield by documenting the impact of the conflict, at great personal cost. Several literally paid with their lives.[50] And then the videos started disappearing. Their accounts were suspended or closed.

In June 2017, Google announced it would use machine learning to detect extremist content, and lauded the fact that just a few months later, 98 percent of violent extremist videos were removed before they ever received a human flag.[51] YouTube removed hundreds of videos related to the Syrian war, including citizen journalism that provided some of the only independent coverage of the region and footage that could be used to document human rights violations or even war crimes. Among these were the Shaam News Network, the Qasioun News Agency, RBSS, and the Idlib Media Center, which lost hundreds of thousands of videos and followers, and the Syrian Archive, which lost hundreds of channels and hundreds of thousands of videos documenting the war in Syria.[52] The account of Orient News was reportedly closed as was the account of a French journalist whose post included an ISIS flag, while Middle East Eye had several videos from Syria removed for violating community standards.[53] Hamza said that RBSS had its Facebook page removed two times and YouTube removed its channels, which often featured footage from ISIS-controlled territories. Hamza said that the stated reason for removal was "repeated or severe violations of the platform's Community Guidelines" and that RBSS had tried to contact YouTube to retrieve the channels several times but were unsuccessful. "We used to contact YouTube to get them back but YouTube has not stopped removing our channels

---

https://www.cpj.org/blog/2016/06/infographic-islamic-states-assault-on-the-press.php; "CPJ Condemns Murder of Raqqa Is Being Slaughtered Silently Journalist," Committee to Protect Journalists, December 16, 2015,
    https://cpj.org/2015/12/cpj-condemns-murder-of-raqqa-is-being-slaughtered-.php.

[49] Syrian Archive, https://syrianarchive.org/en/tech-advocacy (accessed June 3, 2021).
[50] Nadia Massih, "How Islamic State Uses Killings to Try to Spread Fear Among Media," *CPJ.org*, July 13, 2015, https://cpj.org/blog/2015/07/how-islamic-state-uses-killings-to-try-to-spread-f.php; *see also* https://scm.bz/en/missing-memebers (accessed October 1, 2019).
[51] "YouTube: Expanding Our Work Against Abuse of Our Platform," December 4, 2017, https://youtube.googleblog.com/2017/12/expanding-our-work-against-abuse-of-our.html (accessed June 2, 2021).
[52] Tech Advocacy page of the Syrian Archive, https://syrianarchive.org/en/tech-advocacy (accessed May 20, 2019).
[53] "YouTube Criticized After Middle East Video Taken Down over Extremist Content," *Middle East Eye*, http://www.middleeasteye.net/news/youtube-criticised-after-middle-east-video-taken-down-over-extremist-content-1244893230 (accessed May 20, 2019).

until we gave up. We tried many times to verify our YouTube channels, but [they] refused."[54]

The Syrian video removals came following an update to the company's approach for identifying extremist content that relied primarily on natural language processing and machine learning to identify prohibited content for warning or removal. The reliance on artificial intelligence rather than human moderators was intended to more rapidly identify extremist content, but the question of what work has been lost is a "nagging one," according to Jason Stern, a former Middle East researcher for the Committee to Protect Journalists who reported on attacks against journalists and often relied on online videos as part of the verification process. "There are a lot of burning questions about the proper balance on these issues: for me, 127 journalists have died covering the war in Syria, many more have been injured and kidnapped, how much more of their work has been killed by algorithm? They are dodging bullets on the ground but also dodging bullets from terms of service."[55]

Not only are social media platforms important for dissemination and archiving but also for the raw material of the journalistic endeavor. Journalists want to be able to watch the original source material themselves, whether it's a violent video or the speeches by leaders of designated terrorist organizations. They need to review and cross-reference videos of attacks to establish veracity and authenticity, a practice that is particularly important in countries without a free press like Syria, which became too dangerous for foreign journalists to cover after 2014, and Myanmar or China, which restrict access by journalists to their countries and contested territories.

"Why is it that we heard so much about the online documentation of the Syrian war? Well the usual way of reporting to be there in person see with own eyes no longer possible because it is too dangerous to report from the ground," said Stern. "So the only option was to rely on finding videos online, verify it, and report on it that way."

VI. Weaponized Disinformation: The Russian Threat

Following revelations about Russian interference and computational propaganda[56] efforts aimed at influencing the 2016 US presidential election and the

---

[54] Abdelaziz al-Hamza of RBSS interview with the author, December 29, 2017.
[55] Jason Stern interview with the author, May 29, 2019.
[56] Computational propaganda is the use of algorithms, automation, and human curation to purposefully distribute misleading information over social media networks. Definition from Samuel C. Woolley & Philip N. Howard, "Computational Propaganda Worldwide: Executive Summary," Samuel Woolley & Philip N. Howard (eds.), Working Paper 2017.11. Oxford, UK: Project on Computational Propaganda. comprop.oii.ox.ac.uk.

United Kingdom's Brexit vote the same year, the perceived need to regulate online platforms and expand content moderation efforts to stave off antidemocratic interference increased. Although the World Economic Forum had identified the rapid spread of misinformation online as among the top ten risks to society, it wasn't until late 2016 that the extent of Russian interference in the American presidential elections started to be understood and became a serious national security concern.[57] In 2017, the leaders of the three major tech platforms were called to testify before congress.[58] FBI director Christopher A. Wray said at a hearing in August 2018 that Russian efforts to inject divisive misinformation into American social media continued daily,[59] echoing Director of National Intelligence Dan Coats, who said just a few days earlier that Russia was just "a keyboard click away" from a more serious attack on US midterm elections.[60]

Russia has a host of media organizations dedicated to disseminating propaganda, interacting with news and its users, and perpetuating a certain worldview that is not hospitable to journalists or press freedom. Its Internet Research Agency (IRA) reportedly employs hundreds of people to engage on social media platforms and promote a pro-Russian perspective, and it appears to operate a network of pro-Kremlin websites including the Federal News Agency. With a reported budget at the time of at least twenty million rubles (roughly $400,000) a month and competitive salaries, its funding surpassed that of many news organizations.[61] With its extensive workforce and budget, it was able to outperform news outlets in the platformized media ecosystem. In 2016, fake election news articles generated more engagement on Facebook than the top election stories of nineteen major news outlets combined.[62] The IRA was able to spend

---

[57] "World Economic Forum: Outlook Report," http://reports.weforum.org/outlook-14/top-ten-trends-category-page/10-the-rapid-spread-of-misinformation-online/ (accessed June 6, 2020); Craig Silverman, "This Analysis Shows How Viral Fake Election News Stories Outperformed Real News on Facebook," *BuzzFeed News*, November 16, 2016, https://www.buzzfeednews.com/article/craigsilverman/viral-fake-election-news-outperformed-real-news-on-facebook; "Joint Statement from the Department Of Homeland Security and Office of the Director of National Intelligence on Election Security," Department of Homeland Security, October 7, 2016, https://www.dhs.gov/news/2016/10/07/joint-statement-department-homeland-security-and-office-director-national (accessed June 3, 2021). *See also* Office of the Director of National Security. Background to "Assessing Russian Activities and Intentions in Recent US Elections": The Analytic Process and Cyber Incident Attribution, January 6, 2017, https://www.dni.gov/files/documents/ICA_2017_01.pdf (accessed June 3, 2021).

[58] "Full Testimony," *ReCode*, October 30, 2017, https://www.recode.net/2017/10/30/16571598/read-full-testimony-facebook-twitter-google-congress-russia-election-fake-news (accessed June 4, 2021).

[59] Michael D. Shear & Michael Wines, "Russian Threat 'Is Real,' Trump Officials Say, Vowing to Protect U.S. Elections," *New York Times*, August 2, 2018, https://www.nytimes.com/2018/08/02/us/politics/russia-election-security-midterm.html.

[60] Dan Coates, "Russia Election Hack," *Fortune*, August 2, 2018, http://fortune.com/2018/08/02/russia-election-hack-dan-coats

[61] Adrian Chen, "The Agency," *The New York Times Magazine*, June 2, 2015, https://www.nytimes.com/2015/06/07/magazine/the-agency.html (accessed June 16, 2024).

[62] Silverman, *supra* note 57.

hundreds of thousands of dollars on social media ads to promote its junk news articles.[63] An analysis of several elections found that in France users posted one fake election news article for each professionally produced journalistic article; in Germany they shared one fake story for every real story; and in the US state of Michigan, users were sharing fake and real stories at an even ratio.[64]

Journalists and news media struggle for visibility during elections, fighting against better resourced adversaries who game the forcing logic of algorithms to drown out real journalism.[65] The success of misinformation, counterfeit news, and computational propaganda on social media platforms have highlighted the economic incentives embedded in social media platforms that not only helped information operations and "fake news" flourish but effectively de-incentivizes quality journalism. A report by the Global Disinformation Index found that news websites were losing revenue "to click-bait ad farm sites that spread hypersensational, misleading, and sometimes outright false news," because those hyperpolemic stories received higher rates of traffic than reported news stories.[66]

In seeking to combat the proliferation of misinformation on its platform, the tech platforms adjusted their algorithms, reworked their terms of service, and implemented new rules and tools. In addition to expanding the use of automated tools deployed to combat terrorism and violent extremism content (TVEC), Google and Facebook launched partnerships with fact-checking organizations and announced their advertising systems would ban sites that traffic in misinformation and disinformation.[67] Facebook allowed users to report hoaxes, provided related links to reputable publishers next to disputed content, and disincentivized spammy and coordinated inauthentic behavior.[68] Google news and search incorporated a "fact-check" tag and the company launched

---

[63] Scott Shane, "These Are the Ads Russia Bought on Facebook in 2016," *New York Times*, November 1, 2017, https://www.nytimes.com/2017/11/01/us/politics/russia-2016-election-facebook.html; Vindu Goel & Scott Shane, "Fake Russian Facebook Accounts Bought $100,000 in Political Ads," *New York Times*, September 6, 2017, https://www.nytimes.com/2017/09/06/technology/facebook-russian-political-ads.html.

[64] Philip N. Howard & Robert Gwora, "Facebook Could Tell Us How Russia Interfered in Our Elections. Why Won't It?," *Washington Post*, May 19, 2017, https://www.washingtonpost.com/opinions/facebook-could-tell-us-how-russia-interfered-in-our-elections-why-wont-it/2017/05/19/c061a606-3b21-11e7-8854-21f359183e8c_story.html?utm_term=.da50ef901927.

[65] Radsch, *supra* note 2.

[66] Ali Breland, "Fake News Is Getting a Big Boost From Real Companies," *Mother Jones*, May 9, 2019, https://www.motherjones.com/politics/2019/05/fake-news-advertising-networks/.

[67] Adam Mosseri, "Addressing Hoaxes and Fake News," *Facebook Newsroom*, December 15, 2016, https://newsroom.fb.com/news/2016/12/news-feed-fyi-addressing-hoaxes-and-fake-news/; Craig Silverman, "Facebook Is Turning to Fact-Checkers to Fight Fake News," *BuzzFeed News*, December 15, 2016, https://www.buzzfeednews.com/article/craigsilverman/facebook-and-fact-checkers-fight-fake-news; Daniel Funke, "In the Past Year, Facebook Has Quadrupled Its Fact-Checking Partners," *Poynter*, April 26, 2019, https://www.poynter.org/fact-checking/2019/in-the-past-year-facebook-has-quadrupled-its-fact-checking-partners/.

[68] Facebook Newsroom Blog, December 2016, https://newsroom.fb.com/news/2016/12/news-feed-fyi-addressing-hoaxes-and-fake-news/ (accessed June 13, 2021).

Project Owl to improve the quality and recommendations in search and prioritize "trusted sources."[69] It adjusted algorithms to incorporate these signals.[70] Facebook had a human team of editors who curated Trending Topics and made decisions about "injecting" and "blacklisting" topics from the trending feed and which sources were authoritative and trustworthy, relying on a whitelist that included many mainstream news outlets.[71] But accusations that it was suppressing conservative news led to a backlash against the internet behemoth. In response, Facebook tweaked its approach and switched to algorithmic curation, leading to nonjournalistic sources and false or inflammatory articles being promoted.[72]

As Google and Facebook removed problematic accounts, tweaked their algorithms, and sought ways to surface more authoritative content while punishing "inauthentic" behavior, they not only dismantled Russian disinformation sites but also negatively impacted journalistic outlets.[73] Following a January 2018 update to the Facebook newsfeed algorithm designed to combat false or fake news by prioritizing content from friends and family and de-emphasizing news publishers, news outlets experienced an overall decline in referral traffic.[74] This hit nonprofit and investigative outlets and popular niche publications like Slate and Talking Points Memo.[75] The signals platforms use appeared to have marginalized those on the outer edges of the ideological spectrum or freelance journalists in favor of larger, more established and mainstream outlets. Following the announcement of Project Owl in mid-2017, alternative news sites including Democracy Now, the investigative outlet *The Intercept*, WikiLeaks, Alternet,

---

[69] Justin Kosslyn & Cong Yu, :Fact Check Now Available in Google Search and News around the World," *Google Blog*, April 7, 2017, https://www.blog.google/products/search/fact-check-now-available-google-search-and-news-around-world/; "Ben Gomes," *Google Blog*, April 25, 2017, https://blog.google/products/search/our-latest-quality-improvements-search/ (accessed June 4, 2021). Danny Sullivan, "Google's 'Project Owl'—A Three-Pronged Attack on Fake News & Problematic Content," *Search Engine Land*, April 25, 2017, https://searchengineland.com/googles-project-owl-attack-fake-news-273700.

[70] Mike Ananny, "Checking in with the Facebook Fact-Checking Partnership," April 4, 2018, https://www.cjr.org/tow_center/facebook-fact-checking-partnerships.php.

[71] Sam Thielman, "Facebook News Selection Is in Hands of Editors Not Algorithms, Documents Show," *The Guardian*, May 12, 2016, https://www.theguardian.com/technology/2016/may/12/facebook-trending-news-leaked-documents-editor-guidelines; Michael Nunez, "Former Facebook Workers: We Routinely Suppressed Conservative News," *Gizmodo*, May 9, 2016, https://gizmodo.com/former-facebook-workers-we-routinely-suppressed-conser-1775461006.

[72] Sam Thielman, "Facebook Fires Trending Team, and Algorithm Without Humans Goes Crazy," *The Guardian*, August 29, 2016, https://www.theguardian.com/technology/2016/aug/29/facebook-fires-trending-topics-team-algorithm.

[73] Sullivan, *supra* note 69.

[74] Tran, *supra* note 16.

[75] Andrew Gruen & Aisha Townes, "Facebook Friends? The Impact of Facebook's News Feed Algorithm Changes on Nonprofit Publishers," Shorenstein Center on Media, Politics and Public Policy, October 16, 2016; Will Oremus, "The Great Facebook Crash," *Slate*, June 2018, https://slate.com/technology/2018/06/facebooks-retreat-from-the-news-has-painful-for-publishers-including-slate.html (accessed July 15, 2018).

and others experience a massive drop in Google search referrals.[76] A 2018 purge of more than 800 US publishers and accounts from Facebook snared partisan news sites from across the political spectrum and appeared to be mirrored on Twitter.[77] Twitter, in addition to removing offending "fake news" accounts, including those belonging to far right-wing extremists in the United States, refused to verify some accounts and removed their verification status.[78] The impact on news outlets and journalists around the world or working in languages other than English was even more profound.[79]

The political imperative to fight weaponized disinformation and the general scourge of low-quality junk news compelled the technology platforms to seek to mitigate the problem or risk increased regulatory intervention. News outlets have been caught in the middle as they have sought to adjust to the social media–mediated public sphere by producing content to cater to the whims of the algorithmic preferences of the major referral platforms.

VII. The Christchurch Attack and Coordinated Responses

When Brenton Tarrant allegedly set out to murder worshippers at two mosques in Christchurch, New Zealand, on March 15, 2019, he had already emailed out and uploaded his seventy-four-page manifesto online, posting notes on 8chan and Twitter.[80] As he opened fire on the first mosque, he livestreamed the attack on Facebook. Then he moved to the second mosque. For seventeen minutes, he filmed his murderous rampage, and not a single human flagged it; only 200 watched the original.[81] But as soon as it was uploaded it spread exponentially, with 1.5 million copies proliferating on Facebook within the first twenty-four hours as copies were being uploaded to YouTube each second.[82]

---

[76] World Socialist Web Site, "An Open Letter to Google: Stop the Censorship of the Internet! Stop the Political Blacklisting of the World Socialist Web Site!," August 25, 2017, https://www.wsws.org/en/articles/2017/08/25/pers-a25.html; Dan Tynan, "Facebook Accused of Censorship after Hundreds of US Political Pages Purged," *The Guardian*, October 17, 2018, https://www.theguardian.com/technology/2018/oct/16/facebook-political-activism-pages-inauthentic-behavior-censorship.

[77] Taibbi, *supra* note 18.

[78] Courtney Radsch, "Deciding Who Decides Which News Is Fake," Committee to Protect Journalists, March 14, 2017, https://cpj.org/2017/03/deciding-who-decides-which-news-is-fake/.

[79] Radsch, *supra* note 1.

[80] Charlene Wong, "The Manifesto of Brenton Tarrant—A Right-Wing Terrorist on a Crusade," March 15, 2019, https://observer.news/featured/the-manifesto-of-brenton-tarrant-a-right-wing-terrorist-on-a-crusade/.

[81] "Update on New Zealand," *Facebook Newsroom*, https://newsroom.fb.com/news/2019/03/update-on-new-zealand/ (accessed May 4, 2019); E.J. Dickson, "Six Charged in New Zealand for Sharing Mosque Shooting Video Online," *Rolling Stone*, April 15, 2019, https://www.rollingstone.com/culture/culture-news/new-zealand-christchurch-mosque-shooting-facebook-charges-822280/.

[82] Asha Barbaschow, "Christchurch Call: USA Missing from 26 Member Pledge to Eliminate Violent Online Content," May 16, 2019, https://www.zdnet.com/article/christchurch-call-26-members-pledge-to-eliminate-terrorist-and-violent-extremist-content-online/.

Facebook reacted within minutes to reports of the Christchurch killer's video on its site.[83] Google got involved in trying to stem its circulation on YouTube, and Twitter suspended one of the suspect's accounts and sought to remove the video.[84] An official from one of these companies took what they described as the "unprecedented" step of preventing uploads of the video, including by news sites, while Facebook reportedly prevented 1.2 million uploads.[85] Even Reddit finally caved to pressure and deleted the "watchpeopledie" forum with its more than 300,000 subscribers.[86] In New Zealand, the country's chief censor classified the shooter's manifesto as objectionable, making it an offense to possess or distribute it, with no exception for news organizations.[87] Several news articles reviewed for this research revealed embedded content related to the attack that had been removed, including text of the manifesto and explainer videos. The Christchurch attack was specifically designed for social media.

In May 2019, world leaders met in Paris to sign a nonbinding pledge aimed at eliminating terrorist and violent extremist content online and obtain commitments—voluntary at the time of writing—from tech companies to do more on their part. A dozen signed on, including most of the major social media platforms.[88] Microsoft proposed greater industry-wide cooperation to improve the use of hashes and other technology to prevent uploading and viewing of content and called for the creation of a "major event" protocol that would enable tech companies to coordinate in a "joint virtual command center."[89] The language of the post and its proposals uses terminology familiar to the national security sector. At the 2019 UN General Assembly, tech companies announced that the GIFCT would spin off as a separate organization to provide exactly

---

[83] Guy Rosen "A Further Update on New Zealand Terrorist Attack," *Facebook Newsroom*, March 20, 2019, https://newsroom.fb.com/news/2019/03/technical-update-on-new-zealand/ (accessed May 1, 2019).

[84] Courtney Radsch, "Taking Down Terrorism Online While Preserving Free Expression," *New Zealand Herald*, May 15, 2019, https://www.nzherald.co.nz/nz/news/article.cfm?c_id=1&objectid=12230709.

[85] Barbaschow *supra* note 82.

[86] Craig Timberg et al., "The New Zealand Shooting Shows How YouTube and Facebook Spread Hate and Violent Images—Yet Again," *WashingtonPost*, March 15, 2019, https://www.washingtonpost.com/technology/2019/03/15/facebook-youtube-twitter-amplified-video-christchurch-mosque-shooting/?utm_term=.d456b25c7bf7.

[87] "Classification Office Response to the March 2019 Christchurch Terrorist Attack," December 9, 2020, https://www.classificationoffice.govt.nz/news/latest-news/christchurch-attacks-press-releases/#christchurch-attack-publication-the-great-replacement-classified-objectionable (accessed May 12, 2021).

[88] "Text of the Christchurch Call to Eliminate Terrorist and Violent Extremist Content Online," https://www.christchurchcall.com/about/christchurch-call-text (accessed October 30, 2020).

[89] Brad Smith, "A Tragedy That Calls For More Than Words: The Need for the Tech Sector to Learn and Act after Events in New Zealand," *Microsoft Blog*, March 24, 2019, https://blogs.microsoft.com/on-the-issues/2019/03/24/a-tragedy-that-calls-for-more-than-words-the-need-for-the-tech-sector-to-learn-and-act-after-events-in-new-zealand/ (accessed June 3, 2021).

this joint approach and enable smaller companies to tap into its hash database and expertise.[90] They also revealed that the GIFCT had developed a Content Incident Protocol to address livestreaming TVEC that had been tested and deployed numerous times and was not restricted to groups on the UN terrorist designation. Such efforts increase the influence of national security priorities on tech platforms and their policies.

VIII. Conclusion

It is becoming ever more difficult for journalism to escape the deep forcing logic of algorithms and platform policies developed, at least in part, in response to government pressure. As platforms increasingly coordinate between themselves to remove objectionable content and create shared databases of problematic multimedia and textual content, the danger of siphoning off journalistic content increases, particularly in the absence of robust transparency requirements.[91] Journalism, often referred to as the first draft of history, is particularly affected by content moderation during crisis events and coordination among platforms increases the risk that news coverage will be ensnared in efforts to prevent unwanted content. The precedence created through the development of the GIFCT TVEC database for coordinated content moderation by internet companies means that the approaches and technology could be enlisted to address other types of problematic content, such as disinformation or hate speech, which are even more challenging to define that terrorism or extremism. Because there is no independent oversight or audit of the hash database, it is impossible to verify this, and it is also impossible to know whether journalistic material is included in the database, much less to train the artificial intelligence systems to avoid these in the future. Furthermore, news organizations reporting on such issues could end up having their content removed, as there is no ability to audit these databases or consider context in the use of such material. The lack of algorithmic transparency coupled with ever-shifting policies, standards, and priorities means that journalists are in a constant race to keep pace with developments and adapt their products and practices accordingly or risk impediments or erasure.

---

[90] The author attended the closed meeting of heads of state and tech platform executives at the 74th UNGA. For information about the new approach, see Facebook's press release, https://newsroom.fb.com/news/2019/09/next-steps-for-gifct (accessed June 3, 2021).

[91] Radsch, *supra* note 42.

APPENDIX A

Recommendations to Platforms and Governments

Tech platforms and the GIFCT should commit to maintaining a searchable database of hashes and the corresponding content at the minimum at a company level, and ideally by the GIFCT as well. Social media companies should keep a database of all content removed with prefiltering technology or identified by algorithms after it is uploaded, as well as content that is reviewed by a human content moderator. This content should be tagged, and independent experts, researchers and journalists should be able to audit and review this content.[92] The legal and privacy challenges in doing so have been cited as an excuse for inaction by company representatives over three years of dialogues, so it is imperative that policymakers provide clear guidance to companies. In particular, ensuring that the European Union's General Data Protection Regulation (GDPR) does not restrict the ability to maintain a database and share information with researchers and others will require EU policymakers to provide clarity. Companies and policymakers should explore how an accreditation system and the equivalent of an institutional review board could be used to mitigate concerns about privacy violations or unauthorized uses of the data.

Greater algorithmic transparency by social media companies is critical to improve understanding and accountability, but it is not sufficient. The data sets created though content moderation policies and removals must be open to researchers and potential regulators in light of the fact that governments increasingly outsource censorship to the private sector. Attempts to combat online extremist and fight disinformation using machine learning, artificial intelligence, and algorithmic design will not be successful if they result in the removal and censorship of journalism. Ensuring that journalists have access to the raw materials, they need to report and avoiding the inadvertent removal of journalistic content is deeply challenging as outlined in this chapter. Platform-level efforts to counter violent extremism and propaganda online in response to pressure from the United States and Europe has led to censorship of journalistic content, affected citizen journalism from conflict zones, and impacted the ability to use violent imagery in news reporting, yet has not been adequately addressed by either platforms or governments.

Deciding who decides what news is extremist or false is a political question, and one that will empower some actors over others, with significant implications for journalism.[93] As journalism struggles to adapt to the agenda-setting and framing power of algorithms, policymakers must also consider the impact that attempts to address national security concerns online could have on journalists and news content. Equally importantly, journalists must become better attuned to how national security shapes the policies and practices of ostensibly independent private technology companies.

---

[92] Courtney Radsch, "Greater Transparency Welcome but Social Media Sites Should Allow Independent Audits of Content Takedowns," Committee to Protect Journalists, May 18, 2018, https://cpj.org/2018/05/greater-transparency-welcome-but-social-media-site/.

[93] Radsch, *supra* note 78.

Policymakers should avoid outsourcing censorial decisions to private companies without precise guidance, sustained review and oversight, and access to remedy. Governments must avoid seeking quick-fix techniques to address online extremism and recognize that extremism is a social problem that adapts to the dominant media and communication practices of a given era. In seeking to regulate content moderation, policymakers would be well-advised to examine the underlying business models, algorithmic design, and incentives of specific platforms in order to develop tailored solutions that deal with the underlying logic that enables the spread and amplification of extremism and disinformation. Technology platforms, especially the leading social media networks, should avoid acquiescing to political pressure without sufficient legal guidance.

15
Weaponizing Images

Susan D. Moeller

I. Images and Asymmetric Warfare

If you saw a video of a pilot being burned alive in a cage, would you remember it?

On Tuesday, February 3, 2015, the Islamic State in Iraq and Syria (ISIS) posted a twenty-two-minute video across social media. The video followed captured Jordanian fighter pilot, First Lt. Moaz al-Kasasbeh as he walked alone through the rubble of buildings. As he stopped before a line of masked ISIS fighters, the camera zoomed in. Through parallel editing—alternating scenes so that there appeared to be a cause and effect—the video crosscut propaganda footage over the close-up of his face: images of burned bodies of civilians being pulled from the ruins, of dead from coalition airstrikes against ISIS, of Syrian civilians presumptively killed in the raid Lieutenant al-Kasasbeh led when he was shot down on December 24, 2014.

Then came the climactic scene: the lieutenant behind bars, locked in a medieval-style cage, wearing an orange jumpsuit, soaked in fuel. In slow motion a masked terrorist outside lit a torch and ignited a trail of accelerant that licked its way toward the trapped pilot. Swells of music broke over the crackling of the fire; the video lingered on the flames that consumed him. The camera came in for another close-up; viewers saw Lieutenant al-Kasasbeh's contorted face, heard his tortured screams above the roar of the flames, watched his agonized fall to his knees until all that was left was his charred and smoldering remains.

Then the video ended, with a bounty offer: ISIS would give 100 gold coins to anyone who assassinated any of the other coalition Jordanian fighter pilots; it showed their portraits.

If you had seen that video, would you ever forget it? Or forget who was responsible? Denise Grady, a long-time health and medicine reporter at the *New York Times*, early wrote an article for *Discover Magazine* on how the brain makes sense of and remembers what it sees:

Vision, of course, is more than recording what meets the eye: it's the ability to understand, almost instantaneously, what we see. And that happens in the brain. The brain, explains neurobiologist Semir Zeki of the University

---

Susan D. Moeller, *Weaponizing Images* In: *National Security, Journalism, and Law in an Age of Information Warfare.*
Edited by: Marc Ambinder, Jennifer R. Henrichsen, and Connie Rosati, Oxford University Press.
© Oxford University Press 2024. DOI: 10.1093/oso/9780197756621.003.0015

of London, has to actively construct or invent our visual world. Confronted with an overwhelming barrage of visual information, it must sort out relevant features and make snap judgments about what they mean. It has to guess at the true nature of reality by interpreting a series of clues written in visual shorthand....[1]

In Jordan, the December capture of Lieutenant al-Kasasbeh immediately triggered angry protests—men gathering in the streets resented Jordan's military joining an American-led coalition force targeting Muslims. But in the tense weeks that followed, Queen Rania started an Instagram campaign called "We Are All Moaz," and public attitudes began to shift. Public opinion dramatically turned against ISIS after ISIS released a photo and audio on January 24, documenting the beheading of Japanese hostage Haruna Yukawa, and on January 31, after ISIS's media organization, Al Furqan, posted on its Twitter account a minute-long video of the beheading of a second Japanese hostage, journalist Kenji Goto.[2]

When the video of Lieutenant al-Kasasbeh's death appeared on February 3, the Associated Press noted: "The video appeared aimed at pressuring Jordan to leave the coalition that has been battling to roll back the Islamic State group."[3] Instead it did the reverse. "For Jordanians," the *New York Times* wrote, "the extreme brutality of the killing appears to have transformed their country's role in the coalition from a potential political liability to a point of pride." The day of the video's release, Jordanian officials announced that they had learned that the pilot had actually been killed on January 3, even before the two Japanese—a detail that made plain that ISIS's mid-January call for a prisoner exchange had not been in good faith. Within two days of the video's release, King Abdullah publicly offered his condolences to the father of the killed pilot, the nation's warplanes struck ISIS targets inside Syria, and Jordan executed two prisoners already sentenced to death for terrorism—both members of Al Qaeda in Iraq, the terrorist group that had become the present-day Islamic State.[4]

As had been the case with earlier snuff videos from ISIS, the video of Lieutenant al-Kasasbeh's death went viral. ISIS posted the video of the lieutenant's death

---

[1] "The Vision Thing: Mainly in the Brain," *Discover Magazine*, https://www.discovermagazine.com/mind/the-vision-thing-mainly-in-the-brain (accessed October 2, 2023).
[2] Rod Nordland, "ISIS Says It Has Killed 2nd Japanese Hostage," *New York Times*, January 31, 2015, https://www.nytimes.com/2015/02/01/world/middleeast/islamic-state-militants-japanese-hostage.html (accessed October 4, 2023).
[3] "New ISIS Video Appears to Show Jordanian Pilot Burned Alive," *HuffPost*, February 3, 2015, https://www.huffpost.com/entry/muath-al-kaseasbeh-dead_n_6604726 (accessed October 4, 2023).
[4] Ranya Kadri & Anne Barnard, "Jordan, Unabashed, Announces Latest Bombing Raid on ISIS Targets," *New York Times*, February 5, 2015, https://www.nytimes.com/2015/02/06/world/middleeast/jordan-unabashed-announces-latest-bombing-raid-on-isis-targets.html (accessed October 4, 2023).

on YouTube on February 3; Google took it down several hours later. Facebook announced it would do the same if users tried to post the video on its site. But those who had passed on the YouTube link via social media in the early hours of the video's release found another public link to pass on: Fox News in the United States decided to embed the video on its website. Despite Fox's earlier refusal to post previous ISIS videos—for example, the beheading of American journalist James Foley—Fox uploaded the Lieutenant al-Kasasbeh video in its entirety, becoming the only major US news outlet to do so, although Glenn Beck, a former Fox host, also posted the video on his website, The Blaze. Beck defended his decision on his site: "It is time to wake up. This is the enemy of all mankind. Make no mistake, this is a global jihad and it has everything to do with 'their' religion and their fundamental interpretation of the Koran."[5] John Moody, executive vice president of Fox News, explained in more tempered terms why his network posted the video: "After careful consideration, we decided that giving readers of FoxNews.com the option to see for themselves the barbarity of ISIS outweighed legitimate concerns about the graphic nature of the video. Online users can choose to view or not view this disturbing content."[6]

Supporters of ISIS linked to the Fox video page as they cheered the news of the "eye-for-eye" immolation across Twitter and via other social messaging platforms. Activists deplored Fox's choice to post the video. Former Islamist turned anti-extremist activist Maajid Nawaz tweeted out an older photo of Lieutenant al-Kasasbeh in uniform, asking his readers: "Want an image to tweet of burned-alive Jordanian hero Moaz al-Kasasbah? Use this one. Do not use ISIL propaganda."[7] Scholars of terrorism also challenged Fox's decision. ISIS seeks "to strike terror in the hearts and minds of people globally, and by perpetuating these videos and putting them out there into the internet, it certainly expands the audience and potential effects," said Rick Nelson, of the Center for Strategic and International Studies. "These groups need a platform, and this gives them a platform."[8]

---

[5] "Glenn: It Is Time to Wake Up. This Is the Enemy of All Mankind. (GRAPHIC IMAGES)," *Glenn Beck*, February 4, 2015, https://www.glennbeck.com/2015/02/04/glenn-it-is-time-to-wake-up-this-is-the-enemy-of-all-mankind-graphic-images/ (accessed August 1, 2019).

[6] "Fox News Explains Why It Showed Jordan Pilot Video," *BBC News*, February 5, 2015, https://www.bbc.com/news/world-us-canada-31013455 (accessed October 7, 2023).

[7] Thomas Chatterton Williams, "Maajid Nawaz's Radical Ambition," *New York Times*, March 28, 2017, https://www.nytimes.com/2017/03/28/magazine/can-a-former-islamist-make-it-cool-to-be-moderate.html (accessed October 7, 2023); and Joseph Willits [@josephwillits], "#ThisIsMuath We Should Share His Smile Not #ISIS Monstrosity.Jordanian Pilot Muath al-Kasasbeh Http://News.Sky.Com/Story/1420656/Is-Says-Jordanian-Pilot-Burned-Alive-in-Video Http://T.Co/xchdKIsdR5," Tweet, *Twitter*, February 3, 2015, https://twitter.com/josephwillits/status/562658988257722368 (accessed October 7, 2023).

[8] Nicky Woolf, "Fox News Site Embeds Unedited Isis Video Showing Brutal Murder of Jordanian Pilot," *The Guardian*, February 4, 2015, https://www.theguardian.com/media/2015/feb/04/fox-news-shows-isis-video-jordan-pilot (accessed October 7, 2023).

YouTube, Twitter, Instagram, Facebook: all social media platforms used to host, link to, or discuss the video. Within five days of FoxNews.com's posting of the video, two million people had found and watched it—many viewers coming directly to the video from social media links. By February 7, the video accounted for 10 percent of all traffic to FoxNews.com.[9]

But here's what to remember: that traffic wouldn't have occurred—the controversy wouldn't have so dominated the global political arena—if ISIS's news of Lieutenant Kasasbeh's death had been announced using mere words. The images mattered. The visuals—perhaps especially because of the professional production quality of the video—seized the public's attention, were discussed, were passed on to others. The pictures provided a synecdoche of meaning about what ISIS stood for. Social media—with the complicity of mainstream media—brought the inhumanity and the bravura of the lieutenant's execution to the mobile phones of anyone who cared to look.

It's near impossible for individuals and groups today to have their messages rise above the 24/7 flotsam of spam and clickbait and dreck that's out there on the Internet. But a group is more likely to have its agenda noticed if a singular photo or video emerges or is created.[10] As Shayan Sardarizadeh, a journalist at BBC Verify, has noted in his verifications tracking the Israel-Gaza war in the fall of 2023, "it's been really difficult to sift through what is actually genuine footage from what's been going on in Israel and Gaza, and what is either clickbait or unrelated footage or something that is being shared for clicks, engagement or any sort of nefarious intent."[11]

Terrorism is a form of asymmetric warfare; terrorists have long understood that visuals can be force multipliers—even if those photographs or videos are faked or misrepresented. The public still has that kneejerk response to believe that whatever a photograph or video is showing is *real*, whether what is pictures is a "raw" 9/11 photo taken by an eyewitness, or whether it's a photorealistic hallucination invented by a text-to-image AI app, or a propaganda video framed by terrorists or an authoritarian government. Extremists of all stripes know that in today's media environment dramatic images, GIFs and videos of the dead, dying, or injured can be reposted, liked, meme-d, and remixed, used to recruit the interested, rally the others, and strike fear into the rest. Opposition forces,

---

[9] "Islamic State Execution Seen by Millions on Fox News Website," *Wall Street Journal*, https://www.wsj.com/video/islamic-state-execution-seen-by-millions-on-fox-news-website/131DEB82-CB09-45C1-AC22-51037A89A819.html (accessed August 6, 2019).

[10] Rachel Shabi, "Muslims Don't Need Fox to Understand ISIL," https://www.aljazeera.com/opinions/2015/2/7/fox-news-muslims-dont-need-help-to-understand-isil (accessed October 2, 2023).

[11] "BBC Expert on Debunking Israel-Hamas War Visuals: 'The Volume of Misinformation on Twitter Was Beyond Anything I've Ever Seen,'" *Reuters Institute for the Study of Journalism*, https://reutersinstitute.politics.ox.ac.uk/news/bbc-expert-debunking-israel-hamas-war-visuals-volume-misinformation-twitter-was-beyond (accessed October 13, 2023).

too, understand that even allegations of heinous acts as "documented" by images can themselves go viral and become propaganda assets. As Snopes, the verification site, noted in its lengthy investigation of the charges that Hamas beheaded babies in the opening days of the Israel-Gaza war: "The alleged beheadings have been a focus of media attention, appearing in headlines and viral posts, and have been repeated by politicians at the highest levels of government."[12]

In 2015, ISIS in Jordan was the world's latest purveyor of horror porn—not the first, nor the last. For over 150 years, many Americans have proven themselves to be willing takers and spectators of photographs of the worst that can be done to their fellow humans—from the glass-plated photos of the bloated bodies of the Civil War dead of Antietam and Gettysburg taken by Mathew Brady, Alexander Gardner, and Timothy O'Sullivan, to the cartes de visite photos of the mutilated dead on the battlefields of the American Indian wars that late-nineteenth-century Americans back East purchased to gawk at in the comfort of their living rooms.[13] In the twentieth and twenty-first centuries too, Americans were perpetrators and spectators of horrors as recorded by photography: from the Jim Crow lynchings of Black men in the 1920s to the leaked photo documents that were published in 2004 of victims of American torture at Abu Ghraib prison.

In wartime and in times of violence and conflict, there have always been individuals and groups that have taken photos of the desecrated bodies of others. And when the photographers are themselves culpable in that violence, as they were at Abu Ghraib, for instance, the pictures are taken to serve specific needs: the need to believe that the victims are less human than the perpetrators themselves, the need to believe that the perpetrators themselves are more distinguished, and certainly more powerful, than the groups that the dead or victimized belong to. Perpetrators additionally have taken and disseminated images of violence to seduce recruits with evidence of their own power. Such images may also be taken to embolden the perpetrators to engage in egregious abuses because previous images give evidence of impunity. Such images may moreover be taken to tighten the group bonds of the perpetrators, to forestall possible defectors from leaking news of any transgression of social norms.

---

[12] "Were Israeli Babies Beheaded by Hamas Militants During Attack on KfarAza?," *Snopes*, https://www.snopes.com/news/2023/10/12/40-israeli-babies-beheaded-by-hamas/ (accessed October 13, 2023); and see also other verification sites: "Israeli official Says Government Cannot Confirm Babies Were Beheaded in Hamas Attack," *CNN.com*," https://www.cnn.com/2023/10/12/middleeast/israel-hamas-beheading-claims-intl/index.html (accessed October 13, 2023); and "'Beheaded Babies' Report Spread Wide and Fast—But Israel Military Won't Confirm It," *The Intercept*, https://theintercept.com/2023/10/11/israel-hamas-disinformation/ (accessed October 13, 2023).
[13] "Indian Wars," https://www.webpages.uidaho.edu/~rfrey/329indian_wars.htm (accessed October 7, 2023); and "Wikipedia: Featured Picture Candidates/The Mutilated Body of Sergeant Frederick Wyllyams," *Wikipedia*, February 8, 2023, https://en.wikipedia.org/w/index.php?title=Wikipedia:Featured_picture_candidates/The_multilated_body_of_Sergeant_Frederick_Wyllyams&oldid=1138152283.

II. (Social) Media as Amplifier

It was on September 11 that Americans most dramatically encountered the terrorism-publicity calculus. Osama bin Laden already knew of the calculus; that's why the World Trade Center towers and the other targets were selected. In a letter to the Taliban supreme commander, Mullah Mohammed Umar, bin Laden wrote: "It is obvious that the media war in this century is one of the strongest methods [of waging Jihad]; in fact, 90 percent of the preparation for war is effective use of the media."[14]

The morning of 9/11, the US news media inadvertently did more than cover the aftermath of a terrorist attack. The media became the next weapon of the terrorists. What was so diabolical was that Al Qaeda had planned the attacks so that the world would be watching live when the second, third, and fourth planes hit their targets. The first plane striking the World Trade Center would prompt every news outlet in Manhattan to train its cameras on the scene. And then, the terrorists knew, the TV cameras would still be running when the second plane struck the Twin Towers.

As it happened, the cameras not only captured the second attack, they continued to broadcast when, to the shock of the world—including Al Qaeda's—first one, then the other building imploded, with all the loss of life that their collapse implied.

Terrorism live, terrorism constructed so the world could watch, meant that Al Qaeda was not merely a passive beneficiary of the press reporting on the death and destruction. Al Qaeda shaped how media covered 9/11—and in so doing, they "branded" themselves as a global terrorist group, a branding that resulted in a much higher profile and, not coincidentally, a bump in recruits to the terrorists' cause.

The horror of that day in September 2001 went beyond the deaths of thousands; it encompassed the pit-in-the-stomach realization that the attacks had been preplanned to effect maximum casualties, in a place that was the most visible location in the most iconic city in the United States. It was not just the appalling numbers of the dead that changed the world that morning, it was the fact that the world saw the thousands die, in real time—and then again and again and again, as the highlights reels were replayed, that day, that month, that year, and on every anniversary since.[15] "Seeing" terrorism, in all its multivariate meanings,

---

[14] Letter to Mullah Muhammed 'Umar from Bin Laden, Combating Terrorism Center at West Point, https://ctc.westpoint.edu/harmony-program/letter-to-mullah-muhammed-umar-from-bin-laden-original-language-2/ (accessed October 4, 2023). An alternative translation of the second phrase is "its ratio may reach 90% of the total preparation for the battles." It is differently quoted by Williams, *supra* note 7.

[15] Parts of this section are adapted from my book: Susan Moeller, *Packaging Terrorism: Co-Opting the News for Politics and Profit* (Wiley-Blackwell, 2008).

politically, ethically, and morally, helped to shape and (re)shape the next decade of Americans' priorities on national security and foreign policy. "Seeing" terrorism shaped how terrorist and extremist groups understood their remit, causing them to mobilize not just front-line volunteers and tactical strategists, but media and communication experts.

"Jihadists and right-wing extremists use remarkably similar social media strategies." That striking sentence was the subhead to a *New York Times* editorial in the Sunday newspaper before the US holiday of Thanksgiving in November 2018.[16] Terrorists, the late Prof. Paul Wilkinson observed, "thrive on the oxygen of publicity."[17] They also learn the trade and find common cause and fellow travelers on the internet—both on the Dark Web and on those social media sites that regular citizens use to keep up with the Kardashians and share their own travel photos, news of their children's graduations, and videos of their cats' antics.[18]

In short, the internet, taken in all its quotidian murkiness, facilitates both the community-building of everyday people and that of violent extremists. "The fundamental design of social media," wrote the *New York Times* editors, "rewards loyalty to one's own group, providing a dopamine rush of engagement that fuels platforms like Facebook and YouTube, as well as more obscure sites like Gab or Voat. The algorithms that underpin these networks also promote engaging content, in a feedback loop that, link by link, guides new audiences to toxic ideas."[19]

"Social media is not the cause of violent extremism," wrote Shannon Green and Keith Proctor in a report for the Center for Strategic and International Studies, "but a powerful amplifier and accelerant. Digital platforms and increased access to smart phones and internet connectivity help facilitate radicalization and recruitment.... The widespread use of social media has also made violent extremists' plans more difficult to disrupt. Security agencies have to track a much larger number of potential plotters, giving terrorists more space to plan large, complex operations against a higher background level of activity."[20] Or as the *Times*' editors briefly summarized their takeaway: "This is the new shape of extremism: self-directed, internet-inflamed terrorists."[21]

---

[16] The Editorial Board, "Opinion | The New Radicalization of the Internet," *New York Times*, November 24, 2018, https://www.nytimes.com/2018/11/24/opinion/sunday/facebook-twitter-terrorism-extremism.html (accessed October 7, 2023).

[17] Paul Wilkinson, "The Media and Terrorism: A Reassessment," *Terrorism and Political Violence*, 9, no. 2 (June 1, 1997), 51–64, https://doi.org/10.1080/09546559708427402 (accessed October 7, 2023).

[18] "What Is the Dark Web and Should You Access It?," *Investopedia*, https://www.investopedia.com/terms/d/dark-web.asp (accessed October 2, 2023).

[19] The Editorial Board, *supra* note 16.

[20] Shannon N. Green & Keith Proctor, "Turning Point: A New Comprehensive Strategy for Countering Violent Extremism," November 2016, https://csis-ilab.github.io/cve/report/Turning_Point.pdf (accessed October 7, 2023).

[21] The Editorial Board, *supra* note 16.

Four months after that *New York Times* editorial, a terrorist attack in Christchurch, New Zealand, became another signal case. On Friday, March 15, 2019, a gunman opened fire during Friday prayers at the Al Noor Mosque, then left to continue his attack at the Linwood Islamic Centre, ultimately killing fifty-one people and injuring forty-nine.

Prior to the attack, the shooter had teased his upcoming assault on Twitter (later X). Then, at the mosque, he filmed his own attack and live-streamed it to Facebook—a livestream that he had publicized shortly before in a post on the /pol/section of (now former) 8chan, a message board popular with the alt-right. During the livestream, others avidly shared his video, as well as still photos, GIFs, and memes they created from his footage of the shooting. Facebook and Twitter ultimately deleted the gunman's page and profile, but social media had already spread his message. YouTube, Twitter, and Reddit scrambled to take down the proliferating versions on their sites but couldn't keep up with the replicating copies. And some mainstream news sites and broadcasters chose to air excerpts of the gunman's GoPro video in their online and TV news coverage—including Rupert Murdoch's Australian pay-TV channel Sky News.

Back in the previous November, the *New York Times* editorial had noted that a "coherent strategy" did not yet exist for countering violent extremism and domestic terrorism facilitated online. Christchurch made public that lack—but it shouldn't have taken a tragedy of that magnitude. The lack of a strategy to counter terrorists' use of the internet had already been apparent—all it took was a consideration of the global statistics on terrorism and violent extremism. In the United States alone, as the *Times* observed, right-wing extremists, especially white supremacists, "have been responsible for the vast majority of at least 387 domestic terrorist murders in the last decade."[22] And over that decade, their diatribes, hateful memes, photos of their rallies, and videos of their speeches had been circulating online, gathering global attention and followers and stymying efforts to limit their reach.

"Seeing" the terrorism of 9/11 unfold on live TV shaped the next generation of media. The corollary to Wilkinson's observation that publicity as well as death and destruction are terrorists' stock in trade is that media also need and want the public's attention. Across platforms, media hustle to push out stories on tragedies. Mainstream media understand that morally and ethically repugnant events and people are the ultimate in "newsworthiness." Social media engagement also rises following the horrors of terrorist attacks. The Christchurch attacks also made plain how the business models of social media can facilitate those communities and that behavior that feed on fear and hate.

---

[22] *Id.*

III. Seeing Matters

Two decades after the 9/11 attacks, in the aftermath of the January 6, 2020, attacks on the US Capitol and the worst of the COVID-19 pandemic, a majority of Americans had become skeptical of the news they received on social media. In 2022, the Pew Research Center found that 59 percent of Americans felt that any news coming via social media was "largely inaccurate."[23] To further confirm Americans' perception of the problem: 70 percent considered the spread of false information online to be a major threat to the country. To put that number in context, only 54 percent in the same survey believed that climate change was a top threat to the country.[24] In short, Americans have not been oblivious to the crisis of fake news; indeed, according to Pew, by 2022 Americans were much more likely than those of the nineteen other democratic countries Pew surveyed to say that social media has been bad for democracy—64 percent of the Americans said they saw "ill effects of social media on the political system."[25]

It is deeply troubling that two-thirds of Americans believe that social media is undermining American democracy—not because social media isn't by many measures a civic danger, but because the average American spends over seven hours a day online and two and a quarter hours of that on social media.[26] That seeming conundrum—that Americans spend the equivalent of thirty-four days on social media a year, yet believe the platforms are undermining the very political system in which they live—is indicative of the complicated relationship that Americans have had with social media. Two decades after 9/11, half of US adults get their news from social media, according to Pew—a third from Facebook, a quarter from YouTube, and more from other social platforms, including X (formerly known as Twitter) (14%), Instagram (13%), TikTok (10%), and Reddit (8%).[27] And the consequence is, as Pew dryly observed: "Americans who get news mainly on social media are less knowledgeable and less engaged." What Pew meant was this: "U.S. adults who mainly get their political news through

---

[23] "Social Media and News Fact Sheet," *Pew Research Center's Journalism Project* (blog), https://www.pewresearch.org/journalism/fact-sheet/social-media-and-news-fact-sheet/ (accessed October 6, 2023).

[24] Sara Atske, "Climate Change Remains Top Global Threat Across 19-Country Survey," *Pew Research Center's Global Attitudes Project* (blog), August 31, 2022, https://www.pewresearch.org/global/2022/08/31/climate-change-remains-top-global-threat-across-19-country-survey/ (accessed October 6, 2023).

[25] Shannon Greenwood, "Social Media Seen as Mostly Good for Democracy Across Many Nations, But U.S. Is a Major Outlier," *Pew Research Center's Global Attitudes Project* (blog), December 6, 2022, https://www.pewresearch.org/global/2022/12/06/social-media-seen-as-mostly-good-for-democracy-across-many-nations-but-u-s-is-a-major-outlier/ (accessed October 6, 2023).

[26] Rebecca Moody, "Screen Time Statistics: Average in the US vs. Rest of the World," *Comparitech* (blog), June 8, 2021, https://www.comparitech.com/tv-streaming/screen-time-statistics/ (accessed October 7, 2023).

[27] "Social Media and News Fact Sheet," *supra* note 23.

social media tend to be less engaged with news. They follow the news less closely, and they tend to be less knowledgeable on a wide range of current events and broad political-knowledge questions about the U.S."[28]

It's difficult, if not impossible to be certain about cause and effect, but several possibilities occur. One is that the very elements that made the video of the death of the Jordanian pilot go viral also encourage the spread of mis- and disinformation on social media. "Due to the reward-based learning systems on social media, users form habits of sharing information that gets recognition from others," wrote researchers in the proceedings of the National Academy of Sciences. The algorithms of most platforms incentivize users for watching, liking, and forwarding content likely to get others to do the same. "Once habits form, information sharing is automatically activated by cues on the platform without users considering critical response outcomes, such as spreading misinformation." As Wendy Wood, a researcher at USC, succinctly summarized: "[Misinformation is] really a function of the structure of the social media sites themselves."[29]

Social media are not only facilitating the spread of mis- and disinformation, as the Jordanian pilot video made plain, social media with visuals—videos, gifs, photos, memes, and the like—are what are passed on most often. Users engage more with photos and video and graphics than with other forms of media and do so at scale. Consider the global statistics: with roughly three billion monthly active users as of the second quarter of 2023, Facebook was the world's most visited online social network. Its audience and those of other social media platforms dwarf countries and even regions in scale. By July 2023, YouTube had 2.5 billion logged-in users visit its site each month, Instagram had 2 billion, TikTok over 1 billion, Twitter (X) over 560 million, and Pinterest over 460 million—and four of those, YouTube, Instagram, TikTok, and Pinterest, are visual-first and heavily video-dependent media.[30] Even Pinterest, which in 2023 was the world's fourteenth largest social network and grew up as a site for still images, has a growing video focus: users watch close to one billion videos a day on the site.[31] Users are skewing toward engaging with video above all else: by the end of 2022, video

---

[28] "Americans Who Get News Mainly on Social Media Are Less Knowledgeable and Less Engaged," November 16, 2020, https://pew.org/3jSxn4L (accessed October 6, 2023).

[29] David Medzerian, "Study Reveals Key Reason Why Fake News Spreads on Social Media," *USC Today* (blog), January 17, 2023, https://today.usc.edu/usc-study-reveals-the-key-reason-why-fake-news-spreads-on-social-media/ (accessed October 6, 2023).

[30] "We Are Social & Meltwater (2023)," *Global Social Media Statistics*, https://datareportal.com/social-media-users (accessed October 4, 2023).

[31] Hannah Macready, "38 Pinterest Stats That Matter to Marketers in 2023," *Social Media Marketing & Management Dashboard* (blog), February 23, 2023, https://blog.hootsuite.com/pinterest-statistics-for-business/ (accessed October 8, 2023).

accounted for 65 percent of all internet traffic, and data usage from video sites had increased by 24 percent year over year.[32]

The lesson from all that is self-evident—for citizens, for tech companies, for public policy experts, as well as for terrorists and other bad actors. Visual content has come to dominate social media. And only a minimal encounter with visuals is needed for their influence to be felt. Seeing matters online. *That* means that in the realm of national security, the government, the military, regional experts, academics, and Silicon Valley and its ilk all need to track *and understand the implications of* an exponentially growing number and variety of images. As the internet has turned visual, making sense of what's online increasingly means making sense of images.

The dramatic turn toward visual communication has precipitated inquiries across fields: among entrepreneurs interested in monetizing how we construct our visual identity, art historians interested in changing presentations of the self, journalists interested in using visual technologies to bring scenes of the world to their audiences, philosophers interested in unpacking the inclinations of the mind, and neuroscientists interested in unraveling the secrets of the brain. Indeed, neurologists have helped unpack why the internet has evolved from an all-text environment into one where visuals dominate. We're hardwired to prefer *seeing* our information. "Half of the human brain is devoted directly or indirectly to vision," observed Mriganka Sur, Newton Professor of Neuroscience and Director of the Simons Center for the Social Brain at MIT.[33] And John Medina, developmental molecular biologist and *New York Times* best-selling author of *Brain Rules*, noted that "[w]hen people hear information, they're likely to remember only 10% of that information three days later. However, if a relevant image is paired with that same information, people retained 65% of the information three days later."[34]

But *seeing* matters not just because our brains are skewed to visuals. *What we see* and *what we do about what we see* have become preoccupations in part because seeing remains—even in our manipulated, AI, and deepfaked world—a linguistic synonym for knowledge and understanding: "I see what you are saying." As a poster on X (Twitter) argued in a thread about images circulating online of babies being killed in the Israel-Gaza war in 2023: "Everyone saying

---

[32] "In 2022, 65% of All Internet Traffic Came from Video Sites," *Tubefilter* (blog), January 20, 2023, https://www.tubefilter.com/2023/01/20/sandvine-video-data-bandwidth-internet-traffic-report-streaming-video-youtube-netflix/ (accessed October 6, 2023).

[33] "MIT Research—Brain Processing of Visual Information," *MIT News | Massachusetts Institute of Technology*, December 19, 1996, https://news.mit.edu/1996/visualprocessing (accessed October 4, 2023).

[34] "Brain Rules: 12 Principles for Surviving and Thriving at Work, Home, and School—John Medina—Google Books," https://books.google.fr/books/about/Brain_Rules.html?id=G_GbZ 6rDUrsC&redir_esc=y (accessed August 6, 2019).

they can't look.... Stop abdicating your responsibility to acknowledge the truth and take a stand." As photographer Shahidul Alam, one of *Time* magazine's 2018 Persons of the Year, has said: "The reality still is: people do believe photographs. Photographs are used as evidence; photographs are used to validate things. And photographs, particularly in the age of social media, increase engagement, they increase reach."[35]

IV. Images and Cybersecurity

Sundar Pichai, the CEO of Google, said as early as 2017, that Google was now an "AI-first company."[36] The *Economist* similarly observed in a Leader article that same year: "The world's most valuable resource is no longer oil, but data.... [Even] industrial giants such as GE and Siemens now sell themselves as data firms."[37] Most early AI systems were trained to reason via mathematical and logical operations. Today's proliferating AI systems perform visual operations, too, such as rotating and layering images, evaluating patterns, identifying objects, and performing facial recognition. AI's ability to create realistic images and videos has superseded what Hollywood blockbusters have accomplished with CGI technology. Ian Goodfellow, a research scientist at Google DeepMind, Google's lab for AI and artificial general intelligence (AGI) systems, helped advance the field by creating "generative adversarial networks" (GANs): "systems that create photos, sounds, and other representations of the real world." GANs began by setting "a generative network in competition with an image-recognition network, to help both networks improve their performance." In essence, both sides of the network were coded to learn from each other: one side, the generative side, was coded to create images, and the other, the image-recognition side, to evaluate images. According to Yann LeCun, the head of Facebook's AI team in New York City, GANs were "the coolest idea in deep learning in the last 20 years."[38]

But how does one protect the country and the world from bad actors doing bad things—like weaponizing AI in "influence campaigns"?

---

[35] Author interview with Shahidul Alam, Salzburg, Austria, July 17, 2019.
[36] Cade Metz, "Sundar Pichai Sees Google's Future in the Smartest Cloud," *Wired*, https://www.wired.com/2017/05/sundar-pichai-sees-googles-future-smartest-cloud/ (accessed October 7, 2023).
[37] "The World's Most Valuable Resource Is No Longer Oil, but Data," *The Economist*, https://www.economist.com/leaders/2017/05/06/the-worlds-most-valuable-resource-is-no-longer-oil-but-data?fsrc=scn%2Ftw%2Fte%2Frfd%2Fpe (accessed October 7, 2023).
[38] Cade Metz, "Google's Dueling Neural Networks Spar to Get Smarter, No Humans Required," *Wired*, https://www.wired.com/2017/04/googles-dueling-neural-networks-spar-get-smarter-no-humans-required/ (accessed October 7, 2023).

Influence campaigns—they don't sound so bad. But the rather benign-sounding term shares similarities with other national security euphemisms such as "nuclear deterrent," "surgical strike," "collateral damage." Each obfuscates the real meaning of the words: each of those is a reference to a tactic that by itself, or in conjunction with other actions, targets an enemy's vital locations and essential institutions and may well cause injury and/or death. An influence campaign that includes the use of AI and deepfakes might also be doing more than it sounds like: it may work to alter the outcome of an election, threaten the stability of the stock market, or trigger military action.

AI and its twin, cybersecurity, are the future—and the present—of national defense and deterrence. The Russia-Ukraine war, for example, has been the first conflict where AI-enhanced facial recognition software has been used on a substantial scale. Ukraine's defense ministry used Clearview AI's software to "identify dead soldiers and to uncover Russian assailants and combat misinformation."[39] In a cyber-arms race, AI systems can generate cyberattacks and defend against them, as well as support operations by, for example, translating satellite imagery into live intelligence valuable for understanding troop movements, identifying targets, and making damage assessments.

Outside the ground fighting, defense experts expect AI to trigger more and more personal data thefts, epidemics of computer viruses, network penetrations, and deepfakes.

However, as the Israel-Gaza war showed, it doesn't always take deepfakes to mislead the public. As the BBC's Sardarizadeh noted in the opening week of the conflict—a conflict where "the volume of misinformation on Twitter [X] was beyond anything I've ever seen": "I have not seen a single deep fake. There have been a few AI-generated false images, but they were not that good." He further explained, "We saw the same thing with Ukraine. In the first two months of the Ukraine war, there was a deluge of misinformation online and plenty of old videos. So that's definitely the number one category. But there are also videos that are genuine but taken out of context."[40]

In other words, it doesn't always take the most sophisticated technology or campaign to manipulate audiences. Bad actors continue to use old animation techniques, for example, that date back to the mid-twentieth century. Consider two sets of famous cartoons characters: Road Runner and Wile E. Coyote, who started chasing each other in 1949, and Alvin and the Chipmunks, the three lovable rodents who have been familiar radio, TV, and movie stars since 1958. Both cartoon series tapped into a very simple production technique: animators

---

[39] "Ukraine a Living Lab for AI Warfare," *National Defense Magazine*, https://www.nationaldefensemagazine.org/articles/2023/3/24/ukraine-a-living-lab-for-ai-warfare (accessed October 8, 2023).

[40] "BBC Expert on Debunking Israel-Hamas War Visuals," *supra* note 11.

playing with speeding up or slowing down the cartoon audio and film. In the Road Runner and Wile E. Coyote cartoons, that moment during every chase sequence when the coyote runs off the cliff and hangs in midair for several long slo-mo seconds before realizing Road Runner has foiled him again has been a longtime crowd-pleaser. And Alvin and the Chipmunks' immediately recognizable high-pitched voices came to be because the actor who first read their lines and sang their songs had the inspiration to speed up the voices' playback.

Sixty-one years later, in the spring of 2019, using technology not-so-far-advanced in concept, a video of the then US Speaker of the House, Democrat Nancy Pelosi, went viral when a clip of her speaking at a news conference was slowed down. But unlike Alvin and the squeaky Chipmunks, Pelosi's voice in the doctored video was pitch-corrected, so her voice didn't deepen in a telltale way. The manipulation of the Pelosi video, however, was not for entertainment but for political effect.[41] The doctored video was part of an influence campaign. Millions of viewers who saw it first on a pro-Trump Facebook page and then reposted on YouTube and Twitter quickly commented that Pelosi's apparent slurring of her words in the slowed-down video meant she was either drunk or mentally incapacitated.[42] The original caption—"It was very, very, very strange"—obliquely nudged other Facebook commentators into seeing the video as "real." One called Pelosi an "alcoholic old hag"; another queried: "Good Lord lady . . . How many drinks did you have today?"; and a third asked: "Omg is she drunk or having a stroke???"

The juvenile Facebook trolling was perhaps par for the course. But as *New York Times* technology opinion writer Charlie Warzel noted, "the Pelosi fakes weren't newsworthy because they were high-tech, but because the lie [that Pelosi was drunk or incapacitated] was so blatant and spread by powerful individuals."[43]

---

[41] "Kellyanne Conway Defends 'Sped Up' Jim Acosta Video: Occurs 'All the Time in Sports,'" *HuffPost*, November 11, 2018, https://www.huffpost.com/entry/kellyanne-conway-jim-acosta-video_n_5be84f8de4b0e84388990d55 (accessed October 7, 2023). The case of the doctored Pelosi video was not far different than an earlier case from November 2018. As the *Washington Post* reported:

When Fox News' Chris Wallace asked why White House press secretary Sarah Huckabee Sanders tweeted the "clearly altered" video [showing CNN reporter Jim Acosta's interaction with a White House intern during a press conference with President Trump], [White House adviser Kellyanne] Conway downplayed the video's manipulation.

"By that do you mean sped up?" Conway asked. "That's not altered. That's sped up. They do it all the time in sports to see if there's actually a first down or a touchdown."

"I have to disagree with the overwrought description of this video being doctored as if we put someone else's arm in there," she added.

[42] Kevin Poulsen, "We Found the Guy Behind the Viral 'Drunk Pelosi' Video," *Daily Beast*, June 1, 2019, https://www.thedailybeast.com/we-found-shawn-brooks-the-guy-behind-the-viral-drunk-pelosi-video (accessed October 7, 2023).

[43] Charlie Warzel, "Opinion | The Fake Nancy Pelosi Video Hijacked Our Attention. Just as Intended," *New York Times*, May 26, 2019, https://www.nytimes.com/2019/05/26/opinion/nancy-pelosi-video-facebook.html (accessed October 7, 2023).

The video lie had been given credence by President Donald Trump's personal lawyer, Rudolph Giuliani, who tweeted—and later deleted—a link to the doctored video with the caption, "What is wrong with Nancy Pelosi? Her speech pattern is bizarre."[44] And in that same news cycle, President Trump himself tweeted out "PELOSI STAMMERS THROUGH NEWS CONFERENCE"—his tweet copying word for word the crawl underneath a brief Fox News clip from the *Lou Dobbs Tonight* show that cobbled together sound bites from Pelosi's twenty-minute news conference where she had stumbled on words.[45]

Not long after the doctored Facebook video went viral, online and TV news outlets identified it as fake, often running the faked video side by side with the real footage from the news conference.[46] As it turned out, on that occasion, uncovering the malicious manipulation of the Pelosi video was easy. Less clear, as Warzel noted, was how to solve social media's systemic problems made evident by the manipulated video:

> Facebook, the platform of origin for this [Pelosi] video, did exactly what it was designed to do. It brought people with similar interests together, incubated vibrant communities that spawned intense discussion and then gave those communities the tools to amplify their messages loudly across the internet. The rest of the social media ecosystem followed suit....
>
> The mainstream media, designed to document controversy and separate fact from fiction, picked up the story with the best of intentions.... The press identified a story, fact-checked and pointed audiences at the truth. Straight out of the journalism school handbooks.
>
> But if the last few years have taught us anything, it's that you don't bring a handbook to an information war. The distribution mechanics, rules and terms of service of Facebook's platform—and the rest of social media—are no match for professional propagandists, trolls, charlatans, political operatives and hostile foreign actors looking to sow division and blur the lines of reality.[47]

---

[44] Sarah Mervosh, "Distorted Videos of Nancy Pelosi Spread on Facebook and Twitter, Helped by Trump," *New York Times*, May 24, 2019, https://www.nytimes.com/2019/05/24/us/politics/pelosi-doctored-video.html (accessed October 7, 2023); and "Aaron Blake on Twitter: '.@RudyGiuliani Has Apparently Deleted This Tweet in Which He Shared an Obviously Slowed down Video of Nancy Pelosi Https://T.Co/Y1w9TyN7Za' / Twitter," Tweet, *Twitter*. https://twitter.com/aaronblake/status/1131734771518910465 (accessed August 6, 2019).

[45] Donald J. Trump [@realDonaldTrump], "'Pelosi Stammers Through News Conference' Https://T.Co/1OyCyqRTuk," Tweet, *Twitter*, May 24, 2019, https://twitter.com/realDonaldTrump/status/1131728912835383300 (accessed October 7, 2023).

[46] Drew Harwell, "Faked Pelosi Videos, Slowed to Make Her Appear Drunk, Spread across Social Media," *Washington Post*, May 24, 2019, https://www.washingtonpost.com/technology/2019/05/23/faked-pelosi-videos-slowed-make-her-appear-drunk-spread-across-social-media/ (accessed October 7, 2023); and "A Video of House Speaker Nancy Pelosi Was Manipulated to Slow down Her Speech/X," *X* (formerly Twitter), May 24, 2019, https://twitter.com/i/events/1131993009824776192 (accessed October 7, 2023).

[47] Warzel, *supra* note 43.

In fact, not only does one not bring a handbook to an information war, if one were to exist, it is hard to conceive of that reference source staying relevant for long. While the social media titans regularly transmogrify their hardware and software and contend with ever-shifting political environments, so too do "professional propagandists, trolls, charlatans, political operatives and hostile foreign actors." The Pelosi video was not a deepfake in the grand scheme of things: it was a quick and crude effort to slander a politician. But the threat posed by the video was not benign because it came in a simple package.

But although low-tech disinformation campaigns continue to be prevalent, what the defense industry is girding against is the greater harm that can be unleashed with AI in the arsenal. As Daniel Coats, the Director of National Intelligence, early wrote in his 2019 annual report to the US Senate Select Committee on Intelligence: "Adversaries and strategic competitors probably will attempt to use deep fakes or similar machine-learning technologies to create convincing—but false—image, audio, and video files to augment influence campaigns directed against the United States and our allies and partners."[48]

The world has trusted in photographic technologies for almost 200 years. That's a core reason why "deepfakes" are such a threat. "Deepfakes" is a portmanteau combining "fake" with the phrase "deep learning"—deep learning is the engine on which Silicon Valley runs. Deepfakes attack more than an individual or a group. They threaten the credibility of authorities. They threaten our belief in what we see. As the US Department of Defense (DOD) has defined the term: "Deepfakes are AI-generated, highly realistic synthetic media that can be abused to: Threaten an organization's brand; Impersonate leaders and financial officers; Enable access to networks, communications, and sensitive information."[49] The DOD summarized in the fall of 2023: "Threats from synthetic media, such as deepfakes, present a growing challenge for all users of modern technology and communications, including National Security Systems (NSS), the Department of Defense (DoD), the Defense Industrial Base (DIB), and national critical infrastructure owners and operators." The DOD traced the multiplying threats: "Synthetic media threats broadly exist across technologies associated with the use of text, video, audio, and images which are used for a variety of purposes online and in conjunction with communications of all types." AI has given powerful tools to American "adversaries": "the market is now flooded with

---

[48] Daniel Coats, "Statement for the Record: 2019 Worldwide Threat Assessment of the U.S. Intelligence Community," 2019, https://www.dni.gov/index.php/newsroom/congressional-testimonies/congressional-testimonies-2019/3293-statement-for-the-record-worldwide-threat-assessment-of-the-us-intelligence-community-1692377354 (accessed October 7, 2023).

[49] "Contextualizing Deepfake Threats to Organizations," U.S. Department of Defense (.gov) | National Security Agency, Federal Bureau of Investigation, Cybersecurity and Infrastructure Security Agency, September 12, 2023, Cybersecurity Information Sheet, https://media.defense.gov/2023/Sep/12/2003298925/-1/-1/0/CSI-DEEPFAKE-THREATS.PDF (accessed October 7, 2023).

free, easily accessible tools (some powered by deep learning algorithms) that make the creation or manipulation of multimedia essentially plug-and-play. As a result, these publicly available techniques have increased in value and become widely available tools for adversaries of all types, enabling fraud and disinformation to exploit targeted individuals and organizations. The democratization of these tools has made the list of top risks for 2023."[50]

In 2021, after widely disseminated deepfakes videos of Ukrainian President Volodymyr Zelenskyy, a directive in the National Defense Authorization Act instructed the Pentagon to complete an "intelligence assessment of the threat posed by foreign government and non-state actors creating or using machine-manipulated media (commonly referred to as 'deep fakes')," including "how such media has been used or might be used to conduct information warfare."[51] Iyad Rahwan, director of the Max Planck Institute for Human Development in Berlin, noted when he was a professor at MIT's Media Lab, that defending against such attacks necessitated a concerted effort by a broad swath of actors. It's not enough to have the greatest computer minds investing in AI systems: "[E]veryone crucial to protecting the public interest" needs to be "in the control loop of these systems . . . technologists, engineers, the public, ethicists, cognitive scientists, economists, legal scholars, anthropologists, faith leaders, government regulators."[52]

Why all of those? In large measure, because AI technology—especially including its near obliteration of trust in images—intrudes on so many disciplines. "AI could be as big a disruptor to the world as the Industrial Revolution was in the 18th and 19th centuries," Rahwan argued.[53] But an additional reason why "everyone" can and should be in the room is because AI has become "simpler"—all can use it and create with it. That means the dangers are far, far greater because there are far, far more people who can generate credible disrupting images.

The evergreen challenge, then, as Joi Ito, the former director of MIT's Media Lab, phrased it, is: "How can we best initiate a broader, in-depth discussion about how society will co-evolve with this technology, and connect computer science and social sciences to develop intelligent machines that are not only 'smart,' but also socially responsible?"

There are many follow-on questions, and few answers to Ito's question. Even well before the COVID-19 pandemic accelerated concerns about social

---

[50] Id.
[51] Sam Biddle, "U.S. Special Forces Want to Use Deepfakes for Psy-Ops," *The Intercept*, March 6, 2023, https://theintercept.com/2023/03/06/pentagon-socom-deepfake-propaganda/ (accessed October 8, 2023).
[52] "MIT Media Lab to Participate in $27 Million Initiative on AI Ethics and Governance," *MIT News | Massachusetts Institute of Technology*, January 10, 2017, https://news.mit.edu/2017/mit-media-lab-to-participate-in-ai-ethics-and-governance-initiative-0110 (accessed October 4, 2023).
[53] Id.

responsibility, there was general recognition that existential concerns needed to be considered alongside AI research. Ito's lab, for example, together with the Berkman Klein Center for Internet and Society at Harvard, received $27 million in early 2017 to create the Ethics and Governance of Artificial Intelligence Fund.[54] Roughly five years later, the proliferating AI and large language model (LLM) platforms and tools created in academic and corporate labs were ready for prime time. ChatGPT launched to the public on November 30, 2022; it reached 100 million users in two months. On July 20, 2022, DALL-E 2 entered into a beta phase, with invitations sent to 1 million waitlisted individuals, and by a year later, more than 1.5 million users were actively creating over 2 million images a day.[55] A year after that, the *Wall Street Journal* declared in an only slightly over-the-top headline: "Reality Is Broken. We Have AI Photos to Blame."[56]

With the launch of chatbots and generative-AI image platforms, creating deepfakes has become exponentially easier. And as the multimodal LLMs make transformative leaps with each new release, the problems of identifying deepfakes, or even pictures of faces of people that never existed, become ever more whack-a-mole difficult and, for most use-cases, effectively impossible. Even if ninety-nine deepfake moles are successfully whacked (an unlikely record) as they pop up on social media, a hundredth deepfake will slip through to create havoc.[57] And even beyond the specific repercussions of that one deepfake, the survival and spread of any deepfakes, argued Jeffrey McGregor, the CEO of Truepic, a California image-verification company, means that "[s]ociety is going to start distrusting every piece of content they see."[58]

An entire new industry has been birthed to address the growing crisis of distrust: image verification is one approach being tried. McGregor's company together with a number of others, such as Adobe's Content Authenticity Initiative, and Project Origin, a coalition of the BBC, CBC/Radio-Canada, *The New York Times*, and Microsoft, are working on provenance of digital content technologies

---

[54] *Id.* Ito's creation of an Ethics fund took on an ironic cast after news media investigations showed that Ito and other Lab staff continued to accept contributions from convicted sex offender Jeffrey Epstein after Epstein was blacklisted from the university's official donor database. Ito and others actively tried to conceal where the donations came from. Ito resigned from the MIT Media Lab in September 2019, https://www.bbc.com/news/world-us-canada-49623084 (accessed June 28, 2024).

[55] "DALL·E Now Available in Beta," https://openai.com/blog/dall-e-now-available-in-beta (accessed October 4, 2023).

[56] Joanna Stern, "Reality Is Broken. We Have AI Photos to Blame," *Wall Street Journal*, May 26, 2023, https://www.wsj.com/articles/reality-is-broken-we-have-ai-photos-to-blame-de00b23 (accessed October 7, 2023).

[57] Brian Klaas, "Opinion | Deepfakes Are Coming. We're Not Ready," *Washington Post*, May 14, 2019, https://www.washingtonpost.com/opinions/2019/05/14/deepfakes-are-coming-were-not-ready/ (accessed October 7, 2023).

[58] Abigail Summerville, "'Deepfakes' Trigger a Race to Fight Manipulated Photos and Videos," *Wall Street Journal*, July 27, 2019, https://www.wsj.com/articles/deepfakes-trigger-a-race-to-fight-manipulated-photos-and-videos-11564225200 (accessed October 7, 2023).

to permanently mark photos and videos at the moment of their creation with date and location signatures—one method embeds geotagged data of specific cell phone towers or GPS satellites.[59] Others are taking a forensic, postcreation approach to verification, checking preexisting images and videos for anomalies in facial expressions, light, or pixels. Still others are looking to fact-check the content and context shared in images—how are the eyes blinking, is there the right kind of glare on someone's glasses, what do the natural physics of the lighting tell viewers? While many deepfake detectors evaluate a video's raw data, others look for such tells, as the signs of blood flow in a video's pixels of a face. Said Intel about its FakeCatcher technology, part of the chipmaker's responsible AI work: "Blood flow signals are collected from all over the face and algorithms translate these signals into spatiotemporal maps. Then, using deep learning, we can instantly detect whether a video is real or fake."[60] Others doubt that audiences will "be able to tell how manipulated a photo is, what parts are real or fake." The *Wall Street Journal* argued that "our ability to spot true photos might depend on the cooperation of the entire internet."[61] Matt Turek, program director for MediFor (short for "media forensics") at the US Defense Department's Defense Advanced Research Projects Agency, agreed: "I don't think there's one silver bullet algorithm or even technical solution" to discovering deepfakes. "There probably needs to be a holistic approach."[62]

To keep up with AI's increasing capabilities—capabilities that will overtake humans' in arguably all domains of performance—journalists and philosophers are needed to join industry engineers and military strategists in contemplating the essentially infinite combinations of intelligence and goals in AI systems. That intelligence and those goals might be proactively introduced into an AI system design by governments, corporations, terrorists, or sociopaths, or even introduced later through hacking.

The challenge is great: "Until recently," philosopher Regina Rini has said, "video evidence functioned more or less like perception. Most of the time, you could trust that a camera captured roughly what you would have seen with your own eyes. So if you trust your own perception, you have nearly as much reason to trust the video.... Now, with the emergence of deepfake technology, the ability to produce convincing fake video will be almost as widespread as the ability to lie.... [W]e ought to think of images as more like testimony than perception. In

---

[59] Regina Rini, "Opinion | Deepfakes Are Coming. We Can No Longer Believe What We See," *New York Times*, June 10, 2019, https://www.nytimes.com/2019/06/10/opinion/deepfake-pelosi-video.html (accessed October 7, 2023).

[60] Vish Gain, "Intel's New AI Can Detect Deepfakes with 96pc Accuracy," *Silicon Republic*, November 17, 2022, https://www.siliconrepublic.com/machines/intel-deepfake-detector-fakecatcher-ai (accessed October 7, 2023).

[61] *Id.*

[62] Summerville, *supra* note 58.

other words, you should only trust a recording if you would trust the word of the person producing it."[63]

That's the nub of this national-security reciprocal-circularity problem: we are living in a world where images are casually accepted as truthful and used as legal and journalistic evidence, (especially when there is a chain of custody), but also living in a world where images can't be trusted. We need to radically update our ways of thinking about images and consider them as carefully as we do words. Images can show a "truth" or an "hallucination" or be a "deepfake." Images may be AI, miscaptioned, redacted and censored, misleadingly cropped, reframed, and repurposed. They can report on what's unseen and uncover what needs to be learned. When journalists take photos, they are protected by the First Amendment. When trolls unleash them, the visuals can be the levers to take down democratic institutions.

What more is there to do?

We need to be more aware of the reach and power of images, including their power as weapons. "Ironically," as an article in *Harvard Business Review* argued, "our best hope to defend against AI-enabled hacking is by using AI."[64] Democracies depend on a free flow of information communicated via words and images. We must safeguard that flow as well as consider our trust in that information.

The weaponization of images is a policy issue, a security issue, and a social/philosophical issue. What kind of seismic shift is needed for everyone to think of photographic images critically, to consider them, say, as opinions rather than facts? In this brave new world, the likelihood that we the public can shift our thinking is low, but the consequences if we fail to critically evaluate images could be catastrophic.

[63] Rini, *supra* note 59.
[64] Roman V. Yampolskiy, "AI Is the Future of Cybersecurity, for Better and for Worse," *Harvard Business Review*, May 8, 2017, https://hbr.org/2017/05/ai-is-the-future-of-cybersecurity-for-better-and-for-worse (accessed October 7, 2023).

Index

For the benefit of digital users, indexed terms that span two pages (e.g., 52–53) may, on occasion, appear on only one of those pages.

Note: Tables and figures are indicated by an italic *t* and *f* following the page number.

Abd-Ali, Mohammed "Moosa," 189–90, 191
Abu Ghraib prison, 305
active military operations intelligence, 93
Adelson, Sheldon, 153
adversarial journalism, 68–69, 76–77, 83
AggregateIQ, 170–71
Agnew, Spiro, 252
Ailes, Roger, 240–41
Albright, Jonathan, 174
Albury, Terry, 139
algorithmic censorship, xxx, 246–47, 278, 280–81, 298
algorithmic gatekeepers, xxx, 279–83
al-Kasasbeh, Moaz, 301–5
Al Qaeda, 306
American Civil Liberties Union, 99–100
American Israel Public Affairs Committee (AIPAC), 115–16
anonymous sources, 76–77, 101, 136–37, 138, 146, 154, 269
anti-press politics, 43–45
Arab Spring, 279–80
Arendt, Hannah, 278
artificial intelligence (AI)
  ChatGPT, 317–18
  DALL-E 2 system, 311–12, 317–18
  deepfakes, 267–68, 311–12, 313, 316–20
  weaponizing of, 312–20
Assange, Julian (WikiLeaks)
  First Amendment and, 102–4, 105–6, 111–21
  indictments against, 99–105, 121–23, 133
  information anarchy and, 73
  information security and, 144
  journalistic conduct and, 106–9
  liability concerns, 111–21
  media reaction, 99–101
Associated Press (AP), 17–18, 49, 65, 129–30, 141, 302
authority crisis, 26–29, 199–200, 208–9, 210–11, 216–23

Bahrain surveillance case study
  Cellebrite software, 187
  Gamma and, 185–86
  Hacking Team and, 186–87
  introduction to, 182–88
  NSO Group, 187–88
  political economy and, 183–88
  technology use against, 188–91
  Trovicor and, 184–85
Bahrain Watch, 185–86, 188, 190–91
Bannon, Steven, 43, 171–72, 174–75
Barlow, John Perry, 245–46
Baron, Marty, 80
Barstow, Gary, 141
Bezos, Jeff, 153, 245–46, 257–58
bias in news reporting, 77–80, 240–44
Blair, Dennis, 48
Boumediene, Lakhdar, 31
Boyle, Matthew, 80–81
Branzburg v. Hayes, 50–51, 55
Breitbart, Andrew, 246–47
Breitbart News, 246–47, 248–49
Brexit, xvi–xvii, 170–71, 284–85, 291–92
Brin, Sergei, 245–46
Brown v. Board of Education, 235–36
Buchanan, Patrick, 237–38
bulk surveillance, 44, 47, 198–99, 221. *See also* mass surveillance
Buolamwini, Joy, 265
Bush, George H. W., 236–37
Bush, George H.W., 17–18
BuzzFeed, 71–72, 79–80
Byrne, Matthew, 6–7

Cadwalladr, Carole, 173, 175
Cambridge Analytica and US 2016 election
  collaboration efforts, 174–75
  data laundering, 170–71
  data protection rights and, 173–74
  insolvency and bankruptcy, 175–76
  introduction to, 169–70

Cambridge Analytica and US 2016 election (*cont.*)
  lead-up to scandal, 171–73, 176–77
  pro-Trump microtargeting campaign, 248–49
  regulatory failure, 176–77
  transnational impetus for legal challenge, 170–71
  UK Data Protection Act and, xxvi, 170, 173–74, 175–76
Carlo, Silkie, 146–47
Carter, Jimmy, 85–86
Cassidy, John, 75–76
Cellebrite software, 187
censorship, xv, 17–18, 34, 179–80, 183, 246–47, 278, 280–81, 287–88, 298–99, 320
Center for International Media Assistance, 145
Center for International Security and Cooperation, 88–89, 92–93
Center for Nonproliferation Studies, 88–89, 92–93
Center for Strategic and International Studies, 303, 307
Central Intelligence Agency (CIA), 160–62
Chancellor, Joseph, 172
Charlie Hebdo attacks, 284
ChatGPT, 317–18
Chicago Tribune, 128
Christchurch massacre, 278, 279–80, 295–97, 308
citizen journalism, 81, 277–78, 281–82, 283, 288–91, 298
Citizen Lab, 187–88, 190–91
civility, 115
Civil Rights Act, 235–36
Clapper v. Amnesty International USA, 45–46
classified information
  Fourth Amendment Press Clause and, 48, 53–54
  information anarchy and, 63–64, 68–70, 72–73, 79, 82
Classified Information Procedures Act (CIPA), 28, 122–23
Clinton, Bill, 236–37
Clinton, Hillary, 233–34, 242–43, 247–48, 255–56
CNBC, 128
CNN, 70
Coats, Daniel, 291–92, 316
Cold War, 85–86, 231–33, 235–36, 237–38, 258
Collins, Damian, 173–74
Comey, James, 131–32
Committee to Protect Journalists, 128
communicative impact of free speech, 8–9

confidential sources, 135–39, 147–54
constitutional law, 7–8, 13–14
constitutional protections, 200–3
countering violent extremism (CVE), 277–78, 284–91
counterintelligence, 120–21, 133, 214
counterterrorism, 133, 141–42, 214
court proceedings access, 21–22
COVID-19 pandemic, 263–64, 285–86, 309, 317–18
crimes reports, 104–5
criminal law, 7, 9–10, 43–44
criminal trials, 21–22, 23, 34–35, 48–49
Cronkite, Walter, 17–18
Cruz, Ted, 170
cryptographic signatures, 269–70, 273–74, 275
Cuban Missile Crisis, 85–86
culture war and media ecosystems, 237–40
cybersecurity, 127–29, 141–44, 146, 148–49, 152, 233–34, 312–20

DALL-E 2 system, 311–12, 317–18
data laundering, 170–71
data privacy, 149, 169
data protection rights, xxvi, 169–71, 173–74, 175–76, 298
deepfakes, 267–68, 311–12, 313, 316–20
Dehaye, Paul-Olivier, 174–75
Deitz, Bob, 48
Democratic National Committee, 233–34
Denham, Elizabeth, 173–74
Department of Navy v. Egan, 26–27
Detroit Free Press v. Ashcroft, 38
dezinformatsiya, 231–57
Dhiab v. Obama, 26
DigitalGlobe, 93
digital media security
  benefits of cybersecurity, 146–47
  content authentication, 270–72
  corroboration and accountability, 267–68
  cryptographic signatures, 269–70, 273–74, 275
  digital signatures, 272–74
  HTTPS connections model, 270–72
  in information supply chains, 272–75
  internet, as destabilizer of, 262–66
  introduction to, 261–62
  a priori authentication, 268–70
  reactive systems, 266–67
digital publishing, 263–64, 268–69, 272–73, 275
digital signatures, 272–74
digital surveillance
  conceptualizations of, 127–29

confidential sources, 135–39, 147–54
cybersecurity and, 127–29, 141–44, 146, 148–49, 152
digital security and, 146–47
by government, 129–35
information security, 141–47
introduction to, 125–35
journalistic sources, 139–41
new approaches needed, 147–54
Panopticism, 127, 147–48
surveillance assemblage, 127
Trump, Donald and, 131–35
digital surveillance of journalists
bulk surveillance, 44, 47, 198–99, 221
common law protections, 203–4
constitutional protections, 200–3
electronic communications surveillance authorities, 208–23, 209t
introduction to, 197–200
mass surveillance, 22–23, 135, 140, 180, 184–85, 198
protections for, 200–8
regulatory protections, 204–8
statutory protections, 203–4
Discover Magazine, 301–2
Domestic Investigations and Operations Guide (FBI), 54
Downie, Leonard, 109
Dukakis. Michael, 236–37
Dunaway, Johanna, 77–78
Dunning-Kruger effect, 249–50

economic nationalism, 171
Economist, 312
Electronic Communications Privacy Act (ECPA), 213–14
electronic communications surveillance authorities
criminal investigations, 209–13
digital surveillance of journalists, 208–23, 209t
foreign intelligence surveillance and, 216–18
Electronic Frontier Foundation, 134, 221
Electronic Media, 17–18
Ellsberg, Daniel, 3–18, 73–74
Ely, John Hart, 24–25
enforcement investigations, 44–45, 50, 54
Entick v. Carrington, 55
EPA v. Mink, 28–29
Espionage Act (1917)
Assange, Julian (WikiLeaks) and, 101–2
digital surveillance and, 139–40
First Amendment protections and, 155, 156, 158–61, 163–65, 166

Fourth Amendment Press Clause and, 44, 49–50
introduction to, 155–57
journalistic protections and, 163–66, 206
United States v. Jeffrey Sterling, 160–62
United States v. Stephen Kim, 157–60
espionage prosecutions, 114–15
ethics, xvii–xviii, xx, 61–62, 74, 87, 88–89, 95, 146, 153–54, 267
executive branch, 22, 25–27, 28–29, 30–32, 38, 43–44, 66–67, 68–72, 74, 82, 102–3
Executive Order 12333 (EO 12333), 222–23
Export Controls and Human Rights Initiative, 194–95

Facebook/Meta. See also Cambridge Analytica and US 2016 election; social media platform security
Bahrain surveillance case study, 183, 189
digital media security and, 262–63, 266–67
information anarchy and, 78–82
media ecosystems and, 247–49
weaponized images, 302–4, 307–11, 312, 314–15
Fairness and Accuracy in Reporting (FAIR), 239–40
Fairness Doctrine, 238–39
fake news, 67, 71–72, 132, 231, 248–49, 266, 277–78, 279–81, 285–86, 293–95, 309
fascism. *See* surveillance fascism
Federal Bureau of Investigation (FBI), 52–53, 129, 213–16
Federal Communications Commission (FCC), 238
Federal News Agency, 292–93
Federal Trade Commission (FTC), 172
filter bubbles, 246–47, 249–50
FinFisher software, 185–86
First Amendment (US Constitution)
access to national security information, 21–22, 24, 34–37, 157
combating leaks, 102–4, 105–6, 158–59
digital surveillance, 139–41
Espionage Act (1917) and, 155, 156, 158–61, 163–65, 166
freedom of the press and, 3–14
free exercise clause, 12–13
gag orders, 211–12
journalistic protection of, 200–3
publishing classified information, 111–21
substance in Fourth Amendment Press Clause, 55–59
Flynn, Michael, 43–44, 67

Foley, James, 279–80, 284
Forbes, 134
Ford, Corey, 153
foreign intelligence, 48, 120–21, 132–33, 198–200, 202–3, 207–9, 216–22
Foreign Intelligence Surveillance Act (FISA), 45, 46, 218, 221–22
Foreign Intelligence Surveillance Act (FISA) Amendments Act, 198, 217–18, 219–21
Foreign Intelligence Surveillance Act (FISA) PR/TT order, 218–19
Foreign Intelligence Surveillance Court (FISC), 31–32, 59, 218
Foucault, Michel, 127
Fourth Amendment (US Constitution), 134, 200–3, 211–12
Fourth Amendment (US Constitution) Press Clause
  classified information and, 48, 53–54
  constitutional protections, 50–51
  First Amendment substance in, 55–59
  introduction to, 43–45
  leak investigations and, 43–44, 45–54
  NSA surveillance programs and, 45–50
  reasonableness requirement, 45, 55–59
  regulatory protections, 52–54
  statutory protections, 51–52, 53–54
Fowler, Mark, 238
Fox News, 158–59, 240–41, 302–4
Frankfurter, Felix, 114–15
freedom of expression, 47, 55–56, 180–81, 188, 200–1
freedom of information, 188
Freedom of Information Act (FOIA), 14–16, 28, 223
freedom of press, 3–19
Freedom of the Press Foundation, 76–77, 144
free exercise clause (First Amendment), 12–13
French Electoral Commission, 256–57
Frohwerk v. U.S., 114–15
Fukushima Daiichi Nuclear Power Plant meltdown, 89–90
Future Today Institute (FTI), 142–43

gag orders, 53, 207–8, 211–12, 214
Gallup-Knight Foundation, 254–55
Gamma, 185–86
Garland, Merrick, 26
Gebru, Timnit, 265
General Data Protection Regulation (GDPR), 298
generative adversarial networks (GANs), 312
GeoEye, 93

GIFCT protocol, 296–98
Giuliani, Rudy, 174–75, 314–15
Global Disinformation Index, 293
Global Internet Forum to Counter Terrorism (GIFCT), 67–68
Global Science Research Ltd., 172
Globe Newspaper Co. v. Superior Court, 36–37
Goodfellow, Ian, 312–20
Google Transparency Report, 130
Gore, Al, 236–37
governmental digital surveillance, 129–35
Graber, Doris, 77–78
Grady, Denise, 301–2
Grosjean v. American Press Co., 34, 35–36
Guantanamo Bay, 22–23, 26, 31
The Guardian, 125–26, 143–44, 252–53
Gulf War, 17–18

Hacking Team, 186–87
Harvard Business Review, 320
Hennings, Thomas, Jr., 23–24
Herald Company, Inc. v. Board of Parole, 39
high-resolution imaging satellites, 85–88
Holder, Eric, 48, 211
HTTPS connections model, 270–72
Huffington, Arianna, 246–47
Huffington Post, 246–47
Human Rights Watch, 47–48
Hussein, Saddam, 67
hyperspectral imagery, 92–93

Immigration and Nationality Act, 235–36
individual rights, 24, 39, 140–41, 235–36
information anarchy
  classified information and, 63–64, 68–70, 72–73, 79, 82
  journalistic biases, 77–80
  loss of context as consequence, 64–66
  misinformation and, 61–62, 66, 79–80, 81
  power interests and precariousness, 61–64
  Russian efforts to influence election campaign, 64–66
  transparency and, 72–77
  Trump, Donald and, 61–83
  weaponization of information, 63–64, 81, 242–43
information security, 141–47
information supply chain security, 272–75
In re Opinions & Orders, 31–32
In re Washington Post, 38
The Intercept, 143–44
international standards, 4–5
Internet Engineering Task Force (IETF), 271

INDEX   325

Internet Protocol (IP) monitoring, 181–82
Internet Referral Units (IRUs), 285–86
Internet Research Agency (IRA), 248–49, 249f, 292–93
intrusion software, 181–82
Islamic State in Iraq and Syria (ISIS), xix, 242–43, 277–78, 279–80, 281, 283, 284–91, 301–5
Israel-Gaza war, 304–5, 313

Jane's Defence Weekly, 88
Jane's Intelligence Review, 88, 90
Jefferson, Thomas, 32
Jewel v. National Security Agency, 221
jihad, 171, 288–89, 302–3, 306, 307
Jim Crow lynchings, 305
Johnson, Lyndon B., 3–4
Johnson, Ron, 131
journalism/journalists
  adversarial journalism, 68–69, 76–77, 83
  bias against, 77–80
  citizen journalism, 81, 277–78, 281–82, 283, 288–91, 298
  conduct of, 106–9
  confidential source dynamics (*see* confidential sources)
  digital surveillance sources, 139–41
  Espionage Act (1917) protections, 163–66, 206
  parajournalist, 136–37
  privilege of, 13–14
  surveillance technology against, 189–91
  traditional journalism, 81, 116–17, 198–99, 240–41
JSTOR database, 75
judicial branch, 22, 23–32, 38, 41
judicial deference, 27

KalanickTravis, 174
Kasparaov, Gary, 172
Keller, Bill, 119–21
Kelly, Mary Louise, 138
Kendzior, Sarah, 254–55
Kennan, George, 231–32
Kennedy, John F., 3–4
Kim, Stephen Jin-Woo, 49–50, 129, 157–60
Kissinger, Henry, 66–67
Knight Commission, 137–38
Kogan, Aleksander, 172
kompromat ("compromising material"), xxix, 171, 231–33, 241, 256–57
Kyl-Bingaman Amendment (1997), 94–95

Lapowsky, Issie, 173

Las Vegas Review Journal, 153
leaked information, 40, 43–44, 101–2, 115–16
leak investigations, 40, 43–44, 45–54, 69, 158–59, 162, 198, 205, 215
Let's Encrypt, 270–72
LGBTQ community, 239–40
liability for publishing classified information, 111–21
Los Angeles Times, 135–36

machine learning, 79, 82, 152, 264–67, 282, 287–88, 290–91, 298, 316
Macron, Emmanuel, 256–57
Madison, James, 32
Manafort, Paul, 53
Manning, Chelsea, 73–74, 110, 112–13
Mapp v. Ohio, 55–56
mass surveillance, 22–23, 135, 140, 180, 184–85, 198. *See also* bulk surveillance
Matter Ventures, 153
McAfee, John, 146
McCarthy, Joseph, 251–52
McCarthyism, 234–35
McGraw, David, 111
McGregor, Jeffrey, 318
media ecosystems
  bias in news reporting, 240–44
  culture war and, 237–40
  online hyperconnectivity, 244–50
  print journalism decline, 251–57
  Russian efforts to influence election campaign, 64–66, 231–33
  WikiLeaks, 185, 189–90, 233–37
media literacy, 154, 267–68
memorandum of understanding (MOU), 104–5
Mercer, Rebekah, 171–72, 174–75
Mercer, Robert, 248–49
Miller, Judith, 13–14
misinformation
  fake news, 67, 71–72, 132, 231, 248–49, 266, 277–78, 279–81, 285–86, 293–95, 309
  information anarchy and, 61–62, 66, 79–80, 81
  Russian efforts to influence election campaign, 64–66
  weaponized images and, 309–12
Moody, John, 302–3
Morrell, Michael, 120
Mueller, Robert, 247–48
multispectral imagery, 92–93
Murdoch, Rupert, 240–41

Naik, Ravi, 172

Nakashima, Ellen, 215
National Academy of Sciences, 310
National Institute of Standards and
    Technology, 127–28
National Press Club, 48, 141
National Security Agency (NSA)
    digital surveillance and, 125–26, 198
    information anarchy and, 75–76
    liability for publishing classified
        information, 111–21
    surveillance programs, 45–50
National Security Council (NSC), 62–
    63, 66–67
national security information access
    dilemma of, 18–19
    equipping function of, 32–37
    First Amendment and, 21–22, 24, 34–37
    freedom of press and, 14–19
    interbranch function of, 25–32
    introduction to, 21–23
    right of access, 15, 21–25, 26, 32, 34–35,
        37–39, 41
    structural approach to, 23–25
    structural understanding of, 37–40
    US Constitution and, 32–37, 40–41
National Security Letter (NSL), 51–52, 130,
    199–200, 202–3, 207–8, 213–16
national security reporting, viii, 61, 64, 78, 82
The Nation's, 17–19
NATO military operations, 93
Nawaz, Maajid, 303
Near v. Minnesota, 4–5, 117–18
Nelson, Rick, 303
Network Enforcement Act (NetzDG), 285–86
New York Daily News, 261
New Yorker, 158–59
New York Times
    Christchurch massacre, 308
    confidential sources, 138, 151
    cybersecurity and, 129–30
    digital surveillance and, 126–27, 130, 143–
        44, 148
    digital surveillance protections for
        journalists, 205
    financial gains, 257–58
    financial losses, 252–53
    freedom of the press, 4, 6, 9–11, 13–14
    information anarchy and, 64–66, 70, 75–76
    leak cases, 48–49, 111, 119–20
    open source imagery intelligence, 88–89
    Stellar Wind collection program, 119–21
    Trump, Donald on, 163
    The War of the Worlds radio broadcast, 261

weaponized images and, 302
New York Times v. United States. *See Pentagon
    Papers* case
9/11 attacks. *See* September 11, 2001 terrorist
    attacks
Nix, Alexander, 171–72, 173–75
Nixon, Richard, 3–4, 66–67, 131–32
Nofziger, Lyn, 103
North Korea, 62, 69, 88, 91–93, 129
NSO Group, 187–88
nuclear weapons monitoring, 85–86, 88, 91–
    94, 95

Obama, Barack, 48, 74, 79, 111–12, 159–60
objective reporting, 77–78, 238–39, 240–
    44, 256–57
Office of the Inspector General for the
    Department of Justice (OIG), 215
Ogura, Toshimaru, 191–92
online hyperconnectivity, 244–50
open source imagery intelligence, 94–95
    of active military operations, 93
    ethical implications of, 88–89
    Fukushima Daiichi Nuclear Power Plant
        meltdown, 89–90
    high-resolution imaging satellites, 85–88
    hyperspectral imagery, 92–93
    Israel's curtailment of, 94–95
    multispectral imagery, 92–93
    nuclear weapons monitoring, 85–86, 88,
        91–94, 95
    right to privacy and, 93–94
Operation Desert Shield, 17–18
Organisation for Economic Cooperation and
    Development (OECD), 182, 184–86

Page, Larry, 245–46
Panama Papers investigation, 145
Panopticism, 127, 147–48
Papandrea, Mary-Rose, 140
parajournalist, 136–37
Parker, Sean, 245–46
patriotic troublemakers, 128
Pelosi, Nancy, 314–16
Pence, Mike, 43–44
Pen Registers and Trap and Trace Devices (PR/
    TT), 212
PEN Report, 47–48, 180, 256–57
Pentagon Papers case *(New York Times v. United
    States)*
    access to national security information
        and, 29–30
    freedom of the press and, 3–18

leakers of, 73–74
sanctions and, 114
Perot, Ross, 236–37
Pew Research Center, 47–48, 309–10
Pichai, Sundar, 312
platformization of journalism, xxx, 282
Podesta, John, 255–56
PolitiFact, 239–40
Pompeo, Mike, 233–34
Pozen, David, 72
Press-Enterprise I & II, 37
print journalism decline, 251–57
a priori authentication, 268–70
Privacy and Civil Liberties Oversight Board, 56
Privacy International, 186
Privacy Protection Act of 1980 (PPA), 44–45, 51–52, 203–4, 208–9
Proctor, Keith, 307
The Progressive magazine, 4–5
Project Owl, 293–95
propaganda
  Cambridge Analytica and, 173
  confidential sources and, 136–37
  fascism and, 192–93
  by Russians, 231–33, 242–44, 247–49, 256, 258
  social media platform security and, 277–80, 283–85, 286–89, 291–93, 298
  by Soviets, xxix
  weaponizing images and, 301, 303, 304–5
Pruitt, Gary, 129–30, 141
Psychometrics Centre, 172
Public Access to Court Electronic Records (PACER) database, 75
public discourse, 125–26
Putin, Vladimir, 67, 231
PutinCon, 172

Rahwan, Iyad, 317
Rand Corporation, 5–6
Raqqa is Being Slaughtered Silently (RBSS), 289–90
reasonableness requirement of Fourth Amendment, 45, 55–59
religious freedom, 12–13
Religious Freedom Restoration Act, 12–13
Reporters Committee for Freedom of the Press, 99–100
Reuters Institute Digital News Reports, 17–18, 282
Richmond Newspapers, Inc. v. Virginia, 21–22, 34–35, 36–37

right of access to national security information, 15, 21–25, 26, 32, 34–35, 37–39, 41. *See also* national security information access
right to privacy concerns, 93–94
Rini, Regina, 319–20
Risen, James, 48–49, 160
Roosevelt, Franklin D., 234
Roosevelt, Theodore, 251–52
Rosen, James, 49–50, 157–59, 211
Rosenberg, Carol, 22–23
Rosenstein, Rod, 163
Rottman, Gabe, 99–100
RT (Russia Today), 242–44, 248–49
Russian efforts to influence election campaign, 64–66, 231–33, 256, 258, 291–95
Russo, Anthony, 6–7

Salama app, 149–50
Sandberg, Sheryl, 77
Sardarizadeh, Shayan, 304
satellite imagery analysis, xxii, 87, 88–89, 91
satellite journalism. *See* open source imagery intelligence
Satellite pour L'Observation de la Terre (SPOT), 88
satellite technology. *See* high-resolution imaging satellites
Satellogic company, 92–93
Saxbe v. Washington Post Co., 36
Schiff, Adam, 247–48
Schwartz, Aaron, 75–76
SCL Group Limited, 170–71
Second Amendment (US Constitution), 236–37
secrecy in government, 6, 13–14, 18–19, 23–24, 25–26, 28–29, 30–31, 32, 40–41, 48, 54, 70–71, 109–11, 149, 192–94, 209, 214, 216–17
secrecy porn, 70–71
SecureDrop, 76–77, 144
self-censorship, 47, 70, 180
separation of powers, 23, 25–26, 29–32, 38
September 11, 2001 terrorist attacks, 306–7, 308–9
Serviceman's Readjustment Act of 1944 (GI Bill), 234–35
Sessions, Jeff, 43–44, 162
Shane, Scott, 151
Sheehan, Neil, 15
Shehabi, Saeed, 190–91
shield laws, 13–14, 16–17, 44–45, 140–41, 166, 200, 203–4
Sierra, Jorge Luis, 149–50
Sipress, Alan, 215

Slack platform, 148
Snowden, Edward, 75–77, 110, 120, 143–44, 197
social media bots, 243–44, 248–49
social media platform security
   algorithmic gatekeepers and, xxx, 279–83
   Christchurch massacre and, 278, 279–80, 295–97
   countering violent extremism (CVE), 277–78, 284–91
   introduction to, 277–79
   in Syria, 288–91
   weaponized disinformation and, 277–78, 280–81, 284–88, 291–95
Society of Professional Journalists, 107, 138
Soghoian, Christopher, 146
Sotloff, Steven, 279–80, 284
space rocketry, 85–86
special interest cases, 38
Stanford Daily, 50–51, 55, 57
Stellar Wind collection program, 119–21
Stevens, John Paul, 36, 57–58
Stewart, Potter, 4, 15–16
Stored Communications Act (SCA), 51–52, 205–6, 209–12
surveillance assemblage, 127
surveillance authority, 199–200, 208–9, 210–11, 216–23
surveillance capitalism, 192–93
surveillance fascism
   Bahrain case study, 182–91
   introduction to, 179–82
   transnational surveillance fascism, 191–93
surveillance society, 135, 141–42
Syrian Electronic Army, 128

Tarrant, Brenton, 295
Telecommunications Act, 244–45
terrorism
   Christchurch massacre, 278, 279–80, 295–97, 308
   defined, 304–5
   September 11, 2001 terrorist attacks, 306–7, 308–9
   weaponized images of, 301–5
testimonial privileges, xxix
Todd, Chuck, 71–72
traditional journalism, 81, 116–17, 198–99, 240–41
transnational surveillance fascism, 191–93. *See also* surveillance fascism

transparency
   digital surveillance and, 154
   high-resolution imaging satellites and, 87
   information anarchy and, 72–77, 83
Tribe, Laurence, 24–25
Trovicor, 184–85
Truman, Harry, 234
Trump, Donald
   anti-press politics of, 43–45
   campaign news coverage, 255–56
   campaign support, 247–48
   Fox News and, 158–59, 240–41
   information anarchy and, 61–83
   leak frenzy, 131–35
   national security policies, 121–22
   Pelosi, Nancy, 314–15
   US Department of Justice (DOJ) and, 162–63
   WikiLeaks and, 233–37
   See also Cambridge Analytica and US 2016 election
Turek, Matt, 318–19
TVEC database, 296–97

UK Data Protection Act, xxvi, 170, 173–74, 175–76
Umar, Mullah Mohammed, 306
UN General Assembly, 296–97
UN Guiding Principles on Business and Human Rights, 180–81
United Kingdom's National Union of Journalists Code of Conduct, 138
United Press International, 17–18
United States v. Carolene Products Co., 35–36
United States v. Jeffrey Sterling, 160–62
United States v. Nixon, 30
United States v. Stephen Kim, 157–60
UN Universal Declaration of Human Rights (UDHR), 180–81
U.S. v. Julian Paul Assange. *See* Assange, Julian (WikiLeaks)
U.S. v. Rosen, 115–16
USA FREEDOM Act, 213–14
USA PATRIOT Act, 31–32, 46, 132–33, 221–22
US Bill of Rights, 33
US Capitol riots (2021), 61–62, 285–86, 309
US Constitution, 32–37, 40–41, 50–51, 120, 132–33
US Department of Commerce, 93, 194–95
US Department of Defense (DOD), 5–6, 316–17
US Department of Homeland Security, 134
US Department of Justice (DOJ)
   digital surveillance and, 129, 133

digital surveillance protections for journalists, 204–8
First Amendment and, 159–60
mass surveillance and, 198–200
Media Subpoena Guidelines, 52–54, 58
surveillance fascism and, 179–80
Trump, Donald and, 162–63
United States v. Jeffrey Sterling, 160–62
WikiLeaks and, 103–5, 106–7, 111–12, 116–17, 129, 133
user-generated content (UGC), 267, 269
US Foreign Agent Registration Act, 243–44
US State Department, 129
US 2016 election. *See* Cambridge Analytica and US 2016 election

Vietnam War policy, 3–4
viewpoint discrimination, 17–18
violent extremism, xxx, 171, 277–78, 279–81, 284–88, 290–91, 296–97, 298, 307–8
virtual private networks (VPNs), 76–77
Voting Rights Act, 235–36

Wallace, Henry, 234
Waller v. Georgia, 33
Wall Street Journal, 70, 126–27, 252–53, 317–18
The War of the Worlds radio broadcast, 261–62, 275
Warzel, Charlie, 79–80, 314–15
Washington Post
  Bezos' purchase of, 153, 257–58
  confidential sources, 138
  digital surveillance and, 125–27, 130, 144
  financial gains, 257–58
  financial losses, 253–54
  information anarchy and, 68, 70
  leak cases, 49–50, 109, 158–59
  Pentagon Papers case and, 29–30
Wassenaar Arrangement, 181–82, 193–94
Watergate conspiracy, 252
Watergate scandal, 138
weaponized AI, 312–20
weaponized disinformation, 277–78, 280–81, 284–88, 291–95
weaponized images
  asymmetric warfare and, 301–5
  cybersecurity and, 312–20
  deepfakes, 267–68, 311–12, 313, 316–20
  open source imagery intelligence, 94–95
  social media as amplifier, 306–8
  spread of mis-and disinformation, 309–12
weaponized information, 63–64, 81, 242–43
Welles, Orson, 261, 275
Wells, H. G., 261
Wheatland, Julian, 170–71
whistle-blowers, 13–14, 75–76, 125–26, 128–29, 131–32, 136–37, 138, 139, 144, 147, 149, 170, 172, 173–74, 176–77
White, Byron, 4
White supremacy, 171, 235–36, 285–86, 308
WikiLeaks, 185, 189–90, 233–37, 256–57. *See also* Assange, Julian (WikiLeaks)
Wilkes v. Wood, 55
Wilkinson, Paul, 307
Williams, Stephen F., 37
Wilson, James, 25–26
Wiretap Act, 209, 212–13
wiretaps, 6–7, 33, 67, 206, 216–17
Wood, Wendy, 310
World Economic Forum, 291–92
Wray, Christopher A., 291–92
Wylie, Christopher, 173, 174–75

Zelenskyy, Volodymyr, 317
Zurcher v. Stanford Daily, 56–57